PROGRAMMING LANGUAGES,
INFORMATION STRUCTURES,
AND
MACHINE ORGANIZATION

McGRAW-HILL COMPUTER SCIENCE SERIES

RICHARD W. HAMMING
Bell Telephone Laboratories

EDWARD A. FEIGENBAUM
Stanford University

HELLERMAN *Digital Computer System Principles*
ROSEN *Programming Systems and Languages*
SALTON *Automatic Information Organization and Retrieval*
WEGNER *Programming Languages, Information Structures, and Machine
         Organization*

PROGRAMMING LANGUAGES,
INFORMATION STRUCTURES,
AND
MACHINE ORGANIZATION

PETER WEGNER

Department of Computer Science
Cornell University

McGRAW-HILL BOOK COMPANY

New York, St. Louis, San Francisco, Toronto, London, Sydney

PROGRAMMING LANGUAGES, INFORMATION STRUCTURES, AND MACHINE ORGANIZATION

TO SIMON, MARK,
JEREMY, AND MICHAEL

COMMENTARY

ON A

CONCEPT OF PLATO

In performing a computation we do not handle objects of the real world, but merely representations of objects. We are like people who live in a cave and perceive objects only by the shadows which they cast upon the walls of the cave. We use the information obtained from studying the form of these shadows to make inferences about the real world. However, we are not merely passive observers of shadows cast by real objects. We modify reality and observe the new patterns of shadows cast by the new configuration of objects. We go even further, forgetting altogether about the real objects that cast the shadows, treating the patterns of shadows as physical objects, and studying how patterns of shadows can be transformed and manipulated.

Information structures are representations of real objects just like shadows on the walls of a cave. The programmer studies how information structures can be transformed and manipulated and in doing so learns something about objects represented by the information structures. However, the real computer scientist falls in love with information structures and studies their properties not only for what they tell him about the real world but because he finds them beautiful.

PREFACE

This book covers machine language, machine organization, multi-programming systems, assemblers, macros, LISP, ALGOL, PL/I, simulation languages, and many other topics in programming. It treats these topics as part of a single unified discipline, using a unifying framework developed in the text. The author feels strongly that the subject of programming should be treated as a coherent discipline rather than as a loose collection of techniques. Such an approach allows practical problems arising in programming to be analyzed more clearly, and therefore yields practical as well as aesthetic dividends.

There is now a sufficient body of knowledge and experience in the programming field to classify programming techniques and to develop a framework for the characterization of programming languages, programs, and computations. In the present text such a framework is developed, starting from the notions that a program with its data constitutes an *information structure,* and that a computation results in a sequence of information structures generated from an *initial representation* by the execution of a sequence of *instructions.* The information structures which arise during the execution of programs in a number of existing programming languages are analyzed in some detail. Emphasis is placed on the way in which information structures representing programs and their data are modified during execution.

The programming-language literature tends to emphasize source-language structure and compiler design rather than the sequence of *run-time representations* of a program during its execution. This text attempts to demonstrate that it is both feasible and rewarding to directly study the relation between source-language structure and run-time representation. One of the reasons for the neglect of run-time representation was that no sufficiently simple model was available for talking about run-time representations in a machine-independent manner. Such a model is developed in the present text.

There is a close relation between the study of run-time representations and the study of machines which execute programs having the given run-time representation. Chapter 1 considers the relation between machine organization and the run-time representation of programs in machine language, both for simple computers and for large, multiprogrammed computer systems. In later chapters, models of run-time representation for macro systems are compared with models of run-time representation for procedure-oriented languages. Each of the models considered suggests a form of machine organization for computers having instructions of the form required by the model.

The principal reason for studying these models is to develop an insight into the dynamic nature of program execution. The body of the text is concerned with actual programming languages and programming techniques. The models are introduced to give coherence and continuity to the discussion.

A further advantage of this approach is that it allows a common set of concepts to be developed for programming-language theory and automata theory. The run-time representation of a program with its data at a given instant of time is referred to as an *instantaneous description*, by analogy with the corresponding concept of automata theory. The models developed for programming languages may be thought of as automata with a complex structure. Automata theory is concerned with the class of functions computable by various classes of relatively simple devices. It is particularly concerned with devices which compute *subclasses* of the set of all computable functions.† Programming theory takes it for granted that the computational device can compute any desired function, and it is concerned with the specification of devices for efficient program execution, with notations for efficient problem specification, and with the structures which arise during the sequence of transformations that constitute a computation. Although automata theory is outside the scope of the present text, it is, nevertheless, an advantage to develop a conceptual framework which allows the same concepts and terminology to be used at points where the disciplines overlap.

The book is intended to be read at the following levels:

1. As an undergraduate text for a "second" course in programming which emphasizes basic programming concepts during lectures, while assigning programming projects during practical periods. When used at this level the text should be supplemented by a manual for the specific language and computer being used. The book could be used at this

---

† The pastime of defining automata which compute interesting subclasses of the class of computable functions is sometimes referred to as "Turing machine brinkmanship."

level not only at universities but also at technical colleges and two-year colleges which offer more than a single course in programming. It is suited also to industrial training programs.

2. As a graduate text in programming. When used at this level some of the elementary sections in Chapters 1 and 2 would be used principally for review purposes. Less emphasis would be placed on programming assignments in a specific programming language, and more emphasis would be placed on advanced sections in Chapters 3 and 4 and on selected papers in the literature. When the book is used at this level, it is recommended that assignments include a programming project of intermediate difficulty and a term paper which explores some aspect of programming theory in greater depth.

3. As a self-study text for professional programmers with at least one year's programming experience who wish to develop an understanding of the basic concepts of programming theory and to sharpen their ability to read the literature. The book is intended to be sufficiently readable so that working programmers with little formal training in programming will benefit from reading the text.

The text has four chapters which are organized as follows.

Chapter 1 presents a "modern" approach to machine language, machine organization, and multiprogramming, and provides a foundation for understanding the higher-level structures and concepts introduced in subsequent chapters.

Chapter 2 presents a systematic account of assembly techniques and symbol-table techniques. It lays the foundation for the more general discussion of symbol-table techniques in later chapters.

Chapters 1 and 2 can be used as the basis of a first course in machine language, machine organization and system programming. The treatment is more modern than that in other currently available texts on machine-language programming. Although some of the concepts and techniques introduced are usually thought of as "advanced," the overall level of the first two chapters is suited to an elementary course. When used at this level, the text should be supplemented by a manufacturer's manual for the specific language and machine being used for programming assignments.

Chapter 3 deals with generalized macro systems, the lambda calculus, and the representation of functions during their evaluation. It is the most difficult chapter in the book and should be skipped when the book is used as an elementary text. However, its subject matter is fundamental to the theory of programming. This chapter will play a fundamental role in advanced courses on programming theory. A review of the concepts of Chapter 3 may find a place even in an elementary course.

Chapter 4 presents a unified development of the structure of procedure-oriented languages, using ALGOL as the basic model, and indicates how PL/I and other languages relate to the ALGOL model. Emphasis is placed upon reentrant representations of procedures and upon the way which information structures representing functions with their data change during execution.

When used as the basis of a two-course sequence, Chapters 1 and 2 could be covered in the first semester and Chapters 3 and 4 in the second semester.

There are two appendixes. The first appendix is an introduction to syntactic analysis and contains an annotated bibliography of literature in the field of syntactic analysis. The second appendix contains the syntactic definition of ALGOL as given in the ALGOL report, but with the author's personal commentary.

The material in this book relates closely to two of the courses recommended by the ACM curriculum committee in the September, 1965, issue of *Communications of the ACM*. It could be used as a basis for course 2 (computer organization and programming), followed by course 5 (algorithmic languages and compilers). It also contains substantial sections which relate to course 4 (information structures) and course 9 (computer programming systems). However, it should be emphasized that the choice of material was dictated by the internal logic of the subject matter rather than by any existing course outlines.

The text includes a number of sections that contain new concepts, or syntheses of existing concepts, not previously published in the literature. The principal sections containing new material are Sections 1.1, 2.4, 3.1, 3.4, 3.8, 3.10, 3.11, 4.1, 4.6, 4.8, 4.9, 4.10, and 4.11. Section 1.1 gives the overall approach of the text; Section 2.4 gives a classification of modes of identifier assignment and considers table-driven programs; Section 3.1 introduces the notion of substitutive function evaluation, which is elaborated in greater detail in Section 3.8; Section 3.4 brings together a number of notions relating to generalized macro processing; Section 3.10 compares Landin's structure definitions with BNF structure definitions and analyzes the SECD machine; and Section 3.11 relates the notion of the LISP apply function to the notion of a universal Turing machine. Section 4.1 introduces a new approach to the study of procedure-oriented languages; Section 4.6 works this approach out in detail for ALGOL; Section 4.8 brings together some ideas relating to programmer-defined information structures; Section 4.9 analyzes certain features of PL/I, such as the ON statement; Section 4.10 introduces a classification of function modules in terms of control structures; and Section 4.11 compares two alternative strategies for developing simulation languages. Sections 1.10 through 1.13 have been published in substantially their present form as a paper entitled "Machine Organization for Multiprogramming" in the Proceedings of the 22d ACM Conference, Washington, D.C., August, 1967.

The author would like to express his appreciation to the many people who read portions of the manuscript, contributed ideas, and offered suggestions, during the development of this text. Arthur Evans, R. W. Hamming, David Martin, and Andries Van-Dam reviewed the manuscript and did their job very well, each commenting on the manuscript from a different point of view. Others contributing suggestions and ideas include: Bruce Arden, Larry Axsom, Mark Elson, Jerry Feldman, Don Knuth, Doug McIlroy, Calvin Mooers, Bob Rosin, Earl Schweppe, Dana Scott, Tim Standish, Bill Viavant, and Niklaus Wirth. Pat Hauk did a fine job of typing the manuscript. Courses based on this material have been taught at both Cornell University and Penn State University, and the contribution of the captive student audiences attending these lectures is gratefully acknowledged.

PETER WEGNER

CONTENTS

CHAPTER 1

MACHINE LANGUAGE
AND MACHINE ORGANIZATION

1.1 BASIC CONCEPTS

In this section a number of concepts fundamental to the study of programming are introduced. Concepts such as *program, computation computer,* and *information structure* are defined. System concepts such as *interpretation, compilation, loading,* and *multiprogramming* are discussed. In the final subsections concepts such as *name-value correspondence, environment, binding time, syntax,* and *semantics* are developed. The substantive discussion of machine language and machine organization begins in Sec 1.2.

1.1.1 THE REPRESENTATION OF PROGRAMS DURING EXECUTION

A program in a programming language may be thought of as a realization of a *function* f which, given a *data set* x, specifies a *value* $y = f(x)$.†
y is *computed* by *applying* the function f to its data.

Examples: A program "sqrt" for finding the square root of a number is a realization of a function which, when given a nonnegative number x, produces values $y = \text{sqrt}(x)$ by applying the function sqrt to the number x. A program "max" for computing the maximum of a set of n numbers is a realization of a function which, when given a set of n numbers $x_1, x_2, \ldots, x_n$, selects the maximum $x_i = \max(x_1, x_2, \ldots, x_n)$ by applying the function max to the set of n numbers.

The collection of all data sets permitted as inputs to a given program is referred to as the *domain* of the program, while the collection of all outputs that can be produced by the program is referred to as the *range* of the program. The domain of the sqrt program is the collection of all

---

† A function f may be defined as a *rule of correspondence* which for every argument x in the *domain* of the function determines a value $y = f(x)$ in the *range* of the function. A program is a specification of a sequence of steps for computing values of y when values of x in the domain of the function are given.

1

nonnegative numbers.† The domain of the max program is the collection of all n-element number sets for some n. If n is an argument of max, then the domain of max consists of $(n + 1)$-element sets whose first element specifies the number n of elements which follow.

In order to compute $f(x)$, both the function f and its data x must be *represented* in an *information storage medium* in a form that is amenable to computation. A *computation* consists of *applying* a *representation* of f to a *representation* of x in order to compute a *representation* of y.‡

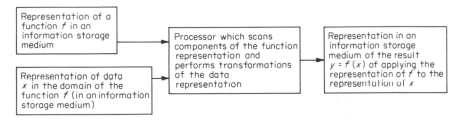

Figure 1.1   Application of a function f to its data x.

A function is usually thought of as a more "active" component in a computation than the data on which it operates. However, in describing how a function is applied to its data on a digital computer, it is convenient to regard both the representation of the function and the representation of its data as "passive" components. The active component responsible for applying a function to its data will be called a *processing unit* or a *processor*. During a computation the processor scans a sequence of components of the function representation (instructions) and performs a sequence of transformations of the data representation, as illustrated in Fig. 1.1. There the representation of the function f is separated from the representation of the data x. However, in many programming languages there is no rigid distinction between functions and data, and it is more appropriate to speak of the representation of a function together

† Whereas a function is said to be undefined for arguments not in the domain of the function, a program normally produces diagnostics for arguments not in the domain of the function to which it corresponds. For example, a program sqrt for computing square roots normally prints a diagnostic for negative arguments such as -4, so that negative arguments may be thought of as being in the domain of the program. However, the domain of a square root function is the set of nonnegative numbers, and the function is undefined for negative arguments such as -4. Conversational programs print out requests for more information if insufficient or wrong arguments are supplied.

‡ A function f can in general be realized in many different ways as a program, and a program may in general be represented in many different ways in an information storage medium. The distinction between an object and its representation or realization is important in certain contexts but merely confusing in others. When there is no confusion, the notions of function, program, and representation of a program will be used interchangeably.

with its data as a single structure. A representation $f(x)$ of a function together with its data will be called an *initial representation*. A *computation* consists of a sequence of transformations which transform the initial representation through a sequence of *intermediate representations* into a *final representation*. The final representation contains a representation of the value y which results from the application of the function f to its data x. This text will consider in some detail alternative strategies for the representation of functions f and their data during successive stages of execution on a computer. This approach will be applied to the study of machine language, machine organization, macro languages, and procedure-oriented languages. This text attempts to demonstrate both that the above approach is a natural one and that it yields a greater insight into the structure of programming languages than do more traditional approaches. Moreover, it is felt that this approach provides a unifying thread to the study of the various topics that constitute programming-language theory.

The current literature in programming languages tends to emphasize (1) the static structure of programs in a programming language and (2) the translation of programs from *problem-oriented languages*, convenient for problem specification, to *machine-oriented languages*, convenient for execution on a computer. In the terminology introduced in previous paragraphs, area 1 is concerned with alternative initial representations of programs, and area 2 is concerned with transformation from one initial representation to another. Neither area 1 nor 2 deals with the process of computation itself but merely with initial representations of information prior to computation.

The study of transformations that occur during a computation should play a more central role in programming-language theory than the study of translation from one initial representation to another. Moreover, the overall characteristics of such transformations are relatively insensitive to changes of initial representation. This means that the characteristics of the evaluation process for a wide class of programming languages can be described in a relatively machine-independent manner.

An understanding of how programs with their data are represented and transformed during their execution yields a direct understanding of how the computers which execute such programs operate. This approach to programming languages therefore has greater relevance to machine organization than the study of translation processes or of static program structures.

1.1.2 INFORMATION STRUCTURES AND DIGITAL COMPUTERS

Programs together with their data constitute examples of *information structures*. The notion of information structure is central to the study of programming languages.   We shall be concerned with the representation and transformation of information structures that constitute programs, together with their data and with the storage of such information structures in information-storage devices.

In order to build up information structures it is necessary to introduce one or more *primitive components* out of which more complex information structures are constructed.   Information structures may be constructed in terms of a single primitive unit of information called the *binary digit* or the *bit*.   A bit is characterized by the fact that it can take on one of two *states*, which will here be represented by 0 and 1.†

Information structures are constructed from bits by grouping ordered sequences of bits into *fields* and by grouping fields into successively larger information units.   Specific fields of an information structure are usually interpreted as identifiable *components* of the object represented by the information structure as a whole.   A specification of an information structure in terms of lower-level components is referred to as a *structure definition*.

Although an information structure may be thought of as an abstract object, any specific instance of an information structure must have a physical existence in some *information-storage medium*.   The information-storage medium contains *primitive information-storage devices* for storing primitive information units.   The primitive information-storage devices are generally grouped into devices for storing information fields.   An information-storage device for storing one or more information fields will be referred to as a *register*.

The principal information-storage medium of a digital computer is the computer *memory*, which usually consists of a sequence of *memory registers*.   The size of a memory register is usually chosen so that it can store commonly occurring information units such as numbers and instructions.

A digital computer is a device for the storage and transformation of information structures.   From a static point of view, a digital computer consists of a set of interacting information-storage devices, a set of devices for transferring information between information-storage components, and a set of devices for transforming information structures.

† The bit is the most common primitive information unit used in specifying information structure within digital computers.   In problem-oriented languages, primitive information symbols are called *characters*, and the set of primitive information symbols is called the *alphabet* of the language.   Characters may be grouped into fields, and fields may be grouped into larger information units, just as in the binary case.   Character sequences of problem-oriented languages can be mapped into binary representations within a computer as described in Sec. 1.2.1.   Structures in two-dimensional languages and languages for the representation of pictures may similarly be built up from a set of primitive information units.

In order to illustrate how a computer operates, we first consider a simple computer which consists merely of a processing unit and a memory, as indicated in Fig. 1.2.   It is assumed that the computer memory consists of a sequence of fixed-length registers and that the information structure which constitutes the program together with its data is represented by a sequence of information fields stored in a contiguous block of registers of the computer memory.   The processing unit is assumed to contain an *instruction pointer* which, during the computation, points to an information field of the information structure being transformed.

During a computation, the processing unit scans a sequence of registers pointed to by the instruction pointer and performs transformations on the information structure determined by the content of the register being scanned.   The content of a register scanned by the processing unit may be thought of as an instruction, and the transformation

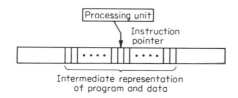

Figure 1.2 **A simple computing device.**

performed when a register is scanned may be thought of as execution of an instruction.

On execution of an instruction, the instruction pointer normally moves one register to the right, so that it is ready to execute the instruction in an adjacent register when execution of the instruction in the current information field has been completed.   However, a subset of the instructions has the property of modifying the instruction pointer so that the next instruction is taken from the field pointed to by the modified pointer.   A further subset of the instructions has the property that when it is encountered by the instruction pointer, it causes the computation to terminate.

The transformation of the information structure that is performed on execution of an instruction may include transformation of one or more of the registers of the computer memory and transformation of information stored in the processing unit.   It may include modification of the content of information fields that are part of the information structure, addition of new information fields, and deletion of information fields.   Addition or deletion of information fields respectively causes the information structure to expand or contract in the computer memory.

The content of all registers in the processing unit and memory of the computer at a given point of the computation will be referred to as an *instantaneous description*.   A computation can be characterized by the sequence of instantaneous descriptions to which it gives rise.   The initial instantaneous description consists of the initial representation of the program and its data in the memory, together with an initialized processing unit with a pointer pointing to the first instruction of the program. The final instantaneous description will contain a component which specifies the result of applying the program to its data.†

An instantaneous description is essentially an intermediate representation of a program and its data, with some additional processing-unit information that specifies the current point of scan of the program.   We have already assumed above that intermediate representations of a program and its data are represented by a linear string of information fields. The complete instantaneous description can be represented by a linear string of information fields by interposing the processing-unit information fields in the intermediate representation immediately to the right of the information field currently being scanned.

The above model of a computer is a particularly simple one which assumes that the program and data for a computation are stored as a linear string in a one-level memory at the beginning of the computation and are successively transformed until a final representation of the information structure is reached.

In actual computers there are a number of qualitatively different information-storage media, and the instantaneous description at a given point of the computation is distributed over these different storage media.   The principal information-storage media for storing components of instantaneous descriptions on an actual computer are illustrated in Fig. 1.3.

Just as in Fig. 1.1, a computation on the computer of Fig. 1.3 is performed by scanning a sequence of information fields in the computer memory and transforming the instantaneous description in a manner determined by the scanned field.   However, the complete instantaneous description of a computation may, in this computer, be distributed over the input medium, output medium, memory, auxiliary memory, instruction-processing unit, and data-processing unit.

---

† The notion of an instantaneous description was first introduced into the literature in connection with the study of Turing machines [18].   The present model of a computer is similar to that of a Turing machine, the principal differences being (1) a Turing machine has an unlimited memory, so that the number of information fields may grow arbitrarily large during the course of the computation; and (2) a Turing machine may modify the information in its memory only in the information field it is currently scanning and may move one field to the right, one field to the left, or remain stationary.

Transformational instructions in this computer can transform only the components of the instantaneous description stored in the instruction-processing unit, data-processing unit, or the memory. In addition to transformational instructions, there are information-moving instructions for input of information from the input medium into the memory, output to the output medium from the memory, and information transfer between the memory and the auxiliary memory.

The input and output media are assumed to be one-dimensional information-storage media that can move in only one direction. The unit of information storage on input and output media is usually referred to as a *record*. The input unit may be thought of as having a *reading head* which, prior to execution of an input instruction, is poised to read the input record under the reading head. When an input instruction is

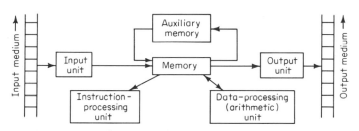

Figure 1.3   Functional components of a digital computer.

executed, the reading head reads the record currently under the reading head into a sequence of one or more registers in the memory and then moves the input medium so that it is poised to read the next input record. Similarly the output unit has a *writing head* which prior to execution of an output instruction points to a blank output record. On execution of an output instruction, the content of a set of memory registers is written on the output record, and the writing head moves to a new blank output record. Input records which have been read and output records which have been written cannot further affect the computation. However, it is convenient to regard such records as part of the instantaneous description. In particular, the result of a computation normally consists of the sequence of output records, so that the output component of the instantaneous description is clearly a very important component.

The auxiliary memory is an information-storage medium for storing information that is not currently in use but is likely to be required at a subsequent point of the computation. Auxiliary memory is necessary principally because the main memory is not always large enough to hold all the information required during a computation. However, the auxiliary memory is used not only for storing overflow information of a single computation, but also for storing repeatedly-used information structures for all computations.   This allows a repeatedly used information structure such as a program to be read in only once through the input medium, to be stored in the auxiliary memory, and to be subsequently read in from the auxiliary memory whenever it is needed.

The auxiliary memory is typically several orders of magnitude larger than the main memory.   However, the time taken to transfer information between the main and auxiliary memories is typically several orders of magnitude longer than the execution time for a single instruction.   As a result, it is important to plan the computation so that components of an instantaneous description to which access is required for the purpose of either execution or transformation are normally in the main memory at the time that access is requested.

1.1.3 SCANNING, INTERPRETATION, COMPILATION, AND LOADING

A digital computer can be thought of as a mechanical device for *scanning* and *interpreting* a sequence of information items stored in its memory and performing a sequence of actions determined by the information items being scanned.   The sequence of information items being scanned is normally in the main computer memory and is referred to as the *instruction sequence*.   The transformations performed include transformation of data items in the data processing unit and/or in the main memory and specification of the next instruction to be scanned.

Interpretation of successive instructions of an instruction sequence which constitutes a program is referred to as *execution* of the program. Programs which can be directly executed by the computer are said to be in *internal machine language*.   However, programs are normally specified by the programmer by character sequences on a sheet of paper.   The programs written by the programmer on a sheet of paper can be thought of as being executed in a number of alternative ways:

1.   By means of a mechanical procedure for directly scanning character strings of the problem-oriented language and performing the transformations as specified.

2.   By simulating direct execution of statements of the problem-oriented language on the computer, i.e., programming the computer to scan character strings of the problem-oriented language and to perform appropriate actions.   This mode of program execution is known as *interpretive* execution of the program.

3.   By translating the problem-oriented program specification into an instruction sequence in the internal machine language of the computer and then executing the resulting program.   The translation from the problem-oriented language to machine language can be performed by a

computer and is referred to as *compiling*.   The translation program is called a *compiler*.

Translation programs play a special role in the theory of programming languages, since the data on which translation programs operate are themselves programs.   The programming language which serves as input to a translation program will be referred to as its *source language*, while the programming language which serves as output of a translation program will be referred to as its *target language* or its *object language*.

When the source language is merely a symbolic representation of the sequence of machine-language instructions, translation into machine language requires little more than transliteration and is referred to as *assembly*.   Programs for performing assembly are referred to as *assemblers* and are discussed in detail in Chap. 2.   Translation of a program from

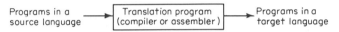

Figure 1.4   Translation of programs from one initial representation to another.

a source to a target language by a compiler or assembler is illustrated in Fig. 1.4.

A translation program may be thought of as a function f which, when applied to data items x representing programs in a source language, produces values $y = f(x)$ representing programs in a target language. The data items x and values y are themselves representations of functions. Thus a translation program is a function which operates on representation of functions.†   Programming languages whose data domain may include representations of functions will be further discussed in Chap. 3.

Translation programs are fairly complex, and translation from a problem-oriented to a machine language involves overhead during which no actual results are being computed.   However, the combined time required for translation and execution of a program is usually less than the time required for interpretive execution, since machine-language instructions can be executed very much faster (say, by a factor of 50) than interpreted instructions, and since program execution normally involves repeated execution of instructions.   Since a translated program

---

† Note that an interpreter for the execution of programs (application of programs to their data) is similarly a function which operates on representations of functions. Translation of a program from a source to a target language may be thought of as a special form of evaluation of the source-language program.   Translation programs are special-purpose interpreters whose output is restricted to programs in some target language.   This point of view is further developed in Appendix 1.

can be repeatedly executed in its translated form, the saving can be even greater.†

When translated programs are immediately executed, then single-stage compilation into internal machine language can be performed as described above. However, in many instances, translated programs are stored in their translated form for later use. In this case compilation results in programs which are close to internal machine language but contain a few parameters whose values are supplied only when the program is finally loaded into memory. The language which results from compilation is referred to as an *intermediate language*. Translation is in this case a two-stage process, the first stage being referred to as *compilation* and the second stage being referred to as *loading* (Fig. 1.5). Compilation consists of translation from a problem-oriented source language to an intermediate language, while loading consists of translation from

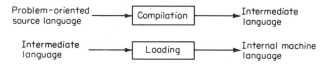

Figure 1.5 Two-stage translation process.

the intermediate language to a representation in internal machine language in memory registers of the computer.

A large program normally consists of a number of interacting program segments, which may be independently programmed and independently modified. It is convenient to allow program segments to be independently compiled. One of the advantages of the two-stage translation scheme is that for an appropriate choice of the intermediate language, program segments can be independently compiled and linked at load time.

In order to allow independent compilation of program segments, the intermediate language must make provision for the representation of information which allows intercommunication between program segments to be established at load time. Facilities for intercommunication between independently compiled program segments are further discussed in Sec. 1.8.

If the intermediate language is properly designed, translation programs can be constructed for the translation of program segments from a number of different programming languages into the same intermediate language, and conventions can be adopted to allow interaction between

---

† If some branches of a translated program are not entered at all, then translation of those branches is all overhead. However, entry to branches of a program cannot in general be predicted at translation time. The saving effected by translation depends on the "average" number of executions of statements of a program.

program segments written in different programming languages. Such conventions allow segments of a large program to be written in different languages in such a manner that each segment is written in the language most suited to programming that particular segment.

Generally available program segments, such as library subprograms, are available in the computer in their intermediate-language form, and can be incorporated into programs which require use of such subprograms using the normal facilities for intercommunication in the intermediate language.

1.1.4 INITIAL REPRESENTATIONS AND INSTANTANEOUS DESCRIPTIONS OF PROGRAMS

The translated program may be regarded as an initial representation of the program before its execution is started. During execution, data items, organizational information, and temporary internal quantities are added to the static information structure and eventually lead to the information items that represent the output. The totality of all information associated with the program may be thought of as changing with every instruction that is executed, since it grows and diminishes during execution. The totality of all the information required to characterize the program at a given instant is referred to as its instantaneous description (see page 6). The instantaneous description of a program contains the information pertaining to the program in the processing unit, main memory, auxiliary memory, and input-output units. Execution of the program is completely characterized by the profile of the instantaneous description through time.

The instantaneous description of a program may be thought of as consisting of three parts:

1.   A program part, representing the program to be executed
2.   A data part, representing the data on which the program operates
3.   A stateword, representing the information in the computer processing unit, including the accumulator, instruction pointer, index registers, etc.

1.1.5 REENTRANT PROGRAMS AND ACTIVATION RECORDS

In early program-execution systems the program part of an instantaneous description was modified during its execution,† and each program part

† The first computers stored only the data in internal memory registers and required successive instructions to be executed either manually (as in the case of desk calculators) or by means of a preprogrammed set of instructions in a storage medium which could not be modified. The advent of computers in which programs as well as data could be stored in the internal computer memory and modified during the computation was hailed as a conceptual as well as a technological breakthrough. It was felt that modification of programs as though they were data would play a

had precisely one data part associated with it during its lifetime, being replaced by a new copy of the initial program part for each instance of use.

In recent program-execution systems, it has been found convenient to allow program segments to be executed by several different higher-level programs simultaneously. This mode of program execution requires each instance of execution to have its own set of registers for storing information that varies for different instances of execution. Each instance of execution of such a program is referred to as an *activation*, and the variable part associated with each activation is referred to as an *activation record*. The fixed-program part of a program whose execution is organized in this way is regarded as an inert text representing an algorithm which may be scanned, interpreted, and executed by any number of higher-level processes with their own set of instruction pointers and their own data. A program part organized in this way is said to be *reentrant* because it can be "reentered" by a second interpreter before execution by a previous interpreter is completed.†

Programs are normally organized in a modular fashion. Each module may be thought of as a function which when executed performs a transformation on the environment in which it is embedded. Program modules which represent functions may be physically embedded in other program modules, as in languages like ALGOL, or may be independently specified, as in languages like FORTRAN.

A program which, during its execution, requires transfer of control between a number of program modules has a sequence of instantaneous descriptions whose structure can be described in terms of the instantaneous descriptions of component function modules. The structure of such composite instantaneous descriptions is discussed in Chap. 4.

Programs are entered reentrantly both when independent processes wish to execute an algorithm represented by the same program part and

---

fundamental role in future computing techniques. However, it was found increasingly that physical modification of programs during their execution led to "unesthetic" programming techniques, which increased the probability of errors. Hardware was developed to allow physical modification of programs to be simulated by varying data parameters rather than by physical embedding of variable information in the program. In recent programming systems increasing emphasis is placed on the separation between "pure (reentrant) procedures," which remain unmodified throughout the computation, and information, which varies during execution. The representation of program segments and complete programs by pure procedures is discussed at length in Chap. 4.

† Reentrantly organized program modules which cause themselves to be reentered during execution are sometimes called *recursive* programs. Execution of recursive program modules is almost always organized reentrantly. However, reentrantly organized programs need not necessarily be recursive.

when a given execution of the algorithm requires recursive reentry into the program part that specifies the algorithm.

An instantaneous description can be considered as an entity that is independent of the interpreter that is executing it.   When the stateword of the instantaneous description resides in a processor and the information required for the next execution step is in the hardware units expected by the processor, the interpreter can perform the next execution step. Otherwise, the process is in a blocked state, and the instantaneous description cannot be modified until required information has been put into required hardware units.

1.1.6 BATCH PROCESSING AND MULTIPROGRAMMING

In previous sections an attempt was made to introduce some of the basic concepts found useful in characterizing the structure of programs and the relation between information structures and the storage media in which they are represented.   In the present section we shall indicate some of the questions which must be considered in representing a number of programs simultaneously within a computer system and in scheduling execution of such programs.

The complexity of the system which controls execution of a set of programs depends heavily on the forms of scheduling of execution of programs in the system.   The earliest form of scheduling of automatic execution of programs is known as *batch processing*.   In the batch-processing mode a sequence of run requests is placed on the input medium, and programs are executed one at a time in the order that the run requests appear on the input medium.   In the batch-processing mode only one program at a time can be in execution and each program is run to completion once it is initiated.

The batch-processing mode of operation has the great virtue of simplicity, but may have the following drawbacks:

1.   The program being executed may be unable to efficiently utilize computer resources while it is being executed.   For example, if a program calls for input of data, the processing unit may be idle while waiting for the data to arrive.

2.   Batch processing may result in an unnecessarily large elapsed time between submitting a program and return of the results.   This elapsed time is referred to as the *turnaround time*.

The first factor affects computer efficiency and will therefore be called a *technological* factor.   The second factor affects user convenience and will be called an *intrinsic* factor.

Inefficient utilization of computer resources may in principle be avoided by allowing several programs to have a sufficient number of components of their instantaneous description in the main computer memory so that their execution can be initiated without recourse to the auxiliary memory or the input medium.   If the program currently being executed cannot effectively continue to use the processor because it is waiting for input, execution of one of the other programs in the main memory can be initiated.

Programming systems which allow several programs to simultaneously occupy portions of the computer memory and compete for processor time will be referred to as *multiprogramming systems*.   They have to cope with the problem of allocating hardware to segments of instantaneous descriptions so that execution can proceed efficiently.

In characterizing multiprogramming systems it is convenient to think of the computer as a collection of resources of different kinds, some of which are in greater demand than others.   Each of the resources is essentially a resource for storing components of information structures, but some resources (the processing unit) have the property that information structures residing in them can be transformed.   It is assumed that the total information-storage capacity of the computer system is sufficient for storage of all information structures (instantaneous descriptions) of programs in the computer system.   However, some classes of resources, such as processing units and the main memory, may become overloaded and cause bottlenecks.

In any given interval of time the useful work done by a multiprogramming system is the sum of the amounts of time spent in computation on programs to which the processor has had access.   The amount of useful work done by the system is referred to as the *throughput*.

A multiprogramming system cannot in general spend all its time doing useful work, since system functions, e.g., initiation of a new program on a processing unit, require instructions to be executed in the processing unit.   The processor time used by the system to perform system functions will be referred to as *system overhead*.

During any given interval of time a given processing unit may be engaged in user computation or system computation or be idle.   The proportion of the time spent in user computation is a measure of the efficiency of use of the processor.

The objectives of a multiprogramming system are not only to maximize technological processor efficiency in the above sense but also to provide a certain quality of service to the user as measured by the turnaround time.   Quality of service may conflict with maximization of technological efficiency, so that the objectives of any given multiprogramming system are usually those of achieving as high a technological efficiency as possible for a given quality of service. The techniques used in current multiprogramming systems for achieving a balance between technological efficiency and quality of service are discussed in later sections of this chapter.

1.1.7 NAMES, DECLARATIONS, AND BINDING TIME

At any given point during execution of a program there is a fixed set of symbols and symbol patterns which is meaningful to the interpreter which executes the program. If the program is a machine-language program and the interpreter is a computer, then the set of meaningful symbol patterns is the instruction set of the computer. The symbol strings which can occur in instructions include operation codes, names of memory registers (addresses), and names of input-output devices. The names of information-storage devices that occur in machine-language instructions may be thought of as names of the information structures currently residing in the information-storage devices. The information structures which can be named in machine language are normally restricted to a predefined set of fixed-length structures, such as integers, floating-point numbers, and character strings.

The meaningful symbol patterns which may occur during direct interpretation of programs in a problem-oriented language similarly include operation codes and names of information structures. The information structures which can be named and manipulated in a problem-oriented language are not in general dependent on the instruction set and hardware facilities of a particular computer. Moreover, names in a problem-oriented language are independent of physical information-storage devices and are associated with information structures independently of where or how they are stored.

Whereas the set of names accessible to a processing unit is that of a *fixed* set of hardware storage devices, the set of names accessible during direct interpretation of a program in a problem-oriented language may be augmented and modified during program execution by *declarations*.

A substring of a program is said to be a *program segment* if it constitutes a unit for purposes of interpretation. It is convenient to classify program segments into two categories:

1. *Imperative* or *executable* program segments, which, when executed, result in transformations of the information structure
2. *Declarative* program segments, which, when executed, result in a change of the mode of interpretation of subsequently interpreted symbols of the symbol string

Executable program segments include complete programs, procedures, statements, and expressions. Declarative program segments specify attributes to be associated with names of variables and symbol strings that occur during program execution. Declarative program segments are normally embedded in executable program segments and may in turn have executable programs embedded inside them.

The set of all symbols and symbol strings which can meaningfully occur at a given point of execution is referred to as the *environment* at that point of execution. The environment E at a given point of execution can be thought of as a list of symbol patterns s_i together with a list of actions t_i which specify the action to be taken when the symbol pattern s_i is encountered during execution. For a program written in a programming language L, there is a set of initial symbol patterns S_L that can meaningfully be encountered. This set of initial symbol patterns can be augmented and modified by declarative program segments during execution.

At the beginning of a computation, we start with an initial instantaneous description I and an initial environment E. The initial instantaneous description contains a pointer to the first symbol of the program string to be interpreted. Interpretation of the program string is initiated using interpretation rules specified in the initial environment E. The interpretation steps can be classified into imperative interpretation steps and declarative interpretation steps. Imperative interpretation steps result in a transformation of the instantaneous description, while declarative interpretation steps result in modification of the environment which may modify the subsequent interpretation rules.

The boundary between imperative and declarative interpretation rules is not always definite. Declarative interpretation rules usually result in a modified instantaneous description at least to the extent of modifying the instruction pointer.

When declarative modifications to the environment are executed, they are usually stored as ordered pairs (s_i, t_i) in a symbol table, where s_i represents a symbol pattern and t_i specifies the action to be taken when the symbol pattern s_i is subsequently encountered during execution. If this symbol table is considered to be part of the instantaneous description, then modification of the environment entails modification of the instantaneous description. The distinction between declarative and imperative program segments is useful when classifying structures of actual programming languages but becomes elusive when attempts are made to express these concepts in terms of more fundamental ones.

Declarations tend to specify structural attributes associated with a name, while executable program segments tend to assign values to components of an information structure. However, the distinction between information structures and values stored in components of an information structure is itself not a fundamental one.   It will be shown in later chapters that information items such as numbers, which are usually represented by values in single information fields, may be represented by "structure components" of structures such as lists. The distinction between declarative and imperative information and the distinction between structure specification and value assignment break down when they are examined closely.

The distinction between declarative and imperative statements is useful because it allows the specification of an information structure to be broken down into two stages.   It is convenient to be able to specify attributes of an information structure that remain invariant during the lifetime of the structure independently of attributes that are modified during execution.   In many applications the number and size of the information fields remain invariant throughout the lifetime of an information structure, and it is convenient to specify these attributes by declarations when the information structure is created.   However, the values of fields of the information structure may be modified during its lifetime.   Such modification is usually specified by imperative program segments.

A program segment which determines attributes of an information structure is said to *bind* these attributes.   The moment during execution at which a given set of attributes is fixed (bound) is said to be the *binding time* of the given set of attributes.   In performing a computation, it is convenient to bind invariant attributes of an information structure at the time of creation of the structure and to bind varying attributes of the structure at the time that they are computed.   Declarations serve to bind invariant attributes of an information structure, while imperative program segments serve to compute varying attributes of an information structure.

The programmer sometimes has a choice as to the time of binding of certain attributes of an information structure.   The following two extreme binding strategies can be used:

1.   Always perform binding at the earliest possible point of time.
2.   Always perform binding at the latest possible point of time.

An example of the first strategy is to specify all invariant properties of all information structures prior to the beginning of the computation. This strategy is normally adopted in FORTRAN, where storage for all information structures is allocated prior to the beginning of the computation.   The second strategy is adopted in ALGOL, where information structures are dynamically created and deleted during execution as they are required.   Binding attributes as early as possible sometimes results in more efficient program execution, since it saves repetition.   However, binding attributes as late as possible allows the decision regarding the bound attributes to be delayed and thereby allows greater flexibility in specifying the attribute.

The distinction between compilation and interpretation may be phrased in terms of the concept binding time.   Compilation results in binding a source-language program to its target-language representation at translation time, while interpretation delays binding the source-language program till execution time.   Here again, early binding results in greater efficiency, since it saves repeated binding, and late binding allows greater flexibility in introducing tracing and other modifications at execution time.

The intermediate language into which a source program is compiled is used because the binding of certain attributes of a source program cannot be performed at compile time but is delayed until load time.   Alternative strategies of binding during the loading process are discussed in later sections of Chap. 1.

The distinction between macros and procedures (elaborated in Chaps. 2 to 4) may similarly be stated in terms of binding time.   When a procedure-oriented language contains macro facilities, macro calls result in physical substitution of the macro definition in the program text prior to execution (see Sec. 2.6).   Procedure calls result in simulated substitution of the procedure definition during execution.   The earlier binding time of macros results in greater efficiency during execution.   However, the delay of binding till execution time allows considerably greater flexibility during execution by delaying the binding of procedure parameters.   The cost is normally only a small proportion of the total execution time of the procedure.

These examples illustrate that the concept of binding time is very useful when distinctions between events occurring at different points of time in a computation are discussed.   The present text emphasizes the sequence of dynamic representations of a program at successive stages of execution, and the concept of binding time is an important one in this context.

The question of binding is relevant not only in the context of creation and deletion of information structures but also in the context of specifying structural forms (templates) for classes of information structure.   At this level, the question arises whether the structural form of program segments and data of a programming language should be specified (bound) at the time of language design or whether the programming language should contain facilities for specifying new structural forms suited to particular problem areas.

Facilities within a programming language for the creation of new structural forms are referred to as *definitional facilities*. Designers of a general-purpose programming language cannot provide suitable program and data structures for all problem areas in which it might be used, so that general-purpose programming languages of the future will probably contain definitional facilities. However, the choice of primitive program and data structures from which nonprimitive structures are to be built up still presents a problem. Languages which contain a relatively small set of primitive program and data structures and rely heavily on definitional facilities are sometimes referred to as *core languages*, while languages which attempt to provide an adequate set of primitives for general-purpose use are sometimes referred to as *shell languages*. The programming languages discussed in Chap. 4, such as ALGOL and PL/I, were developed as shell languages. However, a better understanding of macros (Chaps. 2 and 3) allows macros to be used in developing definitional facilities (see Sec. 3.4). The notion of definitional facilities is extensively discussed in a forthcoming text by Galler and Perlis [21]. Definitional facilities for data structures are discussed and developed by Standish [22].

1.1.8 SYNTAX, SEMANTICS, AND FUNCTION-MODULE REPRESENTATION

In dealing with information structures we are concerned both with inherent structural properties and with the kinds of transformations which the structure may initiate or undergo when it enters into a computation. The inherent structural properties of an information structure are referred to as *syntactic* properties, and the transformational properties of the structure are referred to as *semantic* properties.

It is convenient to have a notation for specifying syntactic and semantic properties of classes of information structures. For example, the set of all representations of programs in a specific programming language is an example of a class of information structures. A notation for specifying the class of programs in a programming language is called a *syntactic notation* for the programming language. A notation for specifying the effect of execution of all programs in a programming language is called a *semantic notation* for the programming language. A specification of the class of programs of a programming language in some syntactic notation is called a *syntax* or a *grammar* of the programming language. A specification of the effect of execution of all programs of a programming language in a semantic notation is called a *semantics* of the programming language.

It should be noted that syntax and semantics as defined above are concerned purely with properties of information structures and not with properties of the functions or other objects *represented* by the information structures. Syntax and semantics are associated with a specific class of *representations* of programs and their data. The syntax and semantics of programs specified in a source language differ from the syntax and semantics of corresponding programs in a machine-oriented target language. However, we shall see, in Chaps. 3 and 4, that there is a strong correspondence between source-language semantics and machine-language semantics for many of the more widely used macro languages and procedure-oriented programming languages.

The syntax of programming languages has been widely studied in the literature, but it is not the primary concern of the present text. A survey of the work on syntax of programming languages, together with an annotated bibliography, is given in Appendix 1. The present text is concerned principally with the direct characterization of the semantics of programming languages.

A program in a programming language is a function which may in turn consist of a number of interacting component functions. Indeed, every executable program segment of a programming language may be thought of as a function which, when it is executed, transforms the instantaneous description of which it forms a part. Executable program segments of a programming language will be referred to as *function modules*.

The semantics of a function module may be specified by the effect of execution of the function module on the instantaneous description in which it is embedded. Let the instantaneous description *before* execution of a function module be denoted by I_B and the instantaneous description *after* execution of a function module be denoted by I_A. Then the effect of the function module for a given environment I_B may be specified by the ordered pair (I_B, I_A). An alternative notation for specifying that I_B is transformed by the function module into I_A is $I_B \rightarrow I_A$. The expression $I_B \rightarrow I_A$ is referred to as a *production*. The notation of productions has been widely used in syntactic specification and is now beginning to be used for semantic specification. Variants of this notation have been widely used by logicians in specifying transformational properties of logical systems.

The set of all transformations which can be performed by a function module can in principle be specified by the set of ordered pairs (I_B, I_A) for every possible I_B or by a corresponding set of productions. In practice the number of ordered pairs required to specify a function module may be very large or even infinite, so that other schemes, such as programs, are frequently used for specifying the correspondence of environments before and after execution of a function module.

Finite sets of ordered pairs are conveniently specified in a computer by *symbol tables*, consisting of a set of entries each of which is an ordered pair. Use of a symbol table during a computation is referred to as *symbol-*

table look-up. The argument for a symbol-table look-up operation is an instance of a first component of an entry of the symbol table, and the value of a symbol-table look-up operation is the corresponding second component. Thus symbol tables are essentially representations of functions defined by a finite set of ordered pairs, and symbol-table look-up constitutes evaluation of such a function for a given argument. Since symbol tables constitute a natural representation of functions having a finite domain, symbol-table techniques figure prominently in Chap. 2 and in subsequent chapters. In Chap. 3 the notion is introduced of semantic specification by symbol-table programs which effectively perform symbol-table look-up to determine the type of function module next to be executed and then perform a transformation to the environment specified by the second component of the symbol-table entry. Symbol tables of this kind effectively determine the *environment* with respect to which the program is interpreted, as indicated in subsection 1.1.7.

Programming languages usually permit specification of function modules of a number of different kinds. Some kinds of function modules, such as simple arithmetic expressions and statements, are normally physically embedded in the program at the point at which they are to be executed. Other kinds of function modules are defined by means of a *function definition* and may be executed at a number of distinct points of the program by means of a *function call*. A further kind of function module has the property of being called *implicitly* when an abnormal condition occurs during execution rather than explicitly by a function call. Such function modules are referred to as *interrupt function modules*.

Function modules may be classified both by the manner in which they are initiated and by the manner in which they may be interrupted by other function modules and subsequently resumed. Each kind of function module may be represented in a number of different ways during execution. Alternative representation strategies result in different kinds of transformations of instantaneous description during execution and therefore in different semantics. A number of alternative strategies for function representation and function execution are considered in the present text, and the transformations of instantaneous descriptions for each of the classes of representations considered are developed in some detail.

The structure of the instantaneous description of a program may be specified in a relatively simple manner in terms of the structure of its component function modules. In Chap. 4 this approach is applied in considerable detail to the specification of the structure of instantaneous descriptions of ALGOL programs and is then applied to PL/I and simulation languages. Chapter 4 is intended to demonstrate that the approach to programming languages adopted in the present text is theoretically and esthetically interesting and at the same time more effective for expository purposes than more traditional approaches.

1.2   THE REPRESENTATION AND TRANSFORMATION OF INFORMATION

In the present section we shall consider how low-level information structures can be represented in a computer and indicate how arithmetic operations can be constructed from lower-level primitive operations. It is pointed out that building hardware for arithmetic operations out of primitive hardware components is analogous to building programs out of a primitive set of instructions, thus emphasizing that building a program out of primitive instructions is in principle a similar activity to building complex hardware units from a set of primitive components. Programming, however, has the advantage of being more flexible than the construction of corresponding hardware units. Moreover, programs stored in the computer can be erased and modified without the necessity for physical rewiring.

1.2.1   BINARY REPRESENTATION OF INFORMATION

When information is represented on a sheet of paper, it is usually represented by sequences of characters chosen from a finite alphabet. Verbal information in a natural language is usually represented by strings of characters of an alphabet, which include uppercase letters, lowercase letters, and standard punctuation symbols. Numbers are usually represented in decimal notation in a language that includes the decimal digits and the decimal point.

In a programming language it is necessary to represent operations on data as well as the data itself, so that the alphabet of a programming language for specifying operations on numbers includes symbols for arithmetic operations. Names of variables and functions of a programming language are usually specified by strings of letters and numbers.

Example: The sequence of 10 characters "$X = A + 2.5 \times B;$" might represent an arithmetic statement in a typical programming language.

Information inside a computer is usually represented by sequences of characters from a two-character alphabet. The two characters will be represented by the symbols 0 and 1 and will be referred to as *binary digits* or *bits*. A two-character alphabet is convenient because two-state physical information-storage devices for distinguishing between characters are more stable and reliable than n-state physical devices for distinguishing between n alternative characters. Two-state devices for storing information include punched cards and paper tape, in which each potential hole may be thought of as representing 1 if it is punched and 0 if it is not punched. The principal storage device for the main memory is currently the magnetic core, which is a two-state device corresponding to two directions of magnetization. Storage devices for auxiliary memory consist of various kinds of magnetic surfaces in which each storage position can be magnetized in one of two directions.

Characters of an alphabet with more than two characters can be represented by groups of binary digits; i.e., two binary digits can be used to distinguish between four alternative characters, three binary digits can be used to distinguish between eight alternative characters, and n binary digits can be used to distinguish between 2^n alternative characters.

Example: Since there are 10 decimal digits, at least four binary digits are required to represent a single decimal digit. In principle, any 10 of the 16 possible four-binary-digit codes could be used for representing the decimal digits. The most common choice of four-binary-digit codes for decimal digits is the following:

Decimal Digit	Binary Code
0	0000
1	0001
2	0010
3	0011
4	0100
5	0101
6	0110
7	0111
8	1000
9	1001

This representation is a *positional* binary notation which associates a weight of 2^n with the $(n + 1)$st digit position, just as the positional decimal notation associates a weight of 10^n with the $(n + 1)$st decimal digit position.

Exercise: How many different ways are there of assigning four-digit binary-digit codes to decimal digits?

There is a considerable body of literature concerned with code assignment [7]. Code assignments should clearly have the property that operations on the items being represented by codes should be reasonably easy to perform. The ease with which operations can be performed on coded items depends considerably on the code chosen. Thus, arithmetic operations can be performed more easily on integers coded in a decimal (or binary) positional notation than on integers represented in the notation for roman numerals.

Exercises: (*a*) Define explicitly an algorithm for addition and multiplication of integers in decimal positional notation and binary positional notation.   (*b*) Define algorithms for conversion from decimal to binary and binary to decimal notation.   (*c*) Define an algorithm for addition and multiplication of integers represented by roman numerals.

A set of n objects can in general be represented by n different patterns of k binary digits, where k is the smallest integer for which $2^k \geq n$. However, it is sometimes convenient to introduce deliberate redundancy into the code so that errors can be detected and corrected.   For example, decimal digits can be represented by five binary digits in a number of alternative ways so that transposition of a single digit from a 0 to a 1 always results in an illegal code not representing a number.

Exercise: Find a set of five-binary-digit codes for decimal digits such that only codes with an odd number of binary 1s represent decimal digits. Find a set of five-binary-digit codes for decimal digits such that only codes with two binary 1s represent decimal digits.

Integers larger than 9 can be represented either by extending the positional notation or by representing each digit individually by a four-digit binary code.   Thus, 12 can be represented in pure binary by 1100 or digit by digit as 0001 0010, while 37 can be represented either by 100101 or by 0011 0111.   A representation of an integer in which each decimal digit is represented by a binary code is referred to as a *binary-coded* representation.

On input into the computer by an input instruction, integers represented externally by decimal digits would initially be represented internally in binary-coded form.   However, in most computers arithmetic operations are performed on integers in positional representation, so that integers must be converted from their binary-coded representation to a positional representation before arithmetic operations are performed on them.

Exercise: Draw a flow diagram for converting an integer from binary-coded representation to positional representation.

Binary-coded representation for digits is a special case of binary-coded representation for characters.   Since there are 10 digits and 10 is less than 2^4, digits can be represented by 4 binary digits.   In general a set of less than 2^k characters can be represented in a k-binary-digit field.

Within a computer, groups of binary digits are used to represent decimal digits, integers, numbers, and many other kinds of information. A group of binary digits which represents a given logical item of information is referred to as a *field*.   Information fields are of different sizes, depending on the number of different items of information that are to be distinguished by the given field.

Example: An address field which distinguishes between 2^n addresses has a size of n binary digits.

The information fields discussed in subsequent sections will include *operation fields*, for specifying the operation codes of instructions; *address fields*, for specifying the location within the computer of an item of information; and *character fields*, for specifying characters of character-coded information. Each of these items of information is represented by a pattern of binary bits. The bit patterns for representing operation codes, address codes, character codes, and number codes are distinguished, not by any inherent property of the code itself, but by the fact that the codes are interpreted by different units of the machine during execution. Thus the operation code will on execution be interpreted by the instruction-processing unit and set in motion a train of events resulting in execution of an operation. An address field is on execution interpreted in the instruction-processing unit and results in access to a given memory location for storage or retrieval of an item of information. Character and number fields are normally operated on in the data-processing unit. The computer system is organized so that the right information field is presented for interpretation to the right computer component at the right time.

1.2.2 LOGICAL OPERATIONS

Since all information in a computer is represented by groups of binary digits, the transformations performed by a digital computer are transfor-

Input	Output
0	1
1	0

not ($\neg$)

Inputs	Output
00	0
01	0
10	0
11	1

and ($\wedge$)

Inputs	Output
00	0
01	1
10	1
11	1

or ($\vee$)

Figure 1.6 Tables which define the logical functions *and, or,* **and** *not.*

mations on binary digits and groups of binary digits. The transformations which can be performed on binary digits are conveniently specified by means of functions which specify for each possible value of the input the value of the output.†

† The set of all possible values of the argument of a function is referred to as the *domain* of the function. The set of all possible values which can be obtained by applying the function to arguments in its domain is referred to as the *range* of the function.

The most common operations on binary digits are the logical operations *and*, *or*, and *not*; *not* has an input domain of one binary digit and is defined in Fig. 1.6 by a two-entry table which specifies the transformation for each element of the input domain; *and* and *or* have input domains of two binary digits and are respectively specified by four-entry tables in Fig. 1.6.

Exercises: (*a*) How many different functions are there having a domain of one binary digit and a range of one binary digit?   (*b*) How many different functions are there having a domain of two binary digits and a range of one binary digit?

1.2.3 HALF ADDERS AND ADDERS

It can be shown that any required function of two binary digits can be constructed by combining the above operations in suitable ways.   For example, addition with carry is defined as a function with two inputs and

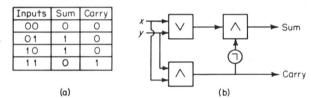

Inputs	Sum	Carry
00	0	0
01	1	0
10	1	0
11	0	1

(a)   (b)

Figure 1.7   (*a*) **Definition and** (*b*) **construction of half adder** h.

two outputs in Fig. 1.7*a* and is constructed in terms of the functions of Fig. 1.6 as indicated in Fig. 1.7*b*.   A device having these functional characteristics is called a *half adder* and will be denoted by h.

In order to add two binary integers, it is necessary to add corresponding digits and consider the carry from the previous position, as in the following example:

$$
\begin{array}{cc}
27 & 11011 \\
29 & 11101 \\
\hline
56 & 111000
\end{array}
$$

Binary addition with carry thus involves three inputs (two plus carry to the preceding digit).   An addition table for two digits with carry is given in Fig. 1.8, together with a specification of how this function can be built up from previously defined functions.   A device having these functional characteristics is called an *adder*.

If the successive digits of a number are added serially, they can be added by a single adder which feeds the carry from the previous digit back into the input through a delay D of one time unit.   Parallel addition would require one adder for each digit position.   Serial addition and parallel addition for three-digit binary integers are illustrated in Fig. 1.9.

This discussion indicates how more complex functions can be built up from the three primitive functions *and*, *or*, and *not* by series connection, parallel connection, and feeding of outputs back into the input.   This

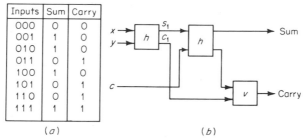

Inputs	Sum	Carry
000	0	0
001	1	0
010	1	0
011	0	1
100	1	0
101	0	1
110	0	1
111	1	1

(a)   (b)

Figure 1.8   (*a*) **Definition and** (*b*) **construction of an adder.**

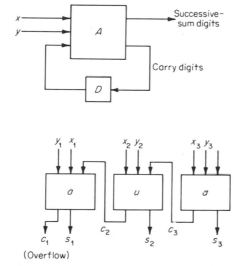

Figure 1.9 Serial and parallel addition. (The sum digit of each addition module serves as output, while the carry digit is fed into the next box on the left.   The carry digit of the leftmost box is an overflow digit.)

development could be continued to show how multiplication and division can be built up from the primitive devices.   Similarly many of the functions which are normally computed by the execution of instruction sequences could be specified in terms of primitive devices and could be realized by means of hardware.   However, it is usual to choose a set of general-purpose instructions as the primitive hardware instruction set of a computer and to arrange that functions for performing specific computations be specified by programs which involve execution of sequences of primitive instructions.

1.2.4 HARDWARE, SOFTWARE, AND MICROPROGRAMMING

The boundary between hardware-implemented functions and functions implemented by programs is somewhat arbitrary. For example, the primitive operations *and*, *or*, and *not* could have been chosen as primitive and addition could have been specified as a program in terms of the primitive *and*, *or*, and *not* instructions. However, this would have involved execution of a long sequence of *and*, *or*, and *not* instructions for every addition or multiplication. Since computers are specifically designed to facilitate rapid operations on numbers, most computers have built-in hardware for arithmetic operations on both fixed- and floating-point numbers. These operations are probably the most complex built-in hardware functions in computers.

Exercise: Write a program for the addition of two binary digits, using only *and*, *or*, and *not* operations.

Some computers have an easily accessible set of primitive operations which are more primitive than the basic instruction set. These primitive operations are normally joined together in a standard way to yield a standard set of instructions, but they can be reorganized relatively easily to obtain a different set of instructions. The instruction set may be thought of as being programmed in terms of the primitive operations by means of a program which is wired in to the computer. Reorganization to obtain a new set of instructions may be thought of as reprogramming followed by "wiring in" of the new program.

A number of computers have specific facilities for redefining the set of basic computer instructions by rearranging the computer logic. This can be accomplished either by physically rewiring the logical circuitry of the computer or by arranging for the logical portion of the circuitry to be detachable or replaceable. For example, the logical circuitry can be represented by a plugboard which can be removed and replaced by a plugboard with different wiring. In some computers such as the IBM 360 model 30, the interconnection between logical components is determined by the pattern of holes in a number of replaceable punched cards. Rewiring the primitive components to form a new set of primitive instructions can in this case be performed by merely replacing the existing set of punched cards by a new set, which establishes the appropriate interconnections.

Definition of the primitive instructions of a computer by establishing a new set of hardware interconnections is referred to as *microprogramming*. Microprogramming certain instructions may result in a considerable saving in execution speed over simulation of the corresponding instructions in terms of a given set of primitive instructions.

Programming is essentially an activity which involves building up a complex functional structure from primitive functional components. The primitive functional components used in programming are normally primitive instructions of a programming language. Those used in microprogramming are hardware modules. The notion of building complex functions out of simpler functional components is basic to both microprogramming and programming in a programming language. Both transformational hardware components and computer programs may be thought of as functions and are therefore to some extent interchangeable. In a digital computer frequently used functions such as addition are built into the hardware, while less frequently used functions are programmed by instruction sequences rather than by physical interconnection of hardware components. However, the distinction between hardware and software is essentially an arbitrary one. The functional effect of *any* given computer program could in principle be achieved more efficiently by physical interconnection of hardware components than by a program.

1.3 REGISTERS, FORMATS, FIELDS, AND THEIR SPECIFICATION

1.3.1 REGISTERS

A given item of information has an inherent logical structure. When it is stored in a computer, on a sheet of paper, or in some other storage medium, the logical structure must be mapped onto a representation in a physical storage medium. The physical storage facilities of a computer are chosen so that a wide variety of logical structures can be stored in the physical structure in such a manner that the logical structure can be simply recovered.

The principal information-storage medium of the computer is the computer memory. It is usually structured into a sequence of *memory registers,*† each of which can hold a fixed number of binary digits of

---

† The term "register" is sometimes reserved in the literature for information-storage devices in the processing unit. In the present text the term register will include information-storage devices in the main and auxiliary memories. The information stored in processing-unit registers is more actively used in determining the course of the computation than that stored in memory registers. Information is usually moved to registers of the processing unit before it is actively used in computation.

information.   This number, called the *length* of the register, is usually chosen so that it can hold a number or an instruction.   Memory registers can be named by *addresses*.   The addresses used to name the registers of a computer memory with N registers are usually the integers 0 through $N - 1$. N is frequently chosen to be a power of 2, say 2^k, so that addresses can be represented efficiently in a k-binary-digit address field.

Other components of a computer, such as the instruction-processing unit and data-processing unit (see Fig. 1.2), contain registers which are used during program execution to store information from memory registers.   The data-processing unit normally contains a register called the *accumulator* (AC), for storing the results of addition and multiplication, and a single-length register called the *multiplier-quotient register* (MQ),

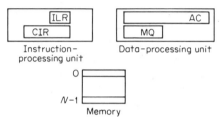

Figure 1.10   **Principal information-carrying registers.**

for holding the multiplier during multiplication and the quotient during division.   The AC and the MQ have arithmetic properties during the execution of arithmetic instruction.   However, they may have other special properties during the execution of instructions on nonnumeric data.†

The instruction-processing unit usually has a register called the *current-instruction register* (CIR), for storing the current instruction being executed, and a register called the *instruction-location register* (ILR), for storing the address of the next instruction to be executed.   When a given instruction is executed on a simple computer, the content of the memory register pointed to by the ILR is moved to the CIR, the content of the ILR is incremented by 1 to point to the next instruction, and the content of the CIR is executed.   The principal registers of the instruction-processing unit, data-processing unit, and main computer memory are illustrated in Fig. 1.10.

† The AC and MQ have an information-carrying capacity similar to other registers of the computer but are distinguished from other registers in that information in these registers can be manipulated more flexibly than information in the main computer memory.

1.3.2 REGISTER DECLARATIONS

When describing a computer, it is convenient to introduce a notation for specifying the number and sizes of all information-carrying registers of the computer.   Such a notation will be introduced and illustrated in the present section.   This notation may be regarded as a fragment of a programming language and may indeed be embedded in a programming language.   Languages of this kind are sometimes referred to as *register-transfer languages* or *computer-description languages*.

A notation for specifying registers of a computer is principally descriptive in nature, since its purpose is to specify the set of computer registers.   However, imperative features are introduced into the notation in order to describe how information stored in registers is manipulated during execution.

A register is an information-storage device, and its principal attribute is the number of bits of information it can store.   A register declaration consists of the word **register,** followed by the register name, followed by a specification of the number of bits in the register.   The MQ of a computer with a 32-bit word can be specified by the following declaration:

register MQ[0:31]   This register declaration specifies a register named MQ having 32 bits named 0 through 31.

The AC of a computer typically has twice as many bits as other registers to accommodate the significant digits of the product in multiplication.†   A 64-bit AC can be specified by the following register declaration:

register AC[0:63]   This register declaration specifies a register called AC with 64 bits named 0 through 63.

The Ith bit of the registers MQ and AC can respectively be referred to as MQ[I] and AC[I].   The complete registers MQ and AC are referred to by MQ and AC without using subscripts.

When there is more than one register of a given kind in the computer, it is convenient to use double subscripting.   Thus the set of registers in a computer memory with 2^{15} 32-bit registers can be specified as follows:

register MEM[0:32767,0:31]   This register declaration specifies that MEM is a set of 32,768 registers named 0 through 32,767 each having 32 bits named 0 through 31.

The conventions will be adopted that MEM[I,J] refers to the Jth bit of the Ith register, MEM[I] refers to the complete Ith register, and MEM refers to the complete memory.   These conventions are an instance

† Sometimes the MQ register serves as the second half of the AC for the purpose of storing the less significant digits of a multiplication.

of the general convention that failure to mention a dimension implies reference to the complete set of elements of the omitted dimension.

A 32-bit current-instruction register CIR and a 15-bit instruction-location register ILR can be specified by the following declarations:

register CIR[0:31]   This register declaration specifies a register named CIR with 32 bits named 0 through 31.

register ILR[0:14]   This register declaration specifies a register named ILR with 15 bits named 0 through 14.   Note that 15 bits in the ILR are sufficient to address a memory with 2^{15} registers.

Computers normally contain a number of additional special registers such as *index registers* (see Sec. 1.6) and a number of indicators such as the *overflow indicator*.   Sizes and names of all information-carrying registers of the computer can be specified by register declarations.

Exercise: Specify the sizes and names of all registers and indicators on a machine of your choice.

There is a fundamental distinction between a register and the information stored in the register at any specified moment, which will be mirrored in the present notation by letting $C(R)$ denote the content of the register R.

Example: $C(MQ)$ denotes the content of the register MQ. $C(MEM(I))$ denotes the content of the Ith memory register.

The above notation will be further extended to allow transfer of information from one register to another.   Thus $C(R) \rightarrow R'$ will denote transfer of the content of register R to register R'.†   Using this extended notation the instruction-execution cycle of a simple computer can be specified by the following sequence of operations:

$C(MEM(ILR)) \rightarrow CIR$ Move the content of the memory register having the address ILR to the CIR.

$C(ILR) + 1 \rightarrow ILR$ Increment the ILR by 1.

EXECUTE(CIR)   Execute the instruction in the CIR.

† In programming languages which use the notation of arithmetic expressions, $C(R) \rightarrow R'$ is written as $R' = R$.   Note that in this case occurrence of the name of a register on the right-hand side of the = sign implies reference to the content of the register while occurrence of the name on the left-hand side of the = sign implies a reference to the named register without regard to its content.   Thus the distinction between register names and their content is *implicit* in such notations.   The distinction between register names and their content is implicit also in machine language, since "LOAD R" or "ADD R" refers to the content of R, while "STORE R" refers to the named register without regard to content.

Execution of the second and third of these operations depends not only on the register size but also on the way in which the information is stored in the register.   The binary digits stored in a register are interpreted in different ways depending on whether the contents are executed as instructions in the instruction-processing unit or operated on as data in the data-processing unit.   The detailed interpretation of specific digits in a register depends on the specific computer.   However, the general principles for interpretation of digits stored in a register are discussed in subsequent sections of this chapter.

The way in which binary digits of a register are organized when representing a given kind of information is referred to as the *information format* for that kind of information.   Information formats are further discussed below.

1.3.3 FORMATS AND FORMAT DECLARATIONS

It is important to distinguish between physical registers of a computer and the information stored in physical registers.   More generally, it is important to distinguish between an information structure and the medium in which it is stored.   An information structure consists of a set of interrelated information fields having a structure that is independent of any storage medium.   The storage medium has a fixed structure determined by register sizes and hardware facilities for automatic interconnections or adjacency relations between registers.

In operating on an information structure, the fields of the structure must be fitted into the fixed storage structure of the information-storage medium.   The information-storage medium is therefore chosen so that commonly occurring information structures such as machine-language instructions or numbers can easily be stored in the storage medium.   In particular, the register size of the computer and the information field size of numbers and instructions are usually coordinated so that numbers and instructions fit precisely into single registers of the computer.

The four principal kinds of data formats in a computer are *integer* format, *floating-point* format, *character* format, and *bit-string* format. Integer format normally has a one-digit sign field and uses the remaining digits to show the magnitude of the number.   Floating-point format requires a field to represent the exponent and a field to represent the mantissa, where each field in turn must specify the sign and magnitude. Character format splits up a register into fields, each having the same number, say n, of digits.   Each n-digit field can be used to represent one of 2^n different characters.   A field which is used to represent a character is sometimes referred to as a *byte*.   A bit may in turn be thought of as a special case of a byte with $n = 1$, so that a bit string is essentially a string of characters chosen from a two-letter alphabet.

The notation for register specification can be extended to the specification of information formats by introducing a class of declarations called format declarations. The register formats for the above data types can be specified by the following format declarations:†

format I(S,MAG)   Defines format of *I* (integer) to be *S* followed by MAG.

format S[0:0]   Defines *S* (sign) to be a one-bit field.

format MAG[0:30]   Defines MAG (magnitude) to be a 31-bit field.

format NUM(E,M)   Defines NUM (floating-point number) to be *E* followed by *M*.

format E[0:7]   Defines *E* (exponent) to be an 8-bit field.

format M[0:23]   Defines *M* (mantissa) to be a 24-bit field.

format B[0:7]   Defines *B* (byte) to be an 8-bit field.

format CHAR(4B)   Defines CHAR (character) to consist of a sequence of 4 bytes.

format CHARS(256B)   Defines CHARS to consist of a string of 256 byte-size characters *B*. This information format requires eight registers when mapped onto physical storage.

A register declaration serves to define a given physical object, while a format declaration defines a template of which many instances may exist simultaneously. This is brought out forcibly in a notation due to Schweppe, who replaces the word **register** in register declarations by "the" and the word **format** in format declarations by "a" or "an." In this notation "**register** AC[0:63]" is replaced by "the AC is [0:63]" while "**format** I[S,MAG]" is replaced by "an I is (S,MAG)".

Instructions may be specified by information formats which specify field sizes for different functional components of the instruction. An instruction format normally consists of an operation field; one or more address fields which address registers in the main memory; one or more special register fields, for addressing groups of special registers; and a mode field, which specifies the mode of execution. There are normally a number of different instruction formats on a computer each associated with a different class of instructions. A typical instruction format is given by the following format declarations:

† The convention is adopted that square brackets are used to enclose length specifications, and parentheses are used to enclose other specifications.

format INSTR(OP,A,X,M)   Defines INSTR (instruction) to consist of the sequence of four fields OP, A, X, M.

format OP[0:11]   Defines OP (operation field) to be 12 bits.

format A[0:11]   Defines A (address field) to be 12 bits.

format X[0:3]   Defines X (special register, i.e., index) field to be 4 bits.

format M[0:3]   Defines M (mode field) to be 4 bits.

Instructions are sometimes classified by the number of main memory references permitted in a single instruction. The above instruction format permits a single reference to the main memory and is said to be a *one-address* instruction format.

In executing the above instruction in the CIR of a computer, the operation field would be examined first and would initiate a chain of actions in which the remaining fields would be used as operands. The address and special-register fields are normally used to determine a main memory address for storage or retrieval of an operand, but they are sometimes used for other purposes.

The notation developed above for specifying register sizes and operations on registers is essentially a very simple programming language in which format specification and concatenation of formated items are emphasized, and transformation of information items plays a secondary role. A more elaborate language which has been widely used for format specification is discussed in [9], and a simple example of a register-transfer language is given in [17].

1.4 INSTRUCTIONS, PROGRAMMING, AND REENTRANT CODE

This section, which is a review of the basic forms of machine-language instructions, is included both in the interests of completeness and in order to discuss machine language in a framework appropriate to the remainder of the chapter. Because this section discusses machine language from a point of view that differs from that of machine-language manuals, it should be read even by persons already familiar with machine language.

1.4.1 INFORMATION-MOVING INSTRUCTIONS

The instructions for a given computer can be classified into the following principal categories:

1. Information-moving instructions
2. Transformational instructions
3. Branching instructions

Information-moving instructions move information between registers of the computer without transforming it. The general format of such instructions may be thought of as having the form

COPY, source, destination

It is assumed that COPY instructions always destroy the information at the destination and do not disturb the copy of the information at the source, so that an extra copy of the information at the source is produced by a copy instruction.

When the source and the destination are both main memory registers, the above instruction requires two address fields for its specification. However, the source or destination of a copy instruction is normally chosen to be a special register or register of the data-processing unit. For example, instructions for loading the AC or MQ registers with information from memory register A might be specified respectively as†

LAC A   Load AC from A $(C(A) \rightarrow AC)$.

LMQ A   Load MQ from A $(C(A) \rightarrow MQ)$.

The destination part of the copy instruction has in this case been absorbed into the operation part of the instruction, and only the source field is specified by an explicit address.

Similarly instructions for storing the content of the AC and MQ in a register A might be specified as

SAC A   Store from AC into A $(C(AC) \rightarrow A)$.

SMQ A   Store from MQ into A $(C(MQ) \rightarrow A)$.

In this case the source part of the copy instruction has been absorbed into the operation code, and only the destination is specified by an explicit address field.

Copy instructions which specify transfer between the computer memory and a special register require only an address field and a special-register field for their specification.

MAI A,I   Move address field of A to index register I $(C(ADDR(A)) \rightarrow I)$.

MIA A,I   Move index register I to address field of A $(C(I) \rightarrow ADDR(A))$.

† Specification of the effect of execution of an instruction in terms of the register- and format-specification language of the previous section is given in parentheses following each instruction.

In this case the class of special register is specified by the operation code, and an address field and special-register field are used to specify the source and destination.

Information-moving instruction may specify transfer of information between memory registers and input or output streams.   In this case a single address may be used to specify the memory register which acts as the source or destination, and the direction of transfer and input-output stream may be specified by the operation field, special-register field, and mode field.

RD A,F   Read from input medium into A in format F (INP(F) → A).

RT A,N,F   Read tape number N in format F into A (TAPE(N,F) → A).

WT A,N,F   Write from A onto tape number N in format F (C(A) → TAPE(N,F)).

RDR A,N,M   Read from drum N words in mode M into N registers starting at A (DRUM(N,M) → A).

WDI A,N,M   Write onto disk N words in mode M starting at A.

Input and output media may be thought of as consisting of sequences of register-size information-storage devices.   Individual registers may in general be addressed, just like registers in the main memory.   However, the above input-output instructions assume that input is performed from an implicit external address currently specified by the reading mechanism and that the external address for output is similarly implicitly specified by a writing mechanism.   If necessary, the external address is assigned by a preceding instruction which "positions" the reading or writing mechanism.   When performing input (output) sequentially from (to) a sequence of contiguous external registers, the positioning instruction is required only initially, and incrementation to position the mechanism for successive contiguous external "registers" is performed automatically.

Exercise: Survey addressing schemes and positioning instructions for magnetic-tape, magnetic-drum, and magnetic-core auxiliary storage.

It is assumed above that input and output consist of a sequence of *logical* information units which are normally of register size.   Actual information input usually consists of physical information blocks, called *records*.   Records are normally read into blocks of registers, called *buffers*, from which they are transferred by a system "read" subroutine to the registers from which they are used.   Similarly information to be output is assembled in a buffer for output and then output when the buffer is full.   In discussing assembly techniques in the next chapter it will be assumed that input is from punched cards and that reading of a single punched card results in a record in the input buffer, whose content is then analyzed by a scanning process.

Move instructions between special registers and data-processing registers and interchange of registers in the data-processing unit are permitted and do not require an address field. It is evident that although information-moving instructions always involve two operands, the operands can be specified using only one memory address field provided there are no instructions for directly moving information between pairs of memory registers. Moving information between two memory registers can be accomplished by a sequence of two move instructions.

1.4.2 TRANSFORMATIONAL INSTRUCTIONS

Transformational instructions perform transformations on information. The most familiar examples of transformational instructions are the arithmetic instructions. However, logical operations, shifting instructions, and instructions which select portions of a register and zero out the remainder may also be thought of as transformational instructions. Arithmetic operations such as addition require two operands as input and produce one operand as output. If the memory registers containing the inputs and the result were specified explicitly in a single instruction, then a three-address instruction with three main memory addresses would be required, having the form "ADD A,B,C". However, the number of explicit main-memory addresses can be reduced if it is assumed that some of the operands use implicitly specified registers.

In one-address computers, one of the arguments is assumed to be in the accumulator, and the result is placed in the accumulator, requiring only one of the arguments to be specified explicitly. A one-address addition instruction usually has the form

ADD A   Add the number in memory register A to the number in the accumulator and store the result in the accumulator $(C(AC) + C(A) \rightarrow AC)$.

When transformational instructions with implicitly specified registers are used, additional instructions must be executed to move the required information to and from the implicitly specified registers. Addition of the two numbers in registers A and B and storage of the result in register C can be specified by the following sequence of three instructions:

LAC A   Load the number in register A into the accumulator.

ADD B   Add the number in register B to the number in the accumulator.

SAC C   Store the content of the accumulator in register C.

The ADD instruction combines information-moving and transformational characteristics, since it moves one of its three arguments from the memory to the data-processing unit and then uses it in a transformation. Instruction codes on some computers† rigidly separate transformational instructions from information-moving instructions and require that transformational instructions such as ADD have all arguments specified implicitly.   Assume that the computer has a data-processing unit with three accumulators called AC1, AC2, AC3 and that the instruction ADD adds the content of AC1 to AC2 and stores the result in AC3.   If the computer has instructions LAC1, LAC2 to load accumulators 1 and 2 and SAC3 to store accumulator 3, then addition of A to B and storage of the result in C can be performed by the following instruction sequence:

LAC1 A   Load AC1 from A.
LAC2 B   Load AC2 from B.
ADD   Add AC1 to AC2 and store in AC3.
SAC3 C   Store AC3 in C.

The instruction ADD is said to be a *zero-address* instruction because zero explicit memory references are required for its execution. All transformational instructions may be specified by zero-address instructions provided information-moving instructions are available to move information into the implicit registers in which the zero-address instruction expects to find its arguments.

Zero-address instructions such as ADD above correspond closely to "pure" operation symbols used in mathematics such as $+$.   The operation $+$ expects to have its arguments specified implicitly immediately preceding and following the symbol $+$ on the sheet of paper on which it occurs, whereas the computer does not require physical closeness but merely a standard set of registers for its operands.

Instead of proliferating registers with independent names such as AC1, AC2, AC3, it is convenient to allocate a structured group of registers called a *stack* for purposes of storing arguments and results of operations. The structure of stacks and their use for storing arguments and results of zero-address operations will be discussed in Sec. 1.5.

1.4.3 LOGICAL INSTRUCTIONS

Computers normally have *logical* as well as *arithmetic* transformational instructions.   These include instructions for left and right shift of the content of a register and for logical bit operations such as *and, or,* and *not* on the set of all bits in a register.

----

† Such as the Burroughs B5500 and the English Electric KDF9.

RS N   Shift the content of the AC N bits to the right.

LS N   Shift the content of the AC N bits to the left.

AND A   Perform a bitwise logical *and* operation on corresponding bits of register A and the AC.

OR A   Perform a bitwise logical *or* operation on corresponding bits of registers A and the AC.

NOT   Complement the bit pattern in the AC.

The right- and left-shift instructions above have arguments that are integers rather than addresses. This is reflected in the internal representation where contents of the field normally used to store the address is actually the *literal* integer specifying the number of places to be shifted.

There are other instances where it is desirable to specify *literal* quantities rather than their addresses. For example, if 10 is to be added to a number, it would be natural to specify an ADD instruction with an argument of 10. Although such specification is normally permitted at the symbolic-language level, an address field in an addition instruction cannot contain the literal quantity to be added. Translation of a symbolic instruction containing a literal quantity results in an instruction whose address field points to a register containing the constant:

ADD = 10   The = preceding the 10 in the address field specifies that the constant 10 is to be added to the quantity in the accumulator. This instruction is translated as an ADD operation with an address pointing to a register containing the constant 10.

The distinction between literals and addresses is an important one.

1.4.4 BRANCHING INSTRUCTIONS

The third class of instructions to be discussed is *branching instructions*. Instructions of a program are normally stored in a sequence of contiguous registers and executed sequentially starting with a given initial instruction. This is accomplished by automatically incrementing the address in the instruction-location register by 1 whenever execution of a given instruction is initiated, so that the next instruction is automatically taken from the next register when execution of the current instruction is completed.

Branching instructions permit explicit specification of where the next instruction is to be taken from. The address field of a branching instruction specifies the address of the next instruction to be executed rather than the address of a data item. The simplest branching instruction is an unconditional transfer instruction and has the form

TRA L   Take the next instruction from register L (L → ILR).

Execution of the above instruction causes the contents of the instruction-location register ILR to be replaced by L, so that the next instruction is automatically taken from L rather than from the register following the transfer instruction being executed. Successive instructions will normally be taken from registers $L + 1$, $L + 2$, etc., until a further branching instruction is encountered.

Most computer instruction sets include a variety of *conditional branching instructions* which branch to the register L when the condition being tested is satisfied and continue with the next instruction in sequence when the condition is not satisfied. These conditions normally include the following:†

TMI L   Branch to L if the AC is negative.

TIR L,I   Branch to L if index register I is zero.

TOV L   Branch to L if the overflow indicator is on and switch the indicator off. This indicator is switched on if there is an overflow as a result of an arithmetic operation.

Conditional branching instructions permit a choice between alternative courses of action depending on whether certain execution-time conditions are satisfied and form the basis of the claim that computers can make intelligent decisions. The TMI instruction above determines alternative courses of action depending on the relative size of two numbers. The TIR instruction can be used to terminate a loop which is to be executed a fixed number of times. It is sometimes replaced by an instruction that combines conditional branching with incrementation of the index register:

TIX L,I,N   Decrement index register I by N. If it is zero then branch to L. Otherwise take the next instruction in sequence $(\text{IND}(I) - N \to \text{IND}(I); \text{IF IND}(I) = 0 \text{ THEN } L \to \text{ILR})$.

The TOV instruction above can be used to detect overflow errors during the computation.

---

† Specification of the effect of conditional branching instructions in our register- and format-specification language requires the introduction of conditional specifications. Using a standard notation for conditional specification, the effect of the three given instructions can be specified as follows:

TMI L   (IF AC = NEG THEN $L \to$ ILR)

TIR L,I   (IF IND(I) = 0 THEN $L \to$ IR)

TOV L   (IF OV $\neq$ 0 THEN $L \to$ IR)

1.4.5 ITERATIVE PROCESSES

Conditional transfer instructions are used when specifying repetitive execution of a sequence of instructions. The flow diagram in Fig. 1.11 illustrates an iterative process which computes successive approximations x_i to the solution of the equation $x = f(x)$ by the formula $x_{i+1} = f(x_i)$ and terminates when the absolute value of $x - f(x)$ is less than the quantity stored in the register E.

In this example the criterion for terminating the repetition of the sequence of instructions is an "internal" criterion based on values generated during execution of the instruction sequence. The criterion allows the computer to exercise judgment as to whether the approximation

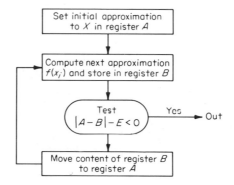

Figure 1.11 Flow diagram of an iterative process.

is adequate. This kind of use of conditional branching instructions provides the basis for the statement that computers can think.

Exercises: (a) Write an instruction sequence to test whether $|A - B| - E < 0$. (b) Write an iterative program to solve the equation $x^2 - A = 0$; i.e., use $f(x) = \frac{1}{2}(x + A/x)$.

The criterion for terminating a repetitive sequence of instructions may be an external criterion specified by a parameter. The flow diagram in Fig. 1.12 illustrates a sequence of instructions which is executed for values $1, 2, \ldots, N$ of an integer I. Here the termination test precedes execution of the instruction sequence. This allows correct execution when the number of repetitions of the instruction sequence is zero.

Exercises: (a) Write a program for the summation of N numbers. (b) Discuss the differences in implementation of the flow diagram in Fig. 1.12 with and without the use of index registers.

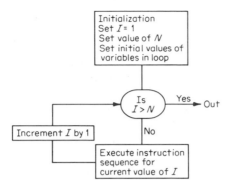

Figure 1.12 Flow diagram for N-fold repetition of an instruction sequence.

1.4.6 PERMANENT AND TEMPORARY INFORMATION

The information associated with execution of a repeatedly executed instruction sequence may be classified into *permanent information*, which does not change between successive execution of the instruction sequence, and *temporary information*, which may change during execution of the instruction sequence or between successive executions of the instruction sequence.

The classification into permanent and temporary information corresponds roughly to the distinction between instructions (which do not change between successive executions) and data (on which the instructions operate). However, there are certain information items for which this distinction becomes blurred. For example, the index I may be used both for instruction modification (either physically or by an index register during execution) and as an integer on which computations are performed.

It is convenient to think of instruction modifiers as data, since they vary during execution, and to store instruction modifiers along with the data rather than within the instruction sequence. If all temporary information generated during the execution of an instruction sequence is stored separately from the permanent information, then a single copy of the permanent information can be executed simultaneously (*reentrantly*) by a number of different programs provided each program makes its own copy of its temporary information.

One of the reasons for the importance of index registers is that they facilitate the specification of programs as reentrant program structures. Before the advent of index registers program modification was accomplished by physical modification of instructions, thus making programs nonreentrant.

1.4.7 SUBROUTINES AND REENTRANT CODE

The instruction sequences which constitute repetitive loops are usually embedded in longer instruction sequences and are not therefore candidates for independent multiple execution.   Segments of code which can be executed as independent entities are referred to as *closed subroutines* or merely as *subroutines*.

A subroutine is an instruction sequence which is entered by a transfer instruction to an entry point.   The transfer instruction to the subroutine is called a *subroutine-calling instruction* and will be denoted by TSR. The program segment in which a given subroutine-calling instruction occurs is referred to as a *calling program* of the subroutine, while the instruction which calls the subroutine is referred to as a *point of call*. On completion of execution of the subroutine, control is automatically transferred back (returned) to the instruction following the calling instruction at the point of call.   The mechanism of subroutine calling is illustrated in Fig. 1.13.

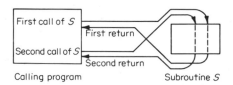

Calling program   Subroutine *S*

Figure 1.13   A subroutine with two points of call.

The information required during execution of a subroutine may be thought of as having a permanent component, consisting of the instruction sequence to be executed, and a temporary component, consisting of data and other information which may vary for successive executions of the subroutine.   The temporary information associated with a subroutine must include a pointer which points back to the calling program.

In early implementations of subroutine calling, such as that in FORTRAN, memory space was assigned at translation time for both the permanent and the temporary information associated with a subroutine. This is adequate provided that the instruction sequence which constitutes the subroutine is never simultaneously executed by more than one calling program.   This precludes not only simultaneous execution of the subroutine by independent programs but also reentrant calling of the subroutine while it is executing itself.

If simultaneous or reentrant execution of a given subroutine is to be permitted, each execution instance of a subroutine must have its own associated temporary information.   An execution instance of a subroutine will be referred to as an *activation* of the subroutine, and the temporary information associated with a given execution instance will be referred to as an *activation record*. Instruction sequences for which the permanent part and temporary parts are rigidly separated to permit multiple and reentrant execution are said to be coded in *reentrant code*.

A subroutine call to a subroutine called SUB can be initiated as follows:

TSR SUB,I   Transfer control to the instruction labeled SUB and store in index register I the address of the instruction currently being executed (ILR $\to$ I; GO TO SUB).

A subroutine may in general require the specification of *parameters*, which vary between successive executions of the subroutine.   A number of alternative conventions can be adopted for specifying the parameters of a subroutine.   The convention adopted in early implementations of subroutine calling is that of storing the *addresses* of all parameters associated with a given subroutine call immediately following the calling (TSR) instruction.   This convention requires that for a subroutine with N parameters, control be returned to the $(N + 1)$st register following the TSR instruction.   This can easily be accomplished inside the called subroutine by appropriate incrementation of the return address transmitted in index register I.

The above convention requires that all quantities specified following the TSR instruction be *addresses* of parameters.   Thus if the first parameter is a constant, the constant will be stored as part of the temporary information of the calling program, and the register following the TSR instruction will contain a pointer to this register.

The above convention is relatively simple but violates the rigid separation between temporary and permanent information, since an address of a parameter may in general be a varying rather than a permanent information item.   Although this violation may be fixed up by means of index-register incrementation of parameters, more recent implementations of subroutine calling tend to store parameter information associated with a given subroutine call as part of the temporary information in the called program rather than as part of the permanent information of the calling program.   This form of program organization will be further discussed in Chap. 4.

Exercise: Write one or more programs in the machine language of your choice, including a program with several subroutines.   Examples of problem areas are sorting, searching, scanning, simple assembly (see Chap. 2 for problem specification); solution of nonlinear equations, tabulation of simple functions, and other iterative problems; simple logical problems.

1.5 BASIC ADDRESS COMPUTATION

1.5.1 INSTRUCTION FETCH AND INSTRUCTION EXECUTION

In execution of an instruction, the operation field is usually thought of as being the active component which initiates execution, while the remaining fields play a passive role, providing auxiliary information which is used principally to determine the address of operands of the operation. Determination of the physical address of an operand from the information fields of an instruction may in general involve execution of a complex sequence of microprogrammed commands and is referred to as an *address computation*. In order to describe the alternative forms of address computation on computers, the instruction-execution cycle will be specified more precisely. It can be split into the following three phases:

1. *Instruction Fetch.* Get the instruction determined by the instruction-location register (ILR) and place it in the current-instruction register.
2. *Data-address Computation.* Use the content of the address field, special-register field, and mode field of the instruction to determine the memory address of data items (if any). If the contents of the resulting register are required for execution of the instruction, move the data to an implicit register for processing in the execution phase. If the address is merely required to store the result of instruction execution, pass on the address itself to the instruction-execution phase.
3. *Instruction Execution.*† Increment the ILR to point to the "next" memory register. Then perform the operation specified in the operation field. The operation may be an arithmetic operation, a data-moving operation between internal registers of the computer, an input or output operation, or one of a number of other kinds of operations. Some operations, such as branching operations, do not operate on data but are concerned with instruction sequencing and other forms of program organization.

The system programmer is interested in the overall information flow during the execution of instruction rather than in the specific action performed by instructions. When discussing machine organization from the point of view of the system programmer, the instruction-execution phase is normally ignored, since it is specific to each instruction.

---

† Phases 1 and 2 can be thought of as the syntactic phase of instruction execution, while phase 3 can be thought of as the semantic phase of instruction execution. A discussion of instruction execution in terms of a syntactic phase, which determines the transformation to be performed, followed by a semantic phase, which performs the transformation, is given in Sec. A1.7 of Appendix 1.

The instruction-fetch phase is relatively trivial on a simple computer. The instruction pointer directly specifies the memory register from which the instruction is fetched and is said to be the *absolute address* of the memory register to which it points.   The mode of addressing of computer memory used during the instruction-fetch phase is called *absolute addressing.*

The data-fetch phase on simple computers allows more sophisticated forms of addressing than the instruction-fetch phase.   The address specified in the address field of an instruction can normally be modified by addition of the content of one of a number of index registers specified in the index-register field, before it is used to reference a memory register. Addresses which are to be modified by the content of another register before being used to reference memory registers are referred to as *relative addresses.*

1.5.2   INDIRECT ADDRESSING

Current computers allow more complex forms of address modification than pure indexing.   In the general case the process of determining an

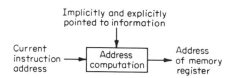

Figure 1.14   Address computation.

address from information in the current-instruction register is referred to as an *address computation.*   The general process of address computation is illustrated in Fig. 1.14.

The address computation makes use of information in the fields of the current-instruction register to designate implicit and explicit registers whose contents are used to compute the address.   An address computation may involve a sequence of computational steps just like any other computation; however, this sequence is completely determined by the hardware of the computer, and the end result is an address which is then used to retrieve a data item from the memory.

If the content of the memory register determined by the instruction address is in turn used to determine a further address, the resulting address is referred to as an *indirect address.*   The register pointed to by the indirect address may in turn be used to compute a further indirect address, resulting in an *indirect-addressing chain* to determine a single physical address.

Indirect addressing is normally specified by the mode part of the instruction word (subsection 1.3.3).   If the mode specifies indirect addressing, the register determined by the current word is used to compute a further indirect address, while if the mode is not set to indirect addressing, the register determined by the current word is used as a data item.

Indirect addressing can be combined with indexing in a number of different ways. In *relative indirect addressing*, the indirect address at each stage of a chain of indirect addressing is the address field modified by the content $C(I)$ of the index register, as indicated in Fig. 1.15. In *absolute indirect addressing*, the indirect address at each stage is taken to be the absolute indirect address, and the index register of the current-instruction register is used to modify the final address determined by the indirect-addressing chain. Other combinations of indexing and indirect addressing are also possible. Since each instruction word has a mode field, a different mode may be used with each level of an indirect-addressing chain.

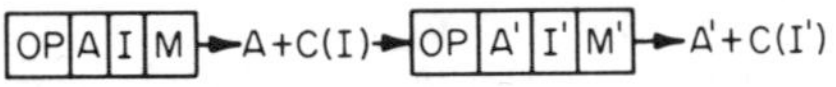

Figure 1.15   Relative indirect addressing.

Indexing and indirect addressing arc normally the principal kinds of operations performed in an address computation on a simple computer. However, computers which have automatic segmentation and paging facilities built into their hardware require more complex address computation for efficient operation.

1.5.3   THE EXECUTE INSTRUCTION

In indirect addressing the operation field is determined by the operation field of the instruction being executed, while the address field is determined by the terminating point of a chain of indexed indirect-address references. If the indirect address is used to determine the operation as well as the data address, the operation code of the initial instruction does nothing to determine the operation actually executed, and the instruction is referred to as an *execute* instruction.

An execute instruction causes execution of the instruction in the register to which it points and may result in a chain of execute instructions. However, on completion of an instruction in the execute mode (other than a branching instruction) the next instruction to be executed is the one in the register following the initial execute instruction and not the one following the instruction actually executed;† i.e., the instruction pointer

† Note that a subroutine call is similar in its effect to an execute instruction. A subroutine call specifies execution out of sequence followed by a return to the sequence at the point of call when execution of the called instruction sequence is completed. Machines which do not have the execute instruction built into their hardware can simulate execute-mode execution by a simple subroutine call.

is incremented by 1 in the normal way (see subsection 1.5.1). If the instruction actually executed results in transfer of control, the next instruction will be taken from the register to which control is transferred.

Indirect addressing will be indicated by * immediately following the operation code. An indexed indirectly addressed load-accumulator instruction would be written

LAC* A,I   Load the accumulator with the quantity whose address is specified by the address, indexing, and mode fields of $A + C(I)$.

The indirect-address computation of an address A can be specified in our computer-description language as follows:

L: A = A + C(I)
   IF (mode = indirect) THEN A(A,X,M) → CIR(A,X,M);
   GO TO L;
   ELSE CONTINUE

The effect of an execute instruction XEQ can be specified as follows:

XEQ A,I   Execute the instruction at $A + C(I)$ $(A + C(I) → CIR)$.

1.5.4 APPLICATIONS OF INDIRECT ADDRESSING

Before leaving the subject of indirect addressing a number of uses of indirect addressing will be briefly mentioned.

1. *Accessing a Two-dimensional Array by a Vector of Indirect Addresses.* Let A be a two-dimensional array stored by rows in the

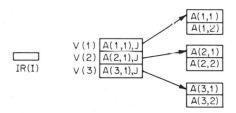

Figure 1.16 Accessing an array by indirect addressing.

computer and V be a vector whose ith element $V(I)$ has an address field which points to the first element $A(I,1)$ of row I, and an index field J. Figure 1.16 illustrates this mode of storage for a 3 × 2 array.

An element $A(K,L)$ can be loaded into the AC by loading the value of K into index register I, the value of L into index register J, and executing the instruction "LAC* V,I".

Example: This technique can be used to access information in an environment which consists of a number of blocks within which relative addresses of components can be predetermined. In the discussion of ALGOL implementation in Chap. 4, addresses are specified by integer pairs (K,L), where K specifies an information block referred to as an *activation record* and L specifies a relative address within this block. During execution a vector V of initial addresses of accessible activation records is maintained. If it is assumed that entries in V are indexed by index register J, then access to the information component having the two-component address (K,L) can be accomplished by loading K into index register I, L into index register J, and executing the instruction "LAC* V,I".

2. *Indirect Addressing to Defer the Memory Allocation (Binding) Time of a Data Structure.* If during compilation of a program segment, the form of a data structure is known but its location is not known or varies during execution, then a fixed address can be set aside to store the base address of the data structure during execution, and the program can be compiled so that all references to the data structure are indirect-address references through this fixed register. This technique allows multiple access to a given data structure to be channeled through a given fixed register. A change in location of the data structure does not require a change in individual references to the data structure but merely a change in the content of the register through which indirect-address references are funneled. The application of this technique to communication between function modules is illustrated in Sec. 1.8.

3. *Access to a Vector of Quantities Whose Addresses Are Specified Relative to an Index Register.* A subroutine must deal with a fixed number of parameters whose storage locations may differ for different calls of the subroutine. Assume that the origin of the block of subroutine parameters is specified by index register I and that access to the Jth parameter is accomplished by the instruction "LAC J,I". In accessing subroutine parameters the convention is sometimes adopted that the block of parameters stores *addresses* of the parameters rather than the parameter values. In this case, access to the Jth parameter would be accomplished by the instruction "LAC* J,I".

Example: In many FORTRAN implementations, addresses of subroutine parameters are stored relative to the point of call of the subroutine. On subroutine call an index register I is loaded with the address of the subroutine, and parameter values can be accessed by indirect-address references relative to this index register.

Indirect addressing is available as a hardware feature on many computers. However, it can be simulated by software with relative ease.

The instruction "LAC* R" may be simulated by the following three instructions:

LAC R   Load AC from R.

SAAC L   Store address of AC in L.

L: LAC **   Load AC with the content of the register whose address was just stored in L.

Even when indirect addressing is implemented by hardware, instructions which involve indirect addressing require an extra memory cycle for each indirect-address reference and therefore take substantially longer to execute than instructions which do not involve indirect addressing. If an instruction involves indirect accessing of a data item, it may be time-wise more efficient to initialize the instruction to be a direct-address reference in order to save a memory cycle on each instance of execution. However, program organization is frequently clearer when indirect-addressing techniques are used, and it is sometimes worth paying a time penalty to obtain a more esthetically packaged program. For example, the machine organization for segmentation and paging, discussed in Sec. 1.13, makes heavy use of indirect addressing for the purpose of increasing the flexibility of access to information.

Exercise: Describe how a three-dimensional array could be accessed by two-stage indirect addressing through a one- and two-dimensional array.

1.6 GENERALIZED REGISTERS AND PUSHDOWN STORES

1.6.1 SHELVES†

In the previous sections it was assumed that registers were of fixed length and that information-moving instructions destroyed the information at the destination while leaving information at the source intact. Instead of the conventional registers discussed above, consider arbitrarily long registers which have the property that storage of new information does not destroy previous information in the register but is merely added to the previous content of the register. Assume that at any given time there is some information in the middle of the register and that information can be added either on the left of the information already in the register or on the right. Let the operations of storing information on the left and right be denoted by LSTORE (left store) and RSTORE (right store). Assume also that individual items of information can be removed from the right or left side of the register by the operation LFETCH (left fetch) and RFETCH (right fetch). Let the two fetch operations be destructive, so

† Knuth refers to shelves as *deques* (double-ended queues).

that an item which is fetched from a register is not merely copied but erased at the source.

Such registers are sometimes called *shelves.*† The register corresponding to the accumulator, which serves as the source of store instructions and the destination of fetch instructions, is sometimes called the *workspace.* Store instructions move information from the workspace to a shelf, and fetch instructions move information from a shelf to the workspace.

The fetch and store instructions defined above in fact represent the intuitive notion of fetching and storing more closely than conventional fetch and store instructions; i.e., the information moved is erased from the source just like a physical object which is moved from a source to a destination. Conventional fetch and store instructions result in two copies of the moved object, one at the source and one at the destination, and are really copying instructions rather than instructions which truly move an object from one place to another.

1.6.2 PUSHDOWN STORES

Now assume that the registers discussed above do not extend in both directions but merely in one direction. Assume that items can be added only at one end, say the right end, and that items can be removed only from the right end.

Items entered into such a register can be removed only in a last in, first out order. Registers of this kind are called *pushdown stores.* A pushdown store is essentially a register that has one closed end and one open end, such that items of data can be added only at the open end and removed only at the open end. Moreover the fetch and store operations appropriate to a pushdown store are of the variety that erase the item being moved from the source and do not erase it from the destination. A pushdown store is somewhat like a stack of plates, since stacked plates must be removed from the stack in a last in, first out order. For this reason pushdown stores are sometimes called *stacks.*

There are two ways of visualizing what happens when an item is stored in a pushdown store. The first, which is suggested by the term "pushdown," visualizes a stack of plates with a false bottom and a top whose level is fixed. When a new plate is put on the stack, the false bottom sinks, so that all plates are "pushed down" one level and the new plate is at the level of the previous top plate. If this model of a pushdown store is simulated in a computer with conventional registers, the top of the pushdown list is identified with a fixed memory register. Insertion of an element at the top of the store would require moving all

---

† This terminology is used by the designers of the COMIT language [17].

existing elements of the store into the next lower register to make room for the new top element.   This procedure is unduly clumsy.

The second approach visualizes a stack of plates with a fixed bottom and a top whose level moves up and down with the number of plates in the stack.   When this model of a pushdown store is simulated in a computer with conventional registers, the top of the stack varies, depending on the number of elements in the store.   Insertion of a new element at the top of the pushdown store does not disturb elements already in the pushdown store, and removal of the top element of the pushdown store merely removes the top element without disturbing other elements.

Since insertion and removal of elements from the pushdown store is so much easier in the second model than in the first, the second model is always adopted when simulating a pushdown store in a computer with conventional registers.   Thus a pushdown store should be visualized as a sequence of consecutive registers with a fixed bottom and variable top register.   Since it is only the top register that is available for computation, this means that the "current" element of the pushdown store has a variable "address."

1.6.3 SIMULATION OF PUSHDOWN STORES

Pushdown stores can easily be simulated in a computer having conventional memory registers and an indexing facility.   The current first free location of the pushdown store is denoted by an address symbol and the content of an index register.   Storing an item in the pushdown store is accomplished by a conventional store instruction followed by incrementation of the index register.   Removal of an item is accomplished by decrementation followed by a conventional fetch instruction.

Pushdown stores are specified by a single address (the *top* of the pushdown store) just like ordinary registers, but they correspond effectively to registers of arbitrary size.   They may be regarded as conventional registers which have a *latent structure;* i.e., when only the top element is used, there is no difference between a conventional register and a pushdown store, but when this register is removed, it automatically uncovers a new register, which may in turn be sitting on top of a further layer of latent structure.

Although no commercially available machines have pushdown facilities built into the memory hardware, there are computers, such as the B5500, whose data-processing unit has an accumulator which operates like the top register of a pushdown store.   Pushdown-store accumulators are particularly useful in the execution of zero-address instructions.   For example a zero-address addition operation could expect to find its two arguments in the top two registers of the accumulator pushdown store (stack) and place the result into the top register of the accumulator stack.

On a machine with an accumulator stack and a zero-address add operation, addition would be accomplished by the following four instructions:

LAC A   Place A on top of the accumulator stack, pushing down the previous top element.

LAC B   Place B on top of the accumulator stack, pushing down the previous top element.

ADD   Remove the two top elements from the accumulator stack and place the sum of the two removed elements on top of the accumulator stack.

SAC C   Store the top element of the accumulator, popping up the previously second element.

Note that each of the first two instructions increases the size of the accumulator stack by one element, while the third and fourth instructions each reduce the size of the stack by one element, so that the net result is to leave the stack in exactly the same state as it was before the beginning of the addition.

If the accumulator stack is simulated on a conventional computer by a set of memory registers starting at X and indexed by I, then the information-moving instructions "FETCH A" and "STORE A" would be simulated as follows:

LAC A   Load AC from A.
SAC X,I   Store AC in $X + C(I)$.
INC I,1   Increment index register I by 1.

DEC I,1   Decrement index register I by 1.
LAC X,I   Load AC with $X + C(I)$.
SAC A   Store AC in register A.

1.6.4 APPLICATION TO ARITHMETIC EXPRESSIONS

Stacks turn out to be a natural structure in a number of different programming applications. In particular, stacks crop up during the evaluation of expressions which are nested in other expressions. Consider an arithmetic expression such as $(a + (b \times (c \uparrow d)))$. In this case the inner nested expression $c \uparrow d$ is to be evaluated first, yielding a value, say R_1. The operator $\times$ must then be applied to b and R_1, yielding a value, say R_2. Finally the operator $+$ is applied to a and R_2.

The above arithmetic expression is said to be in *infix* notation because operators are placed *between* their operands. In order to evaluate the above expression it is convenient to rearrange operations so that they always appear immediately *after* their operands. In *postfix* notation the above expression would have the form "$abcd \times + \uparrow$".

Note that this arithmetic expression can be thought of as being implicitly parenthesized as $(a \ (b \ (c \ d \ \uparrow) \ \times \ ) \ +)$; that is, $\uparrow$ is associated with the two operands c and d, $\times$ is associated with the two operands b and $c \uparrow d$, and $+$ is associated with the operands a and $b \times (c \uparrow d)$.

Execution of an arithmetic expression in postfix notation can be accomplished with the aid of a stack by a single left-to-right scan of the string, using the following rules:

1.   If the symbol being scanned is an operand, move it to the stack and scan the next symbol.

2.   If the symbol being scanned is an operator, apply it to the two top operands in the stack and replace the two operands by the result.

In the above example, the first four symbols to be scanned would be the four operands a, b, c, and d.   On scanning $\uparrow$ the stack would contain the four entries a, b, c, and d, and $\uparrow$ would be applied to the two top entries c and d.   The result R_1 would replace c and d, resulting in a stack a, b, R_1.   The operation $\times$ would now operate on b and R_1 to produce a new stack a, R_2.   Operation of $+$ on a and R_2 would produce a stack with a single entry R.

The expression $((a \times b) + (c \times d))$ would result in a postfix string "$ab \times cd \times +$".   Execution would result in the application of $\times$ to ab, producing a result R_1 followed by application of $\times$ to cd producing a result R_2, followed by application of $+$ to R_1 and R_2.

Exercises: (a) Write out the postfix notation for the arithmetic expression $(a + b) \times (c + d)$.   (b) Write a program for the interpretive evaluation of arithmetic expressions in postfix notation.   (c) Develop an algorithm (write a program) for converting an arithmetic expression in fully parenthesized infix notation into postfix notation.

The structure and evaluation of expressions is further discussed in Chap. 4.

In procedure-oriented languages, nesting occurs not only at the level of arithmetic expressions but also for higher-level program constituents. Moreover nesting occurs not only by *explicit* nesting in the source program but also implicitly whenever a procedure or function call occurs in a program.   A procedure or function call implies simulated substitution of the definition at the point of call; i.e., the program is executed as though the definition were implicitly nested at the point of call.   If the definition itself contains a procedure call, the single call in the source program gives rise to multiple nesting during execution.   Such multiple nesting is conveniently simulated by a run-time stack with one entry for each procedure that has been entered but not yet completed.

When considering procedures with a reentrant program part in Chap. 4, the entries in the run-time stack for each partially executed procedure will be called *activation records* and will contain all data items and organizational items associated with the procedure.   Thus the stacks used in the execution of procedures of procedure-oriented languages have entries that consist of blocks of registers with an internal structure rather than of individual registers.   Structured stacks whose entries are created and deleted in a last in, first out order but which permit access to information below the top of the stack are fundamental in the implementation of programming languages and programming systems.

1.7   INTERRUPTS, TRAPPING, AND DYNAMIC INITIALIZATION

1.7.1   MODES OF INSTRUCTION SEQUENCING

Successive instructions of a program are normally executed in sequence unless a branching instruction is encountered.   An instruction executed by an execute instruction is an exception to this rule, since it does not physically form part of the executed instruction sequence.   Instructions subject to indexing and indirect addressing also use nonsequential information to determine the executed instruction, although less flagrantly than the execute instruction.

A further method of instruction sequencing which has not previously been discussed is that of *interrupting* execution of an instruction sequence by means of a hardware signal known as an *interrupt*.   If A is an instruction sequence being executed and B is a second instruction sequence to which control may be transferred, the relation of interruption to other forms of transfer of control is illustrated by the following table, taken from [10].

Normal sequencing: A keeps control
Branching: A gives control to B
Interrupt mode: B takes control from A
Execute mode: A lends control to B

1.7.2   INTERRUPTS

When an instruction sequence A is interrupted, control is normally transferred to a fixed register, which may be thought of as the first instruction of an *interrupt-handling subroutine*.   The interrupt-handling subroutine stores certain information in the instruction- and data-processing units so that it can itself use these registers, performs an *interrupt action*, and then uses information stored on interruption to return control to the instruction sequence it has interrupted or to transfer control to some other instruction sequence.

Interruption comes into its own in a complex computer system when there are many asynchronously operated interdependent processes. However, it is of use even when only a single process controls all computer operations.   Hardware interrupts, for example, can be used to detect overflow of arithmetic operations and to transfer control to an overflow-handling subroutine when this occurs.   Detection of overflow in the absence of an interrupt facility could be accomplished by the use of a hardware overflow indicator which is set to "on" whenever overflow occurs and can be subsequently tested and set to "off".   In the absence of both interrupts and an overflow indicator, testing for overflow of arithmetic operations would require costly interpretive execution of all operations.

There may in general be a number of different kinds of interrupt on a given computer, each of which results in transfer of control to a different fixed register corresponding to a different interrupt-handling subroutine. Since interrupts may occur asynchronously, care must be taken that interruption of interrupts does not get out of hand and that multiple interrupts of a given kind are adequately taken care of.   The problem of interruption of interrupts can be dealt with by allowing the programmer to inhibit (mask) interrupts while a given interrupt is being executed.   A refinement of this scheme is to associate a priority number with each kind of interrupt and permit interruption during a given interrupt only by an interrupt with a higher priority number.   Both these schemes ensure that a given interrupt will not be interrupted by an interrupt of the same kind.

Multiple interrupts can be dealt with either by associating an interrupt queue with each kind of interrupt, from which interrupts are handled in a last in, first out order, or by stacking interrupts in the devices which originate them.   This method is especially appropriate if the device causing an interrupt cannot proceed with its operations until the interrupt has been dealt with.

Interrupts which physically interrupt the current instruction at the moment of time at which they occur are sometimes referred to as *hard interrupts*.   Interrupts which give rise to an entry in an interrupt queue and are dealt with by a subsequently called system procedure are called *soft interrupts*.   In any programming system there are certain interrupts which must be dealt with within a few instruction cycles of their occurrence and must therefore be implemented by hard interrupts.   There are other interrupts which have no real time constraints and can therefore be implemented by soft interrupts.   The priority of an interrupt is determined by the urgency of the real-time constraint associated with that interrupt.   In order to ensure that high-priority interrupts can be adequately dealt with, the instruction sequences to be executed for high-priority interrupts must be short.   When a high-priority hard interrupt occurs, it is sometimes possible to deal with the immediate real-time requirements of the interrupt in a few instruction cycles and to schedule other computations which result from the interrupt as soft interrupts to be performed at a later point in time.

1.7.3 TRAPPING

Transfer of control to a fixed register of a computer when an exceptional condition (such as an interrupt) is encountered is referred to as *trapping*. The register to which control is transferred is referred to as a *trapping register*. An interrupt by an external device such as an input-output unit may cause trapping to a trapping register. There are also program-caused conditions, e.g., division by zero, that may cause trapping.

A trapping register normally contains the first instruction of a *trapping routine* or *interrupt routine* for handling the condition that caused the interrupt. Since provision must be made for returning to the program which caused the interrupt when handling of the offending condition has been completed, one of the first actions of the interrupt routine is to store the location of the instruction that caused the interrupt. This can be accomplished by an instruction such as the following:

STR A   (*store location and trap*) Store the location of the previously executed instruction in register *A*.

Some computers permit programmer-controlled trapping to a fixed register determined by information bits in the instruction itself. Trapping of this kind is referred to as *fault-mode trapping*. An instruction subject to fault-mode trapping acts as an unconditional transfer instruction to a fixed location when the fault-mode bits are set and is executed as a regular instruction when the fault-mode bits are not set; i.e., the instruction is executed interpretively by means of a trapping routine when the fault-mode bits are set and is executed directly otherwise.

It should be noted that fault-mode trapping is incompatible with re-entrant program organization, since fault-mode bits may be set and reset during execution. In practice, fault-mode bits are separated from the fixed part of the instruction and are associated with activations of the program in which the instruction occurs rather than with the fixed-program part. In multiprogramming systems, fault-mode addressing is used extensively to control memory allocation. The fault-mode bits are stored as part of the linkage information that determines the mapping from logical to physical addresses (see Sec. 1.13).

1.7.4 DYNAMIC INITIALIZATION

One of the principal uses of fault-mode addressing is for *dynamic initialization*, i.e., initialization which occurs at the time of first execution of an instruction or instruction sequence. When fault-mode addressing is available, dynamic initialization is accomplished by having fault-mode bits of an instruction initially set for interpretive execution, performing initialization when the instruction is first encountered and executed interpretively, resetting the fault-mode bits, and then transferring control back to the instruction. Since the fault-mode bits have been reset, the instruction is always directly executed on subsequent occasions.

In the absence of dynamic-initialization facilities, initialization for all instructions which require initialization prior to a given phase of the program would normally be performed in a single initialization phase. Dynamic initialization allows initialization of each instruction to be performed individually at the latest possible moment of time and is for this reason sometimes referred to as *incremental initialization*. Moreover dynamic initialization allows a given instruction to be reinitialized several times during execution of the program without any additional organizational machinery.

1.7.5 APPLICATION TO DYNAMIC RESOURCE ALLOCATION

Dynamic initialization is used heavily in multiprogramming systems for purposes of memory allocation and loading. In a multiprogramming system a given logical segment of the program may occupy different physical memory registers at different times during execution and may reside in auxiliary memory at other times. Logical segments are therefore referenced by a modified form of fault-mode addressing, so that the segment can be automatically brought into the main memory and initialized when necessary, but directly executed once it has been initialized. In this case the fault-mode bits do not physically reside in the instruction that is to be executed but in a register that forms part of the extended address of the instruction. Dynamic initialization must in general be performed repeatedly during execution.

Loading is the process of initializing the logical rather than the physical program. During loading of a program which consists of inter-communicating segments, cross references between segments must be initialized. In early loaders this was performed during an initial loading phase. However, in multiprogramming it has been found convenient to perform load-time initialization dynamically by the dynamic-initialization techniques described above. They not only permit delay in establishing communication links till the latest possible moment but also allow reinitialization during execution at no extra cost. Loading techniques will be further discussed in the next section.

1.8 COMMUNICATION BETWEEN FUNCTION MODULES

1.8.1 THE BLOCK STRUCTURE OF FORTRAN

A large program is normally constructed out of a number of component function modules. The program has a *static* initial source-language representation and is transformed during compilation into a static initial representation for execution. During execution the program together with its data assumes a sequence of *dynamic* representations.

The static and dynamic representations of a program are usually organized so that function modules retain their identity during execution of the program, in the sense that the structure of the program as a whole can be described in a relatively simple way in terms of the structure of the component function modules. Since function modules intercommunicate during execution, facilities must be provided in the static run-time representation for performing such intercommunication. The present section will consider how intercommunication between function modules is organized for FORTRAN-type nonreentrant function modules and briefly indicate how intercommunication between reentrant function modules can be organized. Communication between reentrant function modules is discussed further in Chap. 4.

A FORTRAN program may include the following three kinds of information blocks:

1. A single main program
2. A number of subroutines
3. A number of COMMON data blocks

Information blocks belonging to one of the first two categories are called *program units*.

Figure 1.17   Structure of a FORTRAN program unit.

The run-time environment during execution of a FORTRAN program is conditioned by the fact that the storage requirements of information blocks of a FORTRAN program are determined at translation time. Individual program units of a FORTRAN program are translated independently. Each program unit is translated on the assumption that its program together with its local data will be stored in a contiguous set of registers in the computer memory, as indicated in Fig. 1.17. This assumption implies that the size of all local data items, such as arrays, is known during translation. It also implies a one-to-one correspondence between program blocks and local-data blocks and therefore does not permit programs to be reentrant.

Although the size and relative positions of all information items in a FORTRAN block are assumed known during translation, it is assumed that the actual set of registers in which the program is to reside during execution is not known during translation but is determined at load time immediately prior to execution.   Program units are usually translated assuming that the origin for the first instruction is zero, and a note is made of addresses which constitute references to local data or instructions so that they can be incremented by the true initial address when this becomes known during loading.

In addition to internal cross references, a program unit may contain *external* references to other program units or COMMON data blocks. The relative address of a data item within a COMMON data block is known at translate time, but it is again assumed that the initial register of each of the COMMON data blocks is not known at translation time but specified at load time.   COMMON-data-block references are therefore represented by relative addresses during translation and marked with their COMMON-data-block identification so that they can be incremented by the origin of the appropriate COMMON data block when this becomes known during loading.   References to other programs are similarly left undetermined during translation and must be fixed up at load time by incrementation by the initial address of the program unit to which reference is being made.

Since program units are translated independently, the symbolic names of all external references to program units and COMMON blocks must be preserved at translation time so that matching of names can be performed at load time.   In order to deal with external references the loader establishes an external-symbol table which contains the symbolic names of all externally used symbols together with the addresses assigned to each of the symbols during loading.   When the loading process is complete, true addresses of all external references have been assigned by symbol-table look-up.

A number of alternative schemes can be adopted for keeping track within a program unit of the external references for which substitution is to be made at load time and of the symbols within the program unit to which external reference is made.

1.8.2 DEFINITION AND USE TABLES

It will be assumed that each translated program carries with it a *definition table*, which lists the relative address within the program unit of all symbols to which external reference can be made, and a *use table*, in which the points of use within the program unit of all externally defined symbols are listed.   The format of the definition and use tables of a program unit are shown in Fig. 1.18.

When program units having a use and definition table of the above form are loaded, the definitions from the definition table are collected together into a *load-time definition table*.   If all program units required to run the program have been loaded, the load-time definition table will

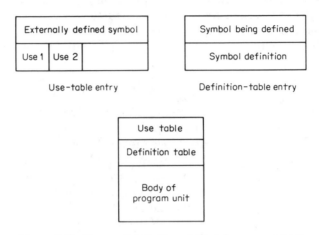

Figure 1.18 Use and definition tables for programs in the intermediate language.

contain definitions for all symbols occurring in the use tables of loaded program units.

1.8.3 THREE METHODS OF LINKAGE TO EXTERNAL SYMBOLS

The definitions in the load-time definition table are then used to set up linkages for all occurrences of all symbols occurring in the use table of any program unit.   This can be done in a number of ways:

Method 1:   Physically substitute the instruction addresses of externally defined symbols for every occurrence in the program unit.

Method 2:   At translate time place indirect-address references to use-table entries at every point in the program unit at which an external symbol is used.   Then at load time place the address of the externally defined symbol into the use table, so that uses of the symbol will result in indirect addressing of the symbol through the use table.

Method 2 requires an extra indirect-address reference every time an external symbol is used.   However, it greatly simplifies the loading process, since the value of an external symbol need be inserted into only one register of the program unit, no matter how often it is used in the program unit.

The use table of method 2 may be regarded as a vector with one entry for each external symbol.   This vector is sometimes called the *transfer vector*, since its principal function during execution is to serve as a funnel through which *transfers* (accesses) to external symbols are accomplished. Figure 1.19 illustrates a subprogram with three uses of an externally defined symbol X.

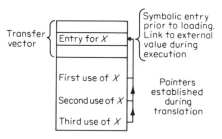

Figure 1.19   Linking by use of a transfer vector. (If transfer vectors must be modified during execution, the transfer-vector section becomes nonreentrant and must be stored as part of the activation record if function modules are implemented reentrantly. External symbols and formal parameters of a subprogram are sometimes linked to their environment by a special *linkage segment*, in which special conventions for linkage of a function module to its environment are adopted.)

Symbolic entries in the transfer vector are required only for establishing linkage to external symbols at load time and are not required during execution.   The addresses which specify the linkage to a given external symbol can therefore be placed in the same register that the symbol occupied in the intermediate-language representation of the program; i.e., since symbolic names of a given external cross reference can be discarded once the value (address) is known, names and values need never be stored simultaneously in the symbol table (transfer vector), and only a single register per symbol-table entry is required.   This register initially stores the name and is replaced at load time by the value of the symbol.

Each entry in the transfer vector allows access during execution not only to the external address specified by the symbol but also to an arbitrary amount of additional information in the environment of that external symbol.   For example, information can be obtained from the external program unit by *relative addressing* relative to the point of external linkage. An even more powerful method of obtaining information in the external block would be to use a convention that allowed access to a symbol table (directory) in the external block, through which additional items could be retrieved by table look-up.

Although method 2 above is a cleaner method of passing externally specified information between program units, it requires an extra indirect-addressing cycle for every execution-time reference to an external symbol. When all program units are loaded before execution into blocks of memory registers that remain fixed throughout execution of the program, the saving of indirect-addressing time using method 1 may on occasion be worthwhile. However, in the time-sharing systems considered below the block of physical memory registers occupied by a given program may change repeatedly during execution, and it becomes mandatory to reduce the loading overhead by a method such as method 2.

Method 3: The overhead of establishing links for cross references between program units can be reduced even further by replacing use-table entries

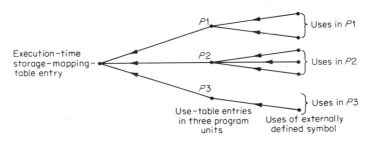

Figure 1.20 Indirect addressing of storage-mapping table.

by indirect-address references to an *execution-time storage-mapping table.* A two-stage indirect-addressing structure which connects uses of an externally defined symbol X in three program units $P1$, $P2$, $P3$ to its definition in the storage-mapping table is illustrated in Fig. 1.20.

In this scheme, moving program units from one set of physical registers to another during execution does not require any change in program units but only a change in entries in the storage-mapping table. Moving the storage-mapping table itself would of course require modification of all use-table entries. However, if a hardware base-address register is available, even moving the storage-mapping table would require merely a change of content of the base-address register.

The above use of indirect addressing is an example of *implicit substitution*. In the absence of indirect addressing, the storage-mapping-table entry would have to be explicitly substituted for all uses of the symbol to which it corresponds. Setting up indirect-address links to use-table entries at translation time and of indirect-address links from the use-table entry to the storage-mapping-table entry at load time has the same effect during execution as direct load-time substitution of the storage-mapping-table entry for all uses of the corresponding symbol. A storage-mapping table which specifies storage mapping for all objects having external names is even more necessary in multiprogramming systems than in batch-processing systems.

1.8.4 COMMUNICATION BETWEEN NESTED FUNCTION MODULES

Setting up linkages between independently compiled blocks has been discussed at some length because it is a special instance of the more general problem of setting up dynamic linkages between independent blocks during execution of a program.† The problem of dynamic linkage and dynamic passing of information between blocks arises in the implementation of time-sharing systems which allow communication between user programs and is also the basic problem of subroutine communication.

The problem of communication between FORTRAN-type function modules has been discussed at some length both because it is historically interesting and because the techniques used for communication between FORTRAN-type function modules do not differ essentially from the techniques used for communication between reentrant function modules.

Whereas FORTRAN-type function modules have a run-time representation consisting of a combined program and data block, reentrant function modules have a run-time representation consisting of a fixed-program block and a data-workspace *activation record* for each activation of the function modules. The fixed-program block associated with a function module must contain instructions for creating the activation record for each instance of execution of the function module.

When the complete program consists of a single function module with other function modules statically nested inside it, as in ALGOL, then cross references between function modules can be specified by relative addresses as described in Chap. 4. When a program consists of a number of independent "external" procedures each having a nested function-module structure, as in PL/I, then a definition table must be used for intercommunication between external procedures and other global‡ symbols, and relative addressing is used within a function module.

† A loader which provides more general load-time linkage facilities and a tree-structured load-time structure for external names is discussed in [20].

‡ A global symbol is one which refers to the same information item throughout the program in which it occurs. Nonglobal symbols (local symbols) may refer to different information structures in different parts of the program.

Exercise: Compare techniques for linkage of external symbols to techniques for linkage of subroutine parameters.

1.9 SIMULTANEOUS INPUT-OUTPUT AND COMPUTATION

1.9.1 CENTRALLY CONTROLLED COMPUTATIONS

In previous sections it was assumed that all actions of the computer were controlled by instructions executed in the instruction-processing unit. It was assumed that actions of the input-output unit as well as the memory and data-processing unit were initiated by a signal from the instruction-processing unit, which was thought of as remaining idle while actions initialized by it were being performed in other components. A signal indicating completion of the action caused initiation of a further action.

Resources of a computer can usually be used more efficiently if actions on different components are sometimes executed in parallel. The earliest and still the most common instance of such parallel execution on computers is simultaneous input-output computation.

1.9.2 DATA CHANNELS AND SATELLITE COMPUTERS

In the earliest computers, input-output instructions were executed directly by the central processing unit, causing the processing unit to remain idle while the information transfer specified by the instruction was being completed. Many large currently available computers contain one or more *central processing units*, capable of executing instructions at the rate of about 1 million per second, and a number of data channels, each of which can independently transmit information between the main memory and various kinds of input-output devices such as drums, disks, tapes, remote-access consoles, and graphical-display consoles. The data channels may be thought of as special-purpose processors for performing information transfers between input-output devices and the main memory. These special-purpose processors are controlled by the central processing unit to perform operations in parallel with it.

The facilities available within a data channel may vary over a wide range. At the simplest level, a data channel must be capable of executing a single input-output instruction transmitted to it by the central processing unit. However, once the concept of a data channel with an independent processing facility is accepted, the idea of making this processing facility successively more sophisticated immediately follows. Thus data channels with the facility of executing sequences of input-output instructions were designed, and became standard equipment on computers such as the 7094. This led naturally to the use of small, cheap, and relatively slow computers, called *satellite computers*, as data channels. One of the advantages of using a satellite computer for this purpose is that input-output conversion as well as input-output itself could be performed on the satellite computer.

1.9.3 DATA-CHANNEL CONTROL AND SYNCHRONIZATION

Since the central processor has control over the operation of its data channels, it must have the facility of initiating execution of input-output instructions on a data channel and of determining whether a computation on a data channel has been completed.   In initiating channel operation it is necessary to specify the channel, the external device, the address on the external device, the mode of information transfer (read, write, binary, binary-coded, formatted), and the internal memory block involved in the information transfer.   The total information required by the channel to initiate an operation is usually specified by a *channel-activation command* which specifies the channel and mode and has the words which specify addresses of the source and destination blocks as an argument. The following is an example of a channel-activation command:

WDBA Y   Write disk in binary mode on channel A, using the auxiliary
        information in the set of registers starting at Y to deter-
  mine the source and destination of the information.   The block of
  information starting at Y could be a program to be executed by the
  data channel.

When the central processing unit has initiated execution of a sequence of input-output instructions on a data channel, it can execute an instruction sequence in the processing unit in parallel with the data channel. The WDBA instruction can be thought of as an instruction which creates and initiates an input-output program on a data channel and then continues the program on the processing unit in parallel with the input-output program.   The dynamic flow of control when the instruction is executed may be thought of as "forking" into two parallel streams.   For this reason instructions which create and initiate new parallel processes are sometimes referred to as *fork* instructions.   The WDBA instruction is an example of a fork instruction for which the two parallel processes are executed on different interpreters.   In multiprogramming and multiprocessing, fork instructions for creating parallel computations on processing units are required.

The complexity of implementing parallel processes depends on the degree to which they can intercommunicate.   Parallel processes which do not intercommunicate do not require synchronization and can be executed independently of each other without any real-time restrictions on the order in which operations are performed.   Processes which have access in the read-only mode to a common data segment are, for practical purposes, independent processes, since one cannot affect the mode of execution of the other. However, as soon as one of the processes can modify information to which the other has access, the processes are said to intercommunicate, since the point of real time at which a commonly accessible information item is modified by one process may affect the course of the computation of the other process.

The input-output computation created by a data-channel command may intercommunicate with computations performed in the main processing unit, since both processes may modify commonly accessible information. If the main computation wishes to use information which has been read in by a data-channel command or reuse memory space from which information has been read out, it must check to see that the required data-channel operation has been completed. This requires an instruction for testing an indicator associated with each channel which is set to "on" when the channel is in operation and to "off" otherwise. Testing the indicator can be performed by an instruction such as the following:

TCA X   Transfer to X on channel A in operation and continue in sequence otherwise.

Let * in the address field denote the address in which an instruction is currently residing.

TCA *   This instruction transfers to itself while channel A is in operation and continues in sequence otherwise.

Channels which execute a sequence of input-output instructions must have internal registers to keep track of the point reached in executing the sequence of input-output instructions. Some computers have instructions for interrogating such internal registers of data channels.

The TCA instruction above requires the main computation to interrogate the channel indicator to determine whether the channel has completed operation. An alternative mode of communication between the processor and data channel is for the data channel to emit an interrupt signal on completion of its task, which causes interruption of the processor and trapping to an interrupt subroutine, which performs bookkeeping operations required on completion of the channel operation, possibly initiates another channel operation, and then returns control to the process which was in execution prior to the interrupt. Interruption has the advantage that checking for channel completion need not be explicitly scheduled but can be implicitly taken care of. Complex systems therefore utilize interrupt hardware rather than indicator testing to indicate explicit completion of input-output commands.

The time taken to execute an input-output command may vary from a few milliseconds to several seconds.   Since central processing instructions are executed at the rate of about 1 million per second, the central processing unit will typically have time to execute many thousands of instructions during execution of one data-channel command.

When a data channel and central processing unit are operating in parallel, they are essentially two independent processors which both have access to a common set of computer resources (memory registers). Conflicts of two different kinds may arise between these processes.

1.   During execution the two processes may wish to use common information channels of the computer.   In particular, both processes may wish to use the memory-selection equipment to retrieve or deposit information in the memory.   When both the data channel and the central processing unit wish to access a memory bank simultaneously, priority is usually given to the data channel since its accesses are much less frequent. The main computation is held up for a memory cycle during the data-channel access.   The data channel is said to *steal* a memory cycle from the main processor.

2.   Modification of registers common to the two processes must be synchronized so that modification of registers by one of the processes is performed only when the other process no longer requires the previous value in that register.   Such synchronization is programmed with the aid of hardware facilities such as interrupts.

In a large computer system it is convenient to regard an input-output process as being under the control, not of the process for which it is performing input-output, but of a higher-level supervisory system, which initiates input-output processes whenever there is any input-output to be performed.

1.9.4 APPLICATION TO BUFFERED OUTPUT

We shall consider below the interaction of a computational process A executed on the central processing unit which performs computations and produces items of output information which it places on an output queue, and a second process B executed on a data channel which takes successive items of information from the output queue and outputs them.   The information items may be individual characters to be output on a typewriter or larger information records with an internal format.   The output process B may either output information in a fixed format or use format information as a parameter to determine output format.   However, it will be assumed that the number of registers required to store each of the output records is fixed.   A group of registers used to store an output record will be called an *output buffer* or merely a *buffer*. It will be assumed that the output queue consists of a fixed number, say n, of buffers numbered 1 through n and that the buffers are chained together in sequence in a loop so that $i + 1$ is the successor of i for $i = 1, 2, \ldots, n - 1$ and 1 is the successor of n.

Initially process B is idle because there is no information to be output. When process A is ready to output its first output record, it places the output record in the buffer. It then calls the supervisory system to initiate a data-channel operation and continues with its computation. An internal *buffer-pointer* indicator keeps track of which buffer in the queue is the next one to be filled. The buffer pointer is incremented (modulo n) whenever a buffer has been filled.

If A generates output records at a faster rate than B can deal with them, A will eventually fill up its buffer queue. When this happens, computation of A must be suspended because there is nowhere for A to place its output. If A produces output at a uniform rate, the rate of real-time computation within the process A is limited by the speed at which B can output information produced by A. However, if A produces output in bursts, the buffer queue serves to smooth out the time profile of actual outputs and permits actual output of information produced by A in a period of high output activity to be distributed over a period of low output activity.

It is assumed that when process B completes output of a record from buffer i, it checks to see whether buffer $i + 1$ (modulo n) has been filled by process A by checking the buffer-pointer register of process A. If buffer $i + 1$ has not yet been filled, there is nothing for process B to do, and it terminates until A completes output of a further record and requests B to be reactivated. If the buffer $i + 1$ has been filled by A, then B automatically continues outputting buffer $i + 1$ (modulo n). B is assumed to have a buffer pointer which points to the buffer from which output is currently being taken.

When A is ready to output a record, it must first verify that there is a free buffer. If not, then A must be terminated until B catches up with its work sufficiently to provide a free buffer for A. If there is a free buffer, A checks whether B is operating and if not, calls the supervisor to initiate B.

Since A might be in a blocked state because of a full buffer, B should check for this condition when it completes output of a buffer and cause A to be reactivated. This results in almost completely symmetrical accessing of the buffer by the computational process A and the input-output process B, as illustrated in the flow diagram in Fig. 1.21.

Although the reason of blockage of the process differs for the two processes A and B, and the form of access differs, the logic is basically the same.   Continuation on completion of access to the buffer queue results in the case of B in a further access to the buffer queue, since the only action performed by B is a sequence of outputs from the buffer queue. In the case of A there is generally some computation before a new access to the buffer queue is required.

The symmetry of the processes A and B arises from the fact that synchronization of each of the processes with the other process is symmetrically performed by checking a state variable of the other process.

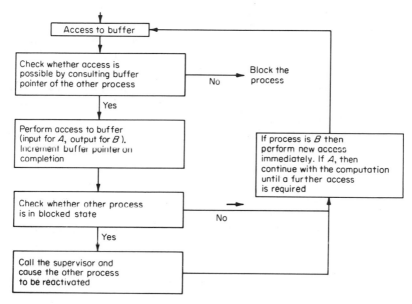

Figure 1.21 Symmetrical access of two processes to a common buffer.

This symmetrical method of synchronization of two asynchronously operating intercommunicating processes is only one of many possible techniques of synchronization.

1.9.5 RACE CONDITIONS FOR SIMULTANEOUS PROCESSES

This algorithm for synchronizing accesses to a common buffer of a computational process A and an input-output process B fails under certain special circumstances.   When B completes output of a buffer, it first checks the buffer pointer of A, and then if the buffer pointer indicates that no further buffers are ready for output, it blocks itself.   Assume that between the time that B checks the buffer pointer of A and blocks itself, A completes a new buffer, checks that B is not blocked, and continues computing without bothering to activate B.   This sequence of events is indicated as follows:

> B completes output, checks buffer pointer of A, finds no buffer waiting.
> A completes new buffer, increments buffer pointer.
> A checks that B is not blocked and continues computing.
> B blocks itself.

If this is the last buffer of output produced by A, then B will never be activated to produce this output.

The problem can be stated in more general terms as follows: B initiates an action based on interrogation of the state of A.   Before B has time to perform this action, A changes its state, interrogates a state indicator of B, and goes into a new state determined by the state of B. B then changes its state, moving into a new state based on an outdated judgment regarding the state of A.

At this point both A and B are in states based on erroneous assumptions about the state of the other, and this may result in situations where the erroneous assumption can never be corrected.

One solution to this problem is to allow processes temporarily to *lock out* other processes from access to information that is common to both of them.   For example, if process B were able to lock out process A from access to the state indicators of both B and A while interrogating A's state indicator and blocking itself, then A could not change its state and interrogate B until B had completed its change to the blocked state. Removal of the lock-out condition could be performed by a higher-level system program on receiving the information that B was blocked.

An alternative approach suggested by Saltzer [11] is to allow the supervisor to recheck the state of A after it has blocked B and to cause B to be reactivated if this second check of the state of A reveals that A has in fact surreptitiously changed its state while B was blocking itself.

1.9.6   MODULARITY OF PROCESSORS

With the development of sophisticated programming systems such as those that arise in multiprogramming, the organizational system activities expand to include scheduling, interrupt handling, and a number of other activities.   This has led to the development of composite computer systems consisting of a relatively slow *foreground machine*, which handles the interface with the user and many system activities, and a fast *background machine*, for performing user computations as rapidly as possible. It is the job of the foreground machine to feed jobs to the background machine so as to maximize its throughput.

Although the above approach appears to simplify the overall problem of system organization by splitting it into two parts, it is not clear that a two-level, two-machine approach is either simpler or more efficient than a one-level approach which assumes that all processors in the computing system have identical properties.   The cost of processing units is only a small fraction of the total cost of a computer system.   If two computers C_1, C_2 with processors P_1, P_2 and memory capacities M_1, M_2 form part of the same computer system, then a single computer system with two identical processors P and a memory capacity $M_1 + M_2$ could be designed to operate more efficiently at little extra cost.†   Moreover, such a computer system would have an added advantage of processor modularity. Programs could be designed without regard to which of the processors they were executed on, and the system could be designed so that it would run even if one of the processors was out of action.   Since the cost of processors is likely to become an increasingly small fraction of total computer cost, it is likely that computer systems with a number of identical processors will become economical.   However, the problem of managing a computer system with multiple processors is formidable. Some of the problems which arise in computer systems with more than one processor have been discussed above.   Computer systems with multiple processors are further discussed in the sections which follow.

1.10   RESOURCE ALLOCATION IN MULTIPROGRAMMING SYSTEMS

1.10.1   MULTIPROGRAMMING, MULTIPROCESSING, AND MULTIACCESSING

Computer systems in which a number of user programs may be simultaneously competing for physical computer resources such as memory registers or processing units are referred to as *multiprogrammed* computer systems.   The set of techniques for realizing multiprogrammed computer systems is referred to as *multiprogramming*.   Multiprogramming may be performed either on a computer with a single processor or on a computer with multiple processors.   The set of techniques for realizing computer systems with more than one processing unit is referred to as *multiprocessing*.   A subfield of multiprogramming is concerned with the problems of computer system organization which arise specifically because of the

† An instructive comparison between the two-machine and one-machine approach can be obtained by comparing the ASP system [27] with the HASP system [28]. The ASP system assumes the availability of a foreground machine for input-output and system organization and a background machine for rapid execution of user programs.   The HASP system is similar in logical organization to ASP but assumes that the processors for performing systems tasks and user computation have the same characteristics.   It appears that HASP will be more efficient and flexible than ASP, even when there is only a single processor, on which execution of the two classes of programs is interleaved.

multiplicity of input-output channels which interface with the system. The problems in this area are referred to as problems of *multiaccessing*.

Both multiprocessing and multiaccessing involve the allocation of scarce computer resources such as the main memory and the processing units among competing user-initiated programs, and therefore are subfields of the general area of multiprogramming. However, multiprogramming may occur even on computer systems with only a single input channel and only a single processor.

Arden [23] distinguishes three kinds of multiprogramming systems:

1. *Special-purpose systems*, in which data may be entered from many different terminals but the program structure remains fixed. The system can service many requests in a short elapsed time, but the requests are restricted to a small number of predefined computations. Airline reservation systems such as the SABRE system [26] are examples of such special-purpose systems.

2. *Limited programming systems*, which allow programs in a number of predefined programming languages to be entered and executed from terminals but have limited user system facilities and limited provision for user interaction or system expansion. The BASIC system [24] and the QUIKTRAN system [25] are examples of such systems.

3. *General programming systems*, which place no restriction on the form of the programs and data that can be entered by the user into his program space, allow flexible intercommunication between users, and provide user facilities for file storage, protection and privacy of information, system expansion, and other facilities. New system facilities normally require the permission and possibly the supervision of system personnel but can be introduced while the system is running. The Multics system for the GE 645 [13] and the TSS system for the IBM 360 model 67 [12] are examples of general programming systems.

The distinction between the above systems can be phrased in terms of increasing diversity of the environment that obtains during the execution of user programs. In special-purpose systems, the environment of programs remains constant, and only the data vary. In limited programming systems, the environment contains a limited number of compilers with system facilities for the execution of compiled programs. In general programming systems, the system environment is much more variable than in the other classes of system, and there are facilities for temporary or permanent modification of the environment built into the system.

In the remainder of this chapter, multiprogramming techniques for general programming systems will be emphasized.

1.10.2 EFFICIENCY VERSUS FLEXIBILITY

A large computer system may be thought of as a utility which is intended to serve a variety of users both flexibly and efficiently. Access to the system by the user should be simple, rapid, and sufficiently flexible to allow the user to suit the mode of access to his needs. For example, an application which requires the computer to make real-time response to an on-line process requires a different mode of operation from that for a batch processing problem whose results are not so urgently required. The mode of operation required to service a user who is debugging a program at a typewriter console and requires small bursts of computation to be performed within a short period of elapsed time must also be catered for.

Program execution in each of the permitted modes of operation should be efficient in terms both of resource utilization and of user requirements. Saltzer [11] has classified the problems of computer-system organization into technological ones, concerned with efficient resource utilization (throughput), and intrinsic ones, concerned with the convenience of the user.   An alternative is to consider the user as one of the resources of the computer system whose efficiency of utilization is determined by the user facilities and the response pattern of the computer system to run requests by that user. Intrinsic problems may in this way be modeled into technological problems; i.e., the intrinsic problems of providing adequate service to an on-line process or to a user at a console can be modeled by the technological problem of providing certain user facilities and computer response patterns for classes of peripheral devices.

1.10.3 TIME SLICING

The hardware of a computer system consists of a collection of physical resources each of which has certain operating characteristics. When considered statically, all computer resources are information-storage devices which at different times are occupied by different items of information. Every resource has a one-dimensional existence through time referred to as its *time line*. The time line of each resource can be subdivided into segments, called *time slices*, corresponding to periods for which the resource is allocated to a particular information item.†   The

---

† The term "time slice" is here used to denote a time interval in the *time space* of a resource. It is also used below to denote time intervals in the time space of an information structure and of a computation. The use of the term for both these concepts must in certain contexts be carefully distinguished. However, there is a sense in which an information structure has just as real an existence as a physical resource. There is a symmetry (duality) between the notion of time slicing of resources among information structures and the notion of time slicing of an information structure in different resources. This symmetry makes it appropriate to use the same name for both notions.

computer resources form a hierarchy such that some are more in demand than others, although the total storage capacity in the computer (including auxiliary memory) is sufficient for information items of all computations.

An any given point of time the computer hardware is occupied by a group of loosely interconnected information structures each of which represents a process at some stage of execution. The term *process* or *computation* will be used to denote the sequence of information structures representing the program and data of a given user during successive stages of execution.† It is convenient to introduce the notion of a *time line for computations*, which measures progress within the computation in terms of the number of executed instructions since the beginning of the computation and has no direct correspondence with real time.

The information structure associated with a computation undergoes transformations as it progresses along its time line. A snapshot of the information structure at a given point of the computation will be referred to as an *instantaneous description*. A computation may be completely characterized by the sequence of instantaneous descriptions to which it gives rise. Individual instructions or executable program segments may be characterized by the effect they have in transforming instantaneous descriptions.

The instantaneous description which constitutes the complete multiprogramming system is structured into a number of interacting but relatively independent component instantaneous descriptions associated with individual users. Each user "sees" a private instantaneous description which contains all accessible information structures. From the system point of view, each active computation may proceed independently subject to certain interlocks and interrupts; and real-time control is passed between user computations in a manner determined by a scheduling algorithm. The mechanism for transfer of control between processes of a multiprogramming system executed on a single processor is similar to that for *coroutines*, discussed in subsection 4.10.3, since each program may create and delete information independently and continues to remain in existence when execution of the program is temporarily suspended.

† The term "user" does not necessarily have human connotations and should be thought of as a group of programs for performing a certain function or a "front" for purposes of accounting rather than as something of flesh and blood. Thus system programs for performing specific system functions may be thought of as users. Users not under the control of the problem programmer are sometimes referred to as *demon users* [11]. It is usually possible to dynamically partition executed instructions so that each is associated with precisely one user. However, there are some fuzzy boundaries in such partitioning for which arbitrary decisions must be made. The partitioning of information structures among users for the purpose of "space accounting" is more complex because certain programs are shared among several users.

However, since the next program is determined by a system-scheduling algorithm, the control mechanism has features similar to that for event notices (see subsection 4.10.4).   Since the order of execution of segments of different processes is largely insensitive to the way in which they are interleaved, the control mechanism has features similar to that for tasks (see subsection 4.10.5).   Finally, the control mechanism has features similar to the interrupt form of transfer of control discussed in subsection 4.9.2.

Exercise: Discuss carefully the forms of control mechanism for transfer of control between user and system programs of a multiprogramming system.

1.10.4 ALLOCATION OF INFORMATION TO RESOURCES

The physical storage registers in which instructions and data reside while they are actually being transformed are referred to as *processor registers*. They are in very great demand during a computation, and the time slice of processor registers allocated to an information item is restricted to the time that the information item is required in transforming the instantaneous description.   When an information item in a processing register is no longer required, it is moved to a register that is less in demand by an *information-moving instruction*.

The speed at which information-moving instructions operate is determined by the accessing characteristics of the information-storage media between which the information is moved.   It is important that instructions which move information in and out of processing registers be rapidly executed, since this constitutes a greater computational bottleneck than the processing time.   Information which has been moved out of the processing registers and is no longer required can be moved to an information medium with slower accessing characteristics by more slowly executed information-moving instructions which do not tie up the processing unit while they are being executed.

The information-storage medium which serves as the direct source and destination of processing-unit information is called the main memory. Information-storage media to which information is moved when it is not directly required by the processing unit are called the auxiliary memory. There may, in general, be several levels of auxiliary memory with different accessing speeds, some communicating directly with the main memory and others communicating with the main memory through one or more intermediate levels of auxiliary memory.

A computer system normally contains a small number of processing units in which processing can be performed and a hierarchy of different memory devices with different accessing speeds.   Information not currently in use is normally stored in a low-speed memory device; information currently being used in processing is stored in processing registers; and information about to be used must be stored in the main memory if the computer is to access it directly.   If an information item accessed by a processing unit is not in the main memory, the processing unit cannot proceed with the computation until a slow information transfer from auxiliary to main memory has been accomplished.   The time for an information transfer from auxiliary to main memory is typically at least 1,000 times as long as the transfer time from the main memory to the processing unit, so that the real time required to execute an instruction whose information is not in main memory is several orders of magnitude greater than that required for an instruction whose information is in main memory.

If a processing unit is to execute a sequence of instructions at its normal processing speed, all components of the instantaneous description accessed during execution of this sequence of instructions must be in the main computer memory.   It is one of the principal tasks of a programming system to organize information transfers between various levels of auxiliary memory so that information is in the main memory when it is required by the processor.   The programming system must allocate time slices of blocks of physical main-memory registers so that information required for processing is usually, though not always, in the main memory before it is used.   At the same time, the memory time slice allocated to an information item should not greatly exceed the time period during which it is used, so that it can be freed for use by other information items. The efficiency of decisions regarding allocation of physical memory to information items is determined by the time pattern of accesses to the information item.   In considering this time pattern, it is important to distinguish the time pattern of access in the internal time scale of a given program and the time pattern in real time when interrupts are to be taken into account.

1.10.5 TIME PATTERNS OF ACCESSING

Time patterns in which information accesses to a given information block occur in bursts separated by long intervals with no accesses allow much greater efficiency of physical-memory allocation than time patterns in which accesses to a large number of blocks are interspersed with each other in a relatively uniform manner.

The real-time pattern of information accesses in a multiprogramming system is inevitably more diffuse than in a batch-processing system because different processes are interleaved with each other on a given processor.

This not only requires information items of a number of interleaved processes to occupy concurrent time slices of the main memory but also requires information items of each of the processes to occupy its time slice for a long period of time.

The index of main-memory utilization by a given computation or set of computations is clearly the product of the number of physical main-memory registers used and the time for which they were used. This index will be referred to as the *memory slice* of the computation or set of computations. An example will show that the memory slice occupied by a set of processes rises sharply with increase in the number of processes being simultaneously executed.

Example: Assume that there are n tasks with similar time and space requirements to be executed on a single processor of the multiprogramming system. Assume also that each process requires m fixed-size blocks (pages) of main memory to operate efficiently and that the internal process time during which the process is required is k seconds for each process. Then the memory slice required for processing the set of n tasks in sequence is kmn units. If, however, the n tasks are interleaved, each task occupies mn blocks for kn seconds, so that the memory slice required to execute the set of tasks is kmn^2 units.

Multiprogramming leads to greater technological efficiency by allowing processor idle time in a given process to be used by another process which is ready for execution. It greatly facilitates more efficient servicing of multiple users requiring real-time responses and short-elapsed-time responses. However, it leads to a greater strain on memory resources even in the case when program characteristics are assumed known and memory-allocation problems are assumed to have been solved.

1.10.6 MATCHING SOFTWARE TO RESOURCE ALLOCATION

In a multiprogramming system with given facilities for allocation of information structures to resources, the system software must be specifically designed to work efficiently under the given allocation scheme. Efficient design of system software can improve overall system efficiency at two levels.

1. If frequently used system programs are constructed to make efficient use of computer resources during their execution, then all programs that utilize scarce computer resources during the execution of these system programs will operate more efficiently, resulting in an overall improvement of system efficiency.

2. Compilers and other programs that determine the run-time representation of user programs should cause programs to have a run-

time representation that makes efficient use of allocation facilities during execution.

If, as has happened in a number of instances, the performance of a given multiprogramming system has been found to be poor, it is difficult to judge whether the poor performance is due to inherently unworkable allocation procedures or to software design which made poor use of the given allocation procedures. A complex system is as weak as the weakest link, and it is not always possible to identify the weakest link in a complex system. Indeed, since components of a system strongly interact, there are usually a number of alternative ways of improving the overall performance of a system, e.g., expanding hardware capacity of critical hardware components, placing restrictions on multiprogramming within the system, providing poorer elapsed-time service to certain classes of users, redesigning software-system modules, redesigning the run-time representation strategy for programs, and redesigning the basic hardware-allocation scheme. In order to determine which of these factors is the critical one, some means of measuring system performance must be devised, and the behavior of the system under changes in system design parameters must be measured. The measurement of system performance will be further discussed in a later section.

1.11 VIRTUAL PROCESSORS

1.11.1 RESOURCE-INDEPENDENT INFORMATION STRUCTURES

One of the principal differences between batch-processing and multiprogrammed programming systems lies in the degree to which a user program has control over physical computer resources during the execution of his program. In batch-processing programming systems machine-language programs are permitted in which the user decides for himself how physical resources are to be allocated during program execution and has complete control over the real-time sequence of events within the computer during execution of his program except in exceptional circumstances which cause interrupts. In a multiprogrammed computer system, the programmer has control over the time sequence of events in his own program but has little explicit control over the allocation of computer resources among different programs in the programming system.

A multiprogrammed system allocates scarce computer resources to programs during execution. Since the physical resources allocated to a program may be different on different instances of execution, it is essential that a multiprogrammed computer system provide facilities for the run-time representation of programs in a manner that is independent of the physical resources they will occupy during execution.

It will be assumed that the physical computer resources are approximately as follows:

1. Several hundred thousand main-memory registers addressable by a linear sequence of integer addresses

2. One or more processing units having access to a common main memory

3. Several hundred million registers of fast auxiliary-memory time with a block access time of a few milliseconds

4. Data channels to a wide unpredictable variety of input-output devices such as tapes, printers, card readers, typewriter consoles, direct data channels to on-line equipment, scopes, etc.

5. A number of meters and clocks for measuring resource utilization

In a batch-processing programming system these resources can be directly addressed at the machine-language level. In a multiprogrammed system the allocation of resources to information structures associated with a particular user is performed dynamically by the programming system. It is therefore convenient to store the information structures in a hardware-independent manner during execution.

1.11.2 VIRTUAL MACHINE LANGUAGE

The hardware-independent run-time representation of instructions will be referred to as *virtual machine language* to emphasize that it is a hardware-independent representation. The computer system is designed to execute programs specified in virtual machine language rather than programs in a more hardware-oriented language. The virtual-machine-language programs may be thought of as being executed *interpretively* by the programming system. As in every interpretive system, a penalty is paid in that there is an interpretive overhead in the execution of individual instructions.† However, the hardware of multiprogrammed computers is designed so as to reduce this interpretive overhead to allow indirect-addressing cycles.

The principal reason for choosing a run-time representation which must be interpreted arises from the requirement that the run-time representation be hardware-independent. However, once the decision for an interpretive run-time representation has been made, other benefits associated with interpretive languages can be exploited. The run-time

† In the multiprogrammed systems considered below only the address field is interpreted, and indirect-addressing hardware is used to reduce the interpretive overhead.

representation can be chosen so that it is a clean and logical language. Additional flexibility of control sequencing, diagnostics, and mode of access can be provided by interpretive control bits encountered during indirect addressing.

Since the purpose of the interpretive language is to provide independence of physical registers, the interpretation will be associated principally with the address fields of virtual-machine-language instructions. The operation fields will normally correspond closely to operations actually performed on the specified operands.

The system programs which interpret instructions of the hardware-independent machine language are referred to as *hardware-management routines*. In a computer system they are equivalent in their effect to microprograms which modify the primitive hardware structure of the computer and give the user the illusion of a more civilized environment. However, hardware-management routines are implemented both by hardware and software and may require a considerable programmed overhead to achieve their effect during execution. The remainder of the present section will describe the static representation of information structures in virtual machine language.

The term "virtual" was introduced above to distinguish the machine language seen by the user from the physical facilities actually used internally to execute computer programs. In the discussion below virtual will be used repeatedly as an adjective to distinguish facilities of the system seen by the user from corresponding physical characteristics.

For example, "virtual memory" will distinguish the memory seen by each user from the physical memory of the actual computer. The concept of a hardware-independent "virtual address" will be defined and distinguished from that of a physical-register address. The concept of a "virtual processor" or "virtual computer" is defined as the computer configuration which each user sees when he writes his program, distinguished from the physical computer that is actually available. It will be assumed that a multiprogrammed physical computer can cope with an indefinite number of identical hardware-independent virtual computers. A virtual computer has hardware-independent *virtual registers* and a *virtual processing unit*. Each programmer programs his virtual computer as though it were a physical computer all of whose resources are dedicated to execution of the program specified by the programmer. The programming system allocates physical facilities of the physical computer to virtual facilities of each virtual computer as they are required.

Although the virtual machine language cannot refer to physical storage registers, some form of addressing must be available within the virtual machine language. The set of all addresses available to the user will be called the *virtual address space*, and individual addresses in the virtual address space will be called *virtual addresses*. All information items accessible in a given program are referred to by virtual addresses. Information that is placed in a given virtual address is assumed to remain in that virtual address unless it is modified or moved, just like information in a conventional computer. However, the programmer has no control over the physical storage medium in which virtual addresses are stored. The correspondence between physical and virtual addresses is completely under the control of the computer system. It is the responsibility of the computer system to move blocks of information about in the physical memory hierarchy so that information appears in the main memory when it is required for processing and is retired to auxiliary memory when no longer required, to make room for other blocks of information.

The programming system must provide facilities not only for moving blocks of information in the physical storage hierarchy but also for accessing the physical register corresponding to a given virtual address when such access is required during execution. The correspondence between virtual addresses and physical addresses is stored for each program in a set of *address-mapping tables*, which are updated whenever a block of information is moved within the physical storage hierarchy and used for table look-up whenever access to information specified by a virtual address is required during execution. The structure of the address-mapping table depends on the relation between the virtual address space and physical address space and also on the hardware facilities available for performing address mapping. The structure of address-mapping tables will be further discussed below.

1.11.3 VIRTUAL-ADDRESS-SPACE ORGANIZATION—TWO-COMPONENT ADDRESSING

Since the virtual address space is hardware-independent, the system designer has considerable freedom in designing it. The following factors must be considered:

1. The virtual address space must be related to the physical address space in such a manner that mapping virtual addresses to physical addresses through the address-mapping table can be performed reasonably rapidly.

2. Within the constraints imposed by factor 1, the virtual address space should be designed for the convenience of the programmer.

Programmers find it convenient to subdivide the information structures of a computation into program and data segments which correspond to logical subdivisions of the problem. The virtual address organization described below structures the address space into a set of *segments* which can be independently named, so that logical segments of a computation can conveniently be mapped into segments of the virtual address space. Information structures within a segment are referred to by a *two-component* virtual address (i,j) where i specifies the segment address (segment name), and j specifies a word-within-segment address.   In the discussion below some of the design considerations which determine the form of a two-component address space are given.

The simplest form of virtual address space is a one-dimensional sequence of virtual addresses running from 0 through $2^n - 1$ for some n. In choosing the size of the virtual address space we are not restricted to the size of any specific physical storage medium.   One of the costs of choosing a large virtual address space is the increase in the number of bits in the address field of virtual-machine-language instructions.   However, it is shown below that enlarging the virtual address space can be accomplished without correspondingly enlarging the number of bits required to denote an address in machine-language instructions.

The number of address bits in an instruction can be reduced if the convention is adopted that the address field contains merely a *displacement* relative to an origin specified in a special register.

If the maximum displacement permitted is 2^l, a main address field of l bits is sufficient, independent of the size of the address space.   Special registers which specify the origin with respect to which displacements are measured are referred to as *relocation registers* or *base registers*.

The number of bits required in a base register to specify the origin for purposes of relocation can be reduced by p bits if the convention is adopted that origins can occur only at registers which are multiples of 2^p. If the maximum displacement is 2^l, it is convenient to choose $p = l$, so that an increment of 1 in a base register is associated with an increment of 2^l in the address space.   When this convention is adopted, addresses in an address space with 2^n addresses can be represented by a k-bit base-register address and an l-bit main-memory address where $k + l = n$.

The above organization structures an address space of 2^n addresses into 2^k blocks each of which contains 2^l words, where $k + l = n$.   The resulting blocks will be referred to as *segments*.†   The contents of the k-bit base register will be referred to as a *segment address*, and the l-bit address in the address field will be referred to as a *word-within-segment* address.

Addressing by means of a segment address and a word-within-segment address is referred to as *two-component addressing*.   Two-component addressing with base-register hardware for implicitly specifying the

---

† The term "segment" is used in different ways by different computer-system designers.   This definition does not allow segments to be truly independent because of carry from the lth to the $(l + 1)$st position.   Truly independent segment naming requires suppression of the carry, as indicated below.

first address component allows a very large address space to be defined without unduly increasing the number of bits in the address field.   For example, in the IBM 360 model 67, an address space of 2^{32} words is defined by 12-bit segment addresses and 20-bit word-within-segment addresses, while in the GE 645 machine an address space of 2^{36} words is defined by 18-bit segment addresses and 18-bit word-within-segment addresses.

In the scheme described above the segments may be thought of as being laid end to end in the address space, so that the last address of one segment is a neighbor of the first address of the next segment.   However, the address spaces associated with different segment addresses may be made truly independent of each other by suppressing carries from the most significant bit of a word address into a segment address and causing either an end-around carry or an error interrupt whenever such a carry occurs.   When this is done, the two address coordinates become truly independent, and the address space becomes a set of independent segment address spaces.

In a virtual address space, physical addresses need be assigned only to those elements of the address space in which information is actually being stored.   This allows extravagant provisions to be made for the possible growth of segments stored in the address space without committing physical resources to unused portions of the segment.   In a virtual address space of this kind the problem of dynamic storage allocation is solved by very sparse use of the address space, so that there is almost always room for structures to expand.   Physical storage for structures in the virtual address space of a given program is provided by a "hidden" allocator, whose characteristics are further discussed below.

Each user programs as though he had his own virtual processor with a private virtual address space.   A set of address-mapping tables is consulted during execution to determine the physical address.†   During the course of the computation a given virtual address may at different times correspond to a number of different physical registers of the memory hierarchy.   The system keeps track of blocks of information by updating the address-mapping tables of the associated virtual computer whenever a block of information is moved.

The use of address-mapping tables not only permits the same virtual address to be represented by different physical addresses at different

---

† Whereas the previous discussion was concerned with the mapping from machine-language instruction addresses to virtual addresses, the present discussion is concerned with the mapping from virtual addresses to physical addresses.   The device used for mapping from machine-language instruction addresses to virtual addresses is the base register, while the device used for mapping from virtual to physical addresses is the address-mapping tables.   These notions are described in greater detail in Secs. 1.12 and 1.13.

points of the computation but also permits addresses of two different virtual memories to denote the same physical address and thereby to have access to the same common information.   In particular, the address space of every virtual processor permits access to a common set of system routines.   The virtual memory of every virtual processor may be thought of as being *initialized* so that it contains a resident standard set of initial system facilities.

1.11.4   AUXILIARY MEMORY AND USER COMMUNICATION

Although the virtual memory of each user is very large, there may still be programs for which the virtual memory is not large enough and for which auxiliary memory is therefore required.   The requirement of hardware independence applies to auxiliary memory as well as to the main memory.   The auxiliary memory accessible to a user will be called the *virtual auxiliary memory.*†

Two alternative approaches can be adopted to auxiliary-memory management:

1.   Each user has a private virtual-auxiliary-memory space.
2.   There is a systemwide virtual-auxiliary-memory space, so that two identical references to auxiliary memory by different users always denote the same information structure.

The second approach is the one adopted in the IBM and Multics systems and will be illustrated below.

The systemwide virtual auxiliary memory, which will be referred to as the *file system,* may be described by a directed graph with an initial vertex called the *root vertex* and a number of terminal vertices.   The terminal vertices correspond to information blocks, and the nonterminal vertices consist of sets of pointers to lower-level vertices.   The sets of pointers associated with nonterminal vertices are referred to as *catalogs* (IBM) or *directories* (Multics).   The directory (catalog) associated with the root vertex of the file-system tree structure is referred to as the *root directory.*‡

The information structures associated with vertices in the file system will be referred to as *files.*   Access to all files in the file system must pass

---

† The term "virtual auxiliary memory" is used to emphasize the fact that the auxiliary memory of the programming system is a "logical" auxiliary memory rather than a physical set of storage devices.   The names of objects in the virtual auxiliary memory are independent of their physical storage locations, just as in the case of virtual main memory.

‡ For further information on the organization of a specific virtual auxiliary memory, see the paper by Daley and Neumann in [13].

through the root directory.   Each file in the file system has a *tree name*, which consists of a sequence of pointers through successive directories terminating in a pointer to the file itself.   The tree name is the address of the file in the virtual auxiliary memory.   A given file in the file system may in general have more than one tree name, corresponding to different paths through the graph structure from the root directory to the file. However, the convention is usually adopted that there are no loops in the graph which represents the file structure; i.e., the vertices of the file system constitute a partial ordering.

The set of physical storage registers in which files of the file system are stored may vary during execution.   The correspondence between addresses in the virtual auxiliary memory and physical registers is determined by a systemwide *file-system address-mapping table*.   The unit which can be named and manipulated in the file system will be referred to as a *segment*, since named information structures become segments when they are mapped into the virtual address space of a user program.   When a user program acquires a file, the file is given a segment number, and a direct correspondence is set up between the segment number and the registers in which the information structure resides. The segment can then be accessed through address-mapping tables in the normal manner.

The systemwide virtual auxiliary memory fulfills the following functions:

1.   It stores information structures private to individual computations which it is inconvenient to store in the main memory.
2.   It serves as a common information base which stores individual program and data segments that are generally available to all computations or selected classes of computations.
3.   It can be used for purposes of communicating between computations.

In order to ensure privacy of information in categories 1 and 3 and freedom from unauthorized modification of information in all categories, there are means of restricting the form of access to information stored in the virtual auxiliary memory.   The modes of permitted access may be a combination of the following:

X The segment may be executed as a program.
R Reading from the segment is permitted.
W Writing information into the segment is permitted.
A Changing the size of the segment is permitted.

The mode of access permitted to a given segment in the auxiliary memory is not determined solely by the segment being accessed but by the relation between the accessing process and the accessed segment. This effect can be achieved by encoding the mode of access in the sequence of pointers that constitute its tree name. For example, the mode of access determined by a sequence of pointers can be taken to be the mode of access associated with the last of the pointers.

These logical attributes of segments in an information structure are represented at the physical level by bit patterns in address-mapping tables which are interpretively interrogated during execution. When a segment is "moved" from auxiliary memory to a given virtual address space, the accessing bit patterns which determine the mode of access are initialized in the address-mapping tables of the virtual processor.

When a user is given permission to use the system, he is allocated a standard initialized virtual processor, with access to a standard set of system programs in his main addressing space and access to a standard set of files in the file system in standard accessing modes. During execution he may build up information structures both in his virtual address space and in the file system. However, he may also wish to request access to information in the file system that is not made available on an automatic basis. Two categories of information in this class may be distinguished:

1.   System files, for which access requests are channeled through the computer operator and made available by an action of the computer operator, possibly after consultation with the system administrator of the computation center

2.   Private files, for which access requests must be made directly to the user having control over these files

The system must contain facilities for granting access to privileged files both by system administrators and by private system users. A set of primitive system operations for allowing such access is discussed in [15].

Mapping an object from the virtual auxiliary memory to the virtual main memory of a virtual computer does not require moving the information itself but merely updating the address-mapping tables of the virtual computer to establish the correspondence between the physical registers of the information item and the virtual main-memory address with which it has become associated. However, in performing a mapping between the virtual auxiliary memory and the virtual main memory, information regarding the mode of access to the information must be preserved. Encoding accessing information in the main-memory address-mapping tables is further discussed in Sec. 1.13.

1.11.5 VIRTUAL COMPUTERS

Each user of a multiprogrammed computer system has at his disposal a virtual computer with a virtual address space which is initialized to have access to a standard set of system facilities.   During the lifetime of a given computation the user may introduce his own information structures from the virtual auxiliary memory into his virtual address space.

A virtual computer has an associated *stateword,* which contains the information that resides in the processing unit when the process is being executed.   However, the stateword has an existence as an information structure independently of whether it is loaded into a physical processing unit.   When the stateword occupies a processing unit, the computation associated with that virtual computer is said to be *active* or *running.* When the stateword is stored in the main or auxiliary memory, the computation is said to be *passive* or *blocked.*

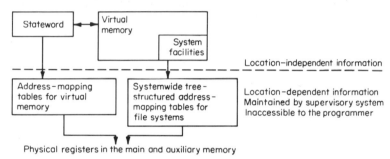

Figure 1.22   A virtual computer with address-mapping tables that determine the physical location of accessible information structures.

The stateword of a virtual computer C contains information stored in processing-unit registers such as the accumulator and instruction-location register.   It also contains a pointer to the address-mapping tables, which determine the correspondence between virtual and physical addresses for the given computation.   The pointer to the address-mapping tables links the stateword to all information structures of the virtual computer associated with the stateword.   The term *computation* will be used to denote the sequence of instantaneous descriptions associated with a given virtual computer.

The transition from a computation C_1 to a computation C_2 on a given processing unit is accomplished by storing the stateword associated with C_1 and loading the stateword associated with C_2 into the processing unit.   Loading the new stateword automatically causes a new set of address-mapping tables to be used in interpreting address fields.   The address-mapping tables are used both in the instruction-fetch phase and in the instruction-execution phase, as indicated in Sec. 1.12.

Moving information in the physical memory during a computation causes changes in the address-mapping tables of the associated virtual computer but not in the virtual addresses of the moved information. Location-independent virtual addresses and location-independent pure-procedure segments are made possible by the expedient of interposing an interpretive address-mapping phase into the computation. The address-mapping tables rather than the address itself are modified whenever the physical address changes during execution.

Figure 1.22 illustrates the relation between the information structure which constitutes a virtual computer and the physical registers in which the information structure is stored.

1.11.6 MEASURES OF SYSTEM EFFICIENCY

When a virtual computer is in execution, it is occupying a time slice of a physical processor. It is also occupying time slices of a number of other resources. It is the job of the computer system to allocate time slices of resources to virtual processors so that computations specified by users can be executed both efficiently and flexibly.

One of the measures of efficiency is the proportion of time a physical processor spends doing computations specified by virtual processors of users. This proportion is less than 1 because a processor may be idle or perform administrative-system functions such as process interchange or memory allocation. System functions such as input-output are provided as a service to the user and charged to the user, and system functions such as accounting or interrupt routines that are not explicitly requested by the user but form part of the system overhead for a computation may also legitimately be charged to the user.† However, certain systemwide computations and certain kinds of excessive administrative overhead due to system inefficiency cannot legitimately be charged to the user.

One of the features of a multiprogramming system is that the user is never charged for idle time on a physical processor. If a given physical processor becomes idle because the information required to execute an instruction is not in the physical main memory, the current computation is interrupted while the information is brought into core, and execution of some other process is initiated on this processor.

More precise data on the factors which affect the efficiency of throughput in a computer system can be obtained by breaking down the time spent in various system functions into categories such as interrupt servicing, resource allocation, resource accounting, etc., and measuring the time spent in each of these activities, the proportion of idle time due

---

† The user of electricity has to pay for the electricity used in running his electric meter.

to each of these activities, and the change in these times brought about by the change of certain design parameters.

Efficiency is measured above in terms of the efficiency of processor utilization.   We shall consider next the effect of the problem mix on the efficiency of processor utilization.

1.11.7 FOREGROUND AND BACKGROUND PROCESSES

Computations which have elapsed-time deadlines for their completion are called *foreground processes*, e.g., real-time computations, interactive computations in which a user at a console expects an "immediate" response, and debugging runs.   Computations for which there is no pressing real-time deadline are referred to as *background processes*, e.g., long production runs and batch-processing runs for which an elapsed time of more than a few minutes is acceptable.   Background processes usually make less stringent demands on resources than foreground processes.   Running programs as background processes can be encouraged both by charging lower rates and by system rules.

Processes within a multiprogramming system are assigned a priority number.   Processes with a high priority number receive faster service but are subject to higher charging rates.   The classification of processes into foreground and background processes is essentially a classification into two priority classes.   In practice, there may be a whole spectrum of priority classes within a programming system.   The choice of a criterion for assigning priorities and for scheduling of jobs having a given structure is discussed in [29].   However, there is as yet insufficient experience to determine how such algorithms perform in practice.

Foreground processes tend to make heavy use of input-output facilities, while background processes tend to make heavier use of processor time.   In order to avoid situations in which a processor is idle because nothing is waiting to be processed, it is desirable to include in the problem mix a number of background processes which make heavy use of the processor and relatively light use of other resources.   Multiprogramming systems are specifically designed to take advantage of variation in the resource requirements of different computations for the purpose of improving the average overall efficiency of resource utilization.

1.12 PROCESSING-UNIT ORGANIZATION FOR TWO-COMPONENT ADDRESSING

1.12.1 REPRESENTATIONS OF IDENTIFIERS

One of the most important problems in programming at all language levels is the representation of identifiers.   At least four levels of representation of names must be considered in a multiprogramming system:

1. *The Source-language Level.*   Names at the source-language level
are symbolic, for example X, $X(I)$.   The association of names with the
objects they denote is determined partially by context and partially by
declarations which specify *attributes* associated with the given name (see
Chap. 4).

2. *The Instruction-address Level.*   The contents of the address and
special-register fields of an instruction determine a rule for computing an
address.   The address is determined both by the contents of address and
special-register fields and by the contents of explicit registers used in the
address computation.

3. *The Virtual-address Level.*   The modified address obtained from
an instruction address by indexing, indirect addressing, and other forms
of address computation results in a virtual address.   In the multiprogrammed computers considered here the virtual address is a two-component address with a segment component and word-within-segment
component.

4. *Physical-register-address Level.*   A physical-register address is the
address of a physical register in the main memory.

The translation from a source-language name to an instruction
address is accomplished by a compiler which translates source language
into object language.   The translation from an instruction address to a
virtual address and from a virtual address to a register address is accomplished by computer hardware during execution.   The translation from
instruction addresses to virtual addresses will be considered in this section, and that from virtual addresses to physical addresses in the following section.

It will be assumed that each processing unit contains a two-component *address register* comprising a *segment register* and a *word register.*
During execution the address register contains the two-component address
of the next instruction to be executed.   The basic instruction execution
cycle is as follows:

1.   Fetch an instruction from the virtual address specified in the
address register.

2.   If a data access is required, fetch the data from the virtual data
address specified by the instruction.

3.   Execute the instruction.

1.12.2 TWO-COMPONENT INSTRUCTION FETCH

The instruction-fetch phase makes use of a register referred to as the
temporary address register, comprising a *temporary segment register* and a
temporary word register.   During the instruction-fetch phase the address

register is moved to the temporary-address register, the word register is incremented by 1, and the content of the temporary register is used to compute the physical register containing the instruction, as illustrated in Fig. 1.23.

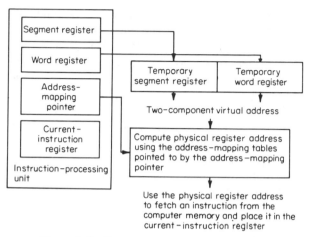

Figure 1.23   The instruction-fetch phase.

Figure 1.24 Two-component instruction-address format. (The resemblance between the last three field names and the name of a well-known computer firm is purely coincidental.)

An address-mapping pointer stored in the instruction-processing unit is used to determine the physical origin of the address-mapping tables to be used in the physical instruction address.

The determination of the virtual address in the instruction-fetch phase is trivial since the two-component virtual address is explicitly stored in the processing unit.   However, the effective address computation in the data-fetch phase involves converting the address fields of a one-address instruction into a two-component physical address and is considerably more complex.   Assume that the one-address instruction has the format shown in Fig. 1.24.   *OP* is the *operation-code field*, *A* is the *address field,* I is the *index-register field,* B is the *base-register field* and is used to point to one of a number of *base registers* containing a two-component base address, and M is a *modifier field.*

1.12.3 TWO-COMPONENT DATA FETCH

The simplest form of address computation occurs when the I, B, and M fields specify no modification.   In this case A is assumed to be an absolute word address in the segment being executed, so that the segment address is automatically taken to be that of the segment register in the instruction-processing unit.

Indexing using an index register pointed to by the I field and indirect addressing using a bit in the M field are assumed to operate on the word address A just as though it were a one-component address.

If no base register is specified, the segment address is always assumed to be that of the currently executed segment.   However, if a base register is specified, the segment component of the base register becomes the segment component of the effective address, and the word component of the base register is used to increment the word component of the effective address, just as though it were an extra index register.

The effective address computed during the data-fetch phase is stored in the temporary segment register and temporary word register, just as in the instruction-fetch phase.   If indirect addressing is specified, the register address corresponding to this effective address is used to replace the A, I, B, and M fields by the $A, I, B,$ and M fields of the fetched instruction and to initiate a further effective-address computation. Otherwise the content of the register address is used as the data item for the current operation.   The address computation during the data-fetch phase is illustrated in Fig. 1.25.

The above machine-language instruction format is basically a one-address instruction format in which the second component is specified by a pointer to a two-component base register.   This requires the segment number to be set by special base-register loading instructions prior to use of a given segment.   The word component of the base register may be thought of as a relocation register which determines a relative initial address within the segment.   Because of this relocation facility the word address can be regarded as a relative rather than absolute word-within-segment address, and the number of address bits in an instruction word need not be the full segment size.

Machine-language programming for a computer with two-component addresses requires the programmer to keep track of both index-register and base-register addresses and is therefore more complex than on a machine with fewer address modifiers.   However, if standard conventions are adopted for intersegment communication, the burden of the machine-

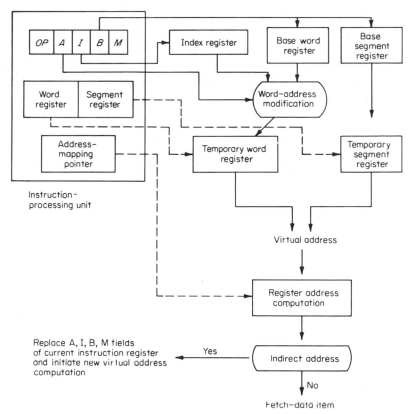

Figure 1.25 Effective address computation during the data-fetch phase.

language programmer can be eased.   Clearly programming in machine
language is the exception rather than the rule.

1.13 PHYSICAL-REGISTER COMPUTATION UNDER PAGING AND SEGMENTATION

1.13.1 MAPPING OF SEGMENTS WITHOUT PAGING

In the previous section it was shown that conversion from virtual to
physical addresses was required during both the instruction-fetch and the
data-fetch phases.   The overall features of this address computation are
similar in both the IBM and GE address computation and will be
described in greater detail below.

Two-dimensional addressing suggests that each segment of a virtual
address space have an independently specified physical origin.   As a
first approximation to an address-mapping scheme we shall assume that
each segment of a process must occupy a contiguous block of registers in

the memory hierarchy.   In this case the initial segment address would completely specify all storage-allocation information about the segment. The address-mapping tables would consist of a *segment table* with one entry per segment specifying the initial address of the segment if it is in main memory and a *segment-not-in-core* marker if the segment is not in main memory.

The stateword of a processor contains a word called the *address-mapping pointer*, which points to the first address of the segment table. The segment-table entry for a particular segment is obtained by relative addressing relative to the address-mapping word.

Such a scheme is clearly impracticable when the segment size is of the same order of magnitude as the number of registers in the main memory.   Since information structures stored in segments normally occupy only a small initial portion of the segment, the scheme would also be very wasteful.   One modification which would make the scheme more practicable would be to allocate memory only to the initial portion of the segment that actually contains information.   This would require a specification of both the initial address and the segment length in the address-mapping table.   On access to the segment the system would first check the segment-not-in-core marker.   If the segment were in core, it would check that the word address was less than the segment length.   Access to the segment would be performed only if these checks were satisfactory.   Otherwise an interrupt would be initiated, causing the system to take some action.

These checks illustrate some of the advantages of interposing an interpretive address mapping between the virtual and physical addresses. Multiprogrammed systems take advantage of this intermediate stage of interpretation in other ways too.

1.13.2   SEGMENT ATTRIBUTES

The entry for each segment in the address-mapping table may be thought of as a "description list" which specifies segmentwide accessing attributes. The accessing attributes so far introduced are location, length, and the property of being in core.   Other attributes which may conveniently be specified in this description list are *mode-of-access attributes*, which restrict the mode of access to the segment.   Four different modes of access may conveniently be distinguished:

1.   Access which involves *reading* words of the segment
2.   Access which involves *writing* words of the segment
3.   Access which involves *executing* words of the segment
4.   Access which involves *adding* or *deleting* words of the segment

These four modes of access are referred to respectively as the *read mode, write mode, execute mode,* and *append mode* and will be denoted respectively by R, W, X, and A. Each mode of access may be controlled by a single bit in the segment description list. If during execution a form of access which is not permitted is attempted, an interrupt occurs, resulting in a system action.

A restriction on the mode of access to a segment may be thought of as a *mode of protection* of that segment from interference by other segments. Since mode of access and mode of protection are reverse sides of the same coin, the terms "access" and "protection" will be used interchangeably.

Although allocation of only the used portion of a segment is a great improvement over allocation of the whole segment, it may still lead to difficulties: variable-sized segments make the problem of storage allocation when a new segment is introduced into the memory very complex, and one or two very large segments may use up the whole of physical memory, thus preventing efficient multiprogramming.

1.13.3 PAGES

In order to avoid both of the above problems it is convenient to choose a fixed-size unit for purposes of storage allocation which is independent of segment size and sufficiently small so that a large number (say 1,000) of these units may simultaneously reside in the main memory. This unit will be called the *page*.

The number of words in a page will be chosen to be a power of 2, say 2^m. If the number of words in a segment is 2^n, $n > m$, then each segment will be subdivided for purposes of storage allocation into 2^k pages, where $k + m = n$. Since each page of a segment can be mapped independently into a block of storage, an initial address and storage-not-in-core indicator is required for each of the pages of a given segment. This information is stored in a *page table*.

When pages are used as the unit of storage allocation, address mapping consists of two stages of indirect addressing through the segment table and the page table associated with the segment. Each stage of indirect addressing may have associated with it certain interpretive tests triggered by indicators stored along with pointer information in the address-mapping tables. Attributes that are associated with the segment as a whole are stored in the segment table. These attributes include the location of the segment page table, the access mode of the segment, the length (number of pages) of the segment, etc. Attributes of individual pages include their location, whether or not they are in core, etc. Thus the two-stage interpretation process permits testing for run-time segment attributes to be separated from attributes associated purely with the storage-allocation process.

The physical memory of the computer is subdivided into pages for purposes of storage allocation. The virtual memory of each virtual processor is also subdivided into pages. When a virtual processor is initiated by placing its stateword into the physical processor, the majority of its pages normally reside in the auxiliary memory. If during execution access to a page which is not currently in core is required, the absence of the page will be discovered during address mapping, and a missing-page fault will occur. The missing-page fault will cause a system program for memory allocation to allocate a page in core for the required page, possibly retiring an existing page to the auxiliary memory to make room for the new page. The virtual processor will become blocked while the memory-allocation mechanism brings in the required page, giving up the physical processor to some other virtual processor that can proceed with its computation. The given processor will be reactivated when the page has been read into the main memory. When it regains possession of a physical processor, it will again access the required page through the address-computation mechanism and this time will succeed.

It is assumed that segments stored in the auxiliary memory occupy a contiguous set of physical registers there. In order to retrieve a missing page from the auxiliary memory, a table must be available which specifies for each segment of a process the tree name or physical auxiliary-memory address for that segment. This table is referred to as the *segment name table*. Thus the relation between virtual and physical addresses is in fact determined by two tables. The segment table will specify physical addresses for segments which are in core, and the segment name table will specify physical addresses for segments that are not in core.

It was assumed above that the page table of the segment containing the page being accessed was in core. The page table of a segment will itself occupy a page of main memory and need be created only when at least one of the pages of the segment is in core. If the page table is not in core, a *missing-segment fault* will occur at the segment-table stage of indirect addressing. A missing-segment fault will cause the system to allocate a page for the page table, create a page table for the segment with missing-page faults in all its entries, and return control to the interrupted program. Note that no information from auxiliary memory is actually required when setting up a page table, so that the page table can be set up by the system by merely borrowing the processor that requires the page table. However, time would be required to retire a page if no pages were available. In order to reduce storage-allocation waiting time associated with pages that are being retired, four or five vacant pages are normally available in the main memory, and a page is retired whenever the threshhold of vacant pages falls below this level.

When the number of segments in the virtual address space is very large, it is no longer possible to have the complete segment table of the virtual processor in the main memory.   This can be avoided by allowing the segment table itself to be paged without any extra machinery as a segment of the virtual processor.

When the segment table is paged, the address-mapping word of the stateword of the virtual processor points not to the segment table but to the page table of the segment table.   Access to a physical register now requires three stages of indirect addressing through the page table of the segment table, the segment table itself, and the page table of the segment.

1.13.4   ADDRESS MAPPING UNDER PAGING AND SEGMENTATION

When both the segment table and the segment address are paged, a two-component virtual address (i,j) effectively becomes a four-component address $(k,m;l,m)$, where the segment-table page table contains 2^k entries, the page tables of individual segments contain 2^l entries, and pages contain 2^m entries.† Since page tables themselves occupy pages of the computer memory, k and l must not exceed m and should be chosen to be m for maximum memory utilization.

Example: If the address space permits 2^{18} segments each having a maximum length of 2^{18}, then a page size of 2^9 would result in page tables with 2^9 entries.   In this case $k = l = m = 9$.

The segment address together with the page component of the word-within-segment address is sometimes called a *virtual page address* since it is the address of a page of the virtual memory.

The three-stage indirect-address computation which results when both individual segments and the segment table are paged is illustrated in Fig. 1.26, from which it can be seen that the address-mapping word of the processor is modified by the first (k-bit) component to determine a page of the segment table.   The initial address of this page is modified by the second component to determine the segment-table entry.   The segment-table entry is incremented by the third component to determine the register which specifies the initial page address.   Finally the initial page address is incremented by the fourth component to determine the physical-register address.

Each of these stages may result either in a missing-information fault or in an accessing fault due to failure of accessing attributes associated with the information access to be met.

---

† Note that this four-component address is essentially a tree name in the four-level tree structure determined by the address-mapping tables.

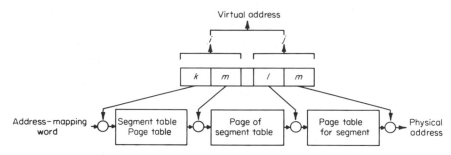

Figure 1.26   Address computation under paging and segmentation.

1.13.5 ASSOCIATIVE REGISTERS

The effectiveness of a system in which memory allocation is performed by paging depends in part on the characteristics of the information structure on which the computation is being performed. Paged storage allocation is most effective for computations in which there are long sequences of instructions whose information requirements are restricted to a small number of pages. If the number of pages to which access is required in a computational sequence is large, the computation will require a large number of in-core pages to run without interruption. In this case a choice must be made between allowing the computation to occupy a disproportionate amount of main memory, thereby impairing the efficiency of other processes, or executing the process in a highly inefficient manner, constantly retiring pages that will again be required at a later point of the process.

The overall efficiency of a computer system under paged storage allocation depends in large measure on the information-accessing charactcristics of the "average" process in the system. If the average process has long computational sequences requiring only a small number of pages, a small number of "memory-eating" processes with large storage requirements can be tolerated. However, if the typical process accesses large numbers of pages intermittently during most of its computational life, paging may not provide a sufficient economy of storage allocation to justify the time and space overhead that it introduces.

Paging introduces a time overhead by requiring extra indirect addressing during execution of individual instructions and by requiring system actions during allocation and retiring of pages. It introduces space overhead by requiring extra space for address-mapping tables and for system programs and their address-mapping tables. One of the factors which determines whether paged storage allocation can succeed is the degree to which the time and space penalties of paging can be reduced.

These penalties can be reduced in part by hardware and in part by efficient system organization.   For example, there is hardware for automatic (nonprogrammed) indirect addressing from the processor addressmapping word through page and segment tables to the physical address. This reduces the time penalty to three memory cycles per memory access. This time penalty can be further reduced by means of a special set of hardware registers known as an *associative register*.

An associative register is one that is addressed by its content rather than by an address.   The associative registers used to speed up the address computation contain direct correspondence between a small number of virtual page addresses and corresponding physical addresses. The content of an associative register is as shown in Fig. 1.27.

A processor typically has eight or possibly sixteen very-rapid-access associative registers in which recently accessed virtual page addresses and corresponding physical addresses are stored.†   Whenever access to a given virtual address is required, the associative memory is scanned for the virtual page address.   If it is found, the physical address is given

Virtual page address	Physical register address	Statistical usage information

Figure 1.27   Associative-register format.

in the physical-register field of the associative register and can immediately be used for accessing purposes without performing multistage indirect addressing.   If the virtual page address is not present in the associative memory, multistage indirect addressing is performed in the normal manner.   The resulting physical address is used not only to access the physical memory but also to establish a new entry in the associative memory for the accessed page, retiring a current entry in the associative memory.   The statistical-usage information is used to determine which of the current entries the new entry is to replace.

The effectiveness of this scheme depends on how often memory accesses can be accomplished through the associative memory, which in turn depends on the size of the associative memory, the rule for replacing segments of the associative memory, and the type of process mix for which computations are being performed.

The technique of allowing rapid access to information on the basis of recency and frequency of use is sometimes referred to as *look-behind*. This is to be contrasted with *look-ahead* techniques, which try to predict

† Note that the virtual page address is a process-dependent quantity and that virtual-actual address correspondences are valid only in the lifetime of the process in which they were loaded.   It is usual to clear the associative registers when replacing one process by another.   However, an alternative scheme is discussed below.

the information which will be required by looking ahead in the instruction sequence.

1.13.6 FACTORS WHICH DETERMINE THE EFFICIENCY OF PAGING SCHEMES

Simulation has shown that a small number of associative registers on a typical computation will require the address computation to be performed less than 20 percent of the time. Thus the time factor for address mapping during accessing can be considerably reduced. However, it has been found that the bottlenecks introduced by paging lie, not in the time penalty during address computation, but rather in space problems in the following categories:

1.   The system facilities for paging eat up a large amount of space for page tables and other purposes.

2.   Problems tend to require a large number of pages for their execution. Accessing does not tend to be localized to a small number of pages over short time sequences (say 10,000 instruction times) but tends to range quite widely, requiring frequent interchange of pages.

3.   The time required by a process to build up a sufficient number of pages in the main memory so that it can run for an appreciable length of time without missing-page faults tends to be quite long, particularly since missing-page faults cause the process to lose control of the processor and since successive pages can never be read in parallel. Thus building up a process in main memory to the point that it can run efficiently represents a considerable real-time investment. The space constraints may well be such that more time is spent building up the memory investment of processes to the point at which they can run efficiently than is spent in the efficient execution of processes.

The memory utilization of a group of programs in a multiprogramming system can conveniently be measured by a *memory-utilization chart*, which measures space along its horizontal dimension and time along its vertical dimension. The total memory space is represented by a fixed horizontal span, a portion of which represents the amount of space occupied by each program. As time moves in the vertical direction, the space utilization of each program is represented by a vertical band. Figure 1.28 shows a memory containing three programs. During the time span indicated in the graph, the leftmost program expands and takes up memory space at the expense of the second program, retains a fixed, large portion of the memory for a given time interval, and then relinquishes the space to the second program. During this time, the third program, possibly a background program, retains a fixed amount of space in the memory throughout the time period.

A profile like this implies that the leftmost program built up pages to a level at which it was able to run with relatively few interruptions, ran at this level for a while, and was then phased out, allowing the middle program to resume operation.   This profile is essentially a healthy one, and page-allocation techniques must allow programs to quickly build up their page requirements to the level at which they can run in an uninterrupted fashion and to maintain their complement of pages at this level for a sufficient time so that the real-time investment required to build up this complement of pages pays off.

In an actual multiprogramming system the number of programs that can simultaneously share portions of the main memory is considerably greater than three.   One significant parameter is the ratio n/k of number of pages n in the main memory and the number of processes k which may simultaneously share the main memory.   It has been found that, for a

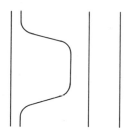

Figure 1.28   Time profile of memory utilization.

page size of 2^{10} words, a ratio $n/k = 10$ allows sufficient freedom for programs to expand their pages at the expense of others, while a ratio $n/k \leq 5$ leads to overcrowding the memory with competing programs.

The dynamic behavior of programs under paging has been simulated in a number of experimental studies such as [16], and the overall conclusion appears to be that "demand paging" for individual pages leads to highly inefficient computer utilization.   It is likely that multiprogramming systems of the future will adopt some form of grouped page-storage allocation, where the group of pages allocated during a single storage-allocation interrupt is determined either by the structure of processes or by the storage requirements during the previous activation of the process.

The efficiency of paged memory allocation would be greatly increased if groups of pages having a high incidence of internal cross referencing and a low incidence of external referencing could be isolated by the supervisory system and moved in and out of memory as a single unit.

Groups of pages which are treated as a single unit for purposes of allocation are sometimes referred to as *hyperpages*.

The problem of efficiently partitioning a problem into hyperpages may be thought of as a *clustering problem* in which individual pages are represented by vertices of a graph and the objective is to group the vertices into clusters having high density of traffic within clusters and low density of traffic between clusters. However, it is not clear that significant clustering patterns could be established at a level at which clusters are significantly smaller than complete programs. Moreover, clustering patterns within programs are likely to vary with time, and it is likely that a look-behind technique for paging of individual processes would be more effective than a static clustering technique.

Clustering techniques are said to be static because they determine groups of pages that remain fixed throughout execution. When comparing look-behind techniques with clustering techniques, it is convenient to think of the set of most recently used pages singled out by the look-behind process as a single cluster which changes in composition through time.

The look-behind techniques discussed above assume a single system-wide set of associative registers which is cleared on every process interchange. Thus a newly activated process has no initial look-behind information, builds up this information as it goes along, and has its look-behind information destroyed as soon as it loses control of the processor. Since the correspondence between logical and physical addresses might change while the process is not in control, this information would not be any use when the process regains control, unless provision were made for updating it. However, the information specifying the cluster of most recently used pages is an important piece of information and could be used for page control if it were available. It is felt that storage of the set of virtual page addresses on termination of a process as part of an extended stateword might be a worthwhile hardware extension.

At any instant of time the associative registers contain only information pertaining to a single process. When the process is terminated, the part of this information that is dependent on physical resources becomes outdated as the system reallocates its resources. However, part of the information tells us about recent page usage of the process and is as relevant when the process is restarted in a year on a different machine as when it is restarted within a millisecond. Careful use of this information could lead to considerably improved paging algorithms.

Problems of paging are caused essentially by the delay till execution time of the binding of information structures to physical registers. This decision requires address-mapping tables during execution and results in more complex accessing during execution, dynamic allocation overheads for user programs, and dynamic allocation overheads for address-mapping tables.

An alternative to execution-time binding of information structures is assignment of fixed relative addresses to information structures at the time of their loading or creation. This approach permits multiprogramming by *partitioning* the memory among several user programs. The overhead of allocating a partition to a program is considerably greater than that of allocating a group of pages, but the overhead during execution is much less.

Some current partitioning systems such as HASP [28] require that partitions be of fixed size and be dedicated to a user program from its initiation till its completion. However, the requirement of fixed-size partitions can be relaxed by allowing overlay as well as expansion into contiguous memory areas during execution; and the time period of allocation can be determined by a time-slicing scheme just as in the case of paged systems.

Whereas paging schemes provide automatic general-purpose relocation facilities for *all* programs, partitioning schemes permit more efficient operation than paging schemes for programs whose storage requirements are known at load time, and treat programs with heavy dynamic storage allocation requirements as a special case. Paging is essentially an elaborate overlay facility which permits overlays to be performed incrementally during every instruction execution. It is not at present clear whether flexibility of allocation can be bought more cheaply by paging or by more traditional allocation methods which require a program to occupy contiguous registers in storage and permit expansion only into contiguous storage areas. This latter approach results in the fragmentation of memory and requires periodic physical shifting of complete partitions in order to compactify the main memory, but avoids allocation overheads during execution.

Exercises: (*a*) Take an existing programming system and analyze its dynamic storage allocation facilities, its facilities for the creation and deletion of user information structures and system information structures, its facilities for creation and deletion of user programs, and its facilities for initiation and termination of execution of user programs.   (*b*) Design and/or implement selected modules of a programming system such as the control-card analyzer, a scheduling algorithm, or a main-memory allocation algorithm.

REFERENCES

1. If this book is being used as a text in a programming course, familiarity with a specific machine language will be required, and manuals for that machine language should be available.

2. Hull, T. E.: "Introduction to Computing," Prentice-Hall, Inc., Englewood Cliffs, N.J., 1966.

3. Wegner, P.: "Introduction to Symbolic Programming," Charles Griffin & Company, Ltd., London, 1963.

4. Wegner, P. (ed.): "Introduction to System Programming," Academic Press Inc., New York, 1964, especially chaps. 5, 7, 14–16, and 18.

5. Rosen, S. (ed.): "Programming Systems and Languages," McGraw-Hill Book Company, New York, 1967.

6. Ash, R.: "Information Theory," John Wiley & Sons, Inc., New York, 1966.

7. Abramson, N.: "Information Theory and Coding," McGraw-Hill Book Company, New York, 1963.

8. Korfhage, R. R.: "Logic and Algorithms," John Wiley & Sons, Inc., New York, 1966.

9. Iverson, K.: "A Programming Language," John Wiley & Sons, Inc., New York, 1962.

10. Buchholz, W. (ed.): "Planning a Computer System," McGraw-Hill Book Company, New York, 1962.

11. Saltzer, J. H.: Traffic Control in a Multiplexed Computer System, Ph.D. thesis, Massachusetts Institute of Technology, Cambridge, Mass., July, 1966 (available from MIT as MACTR-30).

12. IBM Time Sharing System, Concepts and Facilities, IBM System Reference Library, C28-2003-1.

13. *Proc. Fall Joint Computer Conf., Las Vegas*, November, 1965, six papers on various aspects of the Multics programming system.

14. Arden, B., et al.: Program and Addressing Structure in a Time Sharing Environment, *JACM*, January, 1966.

15. Dennis, J. B., and E. Van Horn: Programmed Semantics for Multiprogrammed Computations, *Commun. ACM*, March, 1966.

16. Fine, G. H., et al.: Dynamic Program Behavior under Paging, *Proc. 21st ACM Conf., Los Angeles*, August, 1966.

17. Wilber, J. A.: A Language for Describing Digital Computers, *Univ. Ill. Dept. Computer Sci. Rept.* 197, 1966.

18. Davis, M.: "Computability and Unsolvability," McGraw-Hill Book Company, New York, 1958.

19. Yngve, V.: COMIT, *CACM*, March, 1963.

20. McCarthy, J., et al.: The Linking Segment Subprogram Language and Linking Loader in S. Rosen (ed.), "Programming Systems and Languages," McGraw-Hill Book Company, 1967.

21. Galler, B. A., and A. J. Perlis: Forthcoming text on programming languages.

22. Standish, T. A.: A Data Definition Facility for Programming Languages, Ph.D. thesis, Carnegie Institute of Technology, May, 1967.

23. Arden, B.: Time Sharing Systems—A Review, course notes, Michigan Eng. Summer Conf., 1967.

24. BASIC Language Reference Manual, General Electric Information Systems Division, IPC-202026A, June, 1965.

25. QUIKTRAN Manual, IBM System Reference Library, 520-1071.

26. Evans, G. J.: Experience Gained from the American Airlines SABRE System Control Program, *Proc. 22nd ACM Conf., Washington*, August, 1967.

27. Attached Support Processor System (ASP), System Programmer Manual, IBM System Reference Library, H20-0323-0.

28. The HASP System, IBM, Houston, 67-1495.

29. Shemer, J. E.: Some Mathematical Considerations of Time Sharing Scheduling Algorithms, *JACM*, April, 1967.

CHAPTER 2

ASSEMBLERS,
SYMBOL TABLES, AND MACROS

2.1 BASIC CONCEPTS OF SCANNING AND ASSEMBLY

2.1.1 OVERALL STRUCTURE OF ASSEMBLERS

During execution of a program, the instruction sequence is represented inside the computer by binary instructions in successive registers. However, the programmer specifies instructions symbolically, as we have done in previous sections. The conversion from a symbolic representation of a program to its binary representation inside the computer can itself be performed by a computer program. This is referred to as the *assembly process*, and the program which performs the conversion is called an *assembler* (see Fig. 2.1).

Symbolic programs S → Assembler A → Machine-language programs M

Figure 2.1 The operation of an assembler.

The assembler can be thought of as a function whose domain is the set of symbolic programs and whose range is the set of machine-language programs. Operation of the assembler A on a symbolic program S produces a machine-language program $M = A(S)$. We shall be concerned with the details of implementation of the function A.

Input to an assembler consists of sequences of symbolic instructions each of which consists of a number of symbolic fields. It will be assumed that symbolic instructions consist of a location field, followed by an operation field, followed by an address field, followed by a field for serial numbering. In order to fix ideas it will be assumed that successive symbolic instructions are punched onto individual 80-column punched cards with the following card format:

format CARD(LOC,B,OP,B,ADDR,NUM)   Complete card format.

format LOC[0:9]   Location-field format.

format B[0:0]   Single blank field.

format OP[0:4]   Operation-field format.

format ADDR[0:54]   Address-field format.

format NUM[0:7]   Serial-numbering field.

The location field occupies columns 1 through 10, the operation field columns 12 through 16, the address field columns 18 through 72, and the field for serial numbering columns 73 through 80.

The location field contains the instruction label, if there is one. The operation field contains the symbolic operation code. The address field contains the address and special-register specifications.

During assembly successive lines of symbolic code are read into the computer and are initially stored in a buffer as an 80-byte input record. The assembly program converts successive input records into binary instructions, which will eventually be executed by the instruction-processing unit of the computer. The assembly process can be subdivided into the following three steps:

1. *Scanning* the symbolic input for the purpose of grouping characters into field names and identifying fields which they denote

2. *Transforming* symbolic field names into corresponding binary codes

3. *Assembling* binary fields associated with a single instruction into a single register

2.1.2 SCANNING

The first task above is performed by a program called a *scanner*, which scans successive constituents of a specified string and performs a sequence of actions guided by the constituents being scanned. In this sense the computer as a whole may be regarded as a scanner which scans its instruction sequence, performs actions on data, and moves the contents of the instruction-location register to point to the next executable instruction. However, the scanners used in recognizing constituents of a programming language are more restricted in scope than general scanners for computing any computable function,† and those required to scan the input buffer of an assembler are particularly simple.

† Scanners are essentially syntactic recognizers in the sense that this term is used in Appendix 1. The symbol strings that occur in assemblers can usually be recognized efficiently by special techniques. The more general recognition techniques for context-free languages discussed in Appendix 1 are not therefore required.

It is sometimes convenient to separate the task of recognizing constituents from that of performing the scanning action. When this is done, the constituent-recognizing program (sometimes referred to as a *recognizer*) is programmed as a subroutine which can be called upon by a higher-level program to deliver the next constituent of the scanned string. In analyzing input buffers which contain symbolic instructions it is convenient to specify a constituent-recognizing subroutine with a number of parameters which specify which field of the input buffer is to be recognized.

The characters of the input text are normally packed in successive bytes, so that recognition of individual characters requires unpacking by blanking out all except one of the characters in the word and shifting the character to a standard position for purposes of performing the comparison. Recognition of a field which is stored within a single word of the buffer can be performed by zeroing and shifting applied to the whole field. However, recognition of a field which overlaps word boundaries requires more complex manipulation. In many instances scanning rules specify that blanks be ignored and that the symbol in question consist of the compacted nonblank characters in the field. This requires an even more sophisticated recognition process.

Example: In a computer with 4-byte words, the content of an 80-column card (card image) would be stored in a 20-word block, say BUF to BUF + 19. A three-character symbol in columns 9 to 11 would be stored in BUF + 2 and could be retrieved by picking up the word BUF + 2 and zeroing out the fourth byte. However, a three-character word in columns 11 to 13 would be stored partially in BUF + 2 and partially in BUF + 3 and would require a more complex retrieval process.

Exercises: (*a*) Write a program (draw a flow diagram) to scan an 80-character buffer for successive words separated by one or more blanks, assuming that the number of characters in the longest word does not exceed the number of bytes in a register. Store successive words in a sequence of successive registers. (*b*) Write a subroutine called SCAN which scans a field in an 80-byte buffer BUF whose initial and terminal bytes are specified by integer parameters and which produces the compacted word consisting of all nonblank characters in a sequence of registers specified by a third parameter.

The address field of a symbolic instruction is normally allowed to contain arithmetic expressions which must be scanned and evaluated at assembly time in order to determine the address. This in turn requires an arithmetic-expression recognizer and evaluator to be built into the program. Arithmetic expressions in address fields normally consist of a single symbolic address, a number of constants, and symbols whose values are integers. For example if A is a symbolic address and N is a symbol having an integer value, then "$A + 2 \times N$" is an example of an expression which could occur in an address field.   Symbolic addresses in general denote relative rather than absolute addresses.   Expressions such as $A + B$, where A and B are both symbolic addresses, would cause the relative origin to be added in twice and are therefore prohibited.

When a symbol has been recognized in a location field, operation field, or address field, an action must be performed by the program to which the constituent is delivered.   If the symbol is a location-field symbol, it results in a symbol definition.   If the symbol is in the operation field, it is replaced by the internal binary operation code.   If the symbol is an address-field symbol, it is replaced by a binary address code.

In the remainder of the present section it will be assumed that instructions consist of an optional address symbol in the location field, an operation symbol in the operation field, and a simple address symbol in the address field and that a recognizer is available for scanning symbols in each of these fields.   The process of assembly for instructions having this format will be discussed.

2.1.3 OPERATION CODES, ADDRESS SYMBOLS, AND TWO-PASS ASSEMBLY

The assembler basically has to deal with two kinds of symbols, (1) operation-code symbols and (2) address symbols.   The internal binary codes corresponding to operation-code symbols are specified by an *operation-code symbol table*.   When the binary code corresponding to an operation-code symbol is required, it is determined by symbol-table look-up in the operation-code symbol table.   The structure of symbol tables and techniques of symbol-table look-up will be discussed in the next section.

Address symbols do not have fixed internal codes but have their codes assigned to them by the assembler.   Addresses may be classified into *data addresses*, which are assigned by the assembler according to the storage-allocation scheme used for data, and *instruction addresses*, which are assigned by determining the address of the instruction having the given symbol as its location symbol.

Instructions are normally assembled assuming that they will be placed in a set of contiguous registers during execution.   However, the initial register in which the instructions will be placed is left open, and instruction addresses are normally *relative addresses* relative to the first instruction of the instruction block.

Instruction addresses are specified by an instruction-address symbol table constructed during the assembly process.   In order to ensure that all symbols are defined before they are used, early assemblers were designed to perform assembly in *two passes* over the input data, the first of which constructs the instruction-address symbol table.   In both passes a simulated instruction-location register SLR keeps track of the address of the instruction currently being scanned relative to the beginning of the block.

In translating the address field an address is first looked up in the address symbol table.   If it is found there, its binary value is the value of the corresponding relative address.   Otherwise, it is assumed to be a data address and has a value determined by data storage-allocation techniques.   For example, if data are stored as a data block in a run-time stack, the data address will be a relative address whose origin is dynamically supplied during execution.

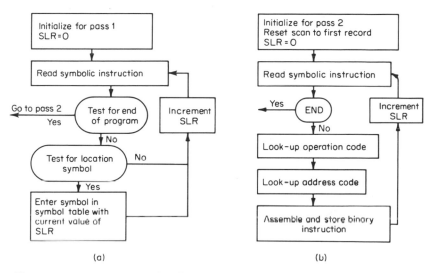

(a)   (b)

Figure 2.2   Operation of a simple two-pass assembler.   (*a*) **Pass 1;** (*b*) **pass 2.**

If the binary instructions of an assembled program can be stored in core during assembly, then assembly can be performed in a single pass by partial translation of instructions which contain undefined symbols as they are encountered.   Core locations of undefined symbols are noted down in an *undefined-symbol table* and are fixed up as location symbols are defined or when translation of all instructions of the program has been completed.

Alternatively, the entry in the instruction-address symbol table can be created when an undefined instruction is first used with a pointer to the occurrence of the undefined symbol, and subsequent undefined occurrences of this symbol can be chained together, so that all undefined occurrences can be accessed and defined when the symbol occurs in the location field.

Both of these techniques must be modified when the program being assembled cannot be completely stored in core.

Exercise: Write an assembly program which assembles sequences of simple symbolic instructions of a kind discussed above for a subset of the operation codes of your local assembly language. Assume that assembly terminates when END is encountered in the operation field.

Assemblers for actual assembly languages have the above structure but must be able to perform evaluation of more complex address fields, the index-register field, the indirect-address symbol, and any other special formats permitted by the assembler.

Project: Write an assembler for a substantial subset of your local assembly language.

2.2 SYMBOL-TABLE LOOK-UP, SEARCHING, SORTING, AND FUNCTION EVALUATION

2.2.1 SYMBOL TABLES AS SETS OF ORDERED PAIRS

In the present section the mechanism of symbol-table look-up will be discussed in greater detail. A symbol table is essentially a sequence of ordered pairs (s_i, t_i) with unique first components s_i. The entry t_i is said to be the value associated with s_i. The problem of symbol-table look-up is essentially that of determining for a given source-code symbol s the symbol-table entry (s, t) with s as its first component, and hence the value t associated with s.

A symbol table may be thought of as defining a function f whose domain is the set S of all s_i and whose range is the set T of all t_i. The discussion of symbol-table look-up techniques below is concerned with efficient ways of representing and evaluating functions of this kind. Following a discussion of the mechanism of symbol-table look-up, we shall indicate a more theoretical approach to symbol-table operations.

When the set of source codes S consists of the set of all 2^k binary digits of a k-bit field, it is unnecessary to represent the codes S explicitly in the symbol table, since the code s_i can be used explicitly as a selector of an entry in a table with 2^k entries. For example, addresses of memory registers are precisely codes of this nature. The set of memory registers may be thought of as a symbol table in which symbol-table look-up is performed by using the source code as a selector.

When source codes of a symbol table are chosen in a redundant manner in the interests of readability, as in the case of operation and address codes for symbolic machine language, the symbol string itself cannot be used directly as a selector.† In this case the symbol-table entry corresponding to a given source code s is found by matching an encoded representation of s against entries s_i within the symbol table itself and taking the value t_i corresponding to a matched s_i. This mode of symbol-table look-up is essentially associative addressing, since selection of the symbol-table entry is determined by matching the *content* of the entry itself.

2.2.2 SYMBOL-TABLE CONSTRUCTION AND SYMBOL-TABLE LOOK-UP

There are many different techniques for symbol-table construction and look-up, some of which are considered below. In the symbol tables we shall discuss, entries will contain an encoded version of the source symbol and a target code, or value, associated with the source symbol. The successor of a given symbol-table entry may be specified either explicitly by a pointer in a pointer field or implicitly by being in an adjacent address or block of addresses. When successive symbol-table entries are linked together by pointers, the symbol table is said to constitute a *linked list*. Linked-list storage permits storage for successive entries in a symbol table to be allocated in a flexible manner, but it may in certain cases lead to less efficient accessing of entries in the symbol table.

If successive entries of a symbol table are arranged in an arbitrary fashion, the average number of entries which must be scanned to find a given first component s in a symbol table of length n is $n/2$, so that the mean search time depends linearly on the length of the symbol table.

Exercise: Draw a flow diagram (write a program) for linear search of a symbol table with n entries. Consider both implicitly and explicitly specified successors.

Search time during symbol-table look-up can be saved by structuring the symbol table during its construction. Four techniques for structuring symbol tables will be discussed:

1. Partitioning entries into pseudo-randomly determined classes by means of a (randomizing) *hashing function*
2. Ordering entries in the table according to lexicographic criteria
3. Structuring the symbol table into a tree or list structure
4. Ordering the symbol table according to expected frequency of occurrence, so that more frequently occurring items appear before less frequently occurring items

† For example, if the symbol space is the set of 26^3 three-letter alphabetic symbols, direct selection would require a symbol table of $26^3 > 2^{14}$ symbols even if only a very small proportion of these is used on any given occasion.

2.2.3 HASHING TECHNIQUES

Hashing techniques partition the set of all source codes by applying a function to them that maps them into a bit pattern with a smaller number of bits. This function, called a *hashing function*, is usually chosen to satisfy the following two criteria:

1. The mapping from a source code to its bit pattern can be rapidly performed.
2. Source codes are mapped into bit patterns in an unpredictable and relatively random manner.

A hashing function partitions the set of all source codes into equivalence classes such that two source codes are in the same equivalence class if and only if they have the same bit pattern.

Example: Source codes consisting of multiple-character strings can be converted into 8-bit target codes by a hashing function which squares the integer representation of the character string and takes the middle 8 bits. This hashing function divides the set of all possible source codes into 256 equivalence classes in a relatively random manner. For example, one-character codes or codes starting with the same set of initial characters will be mapped into equivalence classes in an unpredictable manner.

Hashing permits the equivalence class associated with a given source code to be rapidly determined. However, more than one source code may be mapped into a given target-code class, and a method of selection within target-code classes is required. If the number of classes is such that the average number of entries in each class is small, the method of selection of entries within a class can be relatively inefficient. For example, a method of linear search of entries within a class can be used.

The way in which n-bit hash codes can be used in the searching of symbol tables is described below:

The n-bit code can be used as a relative address in a symbol table with possibly more than 2^n items but only 2^n entry points. Searching the symbol table using a linear search procedure can be started at an entry point determined by the hash code. The n-bit hash code can be used to determine the initial entry of the symbol table for the equivalence class of source codes having this hash code. The large symbol table breaks down into a set of 2^n component symbol tables, each associated with a different hash code. The component symbol tables are sometimes referred to as *buckets*.

Each bucket of a bucket-type symbol table can denote successors within the bucket either implicitly or explicitly. When successors are indicated explicitly, symbol-table entries consist of the following:

1. An encoding of the source-language representation of the symbol s_i
2. The value or target code $v(s_i)$ associated with the symbol
3. A link L_i to the successive entry in the symbol table

Figure 2.3 illustrates a list-structured bucket with n entries s_1, $s_2, \ldots, s_n$ for which the hashing function H computes identical hash addresses $H(s_1) = H(s_2) \cdots = H(s_n)$.

When the number of entries in the hashing table is relatively sparse and there are not too many entries in a bucket, it is more economical to store bucket entries in a linear fashion without the space and time overhead introduced by pointers. Linear bucket storage becomes uneconomical when a bucket overflows its fixed storage allocation and associative address matches require matching not only the entries in the given bucket but also entries in the next bucket, i.e., the one which is physically stored after the present bucket. Bucket overflow can be checked, and a storage allocator can be used to allocate further bucket segments when a

Figure 2.3 List-structured bucket. (The symbol NIL in the third field of the most recent entry S_n is used to denote the absence of a link field.)

bucket overflows. One of the allocation procedures is to use a supplementary hashing function to allocate bucket continuation for buckets which overflow.

Note that hashing functions which produce nonrandomized target-code classes result in inefficient selection procedures for two reasons. Access to an entry in a bucket with a large number of items requires a larger average number of items to be scanned. At the same time, buckets with more entries will be accessed more frequently if access to entries is distributed in a uniform manner, so that long searches will be more frequent than shorter ones.

Exercise: Draw a flow diagram (write a program) for (a) adding a new entry to a hashed symbol table and (b) finding the value of a symbol in a hashed symbol table.

Hashing techniques result in a saving of search time by imposing an unpredictable and somewhat arbitrary structure on symbol-table entries.

The lexicographic techniques discussed below impose a structure on symbol tables that is related to the source codes.

2.2.4   LEXICOGRAPHIC ORDERING AND LOGARITHMIC SEARCHING

Search time can be saved by arranging the entries according to a lexicographic (alphabetic) ordering of source-language symbols, as in a dictionary.   In a symbol table in which entries s_i are listed lexicographically, search for a symbol s can be accomplished by first comparing s with the middle entry to determine whether s is entered into the upper or lower half of the symbol table and then successively bisecting the interval in which s is seen to fall.   The process of bisecting must be adjusted when the interval being bisected contains an odd number of elements.   The process is similar to the way in which a dictionary user would flip pages of a dictionary in performing dictionary look-up.   It can be illustrated by showing how the 365th entry in a 1,000-entry table can be found by 10 successive bisections (Fig. 2.4).

	Test	Success ?	Resulting interval
Test 1:	Is $s_{365} > s_{500}$	No	Lower interval (1-500)
Test 2:	Is $s_{365} > s_{250}$	Yes	Upper interval (251-500)
Test 3:	Is $s_{365} > s_{375}$	No	Lower interval (251-375)
Test 4:	Is $s_{365} > s_{313}$	Yes	Upper interval (314-375)
Test 5:	Is $s_{365} > s_{344}$	Yes	Upper interval (344-375)
Test 6:	Is $s_{365} > s_{360}$	Yes	Upper interval (361-375)
Test 7:	Is $s_{365} > s_{368}$	No	Lower interval (361-368)
Test 8:	Is $s_{365} > s_{364}$	Yes	Upper interval (365-368)
Test 9:	Is $s_{365} > s_{366}$	No	Lower interval (364-365)
Test 10:	Is $s_{365} > s_{364}$	Yes	Result is 365th entry

Figure 2.4   A logarithmic search.

Table look-up in a sorted symbol table takes on the order of $\log_2 n$ comparisons and is therefore called *logarithmic search*.   In a symbol table with 1,000 entries logarithmic search homes in on the required entry in 10 comparisons, while linear search requires an average of 500 comparisons.   However, in order to perform a logarithmic search an initial investment is required to sort the entries in the symbol table into lexicographic order.

2.2.5   SORTING TECHNIQUES

Many of the simpler sorting algorithms used for sorting a set of n symbol-table entries lexicographically require on the order of n^2 comparisons. Among these methods are sorting by moving the largest (lexicographically first) element from an unsorted to a sorted symbol table, and sorting by successive interchange for $i = 1, 2, \ldots , n$ of the ith element s_i with the largest element s_j "following" the element s_i (having $j \geq i$).

Sorting by interchange is illustrated by the flow diagram in Fig. 2.5. This program has an outer loop, which is executed n times, and an inner loop, which is executed an average of $n/2$ times, so that the total number of comparisons required to sort the table is $n^2/2$.

The most efficient sorting methods require only $N \log_2 N$ comparisons for sorting a symbol table with N entries arranged in arbitrary order. Among the more efficient methods is sorting by merging, which merges the symbol-table entries successively into ordered pairs, ordered quadruples, ordered octuples, and ordered 2^n-tuples until 2^n exceeds N. This

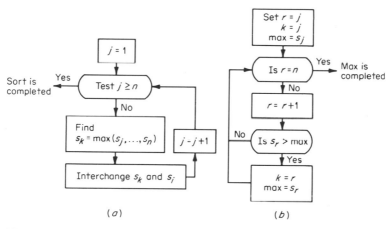

(a)   (b)

Figure 2.5 Flow diagram for sorting by interchange. (a) **Main program;** (b) **max subprogram.**

method requires N comparisons for each merging pass and $\log_2 N$ passes, resulting in $N \log_2 N$ comparisons.

A further sorting method requiring essentially $N \log N$ steps is the *radix sort*, which sorts the symbol table on successive characters of the symbols s_i, starting with the rightmost character. If entries s_i have b binary digits, a radix sort first rearranges entries so that all entries with the last digit zero precede entries with the last digit 1 and repeats this procedure for all digits until the table is completely sorted. This procedure is essentially that used on a sorter for sorting a set of punched cards on successive columns starting with the least significant one. In the binary case the sorting time for b-digit source codes is Nb, since N comparisons are required to sort on a single digit. If all possible b-digit source codes are used, then $N = 2^b$, and $Nb \sim N \log_2 N$. If there is some redundancy in source codes, then $Nb > N \log_2 N$. However, in order for Nb to be as great as $2N \log_2 N$, N would have to be as low as $2^{b/2} = \sqrt{2^b}$, so that we can say that $Nb = kN \log_2 N \sim N \log_2 N$ since the constant k can never be of the order of N.†

Exercises: (a) Draw a flow diagram (write a program) for logarithmic searching of an ordered symbol table.   (b) Draw a flow diagram (write a program) for sorting by moving the largest element and/or sorting by interchange.   (c) Draw a flow diagram (write a program) for sorting by merging and/or radix sorting.

2.2.6 TREE-STRUCTURED SYMBOL TABLES

The symbol-table sorting techniques just discussed can be used to facilitate logarithmic searching of symbol tables only if all symbol-table look-up is performed *after* all symbol-table entries have been created.   In many instances, symbol-table look-up and construction of new symbol-table entries go on side by side.   One solution to this situation would be to keep a lexicographically ordered symbol table of all entries so as to permit logarithmic search and to insert new entries at the correct point in the lexicographic ordering as they are created.   However, insertion of a new entry into the middle of a linearly ordered string is time-consuming, and other forms of symbol-table structure have therefore been proposed.

   If a symbol table is stored as a linear list structure with pointers from one element to the next, it is no longer possible to find the middle of an interval by bisection.   However, the effect of bisection can be achieved by storing the symbol table as a binary tree structure such that each vertex represents a symbol-table entry, all entries less than the given symbol-table entry are reached by going down the left branch starting from the vertex, and all entries greater than the given symbol-table entry are obtained by taking the right branch starting from the vertex. The average number of steps required to find a given entry is the average distance of a vertex from the root of the tree.   A new entry s is added by making comparisons of the new entry with a sequence of entries s_i at vertices starting at the root, moving to the left if $s < s_i$ and moving to the right if $s > s_i$ until a move which does not correspond to an existing vertex is attempted.   The new vertex is attached to the tree at precisely the point corresponding to the first nonexisting vertex in the above process.

   It can be shown [2] that in spite of the fact that paths in the tree will be of unequal lengths, the distance of the average vertex from the root, and therefore the average number of comparisons during a search, is $\log_2 N$.   Further information about tree representation of symbol tables for searching and sorting can be obtained in [2].

   † This survey of sorting is very brief; more information can be found in [2].

2.2.7   STACK-STRUCTURED SYMBOL TABLES

In assemblers, each type of field will have its own symbol table with its own symbol-table look-up procedures.   For example, the set of symbolic operation codes is usually represented by a fixed set of lexicographically ordered entries which can be searched logarithmically.   The address symbol table, on the other hand, is constructed during the assembly process and must be consulted every time a new address is established, to find the value if the address is already in the table and to assign a value if this is the first occurrence of the address.   If a linear search is adequate the symbol-table entries may be placed in the symbol table in the order in which they are first encountered, while if a logarithmic search time is required, a tree-structured symbol table is appropriate.

Symbol tables which arise in simple assemblers usually have a set of entries such that s_i is unique.   However, in symbol tables encountered in macro assemblers and problem-oriented languages, multiple instances of a symbol s_i are permitted, and uniqueness is imposed by selecting the value of s_i associated with the most recently created instance of s_i as the value of s_i.   This class of symbol table will be called a *stack symbol table*.   Such tables cannot be sorted, and scanning of entries to determine the value of a given symbol must always be performed in a last in, first out order.   However, the value associated with a given s_i in a stack symbol table is usually a fairly recent entry, so that the search time is usually better than linear.

2.2.8   FUNCTION EVALUATION BY TABLE LOOK-UP

From a theoretical point of view, a symbol-table look-up operation may be thought of as the application of a function f whose domain is a set of source codes and whose range T is a set of target codes.   In the case of pure encoding, a given predefined function f operates on successive concatenated symbols and in turn defines a function F on strings of symbols having the property that $F(s_1 s_2) = f(s_1)f(s_2)$.   If x is a string of symbols over S and $s \in S$, then $F(xs) = F(x)f(s)$.   Thus encoding a string of symbols may be thought of as the application of a function F which for any string of symbols in the domain of F produces a string of symbols in the range of F.

In assembly languages different classes of symbols are encoded by different functions f_i.   Some of these functions are fixed prior to the assembly process, while others are "growing" functions, whose domains and range grow as new entries are added to the symbol table.

The assembly process as a whole may be thought of as a function A whose domain is a set of programs written in a symbolic language and whose range is a set of programs in machine language.   Given a symbolic program SP in the language of A, the assembler A produces a machine-language program $MP = A(SP)$ in the range of A.   When A is presented with a string of symbols that is not a program, then, if it is a good assembler, it will produce diagnostic information.   Thus the domain of A is not merely the set of well-formed programs of the assembly language but the set of all strings over the input alphabet.   The range of A must similarly be augmented by the set of diagnostics.

Assembly is a special case of translation where the target language can be obtained from the source language by a process that is essentially transliteration.   Translation programs are not in general restricted to transliteration but are, like assemblers, functions which map programs written in a given source language to a target language.   Thus if P is a program written in the source language of a translator T, then $T(P)$ determines the corresponding target-language program.

Most assembly source languages and many translator source languages are universal in the sense that any computable functions can be written in the language.   In particular the function represented by a translation program can be written in a universal source language.   Thus if T_1 is a translator and T_2 is a second translator written in the source language of T_1, then $T_1(T_2)$ is a representation of the translator T_2 in the target language of T_1.   If the target language of T_1 is a machine language, T_1 can be used to translate translators T_2 written in the source language of T_1 into machine language.   The machine-language version of T_2 can then be used to translate programs written in the source language of T_2 to the target language of T_2.   Thus, once a translator from a universal source language to machine language is available, translators for other languages can be written in this source language.   This process is sometimes referred to as bootstrapping [3].

2.3 TABLE-DRIVEN PROGRAMS

2.3.1 FREE VARIABLES, BOUND VARIABLES, AND MULTIPLE DEFINITION

Assemblers normally use a number of different symbol tables, where each symbol table is used to perform transliteration for a different class of symbols.   The symbols which occur in an assembly program can be classified into *free* symbols, whose meaning is determined by the environment in which the program is executed, and *bound* symbols, whose meaning must be defined by means of a symbol-table entry before it can be used.   In simple assemblers the principal free variables are operation codes and control operations (discussed in Sec. 2.5), and the principal bound variables are address fields.

In more general symbol-string processing systems it is convenient to classify symbols into the following categories:

1.   *Constants*, corresponding to free variables whose meaning remains fixed throughout the processing.   Such constants include data constants and syntactic symbols of the programming language which cannot be redefined by the programmer.

2.   *Initialized variables*, which have an initial meaning supplied by the environment but whose meaning can be changed by redefinition.

3.   *Uninitialized symbols*, which must be defined by the programmer. Uninitialized variables may in turn be subdivided into *uninitialized constants*, which may be defined only once, and *variables*, which may be repeatedly redefined.

	Initialized symbols	*Uninitialized symbols*
Single definition	Constants	Uninitialized constants
Multiple definition	Initialized variables	Variables

Constants are specified in the environment either by a fixed set of symbol tables or by programs for supplying the value of the constant or performing the action specified by the constant if the constant is a function.

Initialized variables may be initially specified either by a table entry or a program for supplying the value.   Since initialized variables may be redefined, there must be a mechanism for checking every time an initialized variable is used whether or not it has a defined value or its initial value. This can conveniently be done by means of an indicator bit associated with the initial value which is set for symbol-table searching when the value is redefined.

Uninitialized constants and variables normally have their values defined by symbol-table entries in which the value field is initially undefined.   Uninitialized variables sometimes have their values defined in two stages, the first of which (declaration) results in creation of the symbol-table entry and the second of which (assignment) results in initialization or redefinition of the symbol-table entry.   Identifiers in procedure-oriented languages are usually defined in this way.

2.3.2   DESTRUCTIVE DEFINITION AND PUSHDOWN DEFINITION

Two alternative techniques can be used for redefinition of variables: (1) destructive redefinition, which either physically destroys a previous definition of the symbol or makes it inaccessible or (2) pushdown redefinition, which pushes down the previous definition and replaces it by the new definition but leaves open the possibility of deleting the new definition and reinstating the previous definition. The run-time representation required for pushdown definitions is extensively discussed in Chap. 4.

2.3.3 ATTRIBUTES AND TYPE OF SYMBOL-TABLE ENTRIES

Each entry in a symbol table is essentially an ordered pair which specifies the value associated with a given element of the domain of a function. Symbol tables are convenient for the specifications of functions with finite domains and flexible rules of correspondence between arguments and values.   In Sec. 2.2 it was assumed that the value associated with a given argument was obtained by simple accessing and that the accessed value was output and could not further affect the interpretation process. In general the value associated with a symbol-table argument may be more complex, involving the execution of a function which may cause side effects in the environment that affect subsequent interpretation steps or involving a chain of accesses through pointers internal to the accessed structure.   It is sometimes convenient to associate the following four "accessing attributes" with symbol-table entries:

X Entries that are to be executed when accessed
R Entries to be read when accessed
W Entries to be written when accessed
A Entries which may be structurally changed (augmented) when accessed

A given symbol-table entry may have more than one of the above attributes.   If it is normally accessed in the X mode, it is thought of as a function.   If it is normally accessed in one or more of the other three modes, it is thought of as data.   However, the distinction between functions and data is not very rigid, since some systems execute functions by copying them to a fixed symbol stream prior to execution.

Both function and data types of symbol-table values may in general have an arbitrarily complex internal structure.   However, in practice many symbol tables require values to be in a predefined range, e.g., the set of integers between 0 and $2^n - 1$ for some n.

We have so far assumed the *domain* of symbol-table entries to be a class of simple symbol strings.   The decision procedure to determine whether a given string corresponded to a given symbol-table entry was assumed to be trivial.   However, the set of strings that constitutes names of symbol-table entries may in principle be just as complex as the set of strings that constitutes values.   Symbol-table structures with a complex domain of names arise in pattern-recognition languages.   Languages for string manipulation by pattern matching differ from other languages principally in that they permit symbol tables where the domain of possible names may be arbitrarily complex.   Symbol-table structures with arbitrarily complex names are further discussed in Appendix 1. In the remainder of the present section we shall emphasize the role played by tables in the interpretation process rather than the structure of table look-up operations.

2.3.4   TABLE-DRIVEN PROGRAMS

The term "table" is usually associated with a passive information structure.   However, when the table is interpreted by a higher-level sequencing mechanism in a manner similar to a machine-language program, the distinction between data and program becomes very tenuous.   Data is essentially a relative term.   A given information structure may be a data structure relative to a higher-level interpreter but may play the role of a program relative to a lower-level information structure which it is instrumental in transforming.   For instance, a given computer is an interpreter relative to which all programs constitute data.   Programs on a computer are passive information structures relative to the computer but active information structures when used in transforming data structure in their domain.

Any programming language may be implemented by a table structure to be interpreted by higher-level interpreters; the term "table-driven programs" is used to refer to interpretively executed programs for which successive instructions to be executed are determined by table look up in a table which specifies the interpretation step for every possible instruction format of the language.   There are a number of programming applications both in system programming and at the user level where it is convenient to define new interpretively executed programming languages by means of a table structure and to design an interpreter for sequencing through the table structure.   This approach has been used both at the user level in languages such as TABSOL [4] and at the system-programmer level in designing languages such as TMG [5] for syntactic analysis.

In the case of syntactic analysis (see Appendix 1), the basic operations are pattern-matching operations for string recognitions.   The pattern-matching problem is aggravated by the fact that there may be a number of different ways of locally matching a substring of the string being recognized which are subsequently found to be inconsistent with a larger pattern.   Table-driven languages for syntactic analysis such as TMG are essentially special-purpose programming languages with facilities for pattern matching of symbol strings and for backtracking when local matching is found to be inconsistent with matching at a higher level.

In designing a larger system there may well be a number of different subproblems which are conveniently specified by special-purpose table-driven programming languages, each associated with a different interpreter for sequencing through programs written in the tabular languages. The use of table-driven programming languages makes it possible to write subprograms to deal with subproblems in a language natural to the subproblem.   This not only makes the initial programming job easier but also permits more flexible modification of programs.

If a given sublanguage is found to be sufficiently widely used, the interpreter for the sublanguage can be implemented by means of micro-programs or regular system hardware, so as to save interpretation time.

2.4   INDEX-REGISTER OPTIMIZATION AND RESOURCE ALLOCATION

2.4.1   PROBLEM OF TOO FEW REGISTERS

This section discusses a rather specialized resource-allocation problem relating to assembly and may be omitted on first reading.

The assignment of actual index-register codes to symbolic-index-register names is complicated by the fact that the number of symbolic-index-register names in a program may exceed the actual number of index registers available.   If the number of actual index registers always exceeded the number of symbolic index registers, index-register assignment could be performed by the assembler just like address assignment, and a fixed actual index register could be assigned to a symbolic index register on a one-for-one basis.   However, if there are more symbolic than actual index registers, several symbolic index registers may have to share one actual index register, and a scheme must be devised for storing temporarily the content of an actual index register associated with a given symbolic index register while the actual index register is used to hold information associated with a second symbolic index register.

In symbolic machine language, the responsibility of storing and restoring of index registers lies with the programmer.   However, in more sophisticated programming languages the responsibility of storing and restoring index registers is transferred to the programming system.   In fact the programmer generally does not know which symbolic names will be associated with memory registers and which with index registers.

The problem of automatically associating symbolic index registers with actual index registers so as to minimize the number of store and restore operations during execution is referred to as *index-register optimization*.   This was one of the first compilation problems to be isolated and labeled by compiler writers, and it received a great deal of attention in early compilers.†

The problem of index-register assignment is a special case of the general register-assignment problem when too many symbolic registers are being mapped into too few actual registers. An extreme case of this is the accumulator register. However, in this case it is generally accepted that information must be moved to the accumulator immediately prior to use and be stored immediately after use, so that the optimization problem is solved by insisting on a maximum degree of inefficiency.

The assignment of registers so as to minimize data-moving operations is trivial when there is only a single register to be assigned. When there are a large number of registers (say over 100), it is relatively easy to develop a register-assignment technique for which the amount of time spent in storing and restoring assigned registers is, on the average, small. However, when there are a small number of heavily used special registers of a certain kind, as is the case with index registers, a good assignment technique may well be a considerable factor of efficiency.

2.4.2 RESOURCE ALLOCATION

The register-assignment problem is in turn a special case of the resource-allocation problem. In a computation there generally are resources other than registers which have to be shared among a number of different processes. The number of units of a given resource is fixed in the computation, and a given process is assumed to use an integral number of units of the resource at a given time. The problem of resource optimization is the problem of allocating resources among processes such that some index of throughput through the computer is optimized.

If assignment of an actual register to a symbolic register is viewed as an instance of resource allocation, then storing and restoring the content of the register is essentially the overhead associated with switching this resource from one use to another. The problem of index-register optimization is essentially the problem of allocating resources so that the

---

† Note that the problem of allocating actual index registers to symbolic registers has many points of similarity with the problem of allocating actual memory registers to symbolic names when the total name requirements exceed the capacity of the computer memory. However, index-register optimization has always been conceived of as a translation-time process while memory allocation is performed dynamically during execution on time-sharing computers. If it were considered sufficiently important, then hardware facilities for dynamic index-register optimization could be provided, just as hardware facilities for optimization of main-memory utilization are provided on time-sharing computers. The problem of index-register optimization is not in fact of great practical importance but is of interest because it was one of the first system resource-allocation problems to be isolated and because it illustrates clearly and simply the nature of the resource-allocation problem.

overhead due to switching resources from one purpose to another is minimized.

Before leaving the subject of index-register allocation, some general terminology will be developed which can be used to characterize both concepts which arise in index-register allocation and those which subsequently arise in allocation of physical memory registers to users of a multiprogramming system. Both of these problems are characterized by the fact that a fixed number of identical units of hardware can be named by means of symbolic names by the user. The set of all symbolic names used by users in a program (or collection of programs) will be referred to as the *symbolic name space.*† The set of all internal names denoted by this class of symbolic names will be referred to as the *physical name space.*

In a computation, each element of the physical name space has a one-dimensional existence through time. The one-dimensional chunk of time associated with each element will be referred to as the *time space* of that element.

When the number of elements in the symbolic name space exceeds the number of elements in the physical name space for a given class of hardware units, then elements of the physical name space must be allocated to elements of the symbolic name space in such a way that the time space of an element in the physical name space may be shared by more than one element of the symbolic name space. In the case of index-register allocation the symbolic elements sharing the time space of a given physical element are usually determined during translation, and each symbolic name is associated with only one physical name during the course of the computation. However, allocation can be performed more flexibly if it is performed at run time by means of an allocation mechanism which may assign different physical elements to a given symbolic element at different points in the computation.

A portion of the time space allocated to a given symbolic element is sometimes referred to as a time slice. When there are more symbolic than physical elements, the time space of each physical element is subdivided into time slices such that during a given time slice the physical element is associated with a fixed symbolic element.

When a given symbolic name completes its time slice on a given physical element, it is sometimes necessary to preserve information stored in the physical element. This requires the existence of an *auxiliary physical name space* which is potentially capable of storing as many elements as there are in the symbolic name space. In order to preserve

---

† The symbolic name space refers to the set of symbols actually used within a given function-module program and should be distinguished from the set of all possible names of symbols.

information of a given physical element when its time slice is completed, it is stored in an element of the auxiliary physical name space associated with the symbolic name space of the element. This information can subsequently be moved back from the auxiliary physical name space to the physical name space when a further time slice on a physical element is allocated to the symbolic element.

In the case of index-register allocation the auxiliary physical name space is normally the main core memory, while in the case of memory-register allocation, the auxiliary physical name space is the auxiliary memory.

2.5 CONTROL OPERATIONS

2.5.1 NONTRANSLITERATIVE ASSEMBLY-TIME OPERATIONS

In Sec. 2.1 the basic techniques used in assembly-program construction were discussed. An assembly program was seen to be one which performed transliteration of symbols according to different kinds of rules. Free variables, such as operation codes, were transliterated by means of a fixed symbol table. Bound variables, such as symbolic addresses, were transliterated by a symbol table constructed during the assembly process. When the number of symbolic names exceeded the number of target-language names, as in the case of index registers, allocation techniques had to be used to allocate time slices to symbolic names.

In the present section the concept of an assembler will be broadened to include operations that are not purely transliterative. The kinds of operations appropriate to assembly-time computations will be discussed, illustrating the distinction between purely transliterative transformations and general computations.

Assemblers normally contain *control operations* which, when they are executed, interrupt the process of transliteration and result in the performance of a nontransliterative operation determined by the control operation. In early assemblers, control operations were restricted to editing and simple control functions, as illustrated by the following examples:

COM   The line of code is to be treated as a comment and ignored for purposes of assembly.

START, END   These control operations respectively initiate and terminate the assembly of a program unit.

OCT, DEC, CHAR   These control operations respectively specify that the remainder of the line is to be interpreted as an octal number, a decimal number, or a character.

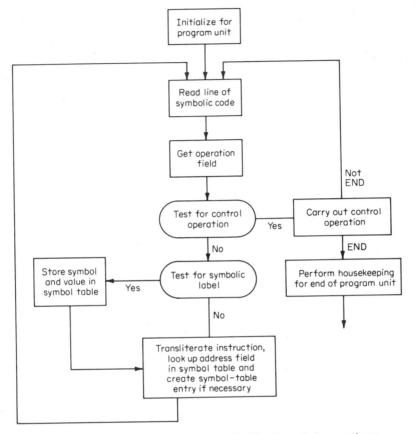

Figure 2.6 One-pass assembler with "editing" control operations.

BLOCK N   This control operation indicates that a block of N registers is to be reserved at this point of the program and causes the content of the simulated-instruction counter to be incremented by N.

A SYM B   This causes the symbol B to denote the same value (address) as the symbol A.

ENTRY A   This specifies that the symbol A is an entry point to the program unit and can be accessed by outside program units.

CALL A($\cdot\cdot\cdot$)   This specifies a subroutine call to an entry point A in another program unit.

    We are not here concerned with the details of individual control operations but with the overall role of control operations in the assembly process.   The role of control operations during assembly is illustrated in Fig. 2.6, which indicates the overall flow of information during the assembly process.

On reading a line of symbolic code, the assembler first determines whether the operation field specifies a control operation.   If not, the assembler performs normal transliteration.   If, however, the operation code is a control operation, the assembler can perform an arbitrary computation determined by the control operation.   Early assemblers restricted control operations to editing operations of the kind indicated above.   We shall consider below two control operations which respectively permit assembly-time assignment of values to variables and assembly-time conditional transfers.

2.5.2 CONDITIONAL AND ASSIGNMENT OPERATIONS AT ASSEMBLY TIME

An assignment statement is one which allows definition and redefinition of the value associated with a given symbol.   For assembly-time assignment statements it is natural to store values of symbols in symbol tables.†   The following control operation increments the value of a symbol stored in a symbol table.

S SET E   Set the value of the symbol S to the value of the expression E.

For example,

S SET 1   Set the value of S to 1.
S SET S + 1   Increment the value of S by 1.

Conditional transfer during assembly can be performed either by conditional transfer to an explicitly labeled line or by skipping a line whenever a certain condition is met.   These two kinds of conditional transfers can respectively be defined as follows:

IF A,B,L   If the value of the symbol A is equal to the value of the symbol B, replace the simulated-instruction counter by the value of L; otherwise increment the simulated-instruction counter by 1.

Transfer to L will cause skipping of a number of symbolic lines if L is the label of a line following the IF instruction and will cause back up and repetition of a number of lines if L is the label of a line preceding the IF instruction.

† The symbol table in which a symbol value is stored must be such that each entry is capable of storing a data item in its value part.   In early assemblers the address symbol was used for storing values of symbols which occurred in assembly-time assignment statements.   However, the value domain of symbols which occur in assignment statements is different from the value domain of address symbols, so that the two classes of symbols may be thought of as being stored in separate symbol tables.

IFF A,B   If the value of the symbol A is equal to the value of the symbol B, increment the simulated-instruction counter by 2; otherwise increment the simulated-instruction counter by 1.

Assembly-time assignment and conditional transfers allow assembly-time computations to be specified in a procedure-oriented notation whose richness is limited principally by the richness of the expressions on the right-hand side of a SET statement. For example, the assembly-time computation of N factorial could be programmed as follows:

```
S  SET       1
K  SET       1
M  IF        S,N,L
K  SET       K × S
S  SET       S + 1
   GO TO     M
L  CONTINUE
```

In the above program the GO TO operation is an assembly-time unconditional transfer, while the CONTINUE operation is a dummy operation used for purposes of attaching a label. The above sequence of lines would cause repetitive execution of the statements "K SET K × S" and "S SET S + 1" until $S = N$ and would result in a final value of N factorial for the symbol K. No lines of object code would be generated by this assembly-time computation.

It is unlikely that any programmer would in fact want to compute N factorial at assembly time, since assembly-time computation is interpretive and therefore slower than computation during execution. However, there are instances where it would be convenient to compute certain functions of an assembly-time parameter during the assembly process.

The SET, IF, and IFF operations provide general assembly-time numeric-computation facilities. We shall next consider a class of control operations which allow substitution of arbitrary strings as "values" of symbolic names. Assembly-time facilities for substituting strings for symbolic names are referred to as *macro facilities*, and the control operations for string substitution are referred to as *macro operations*.

2.6 ASSEMBLY WITH MACRO OPERATIONS

2.6.1 MACRO DEFINITION, MACRO CALL, AND MACRO EXPANSION

Macro facilities allow a programmer to associate names with symbol strings. When macro facilities were first introduced into assembly programs, they were intended to be used to define only symbol strings which represented sequences of symbolic instructions and control operations of an assembly program.   However, it was quickly realized that a macro facility could be used for the definition and manipulation of arbitrary strings.   In the present section we shall develop macro facilities designed specifically for the definition and use of strings which represent lines of symbolic code in an assembly language.   Macro operations for general string manipulation will be developed in Chap. 3.

Macro facilities in an assembler allow the programmer to associate a name with a sequence of symbolic instructions and to subsequently use that name to denote the sequence of instructions.   Consider, for example, the following sequence of three instructions:

```
FETCH X
ADD    Y
STORE  Z
```

If this sequence of instructions occurs frequently in a given program, it is convenient to name it and to denote occurrence of this sequence of three instructions by the abbreviated name.   A name can be associated with a sequence of instructions by means of a *macro definition;* e.g., the name *SUM* can be associated with the above sequence of instructions by the following macro definition:

```
MACRO SUM
        FETCH X
        ADD    Y
        STORE  Z
        END
```

A macro definition is introduced by the control operation MACRO followed by the *macro name.*   Following the macro name are three lines of code, which constitute the *macro body.*   The macro definition is terminated by the END control operation.

A macro definition specifies that the macro name has as its value the symbol string which constitutes the macro body.   When a macro definition occurs in an assembly program, it does not give rise to any lines of generated code but instead causes the macro name and macro body to be entered into a *macro-definition table.*   This table is a symbol table of name-value correspondences for a special class of names called macros. It is organized logically, just like the operation-code symbol table or the address symbol table in an assembler, and is consulted when the value associated with a macro name is to be determined.   However, the range of values which can be associated with macro names is much richer than that which can be associated with operation codes or symbolic addresses.

Use of a macro name in an assembly program causes substitution of the macro body for the macro name and subsequent assembly of the generated lines of code.   Use of a macro name is referred to as a *macro call*. The symbol string generated by a macro call is referred to as the *macro expansion* generated by the macro call.

Thus each use of the macro name SUM in a program with the above macro definition would result in substitution of the three lines of code which constitute the macro body and subsequent transliteration of these three lines of code.

2.6.2 FORMAL PARAMETERS IN MACROS

The above macro is an example of a *parameterless* macro.   Such macros result in the production of precisely the same macro expansion for every macro call.   This is unnecessarily restrictive, and it is usual to allow macro definitions with *formal parameters* for which different *actual parameters* can be substituted in different macro calls.   If in the above example the address fields are treated as formal parameters, the following three-parameter macro definition is obtained:

```
MACRO SUM    X,Y,Z
        FETCH X
        ADD    Y
        STORE Z
        END
```

Macro calls of the above macro must contain three actual parameters.   The macro expansion resulting from a macro call of the above macro definition is obtained by performing two kinds of substitution: (1) that of the actual parameters for the formal parameters in the macro body, and (2) that of the macro body resulting from the first substitution for the macro call.

Thus the macro call

```
SUM A,B,C
```

would result in the macro expansion

```
FETCH A
ADD    B
STORE  C
```

while the macro call

```
SUM  (A,1),(B,1),(C,1)
```

would result in the macro expansion

```
FETCH A,1
ADD    B,1
STORE C,1
```

The parameters of a macro need not be confined to the address field. The following macro has a parameter which is a complete instruction, a parameter which is an operation field, and a parameter which is an address field:

```
MACRO SUM1 X,Y,Z
        X
        ADD  Y
        Z    Y
        END
```

The macro call

```
SUM (FETCH,A),B, STORE
```

would give rise to the macro expansion†

```
FETCH A
ADD    B
STORE B
```

Actual parameters may in general be any strings which result in expansion of well-formed lines of code. In subsequent sections we shall remove the restriction that macro expansions lead to strings of a restricted structure and obtain macro generators that perform arbitrary string substitution.

The formal parameters in a macro definition are *bound variables* in the sense that replacement of all occurrences of a parameter by a symbol which is distinct from all other symbols in the macro will not alter the meaning of the macro. The macro body may be thought of as consisting of a *template* which contains a number of *holes* corresponding to formal parameters into which actual parameters are substituted at the time of call of the macro. Formal parameters serve as *place markers* for these holes. The correspondence between formal and actual parameters is

---

† Actual parameters in parentheses have one level of parentheses stripped off before being substituted for formal parameters. It is assumed also that the macro-expansion mechanism is sufficiently intelligent to recognize that the comma in (FETCH,A) separates an operation code from an address field and must therefore be replaced by a blank on expansion.

determined by the ordinal position of the parameter in the parameter list. The significance of ordinal position is brought out by referring to the parameters as 1st, 2nd, 3rd, etc., rather than by symbolic names, as in the following macro definition.

```
MACRO SUM     1st, 2nd, 3rd
        FETCH 1st
        ADD    2nd
        STORE 3rd
        END
```

The above definition mirrors the internal representation of a macro in the macro-definition table. Macro parameters are assigned fixed internal names according to their ordinal position in the parameter list, since the symbolic names used in the macro definition are irrelevant to subsequent macro calls.

2.6.3 STRUCTURE OF THE MACRO-DEFINITION TABLE

As noted above, macro definitions are stored in a special kind of symbol table referred to as a macro-definition table. Each entry in the macro-definition table consists of the macro name together with an encoded version of the macro body in which formal parameters are replaced by fixed place markers.

Whereas symbols in operation-code or address-field symbol tables have values which can be represented by a fixed number of bits, the values of macro names require a variable amount of space for their representation. Symbol tables with variable-length entries can be represented in a number of alternative ways. For example, storage for values can be separated from storage for names, resulting in a symbol table with fixed-length entries each containing a pointer to the value part. Alternatively the symbol table can be stored as a linked list with each entry containing a pointer to the next entry.

For purposes of the present discussion it will be assumed that each entry is linked to the next entry but that successive entries are linked together in the order of recency of definition such that the *most recently defined* macro is the *first element* of the list. If a pointer to the head of the list is stored in a fixed register, a new element can be added to the list as indicated in Fig. 2.7; i.e., each entry in the definition table has fixed-length LINK and NAME fields and a variable-length BODY field. The last link field in the table contains a special termination marker. When a new entry is added to the list, a pointer in the new top element is set to point to the previous top element, and the pointer to the head of the list is updated to point to the new top element.

When the macro-definition table is searched to determine the value associated with a given macro call, the macro name is matched against successive name fields of the macro-definition table by linking down the set of links specified in the link field.   When a match of names occurs, the corresponding BODY field is used to determine the macro expansion.

This search procedure ensures that if a macro with a given name occurs more than once in the macro-definition table, the macro body corresponding to the most recently defined instance of that macro will be used to determine the macro expansion.   This arrangement allows macro definition and redefinition to be performed just like assignment and reassignment of values to variables during program execution; i.e., redefinition of a macro having a given name causes the old definition to be superseded by the new definition, just as assignment of a value to a variable causes the old value to be superseded by the new value.

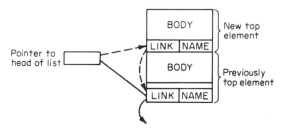

Figure 2.7   Addition of a new entry to the macro-definition table.

A numerical variable is stored in a fixed physical storage register whose content is changed every time a value is assigned to that variable. Redefinition of a macro may result in a value which requires more storage space than the original macro, so that a general solution of the storage-assignment problem for macros requires assignment of a new set of physical registers for each instance of a macro definition.   In an efficient implementation of macro facilities, storage space used for old definitions of macros having a given name can be reclaimed and used for other purposes.   Procedures for reclaiming portions of storage no longer needed by a program are referred to as *garbage-collection procedures* [6].

2.6.4 EXAMPLES OF NESTED AND CONDITIONAL MACROS

A number of examples of macro operations will now be given in order to illustrate the general flavor of programming with macros.   The first example illustrates the use of the conditional control operation within a macro.   The following macro results in the generation of three, two, or one line of code depending on the values of the first and third arguments:

```
MACRO SUM    X,Y,Z
        IFF    X,AC
        FETCH X
        ADD    Y
        IFF    Z,AC
        STORE Z
        END
```

The first IFF operation skips a line if and only if the value of the symbol X is equal to the value of AC, while the second IFF operation skips a line if the value of Z is the same as the value of AC. If the value of AC is assumed to be a code representing the accumulator register, then this macro will result in skipping the STORE instruction if the argument is to remain in the accumulator. This macro is useful for eliminating superfluous FETCH and STORE operations during compilation. More generally conditional assembly operations are useful in macros which may result in the generation of different code sequences for different values of parameters.

The next example illustrates the case of macro definitions which themselves contain macro calls. Consider the following definitions of macros A, B, and C where lines 1 through 6 represent arbitrary lines of code.

```
MACRO A        MACRO B        MACRO C
line 1         line 3         line 5
B              C              line 6
line 2         line 4         END
END            END
```

A call of the macro A would result in the generation of line 1 followed by a call to macro B followed by line 2. The call of macro B would generate line 3 followed by a call to macro C followed by line 4. The call to macro C would in turn generate lines 5 and 6, so that the call of the macro A would result in the generation of six lines of code in the following order:

$$
A \left\{ B \left\{ C \left\{ \begin{array}{l} \text{line 1} \\ \text{line 3} \\ \text{line 5} \\ \text{line 6} \\ \text{line 4} \\ \text{line 2} \end{array} \right. \right. \right.
$$

When considering nested macro calls, it is convenient to define the concept of a *level of nesting* which is zero when not in a macro call, increases by 1 every time a macro is called, and decreases by 1 on completion of a macro expansion.   In the above example the level of nesting is 1 during expansion of the lines of code of macro A, 2 during expansion of B, and 3 during expansion of C.   The levels of nesting of which successive lines of code are generated can be illustrated as follows:

Level 1	Level 2	Level 3
line 1		
	line 3	
		line 5
		line 6
	line 4	
line 2		

When expansion of a macro at a given level is interrupted by a call to a lower-level macro, it is necessary to remember the point reached in the expansion of the interrupted macro.   When expansion of the lower-level macro has been completed, expansion of the interrupted macro is continued at the line following the macro call.   The point reached in the expansion of a given macro is conveniently remembered by a pointer. When a macro at level n is being expanded, $n - 1$ pointers are required to remember the points reached in the partially expanded interrupted macros at levels 1 through $n - 1$.   These pointers are conveniently stored in a pushdown list, since on completion of the expansion of a lower-level macro, expansion of the most recently interrupted macro is always resumed.

2.6.5 THE MACRO-EXPANSION STACK

The information to be remembered for each level of macro expansion includes not only the pointer to the next line to be expanded but also the values of actual parameters for each partially expanded macro.   The pointer and actual parameter information can be stored in a stack, called the *macro-expansion stack*, which contains entries having the format shown in Fig. 2.8.   The pointer to the previous entry contains a special marker if this is the first entry corresponding to level 1 of macro expansion. The values of actual parameters must either be separated by special markers or have pointers pointing to their beginning, since actual parameters may be of arbitrary length.

A macro call always results in a new entry in the macro-expansion stack, while termination of macro expansion at a given level results in deletion of an entry in the macro-expansion stack.   Deletion of the first entry causes normal assembly of a new line of input to be resumed.

| Next line to be expanded |
| Pointer to previous entry |
| Values of actual parameters |

Figure 2.8 Entries in the macro-expansion stack.

2.6.6 RECURSIVE MACROS

Once nesting of macro calls is permitted, it is natural to consider the case of macro definitions which include calls of themselves in the macro body. These are called *recursive macro calls*, and macros which contain calls of themselves are referred to as *recursive macros*.

If recursive macros are permitted, there is clearly the danger of infinite looping by calling of successively deeper levels of a given macro. However, conditional transfers provide a means of terminating recursive calling by a macro of itself after a finite number of levels. The following recursive macro can be used to compute N factorial at assembly time:

```
MACRO FACT, N
      S SET   S + 1
      K SET   K × S
       IFF    S,N
      FACT N
      END
```

In order to call this macro S must be initialized to 0 (or 1) and K must be initialized to 1. The following macro call results in computation of factorial 3.

```
S  SET   0
K  SET   1
   FACT 3
```

The call FACT 3 results in three-level recursive calling of the macro FACT. The call sets S to 1 and K to 1×1 at level 1. Then since $S \neq N$, level 2 is entered, S is set to 2, and K is set to 1×2. Since S is still not equal to N, level 3 is entered, S is set to 3, and K is set to 2×3. Now S equals N, so that assembly of FACT N is skipped at the third level. Since the END instruction is next encountered at the third level, control is returned to level 2, and the entry to the macro-expansion stack at level 3 is deleted. The END operation at level 2 similarly causes deletion of the entry in the macro-expansion stack at level 2 and a return to level 1. Finally the end operation at level 1 causes a return to level 0 and results in reading and assembly of the line of code following "FACT 3" in the assembly program.

It is convenient to think of a recursive macro call as a special case of a nested macro call in which the macro that is called is the one in which the call occurs. Each level of recursive calling may be thought of as a call to a new copy of the macro, so that a recursive call of a macro at level N results, conceptually, in n partially expanded copies of the macro. In practice we can take advantage of the fact that the copies are identical and simulate copies of the macro definition by pointers to the current point of expansion of a single definition. Recursive macro calling essentially results in simultaneous scanning of the string that constitutes the macro definition by several different scanning processes, which also occurs when a given procedure is simultaneously being executed by a number of programs in a time-sharing environment and in other contexts. Simultaneous scanning of a fixed string by a number of processes is always accomplished by associating a pointer to the current point of scan with each of the processes that scans the string.† In the case of recursive macro calls, simultaneously operating partial scans are always interrupted and resumed in at best a last in, first out order.

In implementing nested calls, no distinction need be made between recursive macro calls and other nested macro calls. Each interrupted level of nested macro calling requires storage of a pointer to the partially expanded macro and information about the actual parameters, whether it is a recursively nested macro or a nonrecursively nested macro.

2.6.7 NESTED MACRO DEFINITION

Once macro facilities are introduced into an assembly system, it is convenient if all the structures which can occur outside a macro definition can also occur inside a macro definition. It was indicated above how instructions, macro calls, and standard control operations can occur in macro definitions. In order to complete the picture, the embedding of macro definitions in macro definitions will be discussed. The following example shows macro definition A which contains macro definition B:

MACRO A

· · ·

MACRO B

· · ·

END

· · ·

END

---

† Each of the interpreters must store its private copy of *all* information which differs for different activations (instances of execution). This private copy is referred to as an activation record.

When these lines of text are encountered during assembly, the macro A is defined and the body of macro A is treated as an encoded string of text. A subsequent call of the macro A would result in expansion of A and definition of the macro B. Further calls of the macro A would result in redefinition of the macro B.

Formal parameters of the macro A may occur inside the macro B, resulting in different definitions of the macro B for different actual parameters of A. The macro B may have its own formal parameters. However, a conflict arises when formal parameters of B have the same name as formal parameters of A. This conflict is usually resolved by treating formal parameters of B as bound variables of B which can be renamed independently of whether there is a formal parameter of the same name in an encoding macro. For example, in the following example the parameter X of B together with all occurrences of X in B have been renamed to T without changing the effect of the macro.

```
MACRO A,X,Y              MACRO A,X,Y
. . . . . . . . . .      . . . . . . . . . .
MACRO B,X,Z              MACRO B,T,Z
. . . . . . . . .   ⇒    . . . . . . . . .
END                      END
. . .                    . . .
END                      END
```

The ability to perform the above transformation implies that if a given symbol is a formal parameter of more than one macro definition in a nest of macro definitions, it is bound by the innermost of the macro definitions having that symbol as a formal parameter. Since it can be freely renamed at the innermost level, occurrences of the symbol at the innermost level are completely unrelated to occurrences of the same symbol at other levels.

Implementation of nested macro definitions with correct interpretation of parameters requires careful encoding of macro definitions into the definition table. It is not sufficient to replace all instances of parameter names by fixed internal parameter codes, as previously suggested. One general solution to the problem of parameter naming is to create *two-component* internal parameter names (i,j), where the first component i specifies the depth of nesting of the parameter definition with which the parameter is associated and the second component j specifies the ordinal position of the parameter in the definition. On expansion of a given macro definition, formal parameters whose first component is 1 have actual parameters substituted for them, while formal parameters in inner macro definitions whose first component is greater than 1 have their first components decremented by 1.

Initial encoding of macro definitions from the input string can conveniently be performed with the aid of a *macro-definition stack*, which, for each level of nesting of macro definitions, contains the set of formal parameters associated with that level of nesting. Whenever a new physical level of macro definition is entered, the set of formal parameters associated with that macro definition is placed on the macro-definition stack. Whenever an END operation is encountered, a layer of formal parameters is removed from the macro-definition stack. The END operation associated with the outermost definition results in removal of the final layer of parameters and termination of the macro definition.

Formal parameters are placed on the macro-definition stack together with their values (i,j). During encoding every symbol of the macro definition is compared with successive symbols of the macro definition in a last in, first out order. If there is a match, the (i,j) value of the matched symbol is taken to be the internal representation of the formal parameter. If there is no match, the symbol is not a formal parameter and is encoded in the normal way.

In the above discussion, stacklike structures were introduced in three different places:

1. The macro-definition table, which is a stacklike structure, since it is scanned in a last in, first out order to determine the macro definition corresponding to the given macro call. However, although *reading* of entries in the table is in a last in, first out order, entries never get deleted, so that it is not a true stack.

2. The macro-expansion stack, which is used to keep track of partially expanded nested macro calls.

3. The macro-definition stack, which is used to keep track of formal parameters of nested macro definitions.

The second and third stacks illustrate that stack structures are intimately associated with nested structures. In fact, stacks may be regarded as the *dynamic* counterpart of nested structures, since they are the natural structure for keeping track of information when sequencing "dynamically" through a structure that is statically nested.

The macro definitions discussed above are *explicitly nested*, while macro calls may be regarded as *implicitly nested*, since a given macro call may give rise to an arbitrary number of levels of nesting when it is encountered.

Stack structures such as those introduced above are fundamental to implementation of substitution and assignment in all classes of programming languages and will recur repeatedly in subsequent discussion of dynamic structures required to keep track of information when sequencing through nested static program structures. The macro-definition table, macro-expansion stack, and macro-definition stack are prototypes of three kinds of information which must be saved when executing nested program structures. A number of alternative techniques for handling these classes of information are discussed in Chaps. 3 and 4.

2.6.8   THE OVERALL MACRO ASSEMBLY PROCESS

The details of the overall assembly process in a compiler with macro facilities will now be discussed. A flow diagram for an assembler without macro facilities has already been given in Fig. 2.2. The effect of macro operations on the overall assembly process differs from that of other control operations in that macro operations have a *nonlocal* effect determining the way in which subsequent lines of symbolic code are interpreted. More specifically, a MACRO control operation specifies that lines of code between this control operation and a matching END control operation are to be interpreted as part of a macro definition and placed in the macro-definition table rather than subjected to the standard assembly procedure. A macro call in turn specifies that a number of lines of code are to be inserted at this point from the macro-definition table rather than from the standard input medium.

The mode of operation during macro definition will be referred to as the *macro-definition mode,* while the mode of operation during macro expansion will be referred to as the *macro-expansion mode.* The overall operation of an assembler with macro facilities is illustrated in Fig. 2.9.

This kind of assembler may be thought of as one with two alternative sources of input, depending on whether the macro-expansion switch is on or off and two alternative sources of output, depending on whether the macro-definition switch is on or off. The macro-expansion switch is switched on when the operation field of an instruction is found to be a macro call and is switched off when an END control operation is encountered that reduces the level count to zero. The macro-definition switch is switched on when a MACRO control operation is encountered and is switched off when the line to be encoded in the macro-definition mode is an END control operation matching the MACRO control operation which initiated the current macro definition.

Note that control operations, macro calls, and instruction codes are all denoted by symbol strings in the operation-code field of a symbolic line of code. In Fig. 2.9 the operation field is checked first for being a control operation, next for being a macro call, and finally for being a symbolic instruction. This arrangement implies that macro names cannot be the same symbol strings as control operations, since the symbol would always be interpreted as a control operation before the test for its being a macro call was applied. However, if a macro name is the same as a symbolic operation code, it is interpreted as a macro call. This allows an operation code in a given symbolic program to be redefined as a macro by placing a macro definition at the head of the symbolic instruction sequence.   For example, a given single-precision computation could be redefined as a double-precision computation by placing a pack-

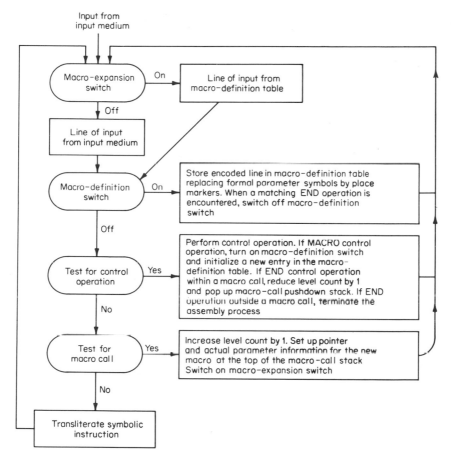

Figure 2.9   An assembler with macro facilities.

age of macro definitions at its head which redefined arithmetic and information-moving instructions as double-precision macros.

It is sometimes convenient to go even further and to write programs that consist completely of macro calls.   This allows programs to be written in a manner that reflects the logic of the problem, independently of the machine language of an actual computer.   The same sequence of macro calls can be converted into the machine language of different computers by merely placing different macro definitions at the head of the sequence of macro calls. Thus macros provide a simple mechanism for writing machine-independent code.

In assembly programs with macro facilities it is usual for the system to include a number of standard *system macros* for performing certain standard system functions. The system macros can be supplied by initializing the assembler to contain a nonempty initial macro-definition table. System macros in the initial macro-definition table have exactly the same logical status as operation codes but in general give rise to a number of lines of code. Among the most common system macros are subroutine entry and exit macros for storing and restoring standard items of information (such as index registers) on entry to, and exit from, subroutines.

A more fundamental use of system macros is that of defining macros whose effect when called is not merely that of substitution of a macro body for a macro call. A macro call may be regarded as a call for performing a function other than substitution. In particular, system macros can be defined whose effect when called is to perform macro definition and other bookkeeping functions of a macro assembler. Generalized macro assemblers which generalize the concept of a macro to permit both more general forms of substitution and arbitrary functional transformations are discussed in the next chapter.

REFERENCES

1. Wegner, P.: "Introduction to Symbolic Programming," Charles Griffin & Company, Ltd., London, 1963.
2. Knuth, D. E.: "The Art of Computer Programming," Addison-Wesley Publishing Company, Inc., Reading, Mass., to be published.
3. Wegner, P.: "Introduction to System Programming," Academic Press Inc., New York, 1964 (see chap. 5 for example of bootstrapping).
4. McLure, R. M.: TMG—A Syntax-directed Compiler, *Proc. 20th ACM Conf., Cleveland*, August, 1965.
5. Kavanagh, T. F.: TABSOL—The Language of Decision-making, *Computers and Automation*, September, 1961.
6. McCarthy, J., et al.: "LISP 1.5 Programmers Manual," The M.I.T. Press, Cambridge, Mass., 1962.

CHAPTER 3

MACRO GENERATORS
AND THE LAMBDA CALCULUS

3.1 SUBSTITUTIVE FUNCTION EVALUATION

3.1.1 MACROS WHOSE DOMAIN AND RANGE ARE ARBITRARY STRINGS

A macro definition can be thought of as a function definition f which for every set of actual parameters $(a_1, \ldots, a_n)$ in the permitted domain determines a value string $f(a_1, \ldots, a_n)$ which consists of the string generated as a result of macro expansion. In the macro assemblers considered in the previous chapter, the domain of actual parameters was normally taken to be a part of a single assembly-language instruction, and the range of the functions defined by macro operations was taken to be the set of sequences of generated assembly-language instructions. However, the function-evaluation techniques developed for macro assemblers can be used also to implement more general macro-type function evaluators where the domain and range of arguments are arbitrary strings. This more general class of function evaluators will be referred to as *macro generators*. Two specific macro generators, GPM and TRAC, will be discussed in some detail. Function evaluation in a "purer" language for function specification, known as the *lambda calculus*, will then be considered.

The lambda calculus is a language sufficiently simple to allow easy comparison of function-evaluation techniques. In Sec. 3.8 macro-type function evaluation by explicit substitution of the value in the function body is compared with function-evaluation techniques normally used to evaluate procedures in a procedure-oriented language. This provides an appropriate transition to the discussion of procedure-oriented languages in Chap. 4.

All programming languages are essentially notations for specifying the application of functions to their arguments, and many also permit function definition and subsequent use of defined functions. Macro facilities are one example of function-definition facilities in a language.

Procedure-definition facilities in procedure-oriented languages are another example of function-definition facilities.

One of the principal differences between macro-type function-definition facilities and procedure-type function-definition facilities is that macros are usually thought of as functions that are physically substituted at the point of macro call when performing evaluation, while procedures are thought of as being executed by transfer of control to a closed subroutine. The difference between macros and procedures is not at the language-definition level but rather in the presumed mode of interpretation of the program at execution time.†

3.1.2 EVALUATION BY PHYSICAL SUBSTITUTION

Macro definitions normally specify functions whose evaluation is accomplished by substitution of string arguments for formal parameters in a macro body. Functions in which evaluation is performed by physical substitution will be called *substitutive functions*. Substitutive function calls may have other substitutive function calls explicitly nested inside them. Evaluation of nested functions is normally accomplished by evaluation of inner functions, substitution of values for function calls, and then evaluation of outer functions as illustrated by the following examples:

$(3 + (4 \times 5))$ The evaluation of this function can be thought of as consisting of a sequence of two substitutions, the first of which substitutes the symbol string 20 for the symbol string (4×5) and the second of which substitutes the symbol string 23 for the symbol string $(3 + 20)$.

$f(x,g(y,z))$ The evaluation of this function can be thought of as a sequence of substitutions which first replaces $g(y,z)$ by its value and then replaces $f(x,g(y,z))$ by the value of the function for its two arguments.

The functions f and g in the above example can be thought of as macros. In "pure" function-evaluation systems such as the lambda calculus (Sec. 3.5) the literal function bodies would be specified in place of the symbols f and g. In the macro systems to be considered in Secs. 3.2 and 3.3, f and g specify the names of the macros, and substitution of macro bodies for macro names is performed automatically. One of the following notations developed by Landin [9] can be used to indicate

† Note that if macro calls executed during translation are compared with procedure calls executed during execution, there is a difference in binding time of the program string which constitutes the function definition. The comparison above is between macro calls and procedure calls executed at execution time.

explicitly that f and g are names which correspond to definitions:

1. $f(x,g(y,z))$ **where** f = [macro definition] **and** g = [macro definition]
2. **let** f = [macro definition] **and** g = [macro definition] **in** $f(x,g(y,z))$

It is usually convenient to have definitions specified *before* the occurrence of the expression in which they are used, so that the second style of definition is more common than the first. In macro assemblers and in the macro generators discussed below, the string which specifies definition of a function must occur prior to the string in which the function is used or as one of the parameters of the string in which the function is used.

3.1.3 MULTISTAGE ARGUMENT SUBSTITUTION AND FUNCTION-BODY SUBSTITUTION

In the above examples the domain and range of the functions considered were assumed not to be functions. However, all the substitutive function evaluation systems considered in this chapter permit both arguments and values of functions to be functions. The rules for substitutive function evaluation are as follows:

1. Substitute actual for formal arguments in the body of the function to be evaluated.
2. Substitute the function body which results from step 1 at the point of function call.
3. Evaluate the substituted function body in the context of the function call.

3.1.4 THE ORDER OF EVALUATION

Since both arguments and values of functions can contain function calls, a decision must be made regarding the order in which function values are to be substituted for function calls. The two principal approaches to the problem of order of evaluation are (1) to evaluate inner function calls before outer function calls, which implies evaluating arguments of a function before substituting them in a function body, and (2) to substitute unevaluated actual arguments for formal arguments and execute the program by interpreting successive symbols in a strictly left-to-right order.

There are many functions which are defined only for evaluated arguments. For example, the function $+$ is normally defined only over a number domain and not over an expression domain, so that $(2 \times 3) + (4 \times 5)$ must be evaluated by first evaluating the inner functions 2×3 and 4×5 before application of $+$. However, indiscriminate evaluation of inner before outer functions may lead to trouble as in the following:

if $3 > 0$ **then** 5 **else** $\frac{0}{0}$;   This function has the value 5.   However, if
inner functions are evaluated before outer func-
tions, $\frac{0}{0}$ will be needlessly evaluated, and the value undefined will be
obtained.

The circumstances under which the evaluation of inner before
outer functions may lead to trouble are discussed in greater detail in
Sec. 3.5.

When evaluation of functions is strictly substitutive, in the sense
that evaluation consists of substitution of actual parameter strings for
formal parameter markers followed by substitution of the resulting string
for the function call, then substitution operations can always be performed
both for unevaluated and for evaluated arguments. Evaluation of
arguments before substitution has the advantage of saving multiple
evaluation when there are multiple substitution instances but results in
needless evaluation when there are zero substitution instances of the
argument.   If there are zero substitution instances of an argument and
the argument is undefined, evaluation before substitution leads to disaster.

The order of evaluation in a function-evaluation system must be
specified as part of the language, since the result may depend on the order
of evaluation when undefined functions occur.   However, in the macro-
generation systems discussed below the result may depend upon the order
of evaluation for still another reason.

Both macro-generation systems below permit not only function calls
but also function definitions to occur in argument strings.   A function
definition is like an assignment statement in that it assigns a value to a
function-valued variable.   The precise point in time at which the function
definition occurs alters the value determined by later calls to that function,
so that the precise point in time of function definitions must be rigorously
specified.

Both of the macro generators discussed in the next two sections perform argument evaluation *before* substitution, and they cause functions
whose definitions occur in argument strings to be defined while the argument is being evaluated prior to substitution in the function body.†
On the other hand, the other macro-evaluation systems such as LISP
(as defined by the LISP APPLY function), macro assemblers, and procedure-oriented languages such as ALGOL have their execution algorithm
defined so that the result of direct evaluation is equivalent to substitution
of unevaluated arguments, followed by evaluation by left-to-right
scanning of the result.

---

† Both macro generators considered permit the effect of substitution prior to
evaluation to be obtained by enclosing arguments in quotes so that evaluation of the
quoted argument yields the unevaluated string.

3.1.5 ALTERNATIVE RUN-TIME REPRESENTATION STRATEGIES FOR SIMULATED SUBSTITUTIVE FUNCTION EVALUATION

In this chapter and the next, the evaluation algorithms for a number of alternative languages are discussed, and a framework is developed for the comparative study of evaluation algorithms. This approach to the study of programming languages is a relatively new one. Programming-language theory has, in the past, tended to emphasize the study of source languages and the study of translation of source languages into an initial target-language representation for purposes of execution. The present approach takes the initial representation for purposes of execution as the starting point and studies the *sequence of run-time representations* during execution of the function. The representation of the function at a given point during execution is referred to as an *instantaneous description*. The process of function evaluation may be characterized by a sequence of instantaneous descriptions.

In Chaps. 3 and 4 the relation will be examined between abstract characteristics of function-evaluation algorithms and the structure of instantaneous descriptions by which algorithms can be realized. The structures considered will be classified into two kinds: (1) substitutive structures, which arise when the initial representation of the function is progressively transformed by physical substitution into a final representation which represents the value of the function, and (2) reentrant structures, which arise when the algorithm specified by the function is represented by a fixed-program part and the point reached in execution of the function is represented by a data part referred to as an activation record. Reentrant structures permit a distinction to be made between the function itself and an instance of execution of the function and permit simultaneous execution of a given function by a number of higher-level interpreters each of which scans successive symbols of the fixed-program part and evaluates the function by successive modification of a private copy of its activation record.

Chapter 3 is concerned with substitutive techniques for function evaluation, while Chap. 4 will be concerned with reentrant techniques of function evaluation.

3.1.6 SYNTAX, SEMANTICS, AND THE SYNTACTIC SPECIFICATION OF SEMANTICS

Sections 3.2 and 3.3 describe the macro generators GPM and TRAC. Section 3.4 discusses a generalization of macros in which macro calls are "patterns" which must be matched against the "templates" of a symbol table in order to determine the macro body to be substituted for the pattern which constitutes the macro call.

Sections 3.5 to 3.7 introduce the syntactic forms and semantic concepts associated with the lambda calculus and give a number of examples of manipulation in the lambda calculus. Although the lambda calculus was first developed as a formal system [4], it is here developed as a programming language with an exceptionally simple syntax and semantics.   Section 3.8 develops a number of alternative models of evaluation of the lambda calculus.   These models are seen to be the prototypes of evaluation models in actual programming languages.

Section 3.9 describes the LISP language and indicates how LISP can be used to specify an interpreter (called the LISP APPLY function) which, when supplied with a LISP program together with its data, will compute the result of applying the program to its data.   The LISP APPLY function may be thought of as a computer for the evaluation of LISP programs together with their data.   More generally, a program written in a language M for applying programs written in a language L to their data can be thought of as a computer whose machine language is L.

When, in Fig. 3.1, the language M is the same as the language L, as in the case of the LISP APPLY function, the program in language M

Program P and data D in language L → Program written in language M for applying programs written in language L to their data → Result of applying the program P to its data D

Figure 3.1   A program for program execution.

for applying programs of the language M to their data is called a *universal program*.   The analogy between universal programs and universal Turing machines is discussed in Sec. 3.11.   Section 3.10 gives a detailed example of a program written in a LISP-like language for the application of lambda expressions to their data.

A program written in the language M for the application of programs written in L to their data may be thought of as a specification of the semantics of the language L in the language M.   This form of semantic specification may be thought of as a *syntactic specification* of the semantics, since the semantics of a language L is specified in terms of syntactic transformations of its instantaneous description during execution.

Let $I(L)$ denote the set of all initial representations of programs of the language L together with their data, and let $C(L)$ (closure of L) denote the set of all instantaneous descriptions which can occur at intermediate stages of application of programs of the language L to their data.   The set $C(L)$ of instantaneous descriptions associated with L is the data space over which the semantics is defined; i.e., a program which specifies the sequence of changes of instantaneous descriptions for transforming elements of $I(L)$ into the result of applying the program to its data is specified in terms of *syntactic transformations* in the elements of $C(L)$. The set of *final instantaneous descriptions*, which corresponds to execution of a halt instruction, will be denoted by $F(L)$. The set $F(L)$ is a subset of $C(L)$. For each final instantaneous description $f \in F(L)$ there is a subset which is called the *output* associated with the instantaneous description f. The relation between $I(L)$, $F(L)$, and $C(L)$ is illustrated in Fig. 3.2.

Exercise: What interpretation is associated with programs that lie in the intersection of $I(L)$ and $F(L)$?

Section 3.11 deals with the special case of semantic specification when the language L used to specify the semantics of a second language M is identical with M. This situation occurs in Sec. 3.9, when specifying LISP in LISP. In Sec. 3.11 it is pointed out that any language able

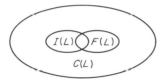

Figure 3.2 Space of instantaneous descriptions for a language L.

to compute any computable function may in principle be used to specify its own semantics and that this question has in fact been extensively studied in the literature in connection with universal Turing machines.

3.2 THE GENERAL-PURPOSE MACRO GENERATOR (GPM)

3.2.1 MACRO DEFINITION AND MACRO CALL

In the present section the characteristics will be developed of a macro-generation language called GPM (general-purpose macro generator), which is due to Strachey [1]. GPM is a *symbol-stream processor* which scans sequences of symbols residing in its input stream from left to right, normally copying them to an output stream but performing special action when certain system symbols are encountered. The special actions in which we are particularly interested are macro calling and macro definition.

Macros in GPM are essentially arbitrary functions. A *macro call* results in an instance of use of a function which has either been previously defined by a macro definition or is initially defined by the system. A *macro definition* results in the definition of a function which can subsequently be used by a macro call.

Functions defined in GPM have *names* and may have *parameters*. Function definitions in GPM require specification of the function name and of the function body. Formal parameters are specified in the function body by means of a set of reserved parameter symbols. Function calls require specification of the macro name and the set of actual parameters to be substituted for formal parameters of the macro definition.

A macro call is introduced by the symbol \$ followed by the macro name, followed by the list of actual parameters separated by commas and terminated by a semicolon:

\$N,A1, . . . ,AK;   This macro call calls a macro named N followed
by K actual parameters $A1, . . . ,AK$ which are
to be substituted for formal parameters into the macro definition of N.

A macro call is executed by first evaluating the string name N and the sequence of strings which constitute the actual parameters A1, A2, . . . , AK and then evaluating the function body corresponding to the evaluated name, substituting evaluated actual parameters for formal parameters. If the values of the name and actual parameter strings are simple symbol strings, their values coincide with the literal strings. However, macro names and actual parameters may themselves contain macro calls and macro definitions. The output from the argument-scanning process is to a special temporary string, which receives the values of the macro name and macro parameters as they are formed. This temporary string is used during evaluation of the macro body and is discarded after that evaluation is completed.

Evaluation of arguments can be delayed by enclosing them in the triangular quotes ⟨ ⟩.

\$N,⟨A1⟩;   This one-parameter macro call is executed by evaluating
the name N and using the literal string $A1$ as the argument
of the resulting macro.

Macro definition is performed by a special system macro DEF. The macro DEF has two parameters, the first of which specifies the macro name and the second of which specifies the macro body.

\$DEF,NAME,BODY;   This macro call results in evaluation of the
name field, evaluation of the body field, and
definition of a macro with the resulting name and body. The name and
body fields can be enclosed in triangular parentheses if they are to be
shielded from evaluation.

Formal parameters in a macro body are denoted by the set of special symbols $\sim i$, where i is an integer. ~ 0 denotes the symbol string which constitutes the macro name, and $\sim i$, $i = 1, 2 \ldots$, denotes the ith formal parameter.†

$DEF,N,⟨A$\sim$1$\sim$2B⟩;   This macro definition defines a macro with two formal parameters ~ 1, ~ 2.

$N,C,D;   This macro call of N yields the string $ACDB$.

The occurrence of a macro call within a macro definition is illustrated by the following example:

$DEF,P,⟨A$N,C,D;$\sim$1⟩;   This macro definition of a macro P contains an inner call of a macro N.

$P,F;   This macro call results in an inner call of the macro N during evaluation of the macro body of P.   If N is as previously defined, the output associated with this macro call is $AACDBF$.

The occurrence of a macro definition nested within an outer definition is illustrated by the following example:

$DEF,X,⟨A$DEF,Y,$\sim$1;⟩;   Definition of a macro X with an inner macro definition Y.

$X,B;   This macro yields the string A and has a side effect of defining the parameterless macro Y with body B.

If in the previous example the quotes are removed from the macro body, the inner macro Y is defined at the moment of call and is deleted when the expansion of the outer macro X is completed.

DEF,X,ADEF,Y,B;;   This macro call results in definition of a macro X whose body is the evaluated second parameter.   Evaluation of the second parameter leads to a value A and definition of a macro Y.   The macro definition of Y is a temporary macro definition, which is deleted when the definition of X is completed.   However, temporary macros defined in parameter strings permit local values to be associated with symbols during a macro expan-

---

† Parameters of macro assemblers are specified by listing the formal parameters in parentheses following the function name but are represented inside the computer by special internal parameter markers.   GPM represents parameters directly by a special class of parameter markers.   In this respect and in a number of other respects GPM is a machine-oriented macro language.

sion followed by reinstatement of a previous value when expansion of
the macro has been completed.

3.2.2 STRING-EVALUATION RULES

The process of evaluation during expansion of a macro may be described
in detail as follows:

1.   On encountering a macro call, the macro name and actual
parameters are evaluated in sequence from left to right.   This process
in turn may involve macro calls, so that the definition of parameter
evaluation is a reentrant one.   Macro definitions which occur during
parameter evaluation result in temporary macro definitions valid only
until the evaluation of the macro body associated with the parameter
has been completed.

2.   When the semicolon terminating the macro call is encountered,
the current list of definitions (known as the *environment chain*) is scanned
in a last in, first out order in order to determine the first occurrence, if any,
of the macro name.   If the name is undefined, an error exit occurs.

3.   The symbol string which constitutes the macro body is now
scanned in the same way as the original input stream except that occurrences, if any, of the symbols $\sim r$, where $r = 0, 1, 2, \ldots$, are replaced
by exact copies of the corresponding actual parameter, which has by
now been evaluated. ~ 0 corresponds to the macro name, ~ 1 corresponds to the first actual parameter, etc.   If r is greater than the number
of parameters supplied, an error exit occurs.   The symbol string comprising an actual parameter is always directly copied without being
subjected to any further evaluation.   The result of the macro call is
the output produced by this scan.

4.   On reaching the end of the defining string, the argument list,
i.e., the macro name and actual parameters, are lost, and any definitions
which may have been added to the environment chain in the course of
argument evaluation are deleted.   Definitions which have been added
during execution of the macro body are not deleted.

5.   Scanning of the input stream is then resumed at the point where
it was interrupted by the final semicolon of the macro call.

3.2.3 EXAMPLES IN GPM

The following examples taken from Strachey illustrate some of the more
interesting effects of macro definition.

$A,X,U,$DEF,A,$\langle\sim 1\sim 2\sim 1\rangle$;;   This macro call defines the macro A
during argument evaluation and then
immediately uses this macro with arguments X and U, producing the
value XUX.   The macro A is then removed from the environment
chain.

This principle is used by Strachey to define the successor macro as follows:

$DEF,Suc,⟨$1,2,3,4,5,6,7,8,9,10,$DEF,1,⟨∼⟩∼1;;⟩;

Given the above definition of Suc, consider the effect of the following macro call:

$Suc,3;   This macro call results during argument evaluation in the temporary definition of a macro with name 1 and defining string ∼3 and then in a call to the created macro with arguments 2, 3, . . . , 10.   The value of this call is therefore 4, and in general the value of $Suc,$r$; $= r + 1$ for $r = 0, 1, . . . , 9$; that is, $Suc,0; will yield the macro name, which happens to be 1, as its value.

Exercise: Show that the following macro definition gives the successor of a two-digit number of the form $α,β$, that is, $successor,$α,β$; yields $(α,β + 1)$ if $β \neq 9$ and $(α + 1,0)$ if $β = 9$:

$DEF,successor,⟨$∼2,$DEF,∼2,∼1⟨,$Suc,⟩

∼2⟨;⟩;$DEF,9,⟨$Suc,⟩∼1⟨;,0⟩;;⟩;

It is evident that GPM allows very complex macros to be defined whose implications are very difficult to disentangle. Moreover, the notation used in GPM when complex nests of functions are defined is not very readable.   In the next section a language is defined which is more readable than GPM at the expense of being more redundant in its notation.   However, before leaving GPM some additional language features and implementation characteristics will be discussed.

GPM contains a system macro, called VAL, which inhibits evaluation of a called string.

$DEF,X,⟨α⟩;   Calling these two macros always produces the string $α$
$VAL,X;   without evaluating constituents of $α$.   The effect is
               the same as that of executing $DEF,X,⟨⟨α⟩⟩; followed
by $X;.

GPM has a macro called UPDATE which can be used to update the value of a name in the environment chain provided the updated value does not require more storage space than the original value.   UPDATE has exactly the same effect as DEF but saves storage space by using existing space within the environment chain.   GPM also has system macros for performing binary-to-decimal and decimal-to-binary conversion and rudimentary facilities for performing binary arithmetic.

3.2.4   IMPLEMENTATION OF GPM

The algorithm for the implementation of GPM is essentially very like that for the implementation of macro-definition and macro-expansion

facilities in macro assemblers.   The six special characters $\langle \rangle$ \$; . $\sim$ are
the counterpart of control operations of an assembly program.   In the
absence of these characters successive symbols are copied directly from
an input string to an output string.   The above symbols cause GPM to
interrupt its normal copying operation and to perform transformational
actions.

The quotation symbols $\langle \rangle$ cause incrementing and decrementing of a
quotation counter q, which is increased by 1 when $\langle$ is encountered and
decreased by 1 when $\rangle$ is encountered.   When $q > 1$, all symbols other
than quotes are ignored.   The outer layer of quotes is always peeled
off and deleted during evaluation.

The symbol \$ initiates parameter evaluation.   The symbol ;
indicates that parameter evaluation at a given level has been completed
and that macro expansion of the given macro can be performed.   The
symbol , is a separator between parameters, and the symbol $\sim$ is a prefix
to formal parameters in a macro definition.   There are also a number of
internally generated control symbols, such as the end-of-string marker ω.

The process of macro evaluation may be thought of as a process of
symbol-stream scanning.   In the absence of a macro definition or a
macro call, the input string serves as the source of the symbol stream,
the mode of interpretation of successive symbols is plain copying, and
the output stream serves as the target stream for evaluated symbols.
When a macro call is encountered, the source stream is switched from the
input medium to the named-symbol stream within the macro-definition
table that constitutes the macro definition.   However, before the macro
body is scanned, a number of temporary actual-parameter symbol
streams are created which will be used as source streams for formal-
parameter replacement during expansion of the macro body.

Scanning of actual-parameter strings or of macro bodies during their
evaluation is similar to scanning of the input stream, except that the
source of the symbol stream differs.   During scanning of actual-parameter strings and macro bodies, symbols are normally copied from the
source stream to a target stream, unless a control symbol is encountered.
Control symbols belong to two categories: (1) those which serve to
initiate a new mode of scanning and push down a previous mode and (2)
those which terminate a given mode of scanning and reinstate a previous
mode.

Scanning modes may be pushed down to an arbitrary level, so that
the sequence of modes to be reinstated must be stored in a stack.   Each
interrupted scanning mode will have a number of temporary information
items associated with it which will be pushed down in the stack along with
the scanning-mode indicator.

The symbol streams which may serve as the source and destination for scanning purposes may be classified as follows:

1. The input stream, which may serve only as a source stream and not as a destination stream.

2. The output stream, which may serve only as a destination stream and not as a source stream.

3. An arbitrary number of created-definition streams, which are created by the programmer on definition of a macro and serve as source streams during call of the macro. Created-definition streams may be subdivided into permanent streams, which cannot be destroyed once they are created but whose values can be destructively reassigned, and temporary streams, whose names and values are assigned and reassigned on a pushdown basis. The first instance of definition of a permanent stream assigns both the name and the value of the stream, while subsesequent assignments assign only its value. In the case of temporary streams, the name and value of the stream are always assigned simultaneously.

4. A number of *system streams* corresponding to initially defined system macros.† Control symbols may also be thought of as represented by system streams. The difference between system macros and control symbols is that system macros may be redefined while control symbols have a fixed meaning.

5. One or more accumulator streams, which contain parameter strings of partially expanded macros, and partially evaluated actual-parameter strings of macros whose expansion has not yet begun. Both macro expansion and actual parameter-string evaluation may be interrupted by a macro call or macro definition. However, all interruptions of the scanning mode are always reinstated in a last in, first out order, so that the set of all parameter strings can be stored within a single accumulator stack.

Since the nomenclature determined by a given macro call comes into effect only when evaluation of its sequence of parameters has been completed, a distinction must be made within the accumulator stack between completed and partially expanded parameter sets. Strachey makes this distinction by visualizing the stack as consisting of two chains of records, referred to as the P chain and the F chain. The P chain contains completed parameter sets associated with a macro expansion that is in progress. The F chain contains partially evaluated parameter

---

† Each of the system streams essentially corresponds to the value field of a symbol-table entry. When value fields of symbol-table entries are subject to interpretation by a higher-level interpreter, it is sometimes convenient to think of them as symbol streams.

sets.   Evaluation of a partially evaluated parameter set can be completed only when it is at the top of the stack.   When this occurs, a new set of nomenclature is established, and the newly completed parameter set is switched from the F chain to the P chain.

The distinction between F and P chains can best be illustrated by considering the occurrence of a DEF macro nested in the actual parameter of an outer macro.

A,XDEF,B,C;Z,Y$B;;   This macro call results in evaluation of actual parameters followed by a call of the two-parameter macro A.   During evaluation, partially evaluated parameters of A are stored in the F chain.   If a macro call is encountered during parameter evaluation, the current F-chain entry is pushed down, and a new F-chain entry is created.   On completion of evaluation of the inner macro the interrupted F chain is popped up, the value of the macro call augments the current parameter being evaluated, and evaluation of actual parameters continues with the semicolon following the macro call.   However, side effects, such as those which occur if the macro call is a DEF macro, are added to the P chain or the environment chain during the macro call.   In the present example evaluation of the parameter X$DEF,B,C;Z would result in temporary pushing down of the F chain during evaluation of the DEF macro.   On completion of execution of the DEF macro the macro definition B with value C would be added to the environment chain, a null value would be placed in the F chain, and complete evaluation of the parameter would result in the value XZ.   Evaluation of the parameter Y$B; would then result in the value YC.   The final semicolon would transfer the macro A from the F chain to the P chain and initiate a call of A with actual parameters X and YC and a temporary macro B.   On completion of the call the value would be placed in the output stream, actual-parameter stream, or macro-definition table, depending on its context, and the complete P chain generated by the macro call including the macro definition for B would be deleted from the run-time stack.

3.2.5 GPM AS A SYMBOL-STREAM PROCESSOR

Macro evaluation may be thought of as a process of scanning symbols in a source stream and moving them to a target stream.   The identity of the source and target streams and the mode of scanning are determined by the *scanning mode*.   The scanning modes that may occur in GPM are the following:

1.   *The Copying Mode.*   In the absence of macro definitions and macro calls the normal scanning mode is the copying mode.   In the copy-

ing mode the source stream is the input stream, the target stream is the output stream, and the scanner performs literal copying.   In assemblers or other transliterative processes literal copying is replaced by transliterative encoding.

2.   *The Macro-expansion Mode.*   This mode is entered when a semicolon terminating a set of actual parameters is encountered.   In the macro-expansion mode the source stream is a macro body in the definition table.   The target stream may be the output stream, the macro-definition table, or the run-time stack, depending on the context of the macro call.

3.   *The Macro-definition Mode.*   This mode is entered on a macro call of the system macro DEF.   The target stream in the macro-definition mode is the macro-definition table.   The source stream may be the input stream, the run-time stack, or the macro-definition table, depending on the context of the macro definition.

4.   *The Parameter-evaluation Mode.*   This mode is entered when a $ sign is encountered in scanning the source stream.   The target stream in the parameter-evaluation mode is the macro-expansion stack.   The source stream may be the input stream, the run-time stack, or the macro-definition table, depending on the context of the macro definition.

5.   *The Parameter-substitution Mode.*   Entered when a formal-parameter marker is encountered during macro expansion, this mode causes switching of the source stream from the macro-definition table to an actual-parameter stream in the run-time stack.   The target stream remains the same as that of the macro expansion in which it occurs.

6.   *The Quote Mode.*   This mode is entered when an opening quote is encountered while in one of the other modes.   It causes copying from the source to the destination obtaining before the quote mode was entered, ignoring all control symbols other than matching quotes.   Exit from the quote mode occurs when a symbol ⟩ matching the opening quote ⟨ is encountered.

3.2.6 GPM EXECUTION ALGORITHM

The operation of GPM is illustrated by the flow diagram in Fig. 3.3. The basic scanning algorithm may receive its input from the input medium or the definition table and may send its output to the definition table, parameter stack, or output medium.   Information in the parameter stack must be moved to the expansion stack before it is used as input. Information input from the expansion stack in the parameter-substitution mode bypasses the basic scanning algorithm, since parameters are assumed to be already evaluated.

In order to complete the specification of GPM actions it is necessary to specify the action determined by each of the control characters.   These actions can be specified as follows:

$ Push down the run-time stack and prepare to evaluate a new set of actual parameters.

; Tag the set of parameters at the top of the run-time stack as being completed, by linking them to the top of the P chain. Find the symbol-table stream associated with the named macro in the macro-definition table. If a macro with this name is found, switch to the

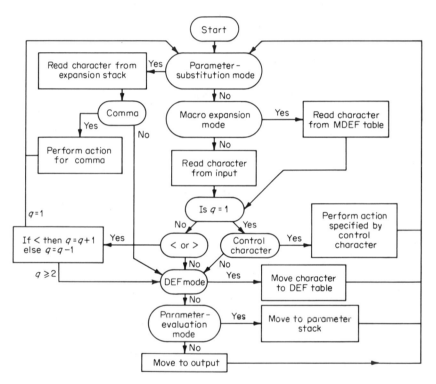

Figure 3.3 Flow diagram for GPM execution algorithm.

macro-expansion mode, using the definition-table entry as the source stream. Otherwise, check list of system macros and execute a system subroutine if this is a system macro. If not, print error diagnostic.

ω This symbol is encountered in the macro-definition table in terminating a macro expansion. Pop up the top layer of parameters on the run-time stack and remove temporary macro definitions. Return to mode of source-string scanning prior to entry to the macro; i.e., if there are no parameter records in the stack, return to the copying mode.

If the top record is a partially completed record, return to parameter-expansion mode. If the top record is a completed record, return to the macro-expansion mode.

,   The comma is a separator between parameters that can be directly copied or transliterated into an internal symbol. It acts as a terminator for parameter evaluation when encountered in the parameter-evaluation mode and as a terminator for substitution when encountered in the parameter-substitution mode.

$\sim$ Parameters $\sim i$ are substituted by actual parameters in the macro-expansion mode and copied otherwise. Thus when $\sim i$ is encountered, a check is made to determine whether the macro-expansion mode is on. If so, the ith actual parameter is substituted without evaluation for the formal parameter, provided there are at least i actual parameters. If there are fewer than i actual parameters, an error diagnostic results. If the macro-expansion mode is off, copy $\sim i$ to the destination without substitution.

<   Increment q by 1.

>   If $q = 1$, print an error diagnostic; if $q > 1$, decrement q by 1.

Exercise: Draw flow diagrams for the actions for each of the control characters and for the system macros DEF, VAL, UPDATE.

Project: Implement GPM or a subset of GPM.

GPM is a general-purpose symbol-stream processor. This discussion of implementation of GPM serves to illustrate both how a substitutive symbol-stream processor can be simulated on a conventional computer and how it could be executed directly on a computer with an arbitrary number of associatively addressed variable-length registers and a structured run-time stack with variable-length entries consisting of sets of actual parameters associated with macro calls. Access to selected items of information in the run-time stack can be accomplished in a read-only mode but not in a read-write mode.

Although GPM is general-purpose, a number of arbitrary decisions were taken with regard to its syntactic form, the order of evaluation of arguments, and the order in which operators are applied to operands. Among these decisions are the following:

1. The strings which constitute the name and arguments of a macro call are always evaluated before being applied to their operands. In the macro-assembly system of Chap. 2 arguments were always substituted for operands in their unevaluated form. It will be seen in the

discussion of the lambda calculus and ALGOL-like language that the question of order of evaluation of operators and operands arises in every function-evaluation language, giving rise to interesting theoretical and practical considerations.

2.   Actual parameters are not reevaluated when they are substituted for formal parameters, since their values are assumed to have been found during the parameter-evaluation phase of macro expansion.

Further details on the GPM system and its evaluation can be found in [1].   In the next section a macro generator with different syntax and evaluation rules is discussed.

3.3 TRAC—A SYSTEM FOR TEXT AND MACRO HANDLING

3.3.1 READ, PRINT, DEFINITION, CALL, AND SEGMENT-STRING FACILITIES

In the present section a system called TRAC† (text reckoner and compiler) developed by Mooers and Deutsch [2, 3] will be considered.   TRAC has an instruction format similar to that of GPM, but it differs from GPM in that there is a clear-cut distinction between system macros and programmer-defined macros.   GPM allows the names of both system macros and programmer-defined macros to occur in the first argument position, while TRAC reserves the first argument position for names of system macros and requires programmer-defined macros to be specified in the second argument position.   The basic instruction format of TRAC is as follows:

$\#(PF,P_1,P_2, \ldots ,P_k)$ Apply the primitive function specified by PF using the parameters $P_1, P_2, \ldots , P_k$.

This instruction format is analogous to the GPM instruction format "$\$N,P_1, \ldots ,P_k;$", where $\$$ corresponds to $\#($ and ; corresponds to).   Both TRAC and GPM allow arbitrary strings to occur in the position corresponding to N, but in TRAC the string must evaluate to one of a fixed set of system function names.   Thus the TRAC symbols $\#($ correspond to the concept "call system macro," while GPM allows either a system macro or a programmer-defined macro to occur following the $\$$ sign.   The first argument field of a TRAC macro may be thought of as

† The name TRAC is a trademark for a specific text-handling language that was developed and is being maintained by the Rockford Research Institute Inc., Cambridge, Mass.   It is implemented at a number of institutions in Europe and the United States.   Since it is machine-independent, an exchange scheme for TRAC programs is in existence.   Serious implementers are urged to get in touch with the Rockford Research Institute in the interests of compatibility.

the operation field of a generalized instruction, where the operations permitted in the operation field are precisely the primitive TRAC functions.

The basic TRAC primitives perform input and output of strings, string (macro) definition and calling, and string segmentation.   Primitive TRAC functions are denoted by two-letter mnemonics as in the following examples:

#(rs)   (*read string*) Read from a typewriter a string of characters up to an end-of-string symbol.   The end-of-string symbol is normally the apostrophe but may be redefined to be any arbitrary character.

#(ps, string)   (*print string*) Print out on a typewriter the string of characters specified by the argument following ps.

The string to be printed as a result of executing a ps instruction is determined by evaluating the second argument and then printing the result.

#(ps,#(rs))   The value of the second argument is the value of the function read in by executing the rs instruction.

#(ps, This is a cat)   In this case the second argument is a constant which yields itself on evaluation.   This expression causes print-out of the text.   "This is a cat".

The rs and ps primitives above are designed to allow TRAC to be used as an interactive language in a time-sharing environment.
String (macro) definition is accomplished as follows:

#(ds,name,string)   (*define string*) Define the string determined by evaluating the second parameters to have as its name the string obtained by evaluating the first parameter.

#(ds,XYZ,#(rs))   Read in a string, evaluate it, and name the string *XYZ*.

#(ds,#(rs),XYZ)   Read in a string, evaluate it, and use it as the name of the string *XYZ*.

String (macro) calling is accomplished by the cl primitive described below:

#(cl,name)   (*call*) Call the expression named in the name field and evaluate it.   Replace this instruction by the resulting value.

#(cl,XYZ)   Replace this instruction by the value of the expression named XYZ.

The above string-definition and string-calling facilities permit storing and loading of unparametrized strings in the TRAC memory. Formal parameters can be associated with strings by means of the following instruction:

#(ss,name,p_1, . . . ,p_k)   (*segment string*) First evaluate the name and parameters. Then call the named string and replace occurrences of p_i in the string by parameter markers for $i = 1, 2, . . . , k$. Then store the resulting string back in the memory. Parameter markers are assigned by first replacing all instances of p_1 by parameter markers from left to right and then replacing all instances of p_i by parameter markers for successive values of i.

#(ss,XYZ,cat)   If the named string XYZ has the form "This is a cat", then the constituent cat is replaced by a parameter marker.

Parameter markers may be replaced by actual parameters using a generalized call instruction.

#(cl,name,a_1, . . . ,a_l)   Call the named string and replace all instances of the parameter marker p_i by the actual parameter a_i. If the number l of parameters a_i in the generalized call instruction is less than the number k specified in the segment-string instruction, segment gaps corresponding to markers p_{l+1} through P_k are replaced by null strings. If $l > k$, excess parameters a_{k+1}, . . . , a_l are ignored.

#(cl,XYZ,dog)   If the form named XYZ has the value "This is a p_1", where p_1 is an internal parameter marker, this instruction has the value "This is a dog".

#(ps,#(cl,XYZ,mouse))   If the form named XYZ has the same value as in the previous example, this instruction results in print-out of the expression "This is a mouse".

3.3.2 ACTIVE-STRING, NEUTRAL-STRING, AND ALTERNATIVE EVALUATION MODES

TRAC may be thought of as a symbol-stream scanner which has three different evaluation modes. The symbol-stream scanning mechanism differs from that of GPM principally in that TRAC always takes as the source stream for evaluative scanning the fixed stream known as the *active-string stack*. Operations such as *read string* and *define string*, which in GPM result in switching to a designated source stream, are implemented in TRAC by first copying the string to be scanned to the top of the active-string stack and then scanning it from the active-string stack. Thus the next instruction to be executed when execution of a given instruction has been completed is always found at the top of the active-string stack.

TRAC permits primitive-function calls in parameters, just like GPM, and therefore requires a stack for pushing down partially and completely evaluated parameter strings. The pointers required to access stack components can be stored either within the stack itself or in a separate parameter-pointer stack. The second alternative was chosen by Deutsch in his TRAC implementation. The run-time stack in which evaluated parameters are stored is referred to in [2] as the *neutral-string stack*.

Primitive-function evaluation in TRAC is triggered† by the control-symbol pair #(, which causes the interpreter to defer evaluation of the current function and to perform parameter evaluation of the inner function until a matching) is encountered. The matching) causes the primitive function specified by the first parameter to be applied, using the remaining parameters as arguments. The application of the primitive function to its arguments may be thought of as producing a "value" and possibly a number of side effects, which include creation of new streams and modification of the value of existing streams. The value produced by application of a primitive function preceded by #(to its arguments is now placed at the head of the active string and is again scanned.

The mode of function evaluation initiated by the control symbols #(is referred to as the *active mode*, since the string resulting from the function evaluation is placed at the head of the active string. Scanning of the active string is resumed, beginning with this new value string. TRAC includes two additional modes of output from string scanning referred to respectively as the *neutral mode* and the *quote mode*. The neutral mode is initiated by the control symbols ##(, and the quote mode is initiated by the control symbol (.

##(PF,p₁, . . . p_k)   Apply the primitive *PF* using the parameters $p_1, \ldots, p_k$, but do not perform further evaluation of the result; i.e., place the value obtained on application of the primitive function to its arguments in the neutral string and continue scanning the active string in the normal manner.

(expression)   If an opening parenthesis not preceded by # is encountered in scanning the active string, copy the active-string symbols to the neutral string, ignoring control symbols (other

† The control-symbol combinations ##(and (introduced below also trigger parameter evaluation.

than parentheses) until a matching closing parenthesis is encountered. Parentheses must be counted in order to find the matching closing parenthesis.

3.3.3 THE IDLING INSTRUCTION

When TRAC executes a sequence of instructions, it is presumed initially to have an instruction of the form "#(ps,#(rs))" in the active string.   This instruction is referred to as the *idling instruction*.   Execution of the idling instruction causes a string terminated by the standard termination character to be read from the typewriter into the active string.   It is then evaluated and printed, leaving a null string in the active string. When the TRAC algorithm finds a null string in the active string, it automatically replaces the null string by a new idling instruction, so that the cycle of read-in, evaluation, and printing is repeated.

3.3.4 THE TRAC EVALUATION ALGORITHM

Execution of a TRAC instruction is performed by scanning successive characters in the active string and performing certain actions depending

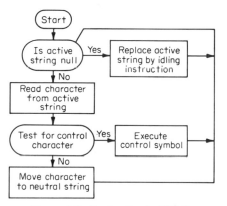

Figure 3.4   Evaluation in TRAC.

on the character being scanned.   Characters are normally copied from the active to the neutral string unless one of a number of control symbols is encountered.   The control symbols in the subset of TRAC so far discussed are the opening function parentheses, #(, ##(, (, the comma, and the terminating parenthesis) .   The basic TRAC evaluation algorithm is given by the simple algorithm shown in Fig. 3.4.

The actions of each of the TRAC control symbols are as follows:

#(Mark the current point in the neutral string as the beginning of a new function to be evaluated in the active mode.

44

4

##(Mark the current current point in the neutral string as the beginning of a new function to be evaluated in the neutral mode.

(If not in the quote mode, initiate the quote mode and copy symbols to the neutral string until a matching end parenthesis is encountered. If in the quote mode, increment a parenthesis counter by 1.

, Mark the beginning of a new argument in the neutral string.

) If in the quote mode, decrement the parenthesis count by 1 and check for termination of the quote mode. Otherwise execute the most recent function call in the neutral-string stack by applying the function which constitutes the first argument to the remaining arguments. When function evaluation is completed, remove the function and its arguments from the neutral stack and place the value produced by execution of this function on the active- or neutral-string stack, depending on whether the evaluation was in the active or neutral mode.

The closing parenthesis initiates execution of primitive functions and thus the bulk of the computation. Execution of primitive functions may in turn be accomplished by table look-up in a primitive-function table followed by transfer of control to a subroutine for executing the primitive function. New primitive functions can be added to TRAC relatively easily by adding new entries in the primitive-function table.

Example: In scanning the idling instruction #(ps,#(rs)), the first instance of #(causes a pointer to be set up to the beginning of the neutral string, indicating a function call. The characters ps, are then moved to the neutral string, the comma resulting in a pointer in the pointer stack pointing to the beginning of a new argument. The second instance of #(results in a pointer to the current point in the neutral string indicating an inner function to be evaluated before the outer function starting at the beginning of the stack. The characters rs are then moved to the neutral string. The symbol) then specifies execution of the most recent function call, which is rs. rs causes an expression to be read into the active string and to be evaluated using the above algorithm. When the expression is evaluated, its value will appear on the neutral string. The final symbol) then activates the function ps (which is now the top function in the neutral string), and ps prints out the evaluated parameter following the comma.

In order to complete the specification of TRAC it is necessary to specify the effect of executing each of the primitive functions. The effect of the five primitive functions introduced above is as follows:

rs Read from the input medium until a terminating character is encountered. If the input medium has no characters waiting to be read in and the terminating character has not yet been encountered, wait for further input.   rs is a parameterless function whose value is the string that is read in.   If rs is executed in the active mode, its value is placed in the active string.   If rs is executed in the neutral mode, its value is placed in the neutral string.

ps   Print into the output medium the value of the first argument.
      ps has a null value, so that there is no difference between active and passive execution.   It has a side effect consisting of the printed string.   However, this side effect cannot influence subsequent computation.

ds   Enter the evaluated second argument of ds into the definition table and christen it with the name specified by the first argument. ds, like ps, has a null value.   It has a side effect of creating a new definition and of destroying previous definitions having that name. The side effect produced by ds may affect the subsequent computation.

ss   In the definition-table string named by the first parameter of ss, successively replace occurrences of the second and following parameters by formal-parameter markers.   ss results in a relatively complex transformation of the string in the definition stack.   The result depends on the order in which parameter markers are substituted for occurrences of parameters in the string.   The function ss has a null value and has the side effect of inserting formal-parameter markers into the defined string with which it is associated.

cl   The value of the function cl consists of the definition-table string named by the first parameter with actual parameters from the neutral string substituted without evaluation for formal-parameter markers.   If the evaluation mode is active, the resulting value is moved to the active string for further evaluation.   If the evaluation mode is passive, the value is placed in the neutral string, and scanning is continued with the next character of the active string.

The rs, ps, ds, and cl functions all involve scanning a source stream and placing the result in a target stream.   However, TRAC replaces direct scanning of a source stream by a multistage operation of first copying into a standard stream (the active-string stack), followed by evaluative scanning from the active string using the neutral string for temporary storage, followed by placing the value in the active-string stack when in the active mode and in the neutral-string stack when in the neutral mode.   The presence of active- and neutral-mode evaluation increases the flexibility of the language but introduces a certain esthetic untidiness, since the notion of neutral evaluation does not seem to fit into a well-defined functional-evaluation pattern.   One of the consequences is that the specification of new TRAC primitives (with active- and neutral-evaluation facilities) in TRAC itself becomes impossible.   It would be convenient if a facility existed whereby TRAC functions defined by the use of ds and ss could be subsequently used as first arguments in the same way as primitive functions so that a defined function fn in the first position followed by actual parameters would have the same effect as a call of the function followed by the same parameters.   However, a number of problems arise in trying to simultaneously make

$$\#(\mathrm{fn},\mathrm{p}_1, \ldots ,\mathrm{p}_k) \equiv \#(\mathrm{cl},\mathrm{fn},\mathrm{p}_1, \ldots ,\mathrm{p}_k)$$
$$\#\#(\mathrm{fn},\mathrm{p}_1, \ldots ,\mathrm{p}_k) \equiv \#\#(\mathrm{cl},\mathrm{fn},\mathrm{p}_1, \ldots ,\mathrm{p}_k)$$

Problem: Develop a scheme for modifying TRAC which allows TRAC functions to be specified in TRAC and called as though they were primitive functions.

The difference in effect between evaluation in the active mode, passive mode, and quote mode is further illustrated by the following example taken from [2].

Example: Assume that the following definitions have been made:

#(ds,A,CAT)	Define A to have the value CAT.
#(ds,B,(#(cl,A)))	Define B to have the value #(cl,A).

The three following instructions illustrate the difference between different forms of evaluation:

#(ps,(#(cl,B)))	Prints out the character string #(cl,B).
#(ps,##(cl,B))	Prints out the character string #(cl,A).
#(ps,#(cl,B))	Prints out the character string CAT.

The TRAC system as described in [2] has a number of additional primitives, namely, two conditional-instruction primitives; a number of primitives for scanning and manipulating parts of forms; two primitives for deleting forms from storage; and primitives for performing arithmetic and Boolean operations, for management of auxiliary storage, and for performing diagnostic and tracing functions.

3.3.5   ADDITIONAL TRAC PRIMITIVES

The two conditional-instruction primitives are as follows:

#(eq,X1,X2,X3,X4)	If $X1$ is equal to $X2$, the function value is $X3$; otherwise it is $X4$.

#(gr,D1,D2,X1,X2)   If the decimal number $D1$ is greater than $D2$, the function value is $X1$; otherwise the function value is $X2$.

In order to perform operations on portions of defined strings (*forms*) in the TRAC memory, each form has an associated *form pointer*, which at any given instant points to a given character of the character string stored in the TRAC memory. There are four instructions for retrieving parts of strings and incrementing the form pointer:

#(cc,N,Z)   (*call character*) Replace this instruction by the character pointed to by the form pointer of the definition named N and increment the form pointer by 1. If the form pointer points beyond the last character of the form, the value of this instruction is Z. Segment gaps are skipped.

#(cn,N,D,Z)   (*call n characters*) Read D characters of the form named N, starting at the character pointed to by the form pointer, and increment the form pointer by D. If D is negative, read characters preceding the form pointer. If no characters are available, the value of the function is Z.

#(cs,N,Z)   (*call segment*) The value of this function is the string from the current position of the form pointer to the end of the next segment gap. The form pointer is moved beyond the segment gap. If the pointer is initially beyond the last character of the form, the value of the function is Z.

#(in,N,X,Z)   (*initial*) Search the form named N for the first occurrence of the string X following the current pointer position in the form named N. If the match is found, the function value is the portion of the form between the form pointer and the matched string, and the pointer is moved to the first character beyond the matched string. If no match is found, the pointer is not moved, and the value of the function is Z.

The "fail" value of Z is in each case placed in the active string and rescanned.

These four functions provide elementary string-processing facilities within forms. Scanning of forms is permitted by character count, by segment-gap recognition, and by general string matching. The form pointer can be reset to point to the beginning of a form by the following instruction:

#(cr,N)   (*call restore*) This null-valued function restores the pointer of the form named N to its initial character.

There are two TRAC functions for deleting definitions:

#(dd,N1,N2, . . .)   (*delete definition*) This null-valued function deletes the definitions named $N1$, $N2$, . . . from the TRAC memory and removes their names from the list of names.

#(da)   (*delete all*) This null-valued function deletes all definitions from the memory and removes their names.

The following example illustrates use of the da primitive within a ds instruction and gives some insight into the order in which evaluation of TRAC instruction is performed.

#(ds,N,##(cl,N)#(da))   Evaluation of ##(cl,N)#(da) results in placing the symbol-table value of N in the neutral string without further evaluation, followed by execution of the null-valued function #(da), which deletes all forms from the TRAC memory. Having evaluated all arguments, the primitive ds is then applied to its arguments, resulting in redefinition of the form N with its value prior to deletion.   If N contains segment gaps, these are replaced by the null string when ##(cl,N) is executed.   The new definition of N correreponds to the old one with segment gaps removed.

TRAC has the following facilities for integer arithmetic:

#(ad,D1,D2,Z)   (*add*) If no overflow, then $D1 + D2$, else Z.

#(su,D1,D2,Z)   (*subtract*) If no overflow, then $D1 - D2$, else Z.

#(ml,D1,D2,Z)   (*multiply*) If no overflow, then $D1 \times D2$, else Z.

#(dv,D1,D2,Z)   (*divide*) If no overflow, then $D1/D2$, else Z.

The following example illustrates how the factorial function can be defined in TRAC:

#(ds,fact,(#(eq,1,n,1,(#(ml,n,#(cl,fact,#(ad,n,-1,0)),0)))))
#(ss,fact,n)

The first line above defines fact to be the function within parenthesis quotes.   The second line identifies n as a formal parameter of the function. Having executed the two statements above, the factorial function can be called as follows:

#(cl,fact,5)   This function call yields the value 120.

The procedure call for the factorial function can be reduced to the form "fact,5" by arranging for the text to be read in under the control of an interpreter which supplies the additional symbols automatically. This interpreter is given by the function embed

#(ds,embed,(#(ps,#(cl,#(rs))(*CR LF*))#(cl,embed)))†

It defines embed as a function which, when it is called, prints the value of the string #(cl,#(rs)), then prints *CR LF*, and finally again calls itself. In order to perform its action, embed reads in a string S, embeds it in an environment #(cl,S(*CR LF*)), and executes the string. If S is "fact,5", then execution of embed leads to evaluation of #(cl,fact,5) followed by a print-out of the result and then a further call to embed. In this simple way it is possible to overlay the basic interpreter provided by the idling instruction by a higher-level interpreter. For many purposes these overlays provide enhanced user convenience by facilitating simple command languages. Such overlays can be stacked to an indefinite number of levels.

TRAC has the following facilities for operations on logical vectors of zeros and ones, expressed in octal notation:

#(bu,V1,V2)   (*Boolean union*) $V1 \cup V2$

#(bi,V1,V2)   (*Boolean intersection*) $V1 \wedge V2$

#(bs,D1,D2)   (*Boolean shift*) Shift $V1$ left $D1$ places. If $D1 < 0$, shift right $D1$ places.

#(br,D1,V1)   (*Boolean rotate*) Rotate $V1$ left $D1$ places. If $D1 < 0$, rotate right $D1$ places.

#(bc,V1)   (*Boolean complement*) $\neg V1$

Forms created by TRAC can be moved to auxiliary storage by the instruction

#(sb,N,N1,N2, . . .)   (*store block*) This null-valued function stores the forms $N1$, $N2$, . . . as a single record of auxiliary storage and calls this flock N. All pointers are saved. A form named N having as content the auxiliary-storage address is set up in the processor.

Information stored by an sb instruction is retrieved by the following instruction:

#(fb,N)   (*fetch block*) This null-valued function fetches from auxiliary storage the forms stored in the block named N.

† *CR* and *LF* respectively denote the function's carriage return and line feed.

Blocks in auxiliary storage can be erased by the following instruction:

#(eb,N)   (*erase block*) This null-valued function erases the block named N in auxiliary storage and any defined block named N.

Because the "hardware address" is accessible through #(cl,N), it is therefore possible to create a great variety of chain- and list-structured types of auxiliary-memory organization, still retaining the facility of retrieval by name.

The diagnostic facilities available in TRAC are the following:

#(ln,X)   (*list names*) List all names in the pair list with each name preceded by string X. If X is the character pair *CR LF*, names are listed in a column.

#(pf,N)   (*print definition*) This function results in print-out of the form named N with its segment-gap markers indicated.

#(tn)   (*trace on*) This null-valued function initiates the trace mode, in which instructions are executed one at a time. Evaluated arguments of each primitive operation are printed out prior to evaluation, and the machine stops. The backspace key or *CR* key causes tracing of the next function. Pressing any other key causes the trace mode to be switched off.

#(tf)   (*trace off*) Switch off the trace mode (programmed exit).

A TRAC system is normally implemented so that execution of individual operation codes is accomplished interpretively by consulting a primitive-function code table and transferring control to a subroutine for executing the primitive function. With this form of organization new primitive functions can be added one at a time as they occur to the user without affecting the rest of the system.

TRAC is a "functional" language which executes instructions by replacing the string of characters constituting the instruction by its value and possibly causing side effects in the TRAC memory, in the input-output medium, or in the state information that determines the mode of operation of the TRAC processor. In functional languages the distinction between instructions and data becomes blurred, since the values which replace instructions may consist either of further instructions to be evaluated or of data items which serve as arguments of higher-level instructions. In the TRAC processor there is a clear distinction between strings which are to be treated as instructions and strings which are to be treated as data. This is made possible by placing strings to be executed as instructions in the active string and those to be used as data in the neutral string. The initial instructions are placed in the active string.   Arguments of an instruction are initially in the active string and thus are treated as instructions when they are encountered.

Evaluation of a string having initial characters #(results in a value which is placed in the active string for further execution.   Evaluation of a string having initial characters (or ##(results in a value which is placed in the neutral string and is thus treated as data.   Evaluation of constants which do not contain control characters results in copying the string to the neutral string, so that constants may be regarded as instruction strings which yield themselves as data items on evaluation.

A TRAC processor for interpreting the TRAC language on a conventional one-address computer is a relatively simple program, consisting of perhaps 2,000 machine-language instructions.   If the TRAC processor is programmed in reentrant code, the processor can be used by a number of users simultaneously.   Thus the TRAC processor can serve as a basis for time-shared use of a computer from a number of different typewriter consoles.   Each user has a private active string, neutral string, storage for form variables, storage for pointers which keep track of the organization of the active and neutral strings, and storage for state variables of the TRAC processor.   The scheduling and allocation of computer processing time for each TRAC user can be performed by a supervisory time-sharing programming system.   If the users all use the TRAC system, the scheduler can be built into the TRAC interpreter.

Exercises: (a) Write a TRAC processor for implementing the basic TRAC scanning algorithm and a selected set of TRAC primitives.   (b) Compare parameter specification techniques in TRAC, GPM, and macro assemblers.

3.4   MACRO TEMPLATES AND SYNTAX MACROS

3.4.1   SYMBOL-TABLE LOOK-UP BY TEMPLATE MATCHING

In the macro languages discussed above it was assumed that macros had simple names and that matching the name associated with a macro call against successive entries of the macro-definition table was a relatively trivial matter.   This requirement placed a restriction on the format of macro calls, requiring them to consist of a name followed by actual parameters or of some other equally simple format.   In the present section the restriction that macro calls have a fixed format will be relaxed. The format permitted on macro call will be allowed to vary widely and will effectively constitute a pattern to be matched by a pattern-matching routine.   A macro definition will consist of two parts:† (1) a macro-definition pattern, called a *template,* consisting of a sequence of fixed (constant) components separated by parameter markers which are

† This format is similar to that of macros in the LIMP language [11].

matched by actual-parameter strings of a macro call and (2) a macro body consisting of a sequence of fixed components separated by parameter markers having the form $\sim i$, where i refers to the ith parameter marker of the corresponding template.

The set of macro definitions is stored in a macro-definition table, just as in more conventional macro generators. The template corresponds to the macro name. A macro call results in an attempt to match successive templates of the macro-definition table by matching fixed components of the templates exactly and matching parameter markers of the template by symbol strings of the macro call. When a template match occurs, the symbol strings of the macro call which are matched against actual-parameter markers become the actual parameters of that call. Macro expansion is accomplished by replacing the symbol string matched by a template by the corresponding macro body with actual parameters substituted for formal parameters $\sim i$ of the macro body.

Let $*$ be a parameter-marker symbol disjoint from other symbols of the symbol string and let ; be the string-termination symbol. The following example gives a macro definition with two parameters followed by three different calls of the macro.

AB$*$CD$*$EF;   This macro definition consists of a template AB$*$
UV$\sim$2XY$\sim$1Z;   CD$*$EF and a body UV$\sim$2XY$\sim$1Z, where $\sim$1
and $\sim$2 refer to the first and second formal parameters of the template. The template has three fixed components separated by parameters.

ABLMNCDPEF   This macro call will match the template AB$*$CD$*$
EF with $\sim$1 = LMN and $\sim$2 = P. On expansion the macro yields $UVPXYLMNZ$.

ABCDEF   This macro call will also match the template with $\sim$1 = $\sim$2 = the empty string. On expansion the macro yields $UVXYZ$.

ABCDCDEFEFEF   This macro call can be matched by the template in a number of alternative ways. A convention must be adopted regarding the order in which matching is attempted.

One possible convention is to match successive fixed components against the earliest possible instance of their occurrence. Using this convention, the template would in the above case match $ABCDCDEF$ with $\sim$1 = null and $\sim$2 = CD.

3.4.2 AMBIGUITY AND BACKTRACKING

Additional conventions are required when two templates with different structure both match a portion of the scanned text starting at the same character. In this case the most convenient convention to adopt is that the most recently defined macro that matches the given string is to be used. This convention is a generalization of the convention that the most recently defined macro having a given name is the one that is current.†

It should be noted that the sequence of fixed components of a template constitutes a generalized macro name. Instead of being given as a single constituent, the macro name is *distributed* throughout the template and is referred to as a *distributed name*. Whereas matching a name consisting of a single constituent can be performed directly, matching a distributed name requires a relatively complex pattern-matching process for its implementation.

A number of string-manipulation languages, such as COMIT [13] and SNOBOL [14], have primitive pattern-matching operations. In such languages matching strings against a sequence of patterns is performed by specifying the sequence of patterns as a program. In the present case, the order in which strings are matched against a sequence of patterns is built into the interpreter. The order in which pattern matching is attempted is determined implicitly by the order in which macros are defined rather than explicitly by means of a program.

Complex pattern matching in template recognition can be avoided by imposing restrictions on the form of template-specification strings and on the form of strings that constitute macro calls. For example, if macro calls are always introduced by a distinguished symbol such as $ and terminated by a distinguished symbol such as ;, the strings that are to be matched against templates are always well defined. However, the problems of ambiguous matching and matching by more than one template still exist in this case.

3.4.3 PATTERN MATCHING WITH KEYWORDS

The problem of matching by more than one template can be avoided by requiring each template to be characterized by a unique keyword. The keyword can be regarded as the name of the macro defined by the template. However, the remaining part of the macro may have fixed portions and parameter markers, allowing for a greater variety of format than in the traditional case.

---

† In some pattern-matching processes, such as syntactic analysis, there is a requirement that the complete string match a given higher-level pattern by successive matching of substrings to lower-level patterns. In this case a given substring may be locally matched by a number of different patterns, but the process of matching the complete string to the higher-level pattern may be possible only for a specific sequence of matching of lower-level patterns. The patterns are usually thought of as being simultaneously defined. If choice of a given pattern is found not to lead to matching at the higher level, a systemic technique of *backtracking* and choosing an alternative pattern is used.

The problem of ambiguity can be avoided by requiring that the alphabet used for specifying fixed components of templates be disjoint from the alphabet for specifying parameters. Although this restriction may appear to be unduly severe, it is a reasonable one in a number of actual applications.

The problem of template matching is made even simpler if the keyword associated with the template is the first symbol string of the macro. This allows the template associated with a macro to be uniquely determined by scanning the initial symbol string. If the remaining symbols of the given string do not match the template, an error has occurred.

Templates with an initial keyword have been used by Leavenworth [10] for the purpose of defining new statement forms within problem-oriented languages such as ALGOL. Macros were initially applied in assembly languages to define new operations within symbolic machine language in terms of sequences of given primitive symbolic instructions. In assembly-language macros the format of new operations was always a name followed by operations. However, in problem-oriented languages it is sometimes convenient to define new composite operations as more complex structures with a number of fixed portions and a number of parameter positions.

3.4.4 TYPE SPECIFICATION FOR MACRO PARAMETERS

In the previous discussion it was assumed that all parameters in a template were of the same type in the sense that the class of actual parameters which could be substituted for each parameter was assumed to be the same. However, it is sometimes convenient to be able to specify that different classes of strings be substituted for different parameter markers. For example, parameters of a new operation format in a problem-oriented language might be required to be integers, simple names (identifiers), arithmetic expressions, or any one of a number of other structures.

In order to permit a number of different predefined parameter types to be specified within symbol strings, it is necessary merely to have a distinguished symbol for each of the parameter types used in templates to indicate that only a parameter of the given type is to be permitted as an actual parameter of the macro call. The template-matching algorithm must include a test to check that successive parameters of a matched template are of the type required by the parameter.

Leavenworth [10] allows parameters of a number of different types to be defined within templates. Moreover, he includes a facility in his macro system for defining the types of actual parameters. Specification of the type of parameter requires specification of the set of strings that is acceptable as an actual parameter.   Thus a notation for specifying sets of strings is required to specify classes of actual parameters.

Leavenworth uses the notation of context-free grammars to specify sets (see Appendix 1).   In his paper he gives examples of specification of new structures in a language that is close to ALGOL.   We shall use the language and grammar developed in Appendix 1 to illustrate Leavenworth's notions.

3.4.5 APPLICATION TO SYNTAX MACROS

The following example of syntax macros parallels one by Leavenworth. It should be skipped by the reader unfamiliar with ALGOL and reviewed after reading Chap. 4 and Appendix 2.

If the **for** statement were not available in ALGOL, iteration could be achieved instead by using conditional statements.   Thus the following two ALGOL programs are equivalent (see Chap. 4):

```
for I := 1 step 1 until N do      begin I := 1;
SUM := SUM + A[I];           L:   if I ≤ N then
                                  begin SUM := SUM + A[I];
                                    I := I + 1;
                                    go to L
                                  end
                             end
```

Generalizing the above equivalence, a template could be defined which allowed users to specify iteration by means of a **for** statement, but resulted in a macro expansion in terms of a conditional statement.   Such a facility could be implemented in an appropriate syntax macro system by the following template and macro body (see Appendix 2):

template for ⟨identifier⟩ := ⟨arithmetic expression⟩ **step** ⟨arithmetic expression⟩ **until** ⟨arithmetic expression⟩ **do** ⟨statement⟩

```
body begin ∼1 := ∼2;
   L:   if ∼1 ≤ ∼4 then
        begin ∼5; ∼1 := ∼1 + ∼3;
          go to L
        end
      end
```

Note that the template contains five parameters of three different types.   If the permitted strings associated with each parameter type are specified by a grammar, as in Appendix 2, checking for correct parameter types can be performed by a syntactic recognizer.

Syntax macros allow new syntactic forms to be introduced into higher-level languages, which on expansion result in instruction sequences of the higher-level language.   They are similar in function to assembler macros but allow a more flexible format both for macro calls and for macro expansion.†

Exercises: (*a*) Given the above *for* template, write out the macro expansion for the following macro call:

for K : = 1 **step** N **until** A[N] **do** X[K] : = Y[K] + Z[K];

(*b*) Compare template specification above with FORMAT specification in [19], emphasizing the alternative methods of identifying and specifying parameters.

3.4.6 PARAMETER TYPES AND SYNTAX SHARING

The introduction of parameter types into a macro language makes the process of matching a good deal more complex, particularly if the templates consist of arbitrary patterns. Matching of a template with parameter types requires checking for compatibility of parameter types at template-matching time. The parameters of such a macro are effectively set-valued variables, and the matching process checks whether the value assigned by the matching process is an element of the specified set.

The use of parameter types allows the fixed components of a distributed name to be interpreted in different ways depending on the context in which they occur in a macro pattern. Consider the macro pattern "$A + B \times C$" where $+$ and $\times$ are the fixed components of the templates and A, B, and C are values in parameter positions of the template. The interpretation of $+$ and $\times$ depends on the parameter types of A, B, and C.

Exercises: (*a*) What is the interpretation of $+$ and $\times$ when A, B, and C are of type *integer, real, complex, array?* (*b*) Under what circumstances can the types of A, B, and C be different in the same expression?

The facility of allowing fixed syntax components to have a different interpretation depending on their context is sometimes referred to as *syntax sharing*. In procedure-oriented languages, the type associated with a given component of the pattern being matched is not always evident from the literal form of the pattern itself but must be inferred from previously given type declarations. In this case pattern matching may require reference to auxiliary information associated with subpatterns corresponding to actual parameters.

Example: The types associated with A, B, and C in a pattern of the form $A + B \times C$ are not evident from the form of the expression itself. In a procedure-oriented language the types would be inferred from previously given declarations. If the expression $A + B \times C$ is regarded

† An alternative approach to the introduction of new syntactic forms into higher-level languages is developed by Brooker and Morris [19]. FORMAT specifications of this system are similar to the template specifications above. The relation between macro-definition facilities and syntactic-definition facilities is further discussed in Appendix 1.

as a macro pattern to be expanded at compile time into a form that takes account of the parameters A, B, and C, then a table which specifies identifier types must be available at compile time. Alternatively, if $A + B \times C$ is executed interpretively by a macro which determines types at execution time, the table which specifies types of identifiers must be available at execution time.

Exercises: (*a*) Design a marco system which has facilities for general macro pattern matching, parameters whose types may be determined either from their literal form or from a declaration, and syntax sharing. (*b*) Discuss the difference between assignment of values and attributes to macro names and macro parameters in various macro systems.

3.5   THE LAMBDA CALCULUS

3.5.1   LAMBDA EXPRESSIONS

The GPM and TRAC languages developed in the previous sections combine facilities for nested-function evaluation with sequential execution of instructions entered from an input medium and contain system functions that are not purely substitutive.   In the present section a language for "pure" function evaluation, known as the *lambda calculus* [4], will be developed.   The lambda calculus has a minimum number of primitives and no explicit facilities for execution of a sequence of instructions. However, the notion of instruction execution is nevertheless firmly embedded in the language.   In the lambda calculus, instruction execution corresponds essentially to substitution of values for bound variables. After showing that the lambda calculus is remarkably insensitive to the order in which instructions are executed (substitutions are performed), a number of alternative strategies for evaluation will be considered, each of which explicitly fixes the order of substitution.   This "pure" language serves to exhibit the basic structural characteristics underlying many existing programming languages and will serve as a model to which other programming languages can be compared.

The basic elements used in building expressions of the lambda calculus are called *variables*.   Variables will be represented by small letters, possibly followed by a subscript.   The set of all variables will be denoted by V.

Variables in a programming language normally take their values in some domain such as the integers, floating-point numbers, two-element set [0,1], etc.   The domain of variables of the lambda calculus is the set of all functions, where functions are represented in a notation to be developed below.   Since any domain of constants (such as the set of integers) can be thought of as a special class of functions, the domain of values of variables in the lambda calculus is broader than that of variables of a given type in a typical programming language.

The symbols in the alphabet of the lambda calculus are the set of variables V and the three special symbols λ (and). The permitted expressions of the lambda calculus are called *lambda expressions*. They are constructed from variables and the basic symbols by these rules:

1. A variable standing by itself is a lambda expression.

2. If M is a lambda expression and x is a variable, then $\lambda x M$ is a lambda expression. λx is said to be the *bound-variable part* of the lambda expression, and M is said to be the *body* of the lambda expression.

3. If F and A are two lambda expressions, then (FA) is a lambda expression. F is said to be the *operator part* of the lambda expression, and A is said to be the *operand part* of the lambda expression.

4. An expression is a lambda expression only if it can be constructed by the above three rules.†

Some examples of lambda expressions follow:

x This lambda expression consists of a single variable.

$\lambda x x$ This lambda expression has a bound variable part λx and a body x.

(xy) This lambda expression has an operator part x and an operand part y.

$(\lambda x x y)$ This lambda expression has an operator part $\lambda x x$ and an operand part y.

$\lambda x(xy)$ This lambda expression has a bound-variable part λx and a body (xy).

$(\lambda x x \lambda y y)$ This lambda expression has an operator part $\lambda x x$ and an operand part $\lambda y y$.

$\lambda x(x(yx))$ This lambda expression has a bound-variable part λx and a body $(x(yx))$.

$\lambda x \lambda y x$ This lambda expression has a bound-variable part λx and a body $\lambda y x$.

$\lambda x \lambda y(x \lambda x \lambda y y)$ This lambda expression has a bound-variable part λx and a body $\lambda y(x \lambda x \lambda y y)$, which in turn consists of a bound-variable part λy and a body $(x \lambda x \lambda y y)$.

3.5.2 FREE, BOUND, AND BINDING VARIABLES

Having defined the class of lambda expressions, we shall next define the rules of computation by which lambda expressions may be transformed

---

† These rules for specifying the form of lambda expressions are an example of a *structure specification*. Methods of structure specification are further discussed in Sec. 3.10.

into other lambda expressions. For this purpose it is convenient to classify variables into three categories, *binding* variables, *bound* variables, and *free* variables:

1. A variable is said to be a *binding variable* if it immediately follows the symbol λ.
2. A given instance of a variable x is said to be *bound* in a lambda expression M if it is a binding variable or if there is a lambda expression M' in M of the form $\lambda x M''$, where M'' includes this instance of x.
3. A given instance of a variable x is said to be *free* in a lambda expression M if it is not bound in M.

A variable x is said to *occur bound* in a lambda expression M if M contains a bound instance of x and to *occur free* in a lambda expression M if M contains a free instance of x.

Example: In the lambda expression $(\lambda x(xy)\lambda y(xy))$ the variable x occurs bound in $\lambda x(xy)$ and occurs free in $\lambda y(xy)$.

3.5.3 THE REDUCTION AND RENAMING RULES

Expressions of the form $\lambda x M$ represent one-argument functions which determine a rule of correspondence between arguments A and values obtained by substituting A for all free occurrences of x in M.† Expressions of the form (FA) are called *operator-operand combinations* and specify the application of the operator F to the operand A. If the operator F is a function of the form $\lambda x M$, then the effect of application of $\lambda x M$ to A is precisely the substitution of A for all free occurrences of x in M; that is, $(\lambda x M A)$ is an operator-operand combination with an operator part $\lambda x M$ and an operand part A. Its value is obtained by substitution of A for all free occurrences of x in M.

The above substitution rule is *the basic evaluation rule* of the lambda calculus and is referred to as a *reduction rule*. A single application of a reduction rule is referred to as a *reduction*, and will be denoted by →. Some examples of reductions are:

$(\lambda x x(yz)) \rightarrow (yz)$
$(\lambda x x \lambda x x) \rightarrow \lambda x x$
$(\lambda x(xy)\lambda z z) \rightarrow (\lambda z z y) \rightarrow y$
$(\lambda x(xx)\lambda x(xx)) \rightarrow (\lambda x(xx)\lambda x(xx))$ yielding a nonterminating reduction

† Occurrences of x in M are free provided they are not bound by an inner lambda expression of the form $\lambda x M$. For example, if $\lambda x M = \lambda x(x\lambda x x)$, the first occurrence of x in $M = (x\lambda x x)$ is free, while the other two occurrences are bound. The outer λx in $\lambda x(x\lambda x x)$ binds only the free occurrences of x in the body M. Inner bound variables may be uniformly replaced by other variables. Thus $\lambda x(x\lambda x x) \equiv \lambda x(x\lambda y y)$.

Lambda expressions may in general contain *free variables* with *externally defined* substitution properties

$$((\lambda x\lambda y((+\ x)y)1)4) \rightarrow (\lambda y((+\ 1)y)4) \rightarrow ((+\ 1)4) \rightarrow 5$$

In this example $+$ is a one-argument free variable which, when applied to an integer i, yields the function $(+i)$. When $(+i)$ is applied to an integer j, the integer $(i + j)$ is obtained.

$$(\lambda f(f(3) + f(4))\lambda x(x \times x))$$

In this example $\lambda x(x \times x)$ is the squaring function. When it is substituted for its two occurrences, the lambda expression becomes $3 \times 3 + 4 \times 4 = 25$.

The two above examples indicate that it is relatively easy to develop nontrivial lambda expressions if free variables with external meanings are permitted. However, in the discussion below, we are interested in the substitutive properties of the lambda calculus rather than in its development as a useful language.

The result of substitution of an argument A for *all* occurrences of a variable x in an expression M will be denoted by $S_A^x M$. In certain cases reduction of $(\lambda x M A)$ to $S_A^x M$ would result in unintended identification of distinct variables.

Examples: If $(\lambda x M A) = (\lambda x\lambda y(xy)(yz))$, then $S_A^x M = (\lambda y((yz)y))$, resulting in unintended identification of the free variable y of A with the bound variable y of M. If $(\lambda x M A) = (\lambda x(x\lambda x(xy))(uv))$, then $S_A^x M = ((uv)\lambda(uv)((uv)y))$, which is clearly not a well-formed expression. If the binding variable x of $\lambda x M$ occurs as a bound variable inside M, the inner bound occurrences of x are intended to denote a different variable.

Because of naming conflicts of this sort the reduction rule of the lambda calculus has the following form:

1. *Reduction Rule.* The expression $(\lambda x M A)$ can be replaced by $S_A^x M$ provided M contains no (inner) bound occurrences of x and provided A does not contain any free variables that are bound in M.

When, in an expression $(\lambda x M A)$, M contains bound occurrences of x or A contains free occurrences of variables bound in M, the reduction rule cannot be applied directly. However, naming conflicts can always be resolved by the following renaming rule for bound variables:

2. *Renaming Rule.* Let M be any well-formed part of a lambda expression other than a variable following the symbol λ. Then if x is a bound variable of M, M can be replaced by $S_y^x M$ provided M contains no free occurrences of x and y does not occur in M.

Examples: If $M = \lambda x(xy)$, then $S_z^x M = \lambda z(zy)$ is a legitimate application of the renaming rule, but $S_y^x M = \lambda y(yy)$ is not legitimate, since y occurs in

M. If $M = (x\lambda x(xy))$, then x cannot be renamed since it occurs free in M. However, if x occurs bound in M, there is always an expression $M' = \lambda xM$ in M which contains no free occurrences of x to which the renaming rule can be applied.

The above renaming and reduction rules completely specify the transformations which can be performed in lambda expressions.† The lambda calculus thus permits a simple specification of the set of permitted lambda expressions and of the way in which these expressions may be transformed. The specification of the set of permitted expressions of a programming language is referred to as its *syntax*, while the specification of the rules for transforming expressions of the language is referred to as its *semantics*. The lambda calculus has both a simple syntax and a simple semantics.

3.5.4 REDUCED FORMS AND VALUE CLASSES

The basic rule of computation of the lambda calculus is the reduction rule, since renaming is used merely to eliminate naming conflicts for the purpose of performing further reductions. A lambda expression to which no further reductions can be applied is said to be in *reduced form*. A lambda expression which is in reduced form can be thought of as an evaluated lambda expression.

Example: $(x(\lambda xx\lambda x(xy)))$ has a reduced form $(x\lambda x(xy))$.

A lambda expression for which there is no finite sequence of reduction rules resulting in a reduced-form expression is said to be *irreducible;* e.g., the lambda expression $(\lambda x(xx)\lambda x(xx))$ is irreducible. However, it can be shown that in general the question of whether a lambda expression is irreducible is undecidable [4].

Two formulas which can be converted into each other by application of renaming rules are said to be *equivalent* up to renaming. The set of all formulas which are equivalent is said to constitute a renaming equivalence class. For any renaming equivalence class a representative element can be chosen by imposing a lexicographic‡ ordering on the set of all variables and selecting names for successive bound variables according to this ordering, omitting free-variable names.

---

† It is relatively easy to pinpoint for a given lambda expression all subexpressions to which renaming can be applied and to pinpoint all subexpressions to which reduction can be applied. The effect of different orders of renaming and reduction for a given lambda expression is further discussed below.

‡ Assume that the set of variables is represented by the set of all strings over a finite alphabet. A lexicographic ordering is obtained by: imposing an "alphabetic" ordering on characters of the alphabet, ordering strings by the number of characters they contain, and ordering all strings having a given length alphabetically.

Example: Let a through z be the first 26 variables of the lexicographic ordering.   Then the lambda expression $\lambda x \lambda y ((xb)y)$ would have as the representative element of its renaming equivalence class the lambda expression $\lambda a \lambda c ((ab)c)$; that is, names are assigned to bound variables in the order of their occurrence when the expression is scanned from left to right.   The first bound variable is renamed a, while the second bound variable is renamed c since b occurs as a free variable of the lambda expression.

If a lambda expression is in reduced form, all lambda expressions which are equivalent up to renaming are also in reduced form.   A renaming equivalence class of reduced-form lambda expressions will be called a *value class*.   All lambda expressions of a given value class may be thought of as representing the same value.   This value is associated also with all nonreduced-form lambda expressions for which a reduction sequence exists reducing them to this value class.†

3.5.5 THE CHURCH-ROSSER THEOREM AND ORDER OF EVALUATION

In general there may be more than one order in which reductions can be applied to a given lambda expression to yield an irreducible lambda expression.   However, the following theorem indicates that two different orders of reducing a given lambda expression to reduced form always yield lambda expressions in the same value class.

Church-Rosser theorem: If a given lambda expression is reduced by two different reduction sequences, and if both reduction sequences lead to a reduced expression, then the two reduced expressions are in the same value class.‡

However, there are instances where one reduction sequence of a lambda expression leads to a reduced form while another reduction sequence is nonterminating.   This situation is illustrated by the lambda expression $(FA) = (\lambda x \lambda y y (\lambda x (xx) \lambda x (xx)))$.

† The lambda calculus can be thought of as a programming language in which the primitive instructions are renaming and reduction rules.   A computation in this programming language consists of the application of a sequence of such primitive instructions.   The computation is said to be complete when there is no way of renaming bound variables such that further reduction rules can be applied.   It is natural to associate values with elements of a programming language to which no further transformations can be applied.   For example, in a programming language that includes arithmetic expressions, the expression $3 + 4 \times 5$ is not thought of as a value since further reduction can be applied.   This expression can be successively reduced to $3 + 20$ and 23.   The symbol string 23 is said to be the value of $3 + 4 \times 5$ since no further reductions can be applied.

‡ This theorem is proved and discussed at some length in Curry and Feys [16]. Note that this theorem essentially states that lambda expressions can be evaluated by *asynchronous multiprocessing* applied in arbitrary order to local subexpressions.

If the first reduction performed is that of substituting the argument $(\lambda x(xx)\lambda x(xx))$ for all occurrences of x in λyy, then the reduced form λyy is obtained. If, on the other hand, an attempt is made to reduce the argument $(\lambda x(xx)\lambda x(xx))$ to reduced form before substituting it, then a nonterminating reduction sequence is obtained.†

In the above example, the lambda expression to be evaluated has the form $(\lambda x M A)$, where A is irreducible and M is reducible and contains no free occurrences of x. The lemma which follows states that these are the only circumstances in which two different reduction sequences yield different results.

Lemma: If, for a given lambda expression, two reduction sequences exist such that one is nonterminating and the other yields a value, then the lambda expression must contain a well-formed subexpression which can be reduced to a form (FA), where A is irreducible, F is of the form $\lambda x M$ with no occurrences of x in M, and M has a reduced form.

Outline of proof: If the lambda expression being evaluated has a subexpression which reduces to (FA) and satisfies the conditions of the lemma, then there is clearly a nonterminating and a terminating reduction sequence. Conversely, a lambda expression for which there is a nonterminating reduction sequence must contain an irreducible lambda expression. The only way in which an irreducible lambda expression can be eliminated is by substitution as an argument into a body in which it has no occurrences.

It is desirable in evaluating lambda expressions to use an algorithm that leads to a nonterminating reduction sequence only when the lambda expression is irreducible. Fortunately, it can be shown that an algorithm which substitutes values for bound variables in the order in which they are encountered in a left-to-right scan has the required property.

Theorem: If a lambda expression is evaluated by successive evaluation of the leftmost operator-operand combination, then the resulting reduction sequence will terminate if and only if the lambda expression is defined.

Outline of proof: If evaluation of successive leftmost operator-operand combinations results in a value, then by the Church-Rosser theorem this is the unique value of the lambda expression. It remains to be shown that if this procedure results in an infinite loop, there is no order of evaluation that leads to an irreducible lambda expression. The latter result follows from the fact that if successive reduction of the leftmost combination yields a nonterminating reduction sequence, there is no way of substituting any

† Church in his original formulation of the lambda calculus avoided this problem by requiring the body M of a lambda expression $\lambda x M$ to contain at least one occurrence of x. However, this restriction is unnecessary in view of the lemma and theorem which follow.

of the leftmost combinations so obtained for a bound variable with a zero number of occurrences. Since, by the lemma, the above condition would have to be met for a terminating reduction sequence to coexist with a nonterminating reduction sequence, it follows that if the leftmost reduction sequence is nonterminating, then all reduction sequences are nonterminating, and the lambda expression is irreducible.

The above theorem indicates that for the pure lambda calculus left-to-right evaluation is a correct mode of evaluation, while evaluation of arguments before substitution may sometimes lead to erroneous results. Since the pure lambda calculus contains no machinery for explicitly indicating delayed evaluation, algorithms which always perform evaluation of arguments before substituting them into the function body of the lambda expression are definitely inadequate.†

The present section has defined the basic structure of the lambda calculus. Examples of the use of lambda expressions for definition of conditional, logical, and arithmetic expressions are given in the next section, which is essentially concerned with machine-language programming in the lambda calculus and should be omitted on first reading. The reader who wishes to follow the thread of the discussion without performing excessive technical manipulation should read subsections 3.8.1, 3.8.2, and 3.8.5 and then continue with Sec. 3.9. An intermediate course of action which allows the examples of the lambda-calculus machines in subsections 3.8.3 and 3.8.4 to be understood is to skip subsections 3.6.1 to 3.6.3 but read subsection 3.6.4 on Church's representation of integers.

Exercise: Show how lambda notation could be used in specifying macro definitions and macro calls in TRAC and GPM. Discuss the limitations of pure lambda notation for this purpose.

3.6 CONDITIONAL, LOGICAL, AND ARITHMETIC OPERATIONS IN THE LAMBDA CALCULUS

3.6.1 REPRESENTATION OF LOGICAL VALUES AND LOGICAL OPERATIONS

A one-argument lambda expression of the form $\lambda x M$ defines a rule of correspondence which for every permitted value A determines a value $S_A^x M$ obtained by substituting A for all free occurrences of x in M. The set of possible values of the actual parameter A is referred to as the

---

† In the terminology of ALGOL developed in Chap. 4, evaluation of arguments prior to substitution corresponds to a call by value, while evaluation of unevaluated arguments corresponds to a call by name. The theorem above indicates that a call by value can lead to premature evaluation of an undefined argument that is never used. In the case of actual programming languages the Church-Rosser theorem does not hold, and the situation is greatly complicated by side effects during evaluation. Mechanical evaluation procedures based on the substitution of unevaluated arguments are shown in Sec. 3.8 and on substitution of evaluated arguments in 3.10.

domain of the function, while the set of all possible values of $(\lambda x M A)$ is referred to as the *range* of the function.   In the case of one-argument lambda expression $\lambda x M$ the domain of arguments A is the set of all lambda expressions, and the range of values of $(\lambda x M A)$ is similarly the set of all lambda expressions.

Two-argument functions are defined by letting the body M of a lambda expression $\lambda x M$ itself be a one-parameter lambda expression $\lambda y N$. By continuing this process, lambda expressions with an arbitrary number of arguments can be defined.   The domain of each of the arguments may in general be an arbitrary lambda expression, and the range of an n-argument lambda expression is over the set of all lambda expressions.

The operations which occur in arithmetic have a domain and range which are restricted to the class of numbers over which they are defined, while the logical operations *and, or, not* have a domain and range restricted to the two-valued domain truth (T) and falsity (F).

In order to represent a given operation by a lambda expression, a representation of operands in the domain of the operation must be chosen. We shall start by choosing a representation of the constants of truth and falsity and then define the functions *and, or,* and *not* so that if they are supplied with arguments denoting truth and falsity, they will, on evaluation, yield a lambda expression which represents the truth value of the result.   This development of representation of conditional and logical expression is based on unpublished notes of Scott [5].

In order to motivate the choice of our representation of T and F, consider the role of the logical expression B in the expression "**if** B **then** S_1 **else** S_2".   Occurrence of this expression in a procedure-oriented language usually implies that S_1 is executed if B has the value T and S_2 is executed if B has the value F.   The value T can be thought of as a selector for the first element of a two-element list (S_1, S_2), while F can be thought of as a selector of the second element of the list.

A two-argument function which selects the first of its two arguments can be represented by $\lambda x \lambda y x$, while a two-argument function which represents the second of its two arguments can be represented by $\lambda x \lambda y y$.   Thus T and F will be represented by the two argument functions $T \equiv \lambda x \lambda y x$ and $F \equiv \lambda x \lambda y y$; that is, T is the function such that $((TP)Q) \to P$, while F is the function such that $((FP)Q) \to Q$.

The logical operations *and, or,* and *not* will now be defined in terms of the above representation for T and F.†   The operation *not* can be represented by the lambda expression $not \equiv \lambda x((xF)T)$.

---

† The operations *and, or,* and *not* are defined to give representations of T and F as values provided they have appropriate representations of T and F as arguments. Nothing is said about the behavior of the lambda expressions representing *and, or,* and *not* for other arguments.

The application of *not* to T yields $((TF)T)$, which results in F, since F is the first argument of the first occurrence of T. In longhand we have

$$(\lambda x((xF)T)\lambda x\lambda yx) \rightarrow ((\lambda x\lambda yxF)T) \rightarrow (\lambda yFT) \rightarrow F$$

Similarly

$$(\lambda x((xF)T)F) \rightarrow ((\lambda x\lambda yyF)T) \rightarrow (\lambda yyT) \rightarrow T$$

The logical operation *and* is a two-argument function, and can be defined as follows:

$$and \equiv \lambda x\lambda y((xy)F)$$

If *and* is applied to T, we get the function $\lambda y((Ty)F) \rightarrow \lambda yy$, which results in T if applied to T and F if applied to F.

If *and* is applied to F, the resulting function $\lambda y((Fy)F) \rightarrow \lambda yF$ yields F independently of the value of its argument.

The function *or* can be defined as $or \equiv \lambda x\lambda y((xT)y)$. In this case a first argument T yields $\lambda y((TT)y)$, which yields T for an arbitrary second argument, while a first argument F yields $\lambda y((FT)y)$, which yields T if applied to T and F if applied to F.

Other logical functions may also be defined. However, the purpose of the above exercise is not just the definition of logical functions. The above definitions are intended to exhibit the essential properties of functions as rules of correspondence even when the notations are unfamiliar. The constants T and F were chosen to be two-parameter functions in an unfamiliar notation, and the operations *not*, *and*, and *or* were chosen to be functions whose domain and range were over the chosen representations of T and F and whose rule of correspondence between arguments and values yields the same result as performing the sequence of operations in a more familiar representation and translating the final value into the unfamiliar representation.

The lambda expressions $T \equiv \lambda x\lambda yx$ and $F \equiv \lambda x\lambda yy$ are interpreted as truth functional constants when considered as arguments and values of logical operations. However, they are also two-parameter functions in their own right which respectively select the first and second arguments of a two-element argument list.

3.6.2 LOGICAL VALUES AS LIST SELECTORS

We now wish to construct iterative functions from the primitives F and T for selecting the ith element of a list. In order to do so both the lambda expressions which constitute the selectors and the form of the lambda expressions on which selection is performed must be defined. Let the selectors be defined as the following lambda expressions:

$$T \equiv \lambda x \lambda y x$$
$$FT \equiv \lambda x \lambda y (y \lambda x \lambda y x) = \lambda x \lambda y (yT)$$
$$F^2 T \equiv \lambda x \lambda y (y \lambda x \lambda y (y \lambda x \lambda y x)) = \lambda x \lambda y (y F T)$$
$$F^{i+1} T \equiv \lambda x \lambda y (y F^i T)$$

Having defined a class of selection operations, we now wish to define a class of lambda expressions on which the above selection operations will perform selection.   Let an n-element list of the required structure be denoted by $\langle \varphi_0, \varphi_1, \ldots, \varphi_{n-1} \rangle$; that is, let $\langle \varphi_0, \varphi_1, \ldots, \varphi_{n-1} \rangle$ be such that $F^i T$ operating on this list yields φ_i when $i \leq n - 1$.

The most obvious form of list data structure is merely a list of the form $\varphi_0(\varphi_1(\varphi_2 \cdots \varphi_{n-1}) \cdots)$.   However FT operating on this list would result in the following value

$$(\lambda x \lambda y (y \lambda x \lambda y x) \varphi_0 (\varphi_1 (\varphi_2 - \varphi_{n-1}) \cdots)) \rightarrow (\varphi_1 (\varphi_2 (\cdots \varphi_{n-1}) \cdots) \lambda x \lambda y x)$$

A mechanism is required for reversing the operator and the operand in the above expression so that $\lambda x \lambda y x$ can be applied to the list $\varphi_1 (\varphi_2 \cdots \varphi_{n-1}))$ to yield the element φ_1.   The following list notation, due to Dana Scott, is accordingly adopted:

$$\langle \varphi_0 \rangle \equiv \lambda x ((x \varphi_0) \psi) \qquad \text{where } \psi \text{ is a dummy function†}$$
$$\langle \varphi_0, \varphi_1 \rangle \equiv \lambda x ((x \varphi_0) \lambda x ((x \varphi_1) \psi)) = \lambda x ((x \varphi_0) \langle \varphi_1 \rangle)$$
$$\langle \varphi_0, \varphi_1, \varphi_2 \rangle \equiv \lambda x ((x \varphi_0) \lambda x ((x \varphi_1) \lambda x ((x \varphi_2) \psi))) = \lambda x ((x \varphi_0) \langle \varphi_1, \varphi_2 \rangle)$$
$$\langle \varphi_0, \varphi_1, \ldots, \varphi_{n-1} \rangle \equiv \lambda x ((x \varphi_0) \langle \varphi_1, \varphi_2, \ldots, \varphi_{n-1} \rangle)$$

Given the above structure for lists, the lambda expression $(\langle \varphi_0, \varphi_1, \ldots, \varphi_{n-1} \rangle F^i T)$ has the value φ_i.   Note that selection of the list element is here performed by applying the list to the selector rather than by applying the selector to the list.   For example,

$$(\langle \varphi_0 \rangle T) = (\lambda x ((x \varphi_0) \psi) \lambda x \lambda y x) \rightarrow ((\lambda x \lambda y x \varphi_0) \psi) \rightarrow (\lambda y \varphi_0 \psi) \rightarrow \varphi_0$$
$$(\langle \varphi_0, \varphi_1 \rangle FT) = (\lambda x ((x \varphi_0) \lambda x ((x \varphi_1) \psi)) \lambda x \lambda y (y \lambda x \lambda y x))$$
$$\rightarrow ((\lambda x \lambda y (y \lambda x \lambda y x) \varphi_0) \lambda x ((x \varphi_1) \psi)))$$
$$\rightarrow (\lambda x ((x \varphi_1) \psi) \lambda x \lambda y x)$$
$$\rightarrow ((\lambda x \lambda y x \varphi_1) \psi) \rightarrow \varphi_1$$

In the above representation, a list is a one-argument function which expects a two-argument selection function as its argument.   When performing selection the list on which selection is to be made is initially regarded as the operator, and the selection function is the operand. However, on application of the operator to the operand, the operand becomes the operator for the next stage of evaluation.   This illustrates

† ψ plays the role of a list terminator and corresponds to the symbol NIL in LISP.

that the distinction between operators and operands is not a basic one in the lambda calculus.

The above list structure specification is very close to that of the LISP language. The function T plays the same role as the LISP operator which has variously been called *car, head,* and *first*. The function F plays the same role as the LISP operator which has been called *car, tail,* and *rest;* that is, T selects the first element (head) of the list, and F selects the rest (tail) of the list.

If L is an n-element list, the expression (LF^2T) is written as $(head$ $(tail(tail\ L)))$ in LISP notation; i.e., instead of writing the successive selection operations in the order in which they are to be performed, LISP requires that a set of nested expressions be written in the reverse order from that in which they are applied. The lambda-calculus notation for lists has been carefully chosen so that a sequence of selection operations applied to the list is written in the order in which they are applied.

The representation of integers and of arithmetic operations on integers will now be considered. Integers can be represented in a number of different ways, two of which will be considered here.

Let the integer i be represented by F^iT. As indicated above, F^iT operating on the list $L = \langle \varphi_0, \varphi_1, \ldots, \varphi_{n-1} \rangle$ selects the element φ_i of the list. Thus integers i in this representation are associated with the ordinal operation of selection.

3.6.3 REPRESENTATION OF THE INTEGER i AS THE iTH LIST SELECTOR

With the above representation, the successor function is the function which given $i = F^iT$ produces $i + 1 \equiv F^{i+1}T$. Such a function can be defined as follows:

$$\text{suc} = \lambda z \lambda x \lambda y (yz)$$

that is, suc applied to any integer $i = F^iT$ yields $\lambda x \lambda y(yF^iT) \equiv F^{i+1}T$.

The predecessor function removes one F if $i \neq 0$† and is undefined when $i = 0$. If U is an arbitrary undefined function, the predecessor function is defined as follows:

$$\text{pred} \equiv \lambda x((xU)\lambda xx)$$

that is,

$$(\lambda x((xU)\lambda xx)F^iT) \rightarrow U \quad \text{if} \quad i = 0$$
$$\rightarrow (\lambda xxF^{i-1}T) \rightarrow F^{i-1}T \quad \text{if} \quad i \neq 0$$

† It is assumed that $F^0T \equiv T$.

In order to define summation for this number representation we first observe that numbers $i = F^i T$ are two-parameter functions which when applied to a pair of arguments a,b exhibit the following behavior:†

$$((ia)b) \rightarrow a \qquad \text{if} \qquad i = 0$$
$$((ia)b) \rightarrow (b(i-1)) \qquad \text{if} \qquad i \neq 0$$

that is,

$$\text{if } i \equiv \lambda x \lambda y x \qquad \text{then} \qquad ((ia)b) \rightarrow a$$
$$\text{if } i \equiv \lambda x \lambda y (y(i-1)) \qquad \text{then} \qquad ((ia)b) \rightarrow (b(i-1))$$

The above result allows definition of the function "sum" by means of the following recursive definition:

$$((\text{sum } m)n) \equiv \textbf{if } n = 0 \textbf{ then } m \textbf{ else } (\text{suc}((\text{sum } m)n - 1))$$

Translated into lambda representation the definition for sum reads:‡

$$\text{sum} \equiv \lambda x \lambda y((yx)\lambda z(\text{suc}((\text{sum } x)z)))$$

When sum is applied to integers $M = F^m T$ and $N = F^n T$, then

$$((\text{sum } M)N) \equiv ((\lambda x \lambda y((yx)\lambda z(\text{suc}((\text{sum } x)z)))M)N)$$
$$\rightarrow ((NM)\lambda z(\text{suc}((\text{sum } M)z)))$$

This expression has the form $((ia)b)$ with $i = N$. If $N = 0$, then this expression has the value M, while if $N \neq 0$, it has the value

$$(b(i-1)) \equiv (\lambda z(\text{suc}((\text{sum } M)z)))N - 1) \rightarrow (\text{suc}((\text{sum } M)N - 1))$$

Evaluation of $((\text{sum } M)N - 1)$ in turn yields $(\text{suc}((\text{sum } M)N - 2)$. Eventually an instance of sum will be reached with the second argument zero. This expression will have the value M, and N-fold application of the successor operation will yield $M + N$.

The product function prod may similarly be defined as follows:

$$\text{prod} \equiv \lambda x \lambda y((yT)\lambda z(\text{sum}((\text{prod } x)z)x))$$

that is, if prod is applied to the two arguments $M = F^m T$ and $N = F^n T$,

---

† The expression $i - 1$, which occurs below in lambda expressions, is assumed to be shorthand for $F^{i-1}T$.

‡ This definition is not a pure lambda expression because it contains the symbol sum, which stands for the complete lambda expression. It can be shown [5] that any lambda expression which contains an explicit reference to itself in the lambda body can be replaced by an equivalent lambda expression not containing an explicit reference to itself. The concept of recursion can be formulated in the lambda calculus in a number of alternative ways, but is not discussed in the present text.

then if $n = 0$, the value of $((\text{prod } M)0) \to T \ (\equiv 0)$.   If $n \neq 0$, the value of

$$((\text{prod } M)N) \to (\lambda z(\text{sum}((\text{prod } M)z)M)(N - 1))$$
$$\to (\text{sum}((\text{prod } M)(N - 1))M)$$

The product of M and N is thus recursively defined as the sum of M and the product of M and $N - 1$.

3.6.4 CHURCH'S REPRESENTATION OF INTEGERS

Sums and products of integers in the above representation have been defined by recursive use of the successor and predecessor functions. However, instead of defining further operations in this representation, an alternative representation of integers will be introduced, and sums and products will be defined in the alternative notation.

An integer will be defined below in terms of n-fold application of a parameter f to a parameter c.   The representation of successive integers is given as follows:

$0 \equiv \lambda f \lambda c c$
$1 \equiv \lambda f \lambda c(fc)$
$2 \equiv \lambda f \lambda c(f(fc))$
$\cdot \ \cdot \ \cdot \ \cdot \ \cdot \ \cdot \ \cdot \ \cdot \ \cdot$

The integer n is defined as n-fold application of the first parameter to the second parameter.   The first parameter can be thought of as representing the successor function, while the second parameter can be thought of as representing the constant zero.

In order to define addition on integers N represented in the above notation, observe first that (Na) is a one-parameter function of the form $\lambda c(a(a \ \cdot \ \cdot \ \cdot \ (ac) \ \cdot \ \cdot \ \cdot))$, while $((Na)b)$ is a zero-parameter function of the form $(a(a \ \cdot \ \cdot \ \cdot \ (ab) \ \cdot \ \cdot \ \cdot))$.

Now consider the result of applying the one-parameter function (Ma) to the constant $((Na)b)$.   This results in substitution of $((Na)b)$ for c in the body of (Ma), and hence to a function $(a(a \ \cdot \ \cdot \ \cdot \ (ab) \ \cdot \ \cdot \ \cdot))$ with $M + N$ occurrences of a.   Thus the sum $[M + N]$ of two integers M,N in the above representation can be defined as follows:

$$[M + N] \equiv \lambda a \lambda b((Ma)((Na)b))$$

Exercise: Verify that the above definition gives the correct result when $M \equiv \lambda f \lambda c(f(fc))$ and $N \equiv \lambda f \lambda c(f(f(fc)))$.

The operation of addition is defined by binding the variables M and N in the above definition; that is,

$$+ \ \equiv \lambda M \lambda N[M + N] \equiv \lambda M \lambda N \lambda a \lambda b((Ma)((Na)b))$$

The product of two integers M and N can be defined as follows:

$$[M \times N] \equiv \lambda a(M(Na))$$

In order to verify that this definition works we observe that substitution of (Na) for all occurrences of f in M results in an expression of the form $\lambda a \lambda c((Na)((Na) \; \cdots \; ((Na)b \; \cdots \;)$, where there are M occurrences of Na. Na itself is of the form $\lambda c(a(a \; \cdots \; (ac) \; \cdots \;))$ with N occurrences of a. From our definition of addition it follows that $((Na)((Na)b))$ is of the same form as $((Na)b)$ but with $2N$ occurrences of a. M applications of Na to b results in an expression of the same form as $((Na)b)$ with $M \times N$ occurrences of a, thus giving the integer $M \times N$.

The operation $\times$ can therefore be defined as follows:

$$\times \equiv \lambda M \lambda N \lambda a(M(Na))$$

The operation of multiplication will now be illustrated for $M \equiv 2$ and $N \equiv 3$. The body M and parameter N of successive substitutions $S_N^x M$ for $(\lambda x M N)$ are underlined.

$$
\begin{aligned}
((\lambda M \; \underline{\lambda N \lambda a(M(Na))} \; \lambda f \lambda c(f(fc)) \,) & \lambda f \lambda c(f(f(fc)))) \\
\rightarrow (\lambda N \; \lambda a(\underline{\lambda f \lambda c(f(fc))}(Na)) \; & \underline{\lambda f \lambda c(f(f(fc)))} \,) \\
\rightarrow (\lambda a(\lambda f \lambda c(f(fc))(\lambda f \; & \lambda c(f(f(fc))) \; a \,))) \\
\rightarrow (\lambda a(\lambda f \; \lambda c(f(fc)) \; & (\lambda c(a(a(ac)))) \,)) \\
\rightarrow (\lambda a \lambda b(\lambda c(a(a(ac)))(\lambda c \; & (a(a(ac))) \; \underline{b} \,))) \\
\rightarrow (\lambda a \lambda b(\lambda c \; \underline{(a(a(ac)))} \; & (a(a(ab))) \,)) \\
\rightarrow \lambda a \lambda b(a(a(a(a(a(ab)) &)))))
\end{aligned}
$$

Exercise: Perform the above computation for $M \equiv 3$ and $N \equiv 2$.

Raising an integer M to the power N can be defined as follows:

$$[M^N] \equiv (NM)$$

This definition can be verified by observing that

$$(\lambda f \lambda c(f(f \; \cdots \; (fc) \; \cdots \;))M) \rightarrow \lambda c(M(M \; \cdots \; Mc) \; \cdots \;)$$

From the definition of multiplication, we have that $M(Mc)$ leads to M^2 occurrences of the first parameter of M, so that an expression of the form $M(M \; \cdots \; (Mc) \; \cdots \;)$ with N occurrences of M yields an expression with M^N occurrences of the first parameter of M.

Exercise: Compute the value of $(\lambda f \lambda c(f(fc))\lambda f \lambda c(f(f(fc))))$.

The example of the previous exercise will be used in the Sec. 3.8 to illustrate the operation of a lambda-calculus machine.

3.7 SYNTAX OF LAMBDA EXPRESSIONS

In the previous two sections the application of the function F to the argument A was represented by the notation (FA), and one-argument lambda expressions were represented by the notation $\lambda x M$.   There are a number of alternative representations of functions that can be used. For example, in normal functional notation, application of a function F to an argument A is denoted by $F(A)$.   This notation has the additional advantage that application of a function F to two arguments can be represented more simply; i.e., instead of writing $((FA)B)$, we can write $F(A)(B)$, and thus adding a new argument can be performed without modifying earlier parts of the expression.   Use of this notation throughout the previous section would modify the syntactic appearance of examples and might in certain instances make them more readable.   However, a mechanical interpreter for evaluating lambda expressions would find the former notation preferable, since in left-to-right scanning it is useful to have information as to whether there is an argument (provided by opening parenthesis) as soon as possible.

Exercise: Rewrite some of the examples of the previous section using $F(A)$ instead of (FA) to denote application of a function to an argument.

There are many different alternative ways of representing the syntax of a lambda expression.   For example, $(\lambda x M N)$ can be represented in the following ways:

M where $x = N$
Let $x = N$ in M
Subst $(x,N)M$;

The first notation specifies the argument value *after* specifying the expression, while the second and third notations specify the argument value before the expression.   Macro languages and procedure-oriented languages such as ALGOL use a variant of the second and third notations, since it is necessary to specify argument values before using them in a one-pass interpretation system.

In practical programming languages it is common to choose a notation convenient to the user when specifying the expressions on which computation is to be performed and to transform this notation into a form convenient for mechanical interpretation by an initial editing phase, sometimes referred to as a compiling phase.   Thus the choice of a representation should be considered in the context of what the representation is to be used for.   It is likely that a representation suited to human needs will differ from a representation suited to the needs of mechanical interpretation.   Since the lambda calculus has been introduced as a language to illustrate mechanical interpretation of pure functions rather than as a language for performing practical computations, no effort has been made to provide a user-oriented representation of lambda expressions. The notation was chosen because it was suited to illustrating mechanical interpretation.

In the next section some algorithms for the mechanical interpretation (evaluation) of lambda expressions will be introduced. As stated in an earlier section, evaluation of a lambda expression is the process of reducing it to a reduced form by a sequence of reductions.

3.8 LAMBDA-CALCULUS MACHINES

3.8.1 ALTERNATIVE STRATEGIES FOR FUNCTION EVALUATION

The lambda calculus is a language for function specification with an exceptionally simple syntax and semantics. Because of the formal simplicity of the language, it is an easy language for which to specify mechanical evaluation procedures which implement the reduction and renaming rules discussed in previous sections. The relative ease of specifying a mechanical evaluation procedure makes it a suitable language for illustrating and comparing alternative evaluation strategies.

In the present section a number of alternative evaluation strategies will be considered for lambda-expression evaluation. These strategies have a direct counterpart in corresponding strategies for macro languages and procedure-oriented languages. The present section is not merely an academic exercise in function evaluation but yields real insight into actual function-evaluation procedures in "real" programming languages.

All the function-evaluation techniques considered in the present section are essentially left-to-right function-evaluation techniques of the kind considered in Sec. 1.1; i.e., it is assumed that the function f and its arguments x are represented as a linear string in an information-storage medium and that the scan pointer of the processing unit that evaluates the lambda expression starts by scanning the leftmost character of the lambda expression, as illustrated in Fig. 3.5. During evaluation a number of information structures that grow and contract independently of the initial representation may be created.

Evaluation consists of matching a sequence of characters pointed to by the scan pointer and transforming the information structure in a manner determined by the matched characters. The alternative evaluation strategies considered perform different transformations on the information structure as successive characters are matched.

The basic transformation rule of the lambda calculus is the reduction rule, which specifies *literal substitution* of arguments for all occurrences of a bound variable in the body of a lambda expression. However, in actual programming languages we find that literal substitution of arguments for bound variables is frequently *simulated*.   The present section is essentially concerned with a number of alternative techniques for *simulation* of substitution of values for bound variables during lambda-expression evaluation.

Each method of simulated substitution results in a different class of intermediate information structures.   The characteristics of intermediate information structures arising for alternative evaluation strategies for

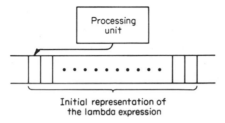

Initial representation of
the lambda expression

Figure 3.5 Initial instantaneous description for the evaluation of lambda expressions.

lambda expressions are closely related to the characteristics of corresponding information structures during the evaluation of procedure-oriented languages.

3.8.2 THE BASIC LAMBDA-CALCULUS MACHINE

The first machine to be described will be called the *basic lambda-calculus machine*.   It is a machine with a single stack, in which substitution of arguments for bound variables x is performed at the moment when the binding expression λx corresponding to the argument is encountered during a left-to-right scan.   However, instead of physically substituting an argument A for occurrences of a bound variable x, a pointer p_i to the argument A is substituted for all occurrences of the bound variable.   It is assumed that replacement of the variable x by the pointer p_i can be made by string substitution without increasing the storage requirements.

Expressions to be evaluated on the basic lambda-calculus machine are first edited (compiled) by performing two operations: (1) all bound variables are replaced by unique internal names different from free variables of the lambda expressions, and (2) for every lambda expression of the form $\lambda x M$ a terminating symbol . is inserted following M and prior to the argument (if any).   The period may be thought of as a closing parenthesis which matches the opening parenthesis λ.   It is introduced as an anchor for insertion of pointers within the lambda expression during the computation.

The lambda-calculus machine to be described has an internal storage area called the *workstack*, which, at the beginning of the computation, contains the edited lambda expression followed by a special termination symbol, say ;.   An output tape is available for output of evaluated portions of the lambda expression.   There is also a parenthesis-count register P which is incremented whenever an opening parenthesis is encountered and is used to distinguish between *active* occurrences of binding expressions λx, which give rise to substitutions of arguments for bound variables, and *passive* occurrences of binding expressions λx, for which no arguments are available.

Computations on the lambda-calculus machine are performed by scanning successive characters at the top of the workstack and performing an action determined by this character.   The actions of the lambda-calculus machine for characters which can be encountered in the workstack are as follows:

Actions by the basic lambda-calculus machine during the left-to-right evaluation of lambda expressions

(Increase parenthesis count P by 1, scan next symbol.

λx If $P > 0$, then the expression at the top of the workstack has the form $\lambda x M.A)$.   Remove λx from the workstack, replace all instances of x in M by pointers p_i to the beginning of A, replace the symbol . by a pointer $\frown$ to the symbol following the closing parenthesis of the combination, and reduce the parenthesis count P by 1.   If $P = 0$, then there is no actual parameter A corresponding to this formal parameter λx.   Create a bound-variable symbol b_j.   Change all occurrences of x in $\lambda x M$. to b_j and move λb_j from the top of the work stack to the output tape.

bound   If the top symbol of the workstack is a free variable or a
variables   bound variable that has not been replaced by a pointer,
b_j or free   print P opening parenthesis on the output tape, set P to
variables x zero, and move the workstack symbol to the output tape.

          In the pure lambda calculus free variables play a purely passive role.   However, in implementations of the lambda calculus free variables may denote predefined system operations such as addition or function definition.

pointer p_i If the top symbol of the workstack is a created pointer p_i, replace p_i by the expression to which it is pointing and move the workstack pointer to point to the beginning of this expression.

) or   If the top symbol of the workstack is a closing parenthesis or a period, move the symbol to the output tape.

⌐⟶   If the symbol on top of the workstack is a pointer inserted in place of a period, erase from the workstack all information preceding the workstack position pointed to and take the symbol in this position as the new top of the workstack.

;   When the symbol ; is encountered, the workstack is empty, and the computation is complete.

A simple computation on the lambda-calculus machine will now be described. The lambda expression $((\lambda x \lambda y(xy)..r)s)$ reduces to the expression (rs) on substitution of the free variable r for x and the free variable s for y. When this computation is performed on the lambda-calculus machine, the workstack initially contains $((\lambda x \lambda y(xy)..r)s)$;, with the next instruction pointer pointing to the first opening parenthesis of the lambda expression and $P = 0$. The basic lambda-calculus machine reduces the expression to (rs) on the output tape by means of the following 12 steps.

Step number	Workstack	Output stack	P	Comment
0	$((\lambda x \lambda y(xy)..r)s)$;	Empty	0	Start with $P = 0$
1	$(\lambda x \lambda y(xy)..r)s)$;	Empty	1	Scan parenthesis
2	$\lambda x \lambda y(xy)..r)s)$;	Empty	2	Scan parenthesis
3	$\lambda y(p_1 y)..\overset{\frown}{r)s)}$;	Empty	1	$p_1 \to r$
4	$(p_1 p_2)..\overset{\frown}{r)s)}$;	Empty	0	$p_2 \to s$
5	$p_1 p_2)..\overset{\frown}{r)s)}$;	Empty	1	Scan parenthesis
6	$rp_2)..\overset{\frown}{r)s)}$;	Empty	1	Substitute for p_1
7	$p_2)..\overset{\frown}{r)s)}$;	$(r$	0	Move r preceded by (
8	$s)..\overset{\frown}{r)s)}$;	$(r$	0	Substitute for p_2
9	$)..\overset{\frown}{r)s)}$;	$(rs$	0	Move s
10	$..\overset{\frown}{r)s)}$;	(rs)	0	Move)
11	;	(rs)	0	Follow ⌐⟶
12	;	(rs)	0	Stop

Substitutions of arguments for bound variables are accomplished in the above machine by two-stage simulation. In the first stage, pointers are substituted for all occurrences of a given bound variable.   Substitution of the argument for the bound variable is performed individually for each instance of the variable when it reaches the workstack top.

Since any computable function can be represented by a lambda expression, the lambda-calculus machine is equivalent to other machines for computing any computable function, e.g., a universal Turing machine.†
The primitive operations on this machine are more complex than those of a Turing machine.   For example, the operation of substitution of pointers for all occurrences of a given variable in a string is a complex operation. However, the lambda-calculus machine simulates substitutive function evaluation more directly than many other universal computing machines. It is significant because it exhibits the underlying structure of machines for performing functional evaluation.

Exercise: Implement the basic lambda-calculus machine.

3.8.3 EVALUATION OF 3^2 ON THE BASIC LAMBDA-CALCULUS MACHINE

In order to illustrate the power and intricacy of computations in the lambda calculus, a more complex example will be discussed.

Let $M = \lambda u\lambda v(u(u(v)))$ and $N = \lambda f\lambda c(f(fc))$.

Then $(NM) = (\lambda f\lambda c(f(fc))\lambda u\lambda v(u(u(uv))))$ has   a   reduced   form $\lambda x\lambda y(x(x(x(x(x(x(x(x(xy)))))))))$.

The main steps of the reduction process are as follows:

1.   The expression $(\lambda f\lambda c(f(fc))M)$ reduces to $\lambda c(M(Mc))$.

2.   Since $M = \lambda u\lambda v(u(u(uv)))$, substitution of Mc for u in the body part of M results in $\lambda v((Mc)((Mc)((Mc)v)))$.

3.   Evaluation of the first instance of Mc results in $\lambda v(c(c(cv)))$.

4.   The   expression $((Mc)((Mc)v))$ is   now   substituted   for v in $(c(c(cv)))$ resulting in $\lambda c\lambda v(c(c(c((Mc)(Mc)v))))$.

5.   Evaluation of Mc again yields $\lambda v(c(c(cv)))$.

6.   This time $((Mc)v)$ is substituted for v, resulting in the expression $\lambda c\lambda v(c(c(c(c(c(c((Mc)v)))))))$.

7.   Evaluation of (Mc) again yields $\lambda v(c(c(cv)))$, and substitution of v for v finally yields $\lambda c\lambda v(c(c(c(c(c(c(c(c(c(cv)))))))))))$.

8.   Renaming yields $\lambda x\lambda y(x(x(x(x(x(x(x(x(xy)))))))))$.

The highlights of the evaluation process for this lambda expression on the basic lambda-calculus machine are as follows:

1. $(\lambda f\lambda c(f(fc))..M)$ reduces to $\lambda c(p_1(p_1c))$.   Where p_1 points to M, λc is encountered in the passive scanning mode ($P = 0$) resulting in λb_i on the output stack and $(p_1(p_1b_1))$.; on the workstack.

† For a proof see Church [4], Curry and Feys [16], or Rosenbloom [17].

2. The first instance of p_1 is replaced by $M = \lambda u \lambda v(u(u(uv)))\ldots$, and λu is scanned in the active mode yielding $\lambda v(p_2(p_2(p_2 v)))$. with p_2 pointing to $(p_1 b_1)$.

3. λv is scanned in the passive mode, yielding $(p_2(p_2(p_2 b_2)))$. on the workstack and $\lambda b_1 \lambda b_2$ on the output tape.

4. The first instance of p_2 is replaced by $(p_1 b_1)$, and p_1 is in turn replaced by M. M is in turn scanned with a parenthesis count of 2 so that both λu and λv are scanned in the active mode. This results in $(p_3(p_3(p_3 p_4)))$ with p_3 pointing to b_1 and p_4 pointing to $(p_2(p_2 b_2))$.

5. The three instances of p_3 are replaced by b_1, and the string $(b_1(b_1(b_1$ is output to the output tape. At this point the workstack contains $p_4)))$ and a sequence of pointers which skip over parameters designated by p_1, p_2, p_3, p_4 but hit two periods corresponding to terminating parentheses for b_1, b_2 and finally point to the ending symbol ;.

6. p_4 is now replaced by $(p_2(p_2 b_2))$, the first instance of p_2 is replaced by $p_1 b_1)$, p_1 is replaced by M, and M is again evaluated with a parenthesis count of 2, resulting in $(p_5(p_5(p_5 p_6)))$ with p_5 pointing to b_1 and p_6 pointing to $(p_2 b_2)$.

7. The three instances of p_5 are replaced by b_1 and moved to the output stack with associated parentheses, leaving p_6 to be evaluated.

8. p_6 is replaced by $(p_2 b_2)$, which is replaced by $((p_1 b_1)b_2)$, which is replaced by $(p_7(p_7(p_7 p_8)))$ with p_7 pointing to b_1 and p_8 pointing to b_2. This causes $(b_1(b_1(b_1 b_2$ to be placed on to the output stack. Further scanning of the workstack causes nine closing parentheses and two periods to be moved to the workstack. The terminating symbol ; is then encountered, causing the machine to stop.

The detailed sequence of computational steps in the computation is given in the table on page 202.

3.8.4 THE LISP LAMBDA-CALCULUS MACHINE

The above method of evaluation of lambda expressions is only one of many methods of evaluation of expression in the lambda calculus. For example, explicit substitution of pointers for bound variables can be avoided if a *definition table*, or *environment*, is introduced for keeping track of correspondences between bound variables and arguments. In the resulting machine occurrence of a binding expression results in addition of a new entry to the definition table having the form (x, A) if there is an argument corresponding to the bound variable and the form (x, B) if the variable is a "passive" bound variable. Occurrence of a variable at the top of the workstack would result in consulting the definition table to determine the argument and replacing the variable by its value if it is present in the definition stack.

Computation of $3^2 = 9$ by the lambda-calculus machine

Step number	Workstack	Output tape	P	Comments
0	$(\lambda f\lambda c(f(fc))..M)$;	Empty	0	$M = \lambda f\lambda c(f(f(fc)))..$
1	$\lambda f\lambda c(f(fc))..M)$;	Empty	1	Read parenthesis
2	$\lambda c(p_1(p_1c))..M)$;	Empty	0	Substitute $p_1 \to M$
3	$(p_1(p_1b_1))..\widehat{M})$;	λb_1	0	b_1 is first bound variable
4	$p_1(p_1b_1)..\widehat{M})$;	λb_1	1	Read parenthesis
5	$\lambda f\lambda c(f(f(fc)))..(p_1b_1)..\widehat{M})$;	λb_1	1	Substitute M for p_1
6	$\lambda c(p_2(p_2(p_2c)))..\widehat{(p_1b_1)}..\widehat{M})$;	λb_1	0	Substitute $p_2 \to (p_1b_1)$
7	$(p_2(p_2(p_2b_2)))..$	$\lambda b_1\lambda b_2$	0	b_2 is second bound variable
8	$p_2(p_2(p_2b_2)))..$	$\lambda b_1\lambda b_2$	1	Read parenthesis
9	$(p_1b_1)(p_2(p_2b_2)))..$	$\lambda b_1\lambda b_2$	1	Substitute for p_2
10	$p_1b_1)(p_2(p_2b_2)))..$	$\lambda b_1\lambda b_2$	2	Read parenthesis
11	$\lambda f\lambda c(f(f(fc)))..b_1)(p_2(p_2b_2)))..$	$\lambda b_1\lambda b_2$	2	Substitute for p_1
12	$\lambda c(p_3(p_3(p_3c)))..b_1)(p_2(p_2b_2)))..$	$\lambda b_1\lambda b_2$	1	Substitute $p_3 \to b_1$
13	$(p_3(p_3(p_3p_4)))..b_1)(p_2(p_2b_2)))..$	$\lambda b_1\lambda b_2$	0	Substitute $p_4 \to (p_2(p_2b_2))$
14	$p_3(p_3(p_3p_4)))..$	$\lambda b_1\lambda b_2$	1	Read parenthesis
15	$b_1(p_3(p_3p_4)))..$	$\lambda b_1\lambda b_2$	1	Substitute for p_3
16	$(p_3(p_3p_4)))..$	$\lambda b_1\lambda b_2(b_1$	0	Move b_1 preceded by one parenthesis
17–20	$p_4)))..$	$\lambda b_1\lambda b_2(b_1(b_1(b_1$	0	Deal with $(p_3(p_3$
21	$(p_2(p_2b_2)))))..$	$\lambda b_1\lambda b_2(b_1(b_1(b_1$	0	Substitute for p_4
22	$p_2(p_2b_2)))))..$	$\lambda b_1\lambda b_2(b_1(b_1(b_1$	1	Read parenthesis
23	$(p_1b_1)(p_2b_2)))))..$	$\lambda b_1\lambda b_2(b_1(b_1(b_1$	1	Substitute for p_2
24	$p_1b_1)(p_2b_2)))))..$	$\lambda b_1\lambda b_2(b_1(b_1(b_1$	2	Read parenthesis
25	$\lambda f\lambda c(f(f(fc)))..b_1)(p_2b_2)))))..$	$\lambda b_1\lambda b_2(b_1(b_1(b_1$	2	Substitute for p_1
26	$\lambda c(p_5(p_5(p_5c)))..b_1)(p_2b_2)))))..$	$\lambda b_1\lambda b_2(b_1(b_1(b_1$	1	Substitute $p_5 \to b_1$
27	$(p_5(p_5(p_5p_6)))..b_1)(p_2b_2)))))..$	$\lambda b_1\lambda b_2(b_1(b_1(b_1$	0	Substitute $p_6 \to (p_2b_2)$
28–33	$p_6)))..$	$\lambda b_1\lambda b_2(b_1(b_1(b_1(b_1(b_1(b_1$	0	Deal with $(p_5(p_5(p_5$
34	$(p_2b_2))))..$	$\lambda b_1\lambda b_2(b_1(b_1(b_1(b_1(b_1(b_1$	0	Substitute for p_6
35–37	$p_1b_1)b_7))))..$	$\lambda b_1\lambda b_2(b_1(b_1(b_1(b_1(b_1(b_1$	2	Substitute for p_2, deal with parentheses
38	$\lambda f\lambda c(f(f(fc)))..b_1)b_2))))..$	$\lambda b_1\lambda b_2(b_1(b_1(b_1(b_1(b_1(b_1$	2	Substitute for p_1
39–40	$(p_7(p_7(p_7p_8))..)))$. $)))$.	$\lambda b_1\lambda b_2(b_1(b_1(b_1(b_1(b_1(b_1$	0	Substitute $p_7 \to b_1$, $p_8 \to b_2$
41–46	$p_8)))$. $)))$. $)))$.	$\lambda b_1\lambda b_2(b_1(b_1(b_1(b_1(b_1(b_1(b_1(b_1(b_1$	0	Deal with $(p_7(p_7(p_7$
47–48	$)))$. $)))$. $)))$. . . . ;	$\lambda b_1\lambda b_2(b_1(b_1(b_1(b_1(b_1(b_1(b_1(b_1(b_1b_2$	0	Move b_2
49–57	. . ;	$\lambda b_1\lambda b_2(b_1(b_1(b_1(b_1(b_1(b_1(b_1(b_1(b_1b_2)))))))))$	0	Move 9 closing parentheses
58–59	;	$\lambda b_1\lambda b_2(b_1(b_1(b_1(b_1(b_1(b_1(b_1(b_1(b_1b_2)))))))))..$	0	Move 2 periods
60	;	$\lambda b_1\lambda b_2(b_1(b_1(b_1(b_1(b_1(b_1(b_1(b_1(b_1b_2)))))))))..$;	0	Stop—empty workstack

Lambda-calculus machines which perform left-to-right evaluation of lambda expressions, keep track of the correspondence between bound variables and arguments in a definition table, and perform physical substitution of arguments for bound variables when they are encountered at the top of the workstack will be called LISP machines because of their

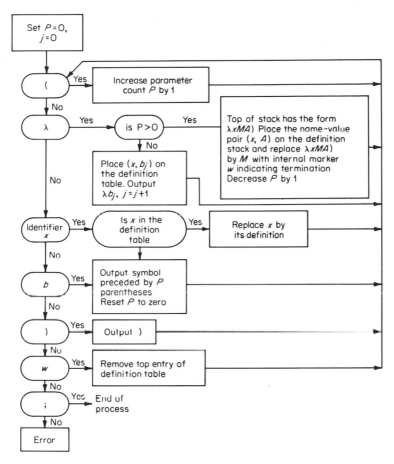

Figure 3.6 Operation of a LISP machine.

similarity to the evaluation mechanism of the LISP APPLY function [6]. The operation of a LISP machine is illustrated by Fig. 3.6, in which the flow diagram is more detailed than corresponding flow diagrams (Figs. 3.3 and 3.4) for GPM and TRAC, since the action for each of the control symbols is explicitly listed. Before making further comparisons between this machine and the GPM and TRAC evaluation mechanisms, a rather subtle point regarding name conflicts between bound variables in the definition stack will be discussed.

Consider evaluation of $(NM) = (\lambda x\lambda y(x(xy))\lambda x\lambda y(x(x(xy))))$ by the above machine. Evaluation of this expression results in the following initial sequence of steps:

Step number		Output tape	P	Comments
0	$(\lambda x\lambda y(x(xy))M)$;	Empty	0	$M = \lambda x\lambda y(x(x(xy)))$
1	$\lambda x\lambda y(x(xy))M)$;	Empty	1	Read parenthesis
2	$\lambda y(x(xy))\omega$	Empty	0	$D_1 = (x,M)$
3	$(x(xy))\omega\omega$	λb_1	0	$D_2 = (y,b_1)$
4	$x(xy))\omega\omega$	λb_1	1	Read parenthesis
5	$\lambda x\lambda y(x(x(xy)))\omega\omega\omega$	λb_1	1	Substitute M for x
6	$\lambda y(x(x(xy)))\omega^3$	λb_1	0	$D_3 = (x,(xy))$
7	$(x(xy)))\omega^4$	$\lambda b_1\lambda b_2$	0	$D_4 = (y,b_2)$
8	$x(x(xy)))\omega^4$	$\lambda b_1\lambda b_2$	1	Read parenthesis
9	$(xy)(x(xy)))\omega^4$	$\lambda b_1\lambda b_2$	1	Replace x by its value
10	$xy)(x(xy)))\omega^4$	$\lambda b_1\lambda b_2$	2	Read parenthesis
11	At this point the rule that a variable should be replaced by the most recent definition-stack entry to which it corresponds results in replacement of x by (xy). However, the required value of x is clearly M, so that the rule of taking the most recently defined value of a definition is not adequate in this case			

This problem of definition-stack bound-variable conflicts is so subtle that it can easily be overlooked by designers of LISP and macro-generating systems. When it is overlooked, the system gives correct results for the very large class of problems in which implicit multiple definition of the above kind does not occur but gives erroneous results whenever computations with the above feature are attempted.

The situation can be corrected in a number of alternative ways:

1. Rename all bound variables of a lambda expression by unique new names whenever it is substituted on the top of the workstack. This ensures that the bound-variable names defined by the symbol table are all different and therefore avoids the possibility of name conflicts. However, renaming during substitution is considerably more time-consuming than substitution without renaming. Since renaming is necessary only a small proportion of the time, this strategy results in many unnecessary instances of renaming.

2. Introduce an explicit mechanism for keeping track of the set of

accessible symbol-table entries, which is updated on encountering a binding expression, on exit from the body of a lambda expression, and on substitution of an argument for a bound variable. This form of organization is essentially similar to that required for the fixed-program machine, which is discussed in greater detail below.

Exercise: What changes are required in Fig. 3.6 to perform renaming during substitution of arguments for bound variables?

Project: Implement a correct version of the LISP machine.

The problem of renaming arises in any completely general function-evaluation system and requires careful symbol-table management to ensure that it is correctly handled. A technique of symbol-table management which adequately handles the renaming problem is described in the next subsection.

3.8.5 FIXED-PROGRAM (REENTRANT) LAMBDA-CALCULUS MACHINES

The LISP machine eliminates substitution of values for bound variables at the time of binding, but requires substitution of values for bound variables when they are encountered at the top of the workstack. However, even this form of substitution can be avoided by thinking of a bound variable as a procedure call and of the argument which constitutes the value of the bound variable as a procedure which is entered by a transfer of control to its first symbol and which returns control to its point of call on completion. Just as in ordinary procedure calls, a procedure call may itself give rise to a procedure call in order to evaluate a bound variable of the lambda expression which constitutes the procedure definition.

When bound variables are treated as procedure calls, the return links must be stored as part of the run-time information structure. Calls are always dynamically nested in the sense that exit from a more recently called procedure always occurs before exit from a less recently called procedure. The return links can therefore be stored in a stack.

Whereas a LISP machine modifies the lambda expression being evaluated, this machine never modifies the initial representation of the lambda expression and keeps track of the currently reached point of execution by a number of run-time structures, such as the symbol and the stack of return links. A machine which uses this evaluation strategy will be called a *fixed-program machine* or a *reentrant machine*.

The run-time structures required to keep track of name-value correspondences and of the current point of execution in a fixed-program machine will now be examined in greater detail.

The fixed program of a fixed-program machine consists of a sequence of nested function modules for which the maximum depth of nesting during execution may be unpredictable.

Exercises: (a) What is the maximum depth of nesting reached during evaluation of 3^2 on the basic lambda-calculus machine? (b) Using Church's representation of integers, develop a formula for the maximum level of nesting required to evaluate m^n. (c) Construct a class of lambda expressions for which the maximum level of dynamic nesting cannot be determined.

Although the maximum dynamic level of nesting during execution may be unpredictable, the number of different bound variables which are accessible at a given point of execution is independent of the dynamic depth of nesting, and depends only on the number of static one-parameter functions in which it is embedded.

The *level of nesting* of a given symbol in a lambda body is defined as the number of nested functions of the form $\lambda x M$ which enclose the symbol. When executing a program at a depth of nesting n, there are at most n bound variables x_i whose values are accessible at that point of execution. The set of accessible values are those which correspond to the most recently executed instances of the n binding expressions λx_i which enclose the current point of execution in the static program.

The lambda body associated with a given binding expression λx is said to be the *scope* of the bound variable x of that binding expression. Symbols of the lambda body are said to be within the scope of the bound variable. A symbol having nesting depth n is within the scope of precisely n bound variables.

A procedure call within the scope of a given set of bound variables may give rise to a chain of procedure calls. Successive procedure calls of such a chain are said to be *dynamically nested* in preceding calls and are sometimes referred to as *inner procedure calls*. Exit from a chain of procedure calls is always in a last in, first out order.

The set of accessible bound variables at the current point of execution will be called the *environment* at that point of execution. The number of accessible elements at a given point of execution of the program is an invariant of the initial representation of the program. We will take advantage of this fact in managing and updating the environment.

The environment undergoes modification at the following points during execution of a program on the fixed-program machine:

1. When a binding expression x is scanned, a new entry is added to the environment. This entry has the form (x, A) if there is an argument which corresponds to x, and has the form (x, b_i) if this binding expression has no associated operand.

2. When evaluation of a given function module is completed, the top entry of the environment is deleted; i.e., the point of execution moves from level of nesting n to a level of nesting $n - 1$, and the number of entries in the environment is decreased by 1.

3.   When evaluating a bound variable x at nesting level n which is defined by a binding expression at level k, the $n - k$ environment elements associated with nesting levels $k - i$ ($i = 1, 2, \ldots, n - k$) must be temporarily pushed down, since they are not accessible in scanning the value string associated with x.   If the value of x is itself a lambda expression with internal levels of nesting, new environment elements $k + 1$, $k + 2, \ldots$ will be created during execution of the value expression but will be deleted before control is returned to the point of call.

4.   On return from execution of a value expression at level k to a point of call at level $n - k$, the $n - k$ environment elements pushed down during execution of the value expression must be restored.

Instead of literally pushing down and restoring name-value pairs during the execution of the value expression associated with a bound variable, it is convenient to store all name-value correspondence in a symbol table whose entries are created in a last in, first out order and to store the current environment at a given point of execution as a vector of pointers to symbol-table entries.†

The symbol table of name-value pairs is a stack with respect to creation and deletion, but allows arbitrarily deep read-only references within the stack by means of environment pointers.   This stack will be referred to as the *symbol-table stack;* it has as many entries as the dynamic level of nesting during execution, and may therefore grow to arbitrary size.

In addition to the symbol-table stack, we need a stack to remember return links when evaluation of the value expression associated with a bound variable is completed, and a stack for pushing down sets of $n - k$ environment pointers when execution of a value expression is initiated. These two stacks can be combined into a single stack, each of whose entries contains a variable number $n - k + 1$ of elements, where $n - k$ elements are pushed-down environment pointers and the remaining element is the return link.   A stack of this form will be referred to as a *procedure stack.*

A symbol-table-stack entry created on execution of a given binding expression remains in existence during all chains of procedure calls originating within the scope of the binding expression, and is deleted when execution of the body which constitutes the scope is completed.   A procedure-stack entry created on entry to a given procedure remains in existence throughout the lifetime of all symbol-table-stack entries of inner (dynamically nested) function modules, and no environment-stack entry can be deleted before deletion of the procedure-stack entry.   It follows that procedure-stack entries and symbol-table-stack entries can be stored in a single stack, which we will refer to as the *run-time stack.*

---

† An alternative is to keep track of the environment by means of a "static chain" as indicated in Fig. 4.10 (p. 270).

The run-time stack contains two kinds of entries:

1.   Entries which specify name-value correspondences are created on execution of a binding expression and are deleted after execution of the body which constitutes the scope of the binding expression.

2.   Entries which specify links and environment pointers are created on call of a value expression and are deleted after execution of the value expression.

Although the run-time stack contains different kinds of entries, all entries in the run-time stack are created and deleted in a last in, first out order.   Access to an arbitrary depth within the run-time stack is permitted in a read-only mode, through the stack of environment pointers, to currently accessible bound variables.

The number of entries in the stack of environment pointers depends on the static level of nesting of the current point of execution.   The maximum number of entries is equal to the maximum level of nesting in the initial program, and is usually fairly small, say, below 100, for programs which might arise in practice.   However, for any given n, a lambda-calculus program can always be found which requires more than n environment pointers.   Thus, no a priori limit can be placed on the size of the stack-environment pointers for lambda-calculus machines.

When the above run-time evaluation strategy is used, it is convenient to subject lambda expressions to a compilation phase which replaces bound variables associated with the ith level of nesting by the reserved symbols $\sim i$.   During execution, the integer i can be used to access the ith entry in the stack of environment pointers, and hence the appropriate entry in the run-time stack.

The above model was developed in some detail because it forms a basis for evaluation strategies in procedure-oriented languages.   In the next chapter, a similar model will be used to describe ALGOL run-time representations.

Exercises: (a) Write out the eleven steps of the example of subsection 3.8.4, assuming that the computation is done on a fixed-program machine. What is the content of the run-time stack at the eleventh step?   (b) Write out the complete sequence of steps required to compute $(NM) = (\lambda x \lambda y (x(xy)) \lambda x \lambda y (x(x(xy))))$ on the lambda-calculus machine.   Indicate the content of the run-time stack at each step.   (c) Compare the above strategy for environment management with the static-chain strategy given on page 270.

Project: Implement a fixed-program machine.   Test it on the example in the above exercises.

3.9 LISP AND EVALUATION OF LISP IN LISP

3.9.1 REVIEW OF PRIMITIVES IN MACRO LANGUAGES

The languages discussed in the present chapter all permit the specification of functions whose domain and range may themselves be strings representing arbitrary functions.   The languages differ principally in primitives that may be used in building up function specifications and in the format of the data strings that serve as function arguments.

The lambda calculus is the simplest of the languages considered. The primitives of the lambda calculus are binding of variables (accomplished by the lambda operator) and reduction by substitution of an actual parameter for all instances of a bound variable in the body of a lambda expression.   Renaming can be added as an additional operation. However, the necessity for renaming can be avoided by judicious management of accessing of variables during reduction.   The lambda calculus is also characterized by the fact that the operand domain is precisely the same as the domain of operators.   Another feature of the lambda calculus is that evaluation of a lambda expression embedded in a larger lambda expression can never yield any side effects.   The evaluation of an operator-operand combination can result only in modification of the symbol string that constitutes the operator-operand combination and can never result in modification of a string external to the combination.   The only side effect possible in the evaluation of lambda expressions is a side effect of control; i.e., if the lambda expression being evaluated has a value, then control on completion of evaluation will return to the evaluator for evaluation of a further lambda expression, while if the lambda expression has no value, control will never return.

The macro generators discussed in the present chapter had a richer set of primitives than the lambda calculus.   One important distinction between lambda expressions and macro generators is that macro generators permit functions to be *named* and subsequently *used* by specification of the name.   Naming of a function may be performed either by *pushdown assignment* or by *destructive assignment*.   Naming by destructive assignment is an operation with essential side effects, since the program action on any subsequent use of that name is automatically modified by assignment of a new value to that name.

3.9.2 SELECTORS, CONSTRUCTORS, AND PREDICATES

In the present section, the lambda calculus will be augmented by a set of primitives which are essentially different from those introduced in the case of macro generators and which are concerned explicitly with string manipulation.

One of the objectives of introducing string-manipulation primitives is to allow direct specification of operations on the program and data strings of a programming language. The string-manipulation operations to be introduced into the language can be grouped into three categories:

1. Selectors, for selecting a substring of a given string
2. Constructors, for constructing new strings
3. Predicates, for testing whether a string belongs to a given class of strings

The prime example of a lambda-calculus–like language with string-manipulation primitives is the LISP language [6]. We shall accordingly use LISP as an example to illustrate some of the interesting features of lambda-calculus–like languages with string-manipulation primitives.

3.9.3 LIST STRUCTURES IN LISP

In LISP the primitive data type is the *list*. The format of a list may be described either at the user level or at a more machine-oriented level. At a user level a list can be described as being either null or consisting of a sequence of list elements separated by commas and enclosed in parentheses. Thus (A,B,C) is an example of a three-element list with the elements A, B, C. The null list will be denoted by the symbol *null*.

The elements of a list may in turn be of two kinds, namely, *atoms*, which denote objects that are not necessarily lists, or *lists*. Thus if A, B, C, D, E denote atoms, $(A,(B,C,D),E)$ denotes a three-element list whose second element is the sublist (B,C,D).

The atoms of LISP may be numbers, symbol strings, or objects with an arbitrarily complex structure. The internal structure of an atom is characterized by a *description list* (DL), which consists of a sequence of attributes of the atom and values associated with each of the attributes. The attributes of an object may be manipulated by a special set of primitives for description-list manipulation which will not be discussed here. A description list is basically a local symbol table for defining properties local to an object.

List entries are usually represented by pointers to the objects they denote. This permits list elements of LISP to be uniformly represented by a pair of pointers, the first pointing to the object associated with the list element and the second pointing to the successor element. List elements which have no successor have a special marker in the successor field, which will here be denoted by NIL. In terms of this representation, the list $(A,(B,C,D),E)$ would be represented by the list structure shown in Fig. 3.7. This model of internal representation helps to visualize how lists specified in LISP are represented at the machine-language level and will subsequently help in visualizing how lists are transformed at the

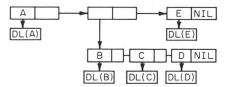

Figure 3.7   Machine-level representation of the list $(A,(B,C,D),E)$.

level of internal machine representation.   However, there is in principle no need to consider this internal representation, since all transformations can be specified purely at the level of external list representation.

3.9.4 LISP PRIMITIVES AND THE REPRESENTATION OF LISP PROGRAMS BY LISTS

There are two primitive selection operation in LISP, called *head* and *tail*, which, by repeated use, can be used to select any component of a list. These two selection operations are both one-argument functions which expect a nonnull list L as an argument.   The result of *head*(L) is to produce as a value the first component of the list L (which may be a list or an atom).   The result of *tail*(L) is to produce as a value the list which is derived from L by removing its first element.   If L is a one-element list, the effect of *tail*(L) is to produce the *null* list.   For example,

$$
\begin{aligned}
head((A,(B,C,D),E)) &= A\\
tail((A,(B,C,D),E)) &= ((B,C,D),E)\\
head(tail((A,(B,C,D),E))) &= (B,C,D)\\
head(head(tail((A,(B,C,D),E)))) &= B
\end{aligned}
$$

Given functions *head* and *tail*, it is convenient to introduce a constructor that acts as an inverse to *head* and *tail* in the sense that it can be used to reconstruct lists from components obtained by the application of *head* and *tail* operations.   This constructor will be called *cons* and will have the property that $cons(head(L),tail(L)) = L$.

The constructor *cons* is a two-argument operator that may have an atom or a list as its first argument and must have a list as its second argument.   The value $cons(A,L)$ is the list which has A as its head and L as its tail.

In terms of the machine-level representation of Fig. 3.7, *head*(L) is the object (*atom* or *list*) pointed to by the first pointer of the first list element of L, and *tail*(L) is the list pointed to by the second pointer of the first list element of L.   The effect of $cons(A,L)$ is to create a new list element whose first pointer points to A and whose second pointer points to L.   Thus *cons* is an operation which requires storage for a new list element to be created during its execution.

Program segments such as *head*(*L*) and *cons*(*A,L*) which consist of primitive operations applied to their arguments can be represented by lists.   Let HEAD, TAIL, and CONS be the names of atoms whose body is a program or mechanism for performing the operations specified by *head, tail,* and *cons*.   Then the program segment *head*(*L*) can be represented by the list (HEAD,L) and the program segment *cons*(*A,L*) can be represented by the list (CONS,A,L) or by the list (CONS,(A,L)).   The machine-level representation of these lists is given in Fig. 3.8.   LISP

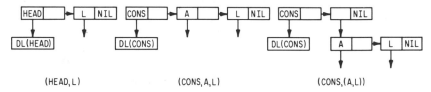

Figure 3.8   List representation of program segments.

uses the representation (CONS,A,L) rather than the representation (CONS,(A,L)) in representing *cons*(*A,L*) as a list.

Since there are two kinds of objects in LISP (lists and atoms), a predicate is required to test whether an object is a list or an atom.   This predicate will be called *atom;* it is a one-argument predicate which yields one of the two special atoms T (true) or F (false) as its value; i.e., the operation *atom*(*A*) has the value T if A is an atom and the value F if not.

A further primitive predicate available in LISP is the two-argument predicate *eq*, which tests whether its two arguments denote the same atom.   That is, *eq*(A_1, A_2) has the value T if A_1 and A_2 denote the same atom and the value F otherwise.

The operations logical *and* $\wedge$, logical *or* $\vee$, and logical *not* $\neg$ are assumed to be available, having predicates as their arguments and producing predicates as their values.

A further selection operation available in LISP is the operation *cond*, which performs evaluation of a sequence of predicates followed by selection of a value corresponding to the first true predicate.   *cond* has a variable number $2n$ of arguments, where odd-numbered arguments are predicates (having a value T or F) and even-numbered arguments are strings.   The effect of "*cond*($P_1, A_1; P_2, A_2; \ldots ; P_n, A_n$)" is to test successive predicates P_i and to take as a value the expression A_i corresponding to the first P_i with value T.   Note that the effect of *cond* is similar to the ALGOL conditional expression "**if** P_1 **then** A_1 **else if** P_2 **then** $A_2 \cdots$ **else if** P_n **then** A_n".

As an example of a program using the above primitives, consider the function ff which, when applied to a list argument, has as its value the first atom of the list.   This function may be specified as follows:

ff$(L) \equiv cond(atom(L),L;T,ff(head(L)))$ If L is an atom, the value of ff applied to L is L. Otherwise the value is ff$(head(L))$.

Thus if $L = ((A,B),C)$, $atom(L)$ is false, so that the value is ff$(head(L))$ = ff$((A,B))$. $atom((A,B))$ is again false, resulting in the value ff$(head((A,B)))$ = ff(A). $atom(A)$ is finally true, yielding the value A.

3.9.5 THE LAMBDA, LABEL, AND QUOTE PRIMITIVES

The function ff can conveniently be specified in the notation of lambda calculus as follows:

$(\lambda,(L),(cond(atom(L),L;T,ff(head(L)))))$ This is a one-argument function which, when applied to an argument L, yields the value ff(L).

The symbol λ, referred to as the binding operator, must be added to the LISP language as an additional primitive. It has two arguments, consisting of a variable and a body, and has the effect of binding all free occurrences of the variable in the body.

In the above lambda expression λ, *cond*, *atom*, and *head* are primitive operations of LISP having a fixed meaning. T and F are primitive constants of LISP, also having a fixed meaning, L is a bound-variable symbol which receives a value when an argument is supplied, and the punctuation symbols are fixed control symbols. The symbol ff is the only symbol in the above expression which does not have a value associated with it. It is convenient to introduce a notation for specifying that a given symbol denotes the function in which it occurs. This is accomplished in LISP by the *label* primitive.

$(label,$ff$,(\lambda,L,(cond(atom(L),L;T,ff(head(L)))))))$ The primitive *label* has two arguments, the first of which is a function name and the second of which is the function which the name denotes. The format of this notation is the same as that of symbol-value macro definitions. However, the function *label* implies a *local* definition, where the name ff denotes the second argument only *within* the second argument itself.

There is one further primitive operator is LISP, known as the *quote* operator, whose purpose is to enclose a list in quotes to shield it from evaluation. The operator *quote* applied to a list L has the effect that evaluation of *quote*(L) always yields the literal string L.†

The operations *atom*, *eq*, λ, *label*, and *quote* may be represented by

---

† The *quote* operator is related to triangular parentheses in GPM and to ##(and (. . .) in TRAC.

atoms, and the strings specifying application of these operations to their arguments may be represented by lists, just as in the case of *head, tail,* and *cons.* In LISP, ATOM, EQ, LAMBDA, LABEL, and QUOTE are the respective names of the atoms corresponding to *atom, eq, λ, label,* and *quote.*

A LISP program consists of a primitive applied to its arguments, where the arguments may consist of primitives applied to their arguments. Thus, if a set of rules exists for transforming primitives applied to their arguments into lists, then a list representation for any LISP program can be developed by repeated application of these rules. For example, the LISP program for ff can be represented by the following list:

(LABEL,ff,(LAMBDA,L,(COND,((ATOM,L),L),(T,(ff,(HEAD,L))))))

Exercises: (*a*) Draw the list structure corresponding to the above list. (*b*) Discuss the relation between the LISP, *label,* and *quote* operators and corresponding operations in TRAC and GPM.

3.9.6   THE EVALUATION OF LISP PROGRAMS IN LISP

When LISP programs are specified as lists, the selectors, constructors, and predicates of the LISP language can be applied to the list structures that represent programs to select program segments, test the type of program segments, and specify transformations on program segments. In particular, LISP can be used to specify the transformations of list structures when LISP primitives are applied to their arguments.

In order to set the stage for specifying the effect of applying LISP primitives to their arguments, the overall run-time environment during the execution of LISP programs will be discussed.

The process of execution of a LISP program is similar to that for the lambda-calculus LISP machine of the previous section. The LISP program will be scanned from left to right, and actions specified by successive symbols will be performed. Primitive functions will result in a transformation of the program that constitutes the list structure, the functions *lambda* and *label* will result in the addition of entries to a symbol table, and bound variables will result in symbol-table look-up and substitution of the value for the name when they are encountered at the top of the program stack.

The LISP primitives may be thought of as being *permanently defined reserved* symbols in the symbol table. This allows the meaning of all symbols encountered during interpretation to be determined by table look-up in the symbol table.

During execution of a LISP program, the principal information structures which grow, diminish, and are transformed are the following:

1.   The program list, sometimes called the *control string*

2. The symbol table, sometimes referred to as the *environment* or *environment chain*

3. A run-time stack used for pushing down information during the evaluation of nested functions

4. An output string

During execution, successive constituents of the program list are scanned in a left-to-right order, and actions specified by successive constituents are performed, including the following kinds:

1. Modify the "top" of the program string either by removing symbols or by adding symbols or both

2. Modify the symbol table (environment chain) by adding or removing symbol-value pairs or both

3. Push down the run-time stack when entering a new level of nesting and pop up on completion

4. Place evaluated strings into the output string

The possible symbols which may be encountered on the top of the program string are the following:

1. A bound variable

2. One of the primitive function symbols QUOTE, HEAD, TAIL, CONS

3. One of the primitive function symbols ATOM, EQ, COND

4. One of the primitive function symbols LABEL, LAMBDA

When a bound variable is encountered on the top of the control string, its value is found in the environment chain and substituted for the bound variable on the top of the program list. Scanning resumes by scanning the leftmost symbol of the substituted string.

When a primitive function symbol of the form QUOTE, HEAD, TAIL, CONS, ATOM, EQ, COND is encountered, the current level of function evaluation is interrupted in order to evaluate the arguments of the function. Then the function corresponding to the primitive-function symbol is applied to the evaluated arguments.

When the primitive-function symbol LABEL is encountered, the unevaluated first argument is paired with the unevaluated second argument and entered as the top entry of the environment chain.

When the primitive symbol LAMBDA is encountered, the unevaluated bound variable is paired with the unevaluated argument and placed at the top of the environment chain.

The process of evaluation of LISP programs is specified by McCarthy

[6] by a two-argument function *eval* having the program list C as its first argument, and the environment chain E as its second argument. The function EVAL(E,C) is specified as a conditional expression which successively tests the first component of E against various primitives and specifies the result of evaluation for each primitive and for bound variables in terms of transformations of the lists E and C and a value which during evaluation of nested functions is passed up to the next higher level of nesting, and which is placed on the output string when the outermost level of nesting is reached.

The detailed specification in LISP of the function EVAL is somewhat technical. Readers interested in the details should consult [6].

Exercises: (*a*) Write out and explain the LISP APPLY function given in [6], or design your own LISP APPLY function. (*b*) Describe the evaluation process for the following list:

((LABEL,ff,(LAMBDA,L,(COND,((ATOM,L),L),

(T,(ff,(HEAD,L)))))),((A,B),C))

3.10   THE SECD MACHINE

3.10.1   EVALUATION OF LAMBDA EXPRESSIONS IN A LISP-LIKE LANGUAGE

LISP can be used to describe the evaluation process both of LISP programs and of any other programming language whose programs are lists. In other words, LISP can be used to specify the semantics of any programming language whose program and data strings are represented in LISP format and whose intermediate structures during evaluation are lists in LISP format.

Landin [9] has used a LISP-like language to specify the semantics of the lambda calculus. He considers a run-time environment with the following four list structures:

1.   A run-time stack S, which stores evaluated arguments of partially executed operations

2.   An environment E, which consists of the symbol-table entries and plays the same role as the environment chain of LISP

3.   A control string C, which plays the same role as the program list of LISP

4.   A dump D, which is used to push down the current state of S, E, C, and D on entering a new level of function evaluation

At any given point of the computation, the state of the machine can be characterized by the four stacks (S,E,C,D). Because of this, Landin calls the machine the SECD machine [9].

One of Landin's most important contributions in developing the SECD machine was a notation for describing structure definitions. This notation, which is essentially a variant of the notation for describing context-free languages, is discussed below.

3.10.2 STRUCTURE DEFINITION, SELECTORS, CONSTRUCTORS, AND PREDICATES FOR LAMBDA EXPRESSIONS

When dealing with structured objects such as lambda expressions whose representations have a complex structure, it is convenient to be able to name and manipulate semantically meaningful components of the representation. Components of a structure can be named by means of *structure definitions* which specify how the structure as a whole is built up out of named substructures. In the case of lambda expressions, there are relatively few semantically meaningful components, so that a structure definition which names semantically meaningful components is relatively simple. We shall use a style of structure definition that is due to Landin [9].

A *lambda expression* consists of a *variable x*; or of a *bound-variable part* B of the form λx, followed by a *body M* which is a *lambda expression;* or of a *combination* C, which consists of an *opening parenthesis, followed by* an *operator F* which is a *lambda expression,* followed by an *operand part A* which is a *lambda expression,* followed by a *closing parenthesis.*

The operator *or* in a structure definition indicates than an alternative form of the structure is about to be specified, while the operator *followed by* indicates concatenation of a further structure component. These components correspond precisely to the vertical stroke and the concatenation operator of the syntactic notation in Appendix 1. The phrases "consists of," "of the form," "which is" all correspond to the horizontal arrow of Appendix 1. The relation between structure definition and syntactic specification is further discussed below.

The above structure definition singles out bound-variable parts λx and bodies M of lambda expressions having the form $\lambda x M$ and singles out operators F and operands A of lambda expressions having the form (FA).† The structure definition is specifically designed to allow operators to be defined for manipulating components named in the structure definition. Landin [9] has classified the operators which operate upon com-

---

† In the above structure definition certain components have been given symbolic names. When the structure definition is used to recognize or manipulate an instance of the structure (see below), these names can be used to denote the substructure components. A further generalization of the above notation suggested by Standish [18] would be to allow parameters to be associated with structure components in a structure definition.

ponents of a structure definition into three categories:

1. Selectors, for selecting components of a structure
2. Predicates, for testing whether a structure is of a given type
3. Constructors, for constructing structures from their components

Given the above structure definition for lambda expressions, it is natural to define the following selectors for selecting components of a lambda expression:

select-bound-variable-part(x)   Select the bound-variable part of the given lambda expression and name it B.

select-body(x)   Select the body of the given lambda expression and name it M.

select-operator(x)   Select the operator part of the given combination and name it F.

select-operand(x)   Select the operand part of the given combination and name it A.

It is natural also to define the following predicates for the above structure definition:

test-variable(x)   Yields the value T if x is a variable and the value F otherwise.

test-lambda-expression(x)   Yields the value T if x is a lambda expression and the value F otherwise.

test-combination(x)   Yields the value T if x is a combination and the value F otherwise.

test-bound-variable-part(x)   Yields the value T if x is a bound-variable part and the value F otherwise.

It is natural also to define the following constructor:

construct-lambda-expression(u,v)   If u is a lambda expression and v is a lambda expression, construct the combination (u,v). If u is a bound-variable part x and v is a lambda expression M, construct the lambda expression $\lambda x M$.

The above operators have been constructed systematically from the names of structure components in the structure definition. It is generally possible to devise a systematic scheme for deriving names of selectors, predicates, and constructors from the names of structure components in the structure definition. The discussion of LISP in Sec. 3.9 illustrates how operators may be used in manipulating the language structures.

In subsection 3.10.3 below, abbreviated names will be used for some of the above selectors, predicates, and constructors. The abbreviations bvpart(x), bodypart(x), rator(x), and rand(x) will be used to denote the respective selectors for the bound-variable part, body part, operator part, and operand part of a lambda expression x. The abbreviations variable(x), λexp(x), combination(x) will denote the respective predicates for testing whether x is a variable, lambda expression, or combination.†

A structure definition is somewhat like a syntactic definition. For instance, using the terminology of Appendix 1, the above structure definition could be replaced by the following syntactic definition:

$$E \to V|\lambda VE|(EE)$$

The above syntactic definition uses the symbol E in every context where a lambda expression can occur, while the corresponding structure definition uses different names in different contexts. However, this can be remedied by replacing the above syntactic specification by the following slightly more elaborate specification:

$lambda$-$expression$ $\to$ $variable|bound$-$variable$-$part$ $body|combination$
$bound$-$variable$-$part \to \lambda$ $variable$
$body$ $\to$ $lambda$-$expression$
$combination$ $\to$ $(operator\ operand)$
$operator$ $\to$ $lambda$-$expression$
$operand$ $\to$ $lambda$-$expression$

This syntactic specification is isomorphic to the corresponding structure definition. Indeed, since the operators of structure definitions correspond precisely to the operators of syntactic specifications, structure definitions can be mapped into syntactic specifications and vice versa.

Exercise: Define a mechanical procedure for mapping structure definitions into syntactic specifications and for mapping syntactic specifications into structure definitions.

Structure definitions allow the syntax of the structure to be specified in an informal way, which encourages use of different names for the same structure when it occurs in different contexts. This in turn allows a richer set of predicates, selectors, and constructors to be used in manip-

---

† Subsections 3.10.3 and 3.10.4 develop a lambda-expression evaluation machine of Landin in detail using his original notation [9]. The present section attempts to illustrate some of the wider implications of Landin's notation for structure definition.

ulating components than if all instances of the same structure were denoted by the same name.†

3.10.3 THE FUNCTION "TRANSFORM" FOR EVALUATION OF LAMBDA EXPRESSIONS

The storage areas S and C of an SECD machine will be thought of as lists and may be acted on by list-processing operations. It will be assumed that all the list-processing operations of LISP are available. Thus $head(L)$ denotes the top element of L; $head(tail(L))$ denotes the second element of L, etc.; $cons(A,L)$ denotes adding a new element to L; $head(L)$ will be abbreviated by hL; $tail(L)$ will be abbreviated by tL; and $cons(A,L)$ will be abbreviated by $A:L$.

The predicate null is defined as follows:

$null(L)$ Has the value T if L is a null list and F otherwise.

In addition to the constructor *cons*, which adds a new list element at the head of a list, it is convenient to define a number of additional construction operations that reflect the construction of new information structures during the evaluation process. The principal intermediate language structure that cannot be simply constructed in terms of existing construction operations is the *value* associated with a lambda expression λxM. The value of such a lambda expression will be called a *closure* and will be constructed by the operation "constructclosure". The constructor constructclosure has three arguments consisting of an environment E, a bound-variable part of a lambda expression, and a body part of a lambda expression and constructs a single object which can subsequently be applied to an argument of a lambda expression or be an argument of a lambda expression. Once a closure has been introduced into the language a predicate "closure(X)" is required for testing whether an object X is a closure, and selectors are required for selecting the environment part, bound-variable part, and body part of a closure. These selectors will respectively be denoted by Epart, bvpart, and bodypart.

The operation of the SECD machine will be defined by a function *transform* which operates on a quadruple (S,E,C,D) and produces a next state (S',E',C',D') by first examining the top symbol $head(C)$ on the control stack C and then performing an operation determined by this symbol. The operation of the SECD machine can be verbally described as follows:

If the top item hC on the control stack is a combination (FA), then

---

† Note that the same effect could have been achieved by using a syntactic algorithm which takes context into account. However, such an algorithm would not necessarily be a bounded-context algorithm in the sense of Appendix 1, since context in structure definitions is specified by structure components, and structure components may in general require arbitrary context to differentiate them.

hC is replaced by the three elements rand(hC):rator(hC):ap, where ap is a special intermediate language symbol which, when encountered, results in application of the top element hS of the stack S to the second element htS of the stack S. If hS is a closure, then application of hS to htS results in evaluation of the one-argument function hS for the argument htS. This is accomplished by pushing down the current state (S,E,C,D) in the dump and initializing the new (S,E,C,D), so that S is empty, E is the environment component of the closure augmented by the bound-variable–actual-parameter pair, C is the body part of the closure, and D is the previous dump with (S,E,C,D) as the new top element.

The only items which can appear on top of the control stack are combinations, the symbol ap, lambda expressions, and variables. Combinations and the symbol ap have already been dealt with. A lambda expression appearing on top of the control stack C results in construction of the closure using the bound-variable part, body, and current environment as parameters and placing the closure on the stack S. A variable encountered on top of the control stack S results in placing of the value of the variable on the stack S, where the value of a variable X in the environment E is denoted by val(EX).

The only other possibility is that the control string is null. A null control string means that evaluation of the current function has been completed. The dump is accordingly popped up so that evaluation of the next recently interrupted function can be resumed at the point of interruption. The function transform can be formally specified by the following conditional expression:†

transform $(S,E,C,D) \equiv$
   if $null(C)$ **then** $(hS{:}S',E',C',D')$ **where** $(S',E',C',D') = hD$
   else if variable (hC) **then** $(\text{val}(E(hC){:}S,E,tC,D)$
   else if λexp(hC) **then**$(\text{constructclosure}(E,\text{bv}(hC),\text{body}(hC)){:}S,E,tC,D)$
   else if $eq(hC,\text{ap})$ and closure(hS)
     then $[(\ ),(\text{bvpart}(hS),htS){:}\text{Epart}(hS),\text{bodypart}(hS),(ttS,E,tC,D)]$
   else if $eq(hC,\text{ap})$ and not closure(hS)
     then $(hS(htS){:}ttS,E,tC,D)$
   else if combination(hC) **then** $[S,E,\text{rand}(hC){:}\text{rator}(hC){:}\text{ap}{:}tC,D]$

The above relatively compact specification of transformations of instantaneous descriptions during the evaluation of lambda expressions has been made possible by a judicious choice of run-time environment and

† Note that this strategy of function evaluation for lambda expressions differs from all those given in Sec. 3.8. Among other things, the present strategy causes operands to be evaluated *before* substitution, whereas all the strategies of Sec. 3.8 cause operands to be evaluated after substitution.

of selectors, constructors, and predicates for specifying transformations of the instantaneous description during evaluation.

Whereas the LISP evaluation function was specified within the LISP language, we have in the present case deliberately allowed considerable freedom in augmenting the language for semantic specification in order to simplify description of semantics of a given programming language. If the language whose semantics is to be described remains fixed, we can by introducing appropriate selectors, constructors, and predicates into the language usually arrange to describe the run-time transformations during evaluation relatively simply. However, if the aim is to describe a language in itself, introduction of new primitives requires specification within the augmented language of the transformation determined by the new primitives, and a point of diminishing returns sets in. The set of LISP primitives appears to be relatively optimal for describing the run-time transformation in terms of the set of primitives.

In the next section it will be shown that the notion of a program for evaluating all programs of a programming language is familiar to logicians and resembles the notion of a universal Turing machine.

The SECD machine described above allows evaluation of expressions that consist of lambda expressions and of operator-operand combinations whose operator part is a primitive operation. The syntax of the class of permitted expressions is

$$E \rightarrow V|\lambda VE|(EE)|\text{pf}E$$

where pf is a primitive function, and the effect of application of pf to E is specified as a primitive within the system.

Expressions of the form pf$E$ are evaluated by the SECD machine as operator-operand combinations by first producing E:pf:ap:C on the control string and then val(pf):val(E):SS on the stack. The symbol ap on the control string then causes hS to be applied to htS. If hS is the closure of a lambda expression, the previous function is pushed down, and a new function is entered. However, if hS is a primitive operation, application of hS to htS is performed directly.

Exercise: Define transform functions for the basic lambda-calculus, the LISP, and the fixed-program machines.

3.10.4   AN EXAMPLE OF EVALUATION ON THE SECD MACHINE

The operation of the SECD machine will be illustrated by showing how the operator-operand $(\lambda f((f3) + (f4))\lambda x(x \times x))$ is evaluated. This operator-operand combination has an operator part that is a one-argument lambda expression with a function-valued parameter and an operand part that is a one-argument function to be substituted for the function-valued parameter.   Evaluation leads to

$$((\lambda x(x \times x)3) + (\lambda x(x \times x)4) = 3^2 + 4^2 = 25$$

In order to evaluate this function on the SECD machine, the arithmetic operations must be specified in prefix form, resulting in the lambda expression

$$(\lambda f((+ (f3))(f4))\lambda x((\times x)x))$$

If the programmer prefers to specify his computations in the previous notation, a compiler for translating from the previous to the present notation can be used.   The prefix representation can be thought of as a machine-language representation of a problem-oriented language in which application of operation to operands is sometimes specified in infix form.

The evaluation of this expression on the SECD machine is illustrated by the 35-step computation on page 224.

3.11   UNIVERSAL PROGRAMS AND UNIVERSAL COMPUTERS

3.11.1   UNIVERSAL LANGUAGES AND UNIVERSAL PROGRAMS

A programming language will be called *universal* if it is sufficiently powerful to specify all computable functions.   Every universal language L permits the specification of a program *apply* which, when presented with a program P in the language L together with its data D, will compute the value $apply(P,D)$ which results from applying P to the data D.   The program *apply* will be called a *universal program* of language L, since it can be used to simulate the application of any program $P \in L$ to any set of data D in the domain of P.

Perlis in his Turing lecture [12] indicates the desirability of designing programming languages so that universal programs can be specified relatively easily.   In the present section we shall briefly characterize universal programs and indicate the relation between universal programs and universal computers.

A universal program may be thought of as specification in L of a set of rules for scanning program strings of L and performing transformations on the data D specified by successive symbols of the program string.   Thus a language L designed to facilitate the writing of a universal program for L in L should contain facilities for scanning program strings and for specifying the syntactic transformations on program and data strings performed during evaluation.

The first language consciously designed to facilitate the specification of universal programs was LISP.   In LISP both programs and data are represented by lists, and the primitive operations of the language include

Step	Comment	S	E
1	Initial state	S	E
2	Combination	S	E
3	Evaluate λ-exp	$\text{cl}(E,\lambda x,((\times\ x)x){:}S$	E
4	Evaluate λ-exp	$\text{cl}(E,\lambda f,(-)){:}\text{cl}(E,\lambda x,(-)){:}S$	E
5	Apply λ-exp	( )	$(f,\text{cl}(E,\lambda x,((\times\ x)x))){:}$ $E = E'$
6	Combination	( )	E'
7	Combination	( )	E'
8	Evaluate 4	4	E'
9	Evaluate f	$\text{cl}(E,\lambda x,((\times\ x)x)){:}4$	E'
10	Apply λ-exp	( )	$(x,4){:}E' = E''$
11	Combination	( )	E''
12	Evaluate x	4	E''
13	Combination	4	E''
14	Evaluate x	4:4	E''
15	Evaluate $\times$	$\text{val}(\times){:}4{:}4$	E''
16	Apply $\times$	$(\times\ 4){:}4$	E''
17	Apply $(\times\ 4)$	16	E''
18	Pop up dump	16:( )	E'
19	Combination	16	E'
20	Combination	16	E'
21	Evaluate 3	3:16	E'
22	Evaluate f	$\text{cl}(E,\lambda x,((\times\ x)x)){:}3{:}16$	E'
23	Apply λ-exp	( )	$(x,3){:}E' = E'''$
24	Combination	( )	E'''
25	Evaluate x	3	E'''
26	Combination	3	E'''
27	Evaluate x	3:3	E'''
28	Evaluate $\times$	$\text{val}(\times){:}3{:}3$	E'''
29	Apply $\times$	$(\times\ 3){:}3$	E'''
30	Apply $(\times\ 3)$	9	E'''
31	Pop up dump	9:16	E'
32	Evaluate $+$	$\text{val}(+){:}9{:}16$	E'
33	Apply $+$	$(+\ 9){:}16$	E'
34	Apply $(+\ 9)$	25	E'
35	Pop up dump	25:S	E

C	D
$(\lambda f((+ (f3))(f4))\lambda x((\times x(x)):C$	D
$\lambda x((\times x)x):\lambda f((+ (f3))(f4)):\mathrm{ap}:C$	D
$\lambda f((+ (f3))(f4)):\mathrm{ap}:C$	D
$\mathrm{ap}:C$	D
$((+ (f3))(f4))$	$D' = (S,E,C,D)$
$(f4):(+ (f3)):\mathrm{ap}$	D'
$4:f:\mathrm{ap}:(+ (f3)):\mathrm{ap}$	D'
$f:\mathrm{ap}:(+ (f3)):\mathrm{ap}$	D'
$\mathrm{ap}:(+ (f3)):\mathrm{ap}$	D'
$((\times x)x)$	$D'' = ((\ ),E',(+ (f3)):\mathrm{ap},D')$
$x:(\times x):\mathrm{ap}$	D''
$(\times x):\mathrm{ap}$	D''
$x:\times:\mathrm{ap}:\mathrm{ap}$	D''
$\times:\mathrm{ap}:\mathrm{ap}$	D''
$\mathrm{ap}:\mathrm{ap}$	D''
ap	D''
$(\ )$	D''
$(+ (f3)):\mathrm{ap}$	D'
$(f3):+:\mathrm{ap}:\mathrm{ap}$	D'
$3:f:\mathrm{ap}:+:\mathrm{ap}:\mathrm{ap}$	D'
$f:\mathrm{ap}:+:\mathrm{ap}:\mathrm{ap}$	D'
$\mathrm{ap}:+:\mathrm{ap}:\mathrm{ap}$	D'
$((\times x)x)$	$D''' = (16,E',+:\mathrm{ap}:\mathrm{ap},D')$
$x:(\times x):\mathrm{ap}$	D'''
$(\times x):\mathrm{ap}$	D'''
$x:\times:\mathrm{ap}:\mathrm{ap}$	D'''
$\times:\mathrm{ap}:\mathrm{ap}$	D'''
$\mathrm{ap}:\mathrm{ap}$	D'''
ap	D'''
$(\ )$	D'''
$+:\mathrm{ap}:\mathrm{ap}$	D'
$\mathrm{ap}:\mathrm{ap}$	D'
ap	D'
$(\ )$	D'
C	D

operations for scanning of lists (selection of list elements) and for performing transformations on the list elements being scanned. These operations are used to specify a universal program in LISP for the evaluation of LISP programs.

3.11.2 UNIVERSAL PROGRAMS AND UNIVERSAL COMPUTERS

Consider next the relation between a program and a computer. A program may be thought of as a specification of a special-purpose computer for transforming data in the domain of the program into values in the range of the program, which has the additional property that primitive operations of the computer correspond to primitive commands of the program. A programming language can be thought of as a specification of a class of computers, where each computer in the class corresponds to a program of the language.

If the programming language permits operations on data structures that constitute program descriptions, the corresponding class of computers must permit operations on data structures that constitute computer descriptions together with their data and produces as output the result of applying the described computer to its data. A computer which corresponds to a universal program will be called a *universal computer*.

The notion of a universal computer U for a class of special-purpose computers C can be defined independently of the notion of a program. A class C of computers will be called universal if there are computers in the class for computing every computable function. A computer U is a universal computer for the universal class C if its domain is the set of ordered pairs (F, A_F), where F ranges over all elements of C and A_F ranges over all elements in the domain of the computer F, and if the result of $U(F, A_F) = F(A_F)$ is the value obtained by applying the computer F to the data A_F.

3.11.3 UNIVERSAL TURING MACHINES

The class of universal computers which has been most extensively studied is the class of Turing machines. It can be shown [15] that for the class of Turing machines there is a universal Turing machine T whose input domain is the set of all pairs (F, A_F), where F is a Turing machine description and A_F is an argument for F, such that $T(F, A_F) = F(A_F)$.

The problem of specifying a universal program in a universal programming language is equivalent to the problem of specifying a universal computer in a universal computer class, illustrating once again the intimate relation between software and hardware representations of functions. In this case the notion of a universal function capable of simulating the behavior of all functions of a given class which includes the function itself was first developed in terms of a hardware model.

The concepts developed for the hardware model can be used to illuminate corresponding properties of a class of software models.

REFERENCES

1. Strachey, C.: A General Purpose Macrogenerator, *Computer J.*, October, 1965.
2. Mooers, C. N.: TRAC—A Procedure Describing Language for the Reactive Typewriter, *Commun. ACM*, March, 1966.
3. Mooers, C. N., and L. P. Deutsch: *Proc. 20th ACM Conf., Cleveland*, September, 1965.
4. Church, A.: "The Calculi of Lambda Conversion," Princeton University Press, Princeton, N.J., 1941.
5. Scott, D.: Handwritten notes on the Lambda Calculus, September, 1966.
6. McCarthy, J., et al.: "LISP 1.5 Programmer's Manual," The M.I.T. Press, Cambridge, Mass., 1962.
7. Wegner, P.: Lambda Calculus Machines and the Run Time Environment of LISP and ALGOL, unpublished manuscript, November, 1966.
8. Landin, P. J.: A Correspondence between ALGOL 60 and Church's Lambda Notation, *Commun. ACM*, February, March, 1965.
9. Landin, P. J.: The Mechanical Evaluation of Expressions, *Computer J.*, January, 1964.
10. Leavenworth, B.: Syntax Macros, *Commun. ACM*, November, 1966.
11. Waite, W.: A Language-independent Macro Processor, *Commun. ACM*, July, 1967.
12. Perlis, A. J.: The Synthesis of Algorithmic Systems, *JACM*, January, 1967.
13. Yngve, V., et al.: COMIT *Commun. ACM*, March, 1963.
14. Farber, D., et al.: SNOBOL—A String Manipulation Language, *JACM*, January, 1964.
15. Smullyan, R. M.: "The Theory of Formal Systems," Princeton University Press, Princeton, N.J., 1941.
16. Curry, H. B., and R. Feys: "Combinatory Logic," North-Holland Publishing Company, Amsterdam, 1958.
17. Rosenbloom, P.: "The Elements of Mathematical Logic," Dover Publications, Inc., New York, 1950.
18. Standish, T.: A Data Definition Facility for Programming Languages, Ph.D. thesis, *Carnegie Tech. Rept.*, May, 1967.
19. Rosen, S.: "The Compiler Building System Developed by Brooker and Morris," in S. Rosen, ed., *Programming Systems and Languages*, McGraw-Hill Book Company, New York, 1967.

CHAPTER 4

PROCEDURE-ORIENTED
LANGUAGES

4.1 INTRODUCTION

4.1.1 REENTRANT PROGRAM REPRESENTATION

There are some obvious notational differences between the macro-like notations for function specification discussed in the previous chapter and the procedure-oriented languages discussed in the present chapter. Although these notational differences do not *require* different function-evaluation strategies to be used, they *strongly suggest* different strategies for evaluation. Macro languages suggest progressive substitution of values for a function with its arguments until a value is obtained. Procedure-oriented languages suggest evaluation by scanning of the function body in a read-only mode, as in the fixed-program machine of Sec. 3.8.

In the present chapter methods of representation of programming languages and evaluation procedures for pure functions will be considered in which the function representation is scanned without being transformed during its evaluation. Instead of transforming the body of the function during its execution, all variable information associated with a partially evaluated function is stored in an information structure referred to as an *activation record* associated with each *instance of execution* of the function. A function is represented by a *fixed-program part*, which may be thought of as representing the "abstract" algorithm independently of its execution. An *instance of execution* of the function is represented by the fixed-program part together with an activation record which contains data and control information that may vary for different instances of execution of the function. During execution the fixed-program part remains fixed, while the activation record may grow, diminish, or be modified.

When functions are represented in this way, a given pure function may be simultaneously executed by a number of independent or coordinated interpreters each of which has a scanning pointer pointing to the point of execution of the function reached in the particular execution instance. Function execution of this form is referred to as *reentrant* function execution, since no special machinery is required to execute functions which reenter themselves during their execution. Functions which require evaluation of themselves during their execution are known as recursive functions. Reentrant representation of functions during their execution facilitates both recursive reentry to functions and other forms of reentrant function execution, such as multiprogramming.

Figure 4.1 illustrates a function module with a single fixed-program part and two instances of activation with associated activation records. The points reached in execution of the two activations are respectively indicated by the statewords $S1$ and $S2$, which point both to the current point of execution in the fixed program and to the activation record. These pointers are normally stored in an instruction-processing unit while the function module is being executed and in the activation record

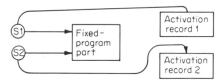

Figure 4.1 A function module with two partially executed activations.

itself if processing of the function module is interrupted. Interruption of a given function module can be caused either explicitly by a call to another function module or (in the case of multiprogramming) implicitly because the system requires the processing unit for another purpose.

In procedure-oriented languages a program consists of a number of interacting function modules having a *static* relation to each other in the initial representation of the source program. During execution, the fixed program representing a set of interrelated function modules gives rise to *dynamic* relations between instances of activation of function modules. These dynamic relations must be reflected by links between the activation records associated with corresponding instances of activation.

The prototype of programming languages with reentrant function modules is the ALGOL 60 language. It was developed as an international language for the specification and communication of algorithms and is specified in its original form in [1] and in a revised form in [2]. The syntax given in [2] is included as Appendix 2 for completeness. For ambiguities and suggested corrections to [2], see [20].

4.1.2 STACKS, TREES, AND NESTED STRUCTURES

In the present chapter a deliberate attempt has been made to minimize discussion of syntactic features of ALGOL and to emphasize the semantics of the language by considering the representation of ALGOL programs during successive stages of their execution. In Sec. 4.2 the symbols which may occur in an ALGOL program are classified from a semantic point of view, and the method of associating identifiers with information structures by means of declarations is considered. In Sec. 4.3 a number of alternative representations of simple expressions and statements are considered, and the run-time operand stack is described.

Expressions may have subexpressions nested inside them to an arbitrary depth. The requirement of an operand stack for expression evaluation is directly related to the fact that expressions are nested in the static program.

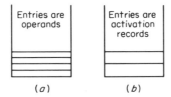

Figure 4.2   Operand stack (a) **and function-module stack** (b).

ALGOL allows nesting both at the level of expressions and at the level of function modules. Static nesting of function modules in the initial program representation results in a *function-module stack* during evaluation for precisely the same reasons that static nesting of expressions results in an operand stack during evaluation. However, individual entries in the operand stack consist of operands, whereas individual entries in the function-module stack consist of activation records, as illustrated in Fig. 4.2.

There is a strong parallel between stack management for operand stacks and function-module stacks. Both grow by one element on entry to an inner level of nesting and diminish by one element when an inner level of nesting is completed.

Nested structures may be converted into tree structures by associating a tree vertex with each nested substructure and letting a vertex B be a descendant of a vertex A if and only if the structure corresponding to vertex B is nested in the structure corresponding to vertex A. The correspondence between nested structures and tree structures is illustrated in Fig. 4.3.

The depth of nesting of a given function module corresponds to the length of the path from the root vertex of the tree to the vertex of the corresponding function module.

During execution of a given function module the activation-record stack contains activation records of the currently executed function module and of all enclosing function modules.   In tree terminology the activation records are those associated with the current vertex and all predecessor vertices.

The function modules of programming languages such as ALGOL may contain procedure calls.   A function module is said to be *implicitly nested* at each of the points at which it is called.   A call of a procedure results in *dynamic nesting* of the called procedure at the point of call. A given procedure call may result in further procedure calls in the called procedure, including recursive calls of the called procedure.   The depth of nesting to which a given implicitly nested procedure call may give rise cannot in general be predicted.   Techniques for implementing implicitly nested function modules are discussed in some detail in Secs. 4.6 and 4.7.

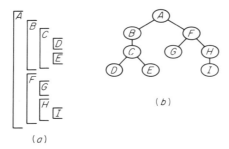

(a)

(b)

Figure 4.3 Correspondence between nested structure (a) **and tree structure** (b)**.**

During execution of a given function module, entry to an inner function module will result in the creation of a new activation record on the activation-record stack.   Evaluation of an expression within the function module will result in the creation of an operand stack during evaluation of the expression.   This operand stack may be stored as part of the current activation record.   The activation record augmented by the operand stack will grow when an operand is added to the operand stack and diminish when an operand is removed from the operand stack.   Evaluation of a given expression is always dynamically nested within a function module, in the sense that exit from expression evaluation must precede exit from the function module.   An operand stack which is placed at the end of the activation record in which the expression occurs will always have room to grow and diminish and will always be deleted before the activation record in which it occurs is deleted.†

† ALGOL permits arguments of expression to be calls of function modules. Expression arguments which are function modules can be dealt with by creating an activation record of the function module at the current point of the operand stack as indicated in Sec. 4.6.   Thus function modules may in turn be nested in the operand stack.

Quantities stored in the activation record of a given function module are said to be *local* to that function module. During execution of a given function module, reference can be made both to local quantities and to selected *nonlocal* quantities stored in previously activated function modules. The set of all quantities accessible during execution of a given function module is said to constitute the *environment* of the current function module. ALGOL is designed so that both reading and writing of selected nonlocal quantities in the environment are permitted. However, writing which alters the size of information structures in the environment is not permitted. Explicit information structures can be created only on entry to function modules and deleted only on exit from function modules. Implicit information structures can be created and deleted during expression evaluation within a function module. All creation and deletion of information is restricted to local information within the function module currently being executed.

Sections 4.4 and 4.5 deal with the forms of expressions, statements, function modules, and block structure permitted in ALGOL and are effectively the sections which describe the principal syntactic and semantic features of the language.

In Sec. 4.6 the run-time representation of ALGOL function modules is described in some detail, special attention being given to methods of storing activation records in a run-time stack and of updating the environment on entry to, and exit from, function modules. A final subsection (4.6.10) indicates how the semantics of ALGOL could be formally specified in terms of an "ALGOL machine" which specifies the transformations of the run-time representation for all symbols (instructions) of the program which may be encountered during execution.

In Sec. 4.7 an analysis is made of the conditions under which the information structure represented by a group of activation records remains invariant. Optimization by combination of such activation records into single composite activation records is discussed. A key role in such optimization is played by procedures which can be guaranteed to be nonrecursive. Graph-theoretic techniques for distinguishing between recursive and nonrecursive procedures are given.

4.1.3 IDENTIFIER ATTRIBUTES AND FUNCTION-MODULE SCHEDULING

Section 4.8 indicates some of the limitations of ALGOL with regard to creation, deletion, and manipulation of information structures and suggests how some of these limitations might be overcome. This discussion in turn leads to a discussion in Sec. 4.9 of the principal structural features of the richer and more elaborate PL/I language. It is shown that the greater richness of PL/I is achieved principally by allowing a greater variety of attributes to be associated with identifiers. Among the additional attributes and language features are a new form of "interrupt" function module defined by the ON statement, the POINTER attribute, the structure declaration, and the controlled storage-allocation attributes. The use of these attributes in the definition and manipulation of lists of structures is discussed.

Although PL/I is a richer language than ALGOL, the order of execution of function modules within tasks of PL/I is required to be nested dynamically so that activation records can be allocated in a single run-time stack. Section 4.10 relaxes this requirement and considers alternative methods of sequencing between function modules. The notion of a *coroutine* is introduced which permits interleaving the execution of function modules. The notion of *scheduling* of function modules by means of *event notices* that contain scheduling parameters is discussed. The notion of *tasks* which can be executed in parallel on simultaneously operating interpreters is introduced, and problems of synchronization are considered. It is shown that coroutines are most naturally implemented by a separate stack for each coroutine which grows and diminishes independently of stacks for other coroutines. Tasks are most naturally implemented by means of a tree-structured (forked) stack. When a task is created, it has access to the already existing portion of the stack of the creating task. However, portions of the stack created during execution of the task are private to the task.

In the final section the scheduling of function modules using a single linear scheduling parameter (system time) is examined in greater detail. Languages built around such a scheduling mechanism are referred to as *simulation languages*. The two simulation languages SIMSCRIPT and SIMULA are described and compared by programming the job-shop scheduling problem in each of the languages. This comparison illustrates the use of controlled storage allocation, coroutines, and a number of other advanced features of programming languages.

4.2 SYSTEM SYMBOLS, IDENTIFIERS, AND TYPE SPECIFICATIONS

4.2.1 THE STRUCTURE OF ALGOL PROGRAMS

Syntactically any program consists of a linear string of symbols chosen from a finite alphabet (see Appendix 1). The finite alphabet used in the specification of an ALGOL program contains 116 symbols, including alphabetic characters, decimal digits, operation and punctuation symbols, and a number of symbols represented by character strings in a special alphabet.

The basic symbols of ALGOL can be used to build up successively larger constructs of the language, such as constants, variables, expressions, statements, etc. The strings which represent these constructs are in turn components of function modules of the language (blocks and procedures). A complete ALGOL program consists of a single function module (block), which may have other function modules nested inside it. The detailed syntax of ALGOL is given in Appendix 2.

An ALGOL program will be thought of as a symbol string which is executed by scanning successive symbols and performing transformations determined by the symbols being scanned.† The information structure at any given point of the computation will be called an instantaneous description. The semantics of any executable program segment will be specified in terms of the effect it has in transforming instantaneous descriptions.

For semantic purposes it is convenient to choose a slightly higher-level set of basic symbols than the 116 basic characters. The set of basic symbols will include an unbounded set of names (identifiers) which can be used by the programmer to specify and transform information structures and an unbounded set of constants representing integers and decimal numbers.

4.2.2 CLASSIFICATION OF PRIMITIVE PROGRAM CONSTITUENTS

The set of primitive program constituents can be classified into two categories:

1. *System symbols* which have a *fixed meaning* specified by the system and include control symbols, operators, and data constants of the language. Some, like +, consist of single characters, while others, like 11.63, consist of character strings. Still others, like **begin**, **if**, and **for**, have precisely the same status as single characters in spite of the fact that they are represented by character strings in a special alphabet.

2. *Identifiers* which serve as names of information structures of the language. There are mechanisms in the language for defining both the structure and the value of an identifier and for redefining the values of certain classes of identifiers. ALGOL contains a small subset of identifiers (such as the standard functions sin and cos) which are *initialized identifiers* in the sense that initial definitions for these identifiers are supplied by the system.

The symbols scanned during execution of an ALGOL program are either system symbols or identifiers. System symbols result in an action determined by the system, while identifiers result in access to the named information structure for purposes of storage, retrieval, or execution.

† Note that this point of view can be adopted both for ALGOL source programs and for programs in a machine-oriented representation.

4.2.3 ATTRIBUTES OF SYSTEM SYMBOLS AND IDENTIFIERS

The effect of encountering a symbol during execution is determined by its *attributes*. The attributes of system symbols are implicitly given and need never be explicitly specified by the programmer. However, attributes of uninitialized identifiers must be specified by the programmer, and ALGOL therefore has a notation for defining identifiers and associating attributes with identifiers. A specification of an identifier together with its attributes is referred to in ALGOL as a *declaration*.

The principal attribute which the user may specify for an identifier is the *domain* of information structures which the identifier may denote. ALGOL identifiers are classified into a number of *types*, each of which may have a specific class of information structures as its values. Programming languages normally use one of the following techniques for specifying the type of identifier:

1. Using different classes of names for different classes of identifiers. This technique is used in FORTRAN to distinguish between identifiers (variables) representing integers and identifiers representing floating-point numbers.
2. Examining the context in which a name is used; i.e., if x occurs as part of an arithmetic expression $x + y$, it is assumed to be an identifier having numerical values, while if it appears as part of a logical expression $x \wedge y$, it is assumed to have logical values.
3. By means of explicit *declarations* which specify the class of values that may be associated with the name. This is the form of identifier specification used in ALGOL.

4.2.4 PRIMITIVE ALGOL DATA TYPES

Identifiers in ALGOL consist of a letter followed by an arbitrary number of letters or digits. ALGOL permits the following three primitive data-type specifications:

integer x;   This declaration specifies that the value associated with the identifier x must be chosen from the set of integers. More specifically the value of the integer x must be within the range permitted by the implementation.†

† In the ALGOL report, it is stated that there is no restriction on the length of an integer. However, implementation of arithmetic for integers of unrestricted length is not usually included in ALGOL implementations, and the size of integers and floating-point numbers is normally determined by the size of the memory register. Languages like PL/I explicitly specify that number length is determined by the implementation.

real x;   This declaration specifies that the value of the identifier x is a floating-point number lying in the range permitted by the implementation.

Boolean x;   This declaration specifies that x is a two-valued (Boolean) variable having one of the two values **true** or **false**.

The information structures associated with identifiers of type **integer** and **real** could be specified in terms of lower-level attributes, such as the number of bits in component fields of the structure. For instance, "**real**[0:7,0:23]x" could be used to specify a floating-point number with a 24-bit mantissa and an 8-bit exponent. However, it is assumed that the field specifications for items of type integer, real, and Boolean are automatically supplied by the system and need not be supplied by the user. This is precisely what is meant by the statement that **integer**, **real**, and **Boolean** are *primitive* data types of the system.

4.2.5   ARRAY AND PROCEDURE DECLARATIONS

Rectangular arrays whose elements are primitive data types can be specified in ALGOL by *array declarations*.

real array A[1:m, −2:2];   This declaration specifies that the identifier A has as its value an information structure consisting of a two-dimensional array of real-valued quantities. The first dimension has a lower bound 1 and a variable upper bound which is determined by the value of m at the time of declaration. The second dimension has five elements with subscripts $-2, -1, 0, 1, 2$.

Array declarations consist of the symbol **array**, prefixed by a type specification **integer**, **real**, or **Boolean**, specifying the type of the elements of the array, followed by the array name, followed by a *subscript specification* enclosed in square brackets. The subscript specification consists of a lower-bound and upper-bound specification for each subscript, where lower- and upper-bound specifications must be integer-valued expressions. Arrays declared by array declarations are *used* by specifying the array name and subscript values.

$A[I+2\times J, K]$ When this array variable is encountered during evaluation, the integer expressions in each subscript position are evaluated, and the resulting integer is taken to be the value of the subscript. If the subscript is outside the bounds specified in the declaration, a good ALGOL system will cause a run-time diagnostic.

The fifth form of identifier declaration is the procedure declaration, which has the form:

procedure name (P1, . . . ,PN) specification body   A procedure declaration consists
of the system symbol **procedure** followed by the procedure identifier,
followed by a list of formal parameters separated by commas and
enclosed in parentheses,† followed by a *specification* which specifies the
types of formal parameters, followed by the *procedure body* which specifies the action to be performed on execution of the procedure.   Examples of procedures will be given in Sec. 4.5.

ALGOL also permits identifiers to be of type **label**.   However, identifiers of type label are not explicitly declared in ALGOL but recognized by
their context.   This is somewhat of an anomaly, and an explicit label
declaration will therefore be introduced for purposes of exposition.

label L;‡   This declaration (which is not permitted in ALGOL 60)
could be used to declare L to be an identifier having a label
as its value.

At any given point during the execution of an ALGOL program the
set of symbols which can meaningfully be used consists of the fixed set
of system symbols, a set of *current* programmer-defined identifiers, and
those initialized identifiers which do not conflict with current programmer-
defined identifiers.   This set of symbols together with their attributes is
referred to as the *current environment*.   During execution of the program,
declarations cause the current environment to be augmented.   Subsequent uses of symbols cause access to the current environment for purposes
of execution, storage, or retrieval.   Different classes of symbols require
different modes of access to the current environment when they are
encountered.   One of the aims of the present discussion of ALGOL is to
classify and describe the different modes of access to the environment for
the different classes of symbols that occur in ALGOL.

4.3   THE STRUCTURE AND EVALUATION
OF SIMPLE EXPRESSIONS AND STATEMENTS

4.3.1   PREFIX AND INFIX NOTATION

Identifiers are used in a program to access information items in the
environment.   The principal reason for access to information associated
with identifiers is to modify values of identifiers by performing operations

---

† A procedure with zero parameters, referred to as a *parameterless procedure*, has
no parameter list.

‡ Although declarations of type **label** are not permitted, procedure parameters
may be specified to be of the type **label** in the specification part of the procedure (see
Sec. 4.5).

on them.   Operations on information items are specified by *expressions* containing *operators* and *operands*.

The juxtaposition of operators and operands in an expression is determined by the rules of syntax for forming expressions.   Common syntactic forms for specifying the application of operators to operands will now be discussed.

In prefix notation the operator *precedes* its operands.   The operands may be separated by commas and enclosed in parentheses or merely listed in sequence.

$f(x_1, x_2, \ldots, x_n)$ These are two alternative notations for specifying
$f x_1 x_2 \ldots x_n$ the application of an operator f with n arguments
      to its operands.

An argument may itself be an operator applied to its operands. Thus x_2 could have the form $g(y_1, y_2)$ (or $g y_1 y_2$), where g is a two-argument operator.   An expression may in general contain operators applied to operands nested to an arbitrary level.

An operator with n arguments is usually called an *n-ary operator*, an operator with two arguments is usually called a *binary operator*, and an operator with one argument is usually called a *unary operator*.†   An operator with no arguments is called a *nullary operator*.   A constant may be thought of as a nullary operator.   It is sometimes convenient to do away with the distinction between operators and operands and think of operands as a special class of operators which happen to be nullary.

The number of arguments of an operator will be called its *degree*. The degree of an operand is always zero.   Note that if the degree of every operator and operand in a prefix expression is known, the operands of every operator are uniquely determined, and it is unnecessary to use parentheses to indicate the operands associated with a given operator. For this reason prefix notation is sometimes referred to as a *parenthesis-free notation*.

Expressions containing binary operators frequently have a syntactic form in which operators are written *between* the operands.   Such a notation is referred to as *infix* notation.   For example, arithmetic expressions which contain arithmetic operations such as $+$ and $\times$ are usually specified in infix notation.   Many of the basic operations of ALGOL are specified in infix notation.

Careful conventions are required to specify the order of evaluation of infixed expressions.   For example, an explicit rule is required to specify that in the expression "$a - b + c$" the minus operation is applied to its

---

† Operators (functions) with 1, 2, n and many arguments are sometimes referred to as *monadic*, *dyadic*, *n-adic*, and *polyadic* operators (functions).   Functions with a varying number of arguments are sometimes referred to as *variadic* functions.

operands before $+$ is applied to $a - b$ and c, while in the expression "$a - b \times c$" multiplication is applied to its operands before $-$ is applied to a and $b \times c$. In prefix notation these two expressions are respectively specified as $+(-(a,b),c)$ and $-(a,\times(b,c))$ (or in parentheses-free notation, $+-abc$ and $-a\times bc$), and the identification of the operands associated with a given operator is much clearer. Evaluation rules for expressions in infix notation will be further discussed in subsection 4.3.7.

4.3.2 THE TREE STRUCTURE OF EXPRESSIONS

Prefix and infix notation are two alternative linear representations of a structure that is most naturally represented by a tree. The two arithmetic expressions of the previous paragraph have the tree representations shown in Fig. 4.4.

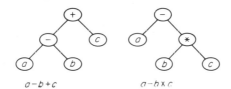

Figure   4.4 Tree   representation   of $a - b + c$ **and** $a - b \times c$.

The tree representation of an arbitrary expression consisting of operators applied to operands is built up by representing a subexpression of the form $f(x_1,x_2, \ldots ,x_n)$ by a subtree with f as the root and x_1, $x_2, \ldots , x_n$ as terminal vertices. Arguments x_i which are themselves operators applied to operands consist of subtrees rather than simple terminal vertices.

Given the tree representation of an expression, the order in which vertices occur in the corresponding prefix representation can be specified as follows: Start by listing the root vertex. List the leftmost descendant of the most recently listed vertex whenever possible. Whenever the vertex which has just been listed has no further unlisted descendants, back up to the most recent predecessor which has an unlisted descendant and list its leftmost unlisted descendant. This procedure can terminate only when all descendants have been listed.

Exercises: (a) Draw a flow diagram for determining the prefix representation of an expression given the tree representation of an expression, assuming that operations such as predecessor, successor, and leftmost unlisted descendant are primitive operations.   (b) Discuss how the tree-structured representation might be represented in a computer and how the above tree-accessing primitives might be implemented. (*c*) Develop an algorithm for going from a tree representation of an arithmetic expression having only binary operations to the corresponding infix expression. (*d*) Develop an algorithm for constructing the tree associated with an expression from its prefix representation.

4.3.3 GENERALIZED DEGREE

The well-formedness of an expression in prefix notation can be completely determined by examining only the sequence of degrees i associated with each of the constituents in the expression. Given a prefix notation expression such as $+a \times bc$, the well-formedness of this expression can be determined by examining the sequence of integers 20200. The rule for determining well-formedness is as follows:

Let $i_1, i_2, \cdots , i_n$ be the sequence of argument counts of successive symbols on an n-element prefix expression. Then the expression is well formed if $1 + \sum_{k=1}^{n} (i_k - 1) = 0$ and every partial sum from $k = 1$ through $j, j = 1, 2, \ldots , n - 1$, is greater than zero.

When the sequence is 20200, successive partial sums are 2, 1, 2, 1, 0, so that the above conditions are satisfied.

The number $1 + \sum_{k=1}^{j} (i_k - 1)$ represents the number of arguments still required by the prefix expression whose first j symbols require i_1, $i_2, \ldots , i_j$ arguments. This number is referred to as the *generalized degree* of the expression.† When a new symbol requiring i_{j+1} arguments is added as the $(j + 1)$st symbol, the generalized degree of the prefix expression is clearly changed by $i_{j+1} - 1$.

4.3.4 STATIC AND DYNAMIC TYPE TESTING

The notion of a generalized degree allows us to check whether an expression in prefix notation has the right number of arguments. However, in order to evaluate an expression, the additional requirement must be satisfied that each of the arguments must have a value in the domain expected by the operator which operates upon it. Checking that the domain of an operand specified by an identifier is of the type expected by the operator is more complex than merely checking for the right number of arguments. These checks may in principle be performed prior to execution by examining an initial representation of the program, but they are sometimes delayed until execution. ALGOL and most other currently existing procedure-oriented languages are designed

---

† Degrees are associated only with individual operators, while generalized degrees are associated with initial substrings of an expression.

specifically with a view to allowing a check for operator-operand compatibility to be performed on the initial program representation; i.e., the type of a specific occurrence of an identifier can be determined from the initial program representation and does not change for different instances of execution of that identifier.   However, programming languages may be designed which do not permit testing for operator-operand compatibility by checking the initial program.   Thus if type assignment and reassignment statements can be executed at arbitrary points of the program like regular assignment statements, there is no general algorithm for determining from the initial program representation whether operators will be compatible with operands in all instances of execution.

4.3.5 EVALUATION OF EXPRESSIONS IN POSTFIX NOTATION

It was shown above that prefix and infix notation are two alternative linearizations of the tree structure which constitutes an arithmetic expression.   Still a third linearization of the tree structure which constitutes an arithmetic expression is postfix notation, in which the operators occur immediately after the operands which they operate.   Thus $a - b + c$ would be specified in postfix notation as $ab-c+$ and $a - b \times c$ would be specified in postfix notation as $abc\times -$.

As indicated in subsection 1.6.4, postfix notation is the most convenient notation for direct execution of arithmetic expressions by left-to-right scanning with the aid of a single run-time operand stack.   Execution can be accomplished by moving operands to the operand stack and applying operators to operands at the top of the operand stack. The sequence of steps to be performed on execution of an expression in postfix form stored in positions $C(1), C(2), \ldots, C(n)$ of a control string C is specified by Fig. 4.5; i.e., if the symbol currently being scanned is an operand, determine the value of the operand in the environment and place the value on top of the operand stack, increasing the number of elements in the operand stack by 1.   If the currently scanned symbol is an operator expecting n arguments, apply the operator to the n top operands in the operand stack, erase the n arguments from the operand stack, and place the value which results from application of the operator to the operands on top of the operand stack.

An n-ary operator reduces the size of the operand stack by $n - 1$. If operand types have not been checked for compatibility with operators prior to execution of the program, the compatibility of operand types with the operator may be determined dynamically on application of the operator to the operands.

Exercises: (a) Develop a model similar to the SECD machine for execution of expressions in postfix notation.   *Hint:* The model will have a

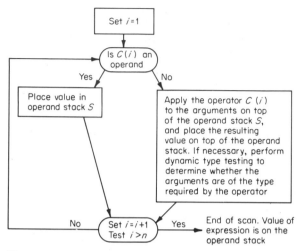

Figure 4.5 Evaluation of expressions in postfix notation.

stack S, a fixed environment E, and a control string C. No dump component is necessary since execution of function modules cannot be interrupted. (b) What happens if the expression being evaluated is not well formed? Suggest a method for testing for well-formedness.

4.3.6 EVALUATION OF EXPRESSIONS IN PREFIX NOTATION

Left-to-right evaluation of expressions in prefix notation is more complex than left-to-right evaluation of expressions in postfix notation. However, such evaluation may be specified relatively economically with the aid of an operator stack in which operators together with auxiliary information can be pushed down while arguments are being evaluated. The principal item of auxiliary information is an argument count which is initially n for an n-ary operator, is reduced by 1 whenever an operand for that operator is placed in the operand stack, and triggers application of the operator to its operands when it reaches zero. Figure 4.6 illustrates the evaluation of a prefix expression of length n stored in positions $C(1), C(2), \ldots, C(n)$ of a control string C. Note that the algorithm allows operators to have zero arguments. An operator with zero arguments is immediately evaluated and has its value placed on the operand stack. If all operands are treated as zero-argument operators, the test to determine whether the current constituent is an operand and the action specified when an operand is encountered can be eliminated from the flow diagram. Although such elimination would simplify the flow diagram, the present flow diagram corresponds more closely to our intuitive notions of expression evaluation than the simplified one.

Exercise: How is the flow diagram changed when operands are treated as zero-argument operators?

The algorithm in Fig. 4.6 can be changed to an algorithm for conversion from prefix to postfix notation by merely changing the application box to one which places the operator in the operand stack instead

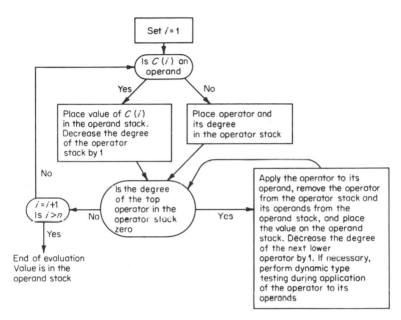

Figure 4.6   Evaluation of expressions in prefix notation.

of applying it to its operands.   Conversion from prefix to postfix notation may be thought of as a special form of evaluation of prefix expressions in which the rules of application of an operator to an operand differ from the standard rules.

4.3.7 PRECEDENCE AND EVALUATION OF EXPRESSIONS IN INFIX NOTATION

Evaluation of expressions in infix form is more complex than in prefix and postfix form but may similarly be performed with the aid of an operator and operand stack.   It will be assumed that each binary operator has associated with it a *precedence number p* and that expressions are evaluated by first applying operators of highest precedence to their operands in a left-to-right order and then applying operators of successively lower precedence to their operands in a left-to-right order. Parentheses can be used to define subexpressions for which internal evaluation according to the above rules takes precedence over use of the resulting value as an operand for further evaluation.

Example: Consider arithmetic expressions in infix notation in which the five operators $+$ $-$ $\times$ $/$ and $\uparrow$ are permitted. Let $+$ and $-$ have the precedence number $p = 1$, $\times$ and $/$ the precedence number $p = 2$, and $\uparrow$ the precedence number $p = 3$. Evaluation of arithmetic expressions without parentheses is accomplished by first applying all instances of the exponentiation symbol $\uparrow$ to its operands in a left-to-right order, then applying all instances of multiplication and division in a left-to-right order, and then applying all instances of addition or subtraction in a left-to-right order. If parentheses are present, this evaluation procedure is applied within the parentheses, and the resulting value enters as an evaluated operand in further evaluation.

Evaluation of infix expressions containing operators with precedence in the absence of parentheses can be accomplished by a left-to-right evaluation scan for each level of precedence, starting with operators of highest precedence. When parentheses are present, such a multipass evaluation process can be performed within each level of parentheses. However, an algorithm will be given for evaluation of any expression of the above form in a *single pass* over the expression string. This algorithm will make use of an operand stack for storing operands and an operator stack for storing operators together with their precedence numbers. The algorithm is specified by the flow diagram in Fig. 4.7.

An opening parenthesis is automatically placed on the stack when it is encountered. It is assumed that the precedence number associated with an opening parenthesis is less than that of any existing operator, so that an operator which finds an opening parenthesis on top of the operator stack pushes down the operator stack and cannot cause application of the opening parenthesis to operands. Opening parentheses are removed from the operator stack by the occurrence of matching closing parentheses.

Like the algorithm for evaluation of prefix notation, that for evaluation of infix notation can be converted to an algorithm for conversion from infix to postfix notation by defining application of an operator to its operands to consist of placing the operator into the operand stack.

Exercises: Specify the sequence of steps performed during evaluation of the following expressions by the above algorithm:

$x + y \times z \uparrow 2$

$a \times b - c \times d + e \times f$

$a \times (b - c) \times (d + e) \times f$

Convert each of the expressions to (*a*) prefix and (*b*) postfix notation and specify the sequence of evaluation steps in the respective algorithms.

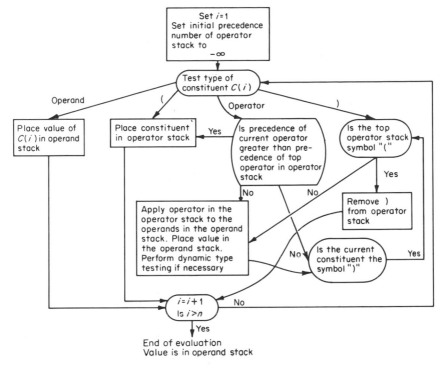

Figure 4.7   Evaluation in infix notation.

4.3.8 ASSIGNMENT OPERATORS AND SIDE EFFECTS

It has been assumed above that all operators and operands access the environment in a read-only manner or in an execute-only manner and that execution of successive symbols cannot therefore modify the values associated with programmer-defined identifiers.   However, programming languages usually contain operators which may modify the environment. The most common of these operators is the *assignment operator* which is denoted in ALGOL by := .   Thus a statement such as "$x := 3$;" modifies the environment in the sense that it changes the value of the information structure named x and determines the value that is retrieved when x is subsequently accessed in the read-only mode.

Note that the operator := is, syntactically speaking, a binary infixed operator, just like the binary arithmetic operators.   However, the assignment operator differs semantically from other operators in that it permits writing into the environment.

An expression which contains an infixed assignment operator can be converted to a postfix notation for purposes of execution.   Thus

$x := a - b \times c$ has the postfix representation 'x'$abc\times -:=$.† This expression can be evaluated by scanning from left to right, placing values of operands in the operand stack, and applying operators to operands at the top of the operand stack. When the assignment operator is encountered in the evaluation process, the two operands in the operand stack will be 'x' and the value of the expression $a - b \times c$. The effect of applying the assignment operator to the two top operands in the stack is to store the value of the expression $a - b \times c$ at the point in the environment specified by x and to remove the two arguments of the assignment operator from the operand stack.

In applying an operator to its operands the quantity that replaces the operands at the top of the operand stack is usually referred to as the *value* or *result* of the operation. Arithmetic operators such as $+$ and $\times$ produce as their value a quantity (information structure) that is numerical. The assignment operator $:=$ merely removes both its arguments from the operand stack without replacing them with a value and is therefore said to have a *null value*. Whereas the principal effect of an *arithmetic operation* is to produce a value to be used as an argument by subsequent operators, the principal effect of an *assignment operation* is to modify the environment. Modification of the environment during application of an operator to its operands is sometimes referred to as a *side effect,* since the principal effect of an operator is assumed to be the value it produces. The distinction between *values,* which represent intermediate temporary results during expression evaluation, and *side effects,* which modify the environment, will become clearer in Sec. 4.6, when side effects of procedures and the distinction between call by value and call by name is discussed.

Expressions whose principal effect is that of producing a side effect are referred to as *statements.* There is no fundamental syntactic distinction between the expressions and statements of a language but merely a semantic one. The values produced in the absence of side effects may be thought of as temporary quantities, while side effects may be thought of as methods of recording the result of a sequence of transformations in the permanent environment, thereby making it unnecessary to carry the information in the temporary environment.

In the above discussion, expression evaluation has been discussed

---

† The single quotes around the symbol x imply that, on execution, the address of x is placed in the operand stack rather than the value of x. It is assumed that the compiler which converts an expression from infix to postfix form has some means of marking identifiers immediately preceding an assignment operator to indicate that the address rather than the value is to be placed in the stack. The address is sometimes referred to as the *left-hand value* of the identifier since it is the value placed in the operand stack when the identifier occurs on the left-hand side of an assignment statement.

from a relatively machine-dependent point of view in order to develop an intuitive understanding of the information structures that arise during expression evaluation. The operand stack may be thought of as a generalized accumulator, and placing a value in the operand stack may be thought of as an operation that changes the state of the main memory and thereby affects the value retrieved on subsequent access to the main memory.

In the next section the syntax and semantics of expressions and statements in ALGOL will be developed. The machine-oriented model developed in the present section will be found useful in understanding how evaluation of ALGOL expressions and statements introduced in the next section might be implemented.

4.4 EXPRESSIONS, STATEMENTS, AND SIDE EFFECTS IN ALGOL

4.4.1 ARITHMETIC EXPRESSIONS AND TRANSFER FUNCTIONS

The principal information structures in ALGOL manipulated during expression evaluation are quantities of type **integer**, **real**, and **Boolean**. An ALGOL expression is said to be of type **integer**, **real**, or **Boolean** if the value produced on evaluation of the expression is respectively of type **integer**, **real**, or **Boolean**.

Operators in ALGOL can be classified in terms of their *domain* and *range*. Arithmetic operators expect arguments that are of type **integer** or **real** and produce values that are of type **integer** or **real**. In the following examples m is assumed to be of type **integer** and x, y, z are assumed to be of type **real**.

m + 1   This integer expression results in a value 1 greater than the value of m.

x + y × z   This real-valued expression results in the value $x + yz$.

The operation + has a different meaning in the two examples above and would be denoted by a different operation code at the machine-language level even though it is denoted by the same symbol at the source-language level. In the first example + denotes addition of integers, while in the second example it denotes addition of floating-point numbers. The type of identifiers can be determined from the initial representation of an ALGOL program, so that the two instances of + can be distinguished from each other and replaced by an appropriate machine-language operation code prior to execution.

ALGOL permits mixed expressions containing both integer and real operands, such as $x + m$. When an arithmetic operator has one operand of type real and one operand of type integer, the integer-valued operand is transformed to the corresponding real (floating-point) value by a special function T, called a *transfer function*, so that $x + m$ is transformed to $x +_f T(m)$ where $+_f$ is floating-point addition. A transfer function is a function which maps a class of values from one value domain into another. Other instances of the use of transfer functions in ALGOL will be introduced below.

The six arithmetic operators permitted in ALGOL are $+ - \times / \div$ and $\uparrow$. The first four operators are standard addition, subtraction, multiplication, and division operators. The operator $\div$ is integer division. The arguments of $\div$ must be integers, and the value of $m \div n$ has the same sign as m/n but has a magnitude part equal to the truncated absolute value; that is, $3 \div 2$ has the value 1, and $4 \div (-3)$ has the value -1.[†] The operator $\uparrow$ denotes exponentiation. However, the implementation of $\uparrow$ depends on its second argument. If the second argument is a small integer n, the value of $x \uparrow n$ is computed by a sequence of multiplications, while if the value of the second argument n is *real* or is a large integer, then $x \uparrow n$ could more efficiently be computed by the formula $e^{n \log x}$.

Exercise: If n is an integer, then $x \uparrow n$ may in general be computed in fewer than n multiplications. Develop an algorithm for computing $x \uparrow n$ for which the number of multiplications is of the order $\log_2 n$ for large n. *Hint:* Use the binary representation of n to determine how multiplications are to be performed.

4.4.2 BOOLEAN EXPRESSIONS

ALGOL permits identifiers to be of type Boolean. Boolean identifiers take their values in the two-element set of Boolean constants denoted in ALGOL by **true** and **false**.

ALGOL contains four binary Boolean operators and one unary Boolean operator for mapping Boolean arguments into Boolean values. The binary Boolean operators are Boolean equivalence $\equiv$, Boolean implication $\supset$, logical *or* $\vee$, and logical *and* $\wedge$. The unary operator is logical *not* $\neg$. The operators have been listed above in increasing precedence.

a $\equiv$ b $\supset$ c $\vee$ d $\wedge$ $\neg$ e   By virtue of the precedence relations
a $\equiv$ (b $\supset$ (c $\vee$ (d $\wedge$ ($\neg$ e))))   between Boolean operators, the first
                                                             of these expressions has the implicit
parenthesis structure given in the second.

4.4.3 RELATIONAL OPERATORS

Arithmetic and Boolean operators yield values of the same type as their arguments. There is a class of operators in ALGOL known as *relational*

[†] ALGOL contains a transfer function *entier* for mapping reals onto integers according to the above rule. Note that the transfer function entier is a many-one function mapping many reals onto the same integer.

operators which take arithmetic expressions as their arguments and yield a Boolean value. The six relational operators in ALGOL are $\leq$ < = $\neq$ > and $\geq$.

x > y   This expression has the value **true** if $x > y$ and the value **false** otherwise.

2 > 3   This expression always has the value **false**.

x = y + z ↑ 2   This expression has the logical value **true** if the identifier x has the same value as the expression $y + z \uparrow 2$. Note that this expression is evaluated as though there were parentheses $(x = (y + (z \uparrow 2)))$; i.e., all arithmetic operators take precedence over all relational operators.

In ALGOL the additional convention is adopted that all relational operators have the same precedence and all Boolean operators have lower precedence than relational operators. Thus arithmetic, relational, and Boolean operators may meaningfully occur in the same expression.

Exercise: Insert parentheses in the following expression to indicate the order of application of operators to operands and indicate the implied type of each variable:

$$x \wedge y < a + b$$
$$a \equiv b \supset c \vee d \wedge \neg e > f + y \times h \uparrow i$$

The above conventions about precedence result in a nine-level precedence hierarchy for ALGOL expressions where the operators at each precedence level are as follows:

1. $\equiv$	4. $\wedge$	7. $+$ $-$
2. $\supset$	5. $\neg$	8. $\times$ / $\div$
3. $\vee$	6. $\leq$ < = $\neq$ > $\geq$	9. $\uparrow$

Exercises: (*a*) Using the techniques of Sec. A1.6 of Appendix 1, develop a context-free grammar for ALGOL expressions which reflects these nine levels of precedence. (*b*) Is it necessary to introduce precedence conventions for operators of infixed binary expressions? What would be the effect of doing away with precedence relations?

4.4.4 ASSIGNMENT STATEMENTS

When an expression has been evaluated, the value is normally assigned to an identifier by an *assignment statement*.

x := 5;   This assignment statement assigns the value 5 to the identifier x.

x := y + z;   This assignment statement assigns the value of $y + z$ to the identifier x.

a := b ∧ c;   This assignment statement assigns the value **true** to the Boolean variable a if the variables b and c have the value **true** and the value **false** otherwise.

The general form of an assignment statement is as follows:

V := E;   Evaluate the expression E and assign the resulting value to the variable V.

The type of the variable on the left-hand side of an assignment statement is usually the same as the type of the expression on the right-hand side of the statement. However, certain differences in type are permitted. For example, if the right-hand side is of type real and the left-hand side is of type integer, the expression E is truncated to the next lower integer, and the result is assigned as the value of the variable V. More generally type conversion may be thought of as being accomplished by a transfer function which maps elements in the value domain of the *source type* to elements in the value domain of a *target type*.

As indicated in Sec. 4.3, the principal purpose of an assignment statement is to make a permanent record of quantities computed during expression evaluation by storing them in the environment. Identifiers which occur as arguments of arithmetic, Boolean, and relational operators during expression evaluation access the environment in a read-only mode, while identifiers which occur on the left-hand side of an assignment operator cause modification of the environment so that subsequent read-only accesses to that identifier are affected.

4.4.5 LABELS, SWITCHES, AND UNCONDITIONAL TRANSFER STATEMENTS

Assignment statements may be labeled as in the following example:

L: x := S;   This assignment statement has a label L.

All statements in ALGOL may be labeled. Labels precede the statement and are separated from the statement by a colon, as in the above example. Statements may have multiple labels, as in the following example:

L: M: x := S;   This assignment statement has two labels, L and M. Use of either of these labels in a **go to** statement (see below) will result in a transfer to this statement.

A labeled statement is an example of a statement. Thus the above example may be thought of as a statement $M: x := S$; having the single label L.

Although there are no facilities for declaring identifiers to be of the type label in ALGOL or facilities for assigning labels as values of variables by means of assignment statements, there are facilities for defining arrays of labels and selecting an element of a label-valued array by means of array subscripts.   A label-valued array is declared by means of a *switch declaration.*

switch S := L1,L2,L3,L4;   This declaration declares S to be a label-valued array with $S(1) = L1$, etc.

Transfer of control to a labeled statement is accomplished in ALGOL by a **go to** statement:

go to L;   Transfer control to the statement labeled L.

go to S (I);   Transfer control to the statement whose label is the Ith label on the right-hand side of the switch declaration.
Note that this use of switches is a cross between the assigned go to and the computed go to of FORTRAN.

The **go to** statement is an example of an ALGOL statement that is not an assignment statement.   There are other kinds of statements in ALGOL, including conditional **if** statements, for choosing between alternative courses of action, and iteration **for** statements, for repetitive execution of a sequence of instructions.

4.4.6 CONDITIONAL STATEMENTS AND CONDITIONAL EXPRESSIONS

Conditional statements have one of the following two forms:

if B **then** S_1 **else** S_2 If the Boolean expression B has the value **true,** then execute the statement S_1.   Otherwise execute the statement S_2.   If the statements S_1, S_2 are **go to** statements, the conditional statement results in transfer to one of two alternative labels.   However, the statements S_1, S_2 may be other kinds of statements, the only restriction being that S_1 must not itself be a conditional statement.   If S_2 is a conditional statement, the statement is said to be a multiple conditional statement.

if B **then** S   This statement results in the execution of S if the Boolean expression B has the value **true** and continues with the statement following S if B is **false;** i.e., it is like the previous conditional statement with a null statement in its second branch.

Conditional statements result in a choice between execution of two alternative statements depending on the value of a Boolean variable. ALGOL also permits *conditional expressions* for choosing between execution of two alternative *expressions* depending on the value of a Boolean variable.

if B **then** E_1 **else** E_2 — If the Boolean expression B has the value **true**, then the value of this conditional expression is E_1; otherwise the value of the conditional expression is E_2.

The difference between conditional expressions and conditional statements is illustrated by the following examples:

if x = 0 **then** y := y + 1 **else** y := y − 1; — This conditional statement increments y by 1 if $x = 0$ and decrements y by 1 if $x \neq 0$.

y := **if** x = 0 **then** y + 1 **else** y − 1; — This statement has the same effect as the previous one. Evaluation of the conditional expression yields $y + 1$ or $y - 1$, depending on the value of x, and this value is assigned to y.

y = y + (**if** x = 0 **then** 1 **else** −1); — This statement has a conditional expression as one of the arguments on its right-hand side. It increments y if $x = 0$ and decrements y otherwise.

The following example illustrates the use of a label-valued conditional expression:

go to if A > B **then** L1 **else** L2; — This **go to** statement results in transfer to the label $L1$ if $A > B$ and to the label $L2$ otherwise.

4.4.7 ITERATION STATEMENTS

Iteration statements have the following form:

for V := for list **do** S — Execute the statement S for values of the variable V specified in the for list. It will be seen below that statements S may consist of arbitrarily complex nests of other statements, so that the restriction that the range of iteration be restricted to a single statement is not so severe as it appears.

The for-list elements may have one or more of the following three forms:

1. Individual expressions E.
2. Expressions of the form "E_1 **step** E_2 **until** E_3" indicating execution of S for values of V starting with E_1 and moving by increments of E_2 until E_3 is exceeded. Modification of E_2 and E_3 during execution of the statement S is permitted but not advised, since it may lead to trouble.
3. Expressions of the form "E **while** B", which specify execution of S with $V = E$ as long as the value of B is **true.** In this case the statement S

must be such that it can change the value of B to accomplish loop termination. S will normally also modify E when necessary.

The following example illustrates the use of a **for** statement to scan an N-element vector:

SUM := 0;
for I := 1 **step** 1 **until** N **do**
SUM := SUM + A[I];

There is a fundamental difference in ALGOL between *statements* and *expressions*. The principal result of evaluation of an expression is to produce a value which may in turn be used as an argument of a larger expression. The principal effect of a statement is to change the environment. Thus an assignment statement results in a change in the value on its left-hand side, a go to statement changes the value of the scan pointer which determines the next instruction to be executed, a conditional statement results in execution of one of a number of alternative statements, and an iteration statement results in repetitive execution of a statement.

4.4.8 MULTIPLE ASSIGNMENT

Statements may be regarded as special kinds of expressions which, on evaluation, yield a null value and affect the course of the subsequent computation by the side effect they produce. However, in certain instances it is convenient to think of statements as having values given by the last information item which was assigned as a value in the environment during execution of the statement. This convention is used, for example, in multiple assignment statements.

x := y := S;   This statement assigns the value S to the variables x and y. Execution of this multiple assignment statement can be thought of as a process which first executes the assignment statement $y := S$;, leaving behind a value S rather than a null value, and then executes the statement $x := V$, where V is the value left behind on execution of the first assignment statement.

The notion of a statement which leaves behind a value has been systematically exploited in the Euler language [3].

4.5 THE BLOCK STRUCTURE OF ALGOL

4.5.1 COMPOUND STATEMENTS

The statements and expressions discussed in the previous section constitute the principal lower-level machinery for performing computations in

ALGOL.   In the present section higher-level constructs of the language will be introduced for grouping statements into function modules and for defining the range of statements over which a given identifier is associated with a given information structure.

A group of statements can be grouped into a single functional unit by enclosing them in the system symbols **begin, end.**   Such a grouping is referred to as a *compound statement.*

begin
   x := 5;   This compound statement assigns values to both the identi-
   y := 4;   fiers x and y.
end

Compound statements can occur in any context in which statements can occur.   In particular, compound statements can occur as branches of conditional expressions or as the statement over which iteration is performed.   The symbols **begin** and **end** act as statement parentheses and cause the group of statements inside the parentheses to be treated as a single statement in precisely the same way that expression parentheses cause a complex expression to be treated as a single factor.

Execution of a compound statement results in a null value.   The side effects associated with execution of a compound statement may result in the modification of several identifiers in the environment.

4.5.2   BLOCKS

The **begin, end** statement parentheses are used in ALGOL not only to group statements but also for the purpose of determining the range of statements over which identifiers retain their meaning.

The basic module for specifying the range over which identifiers have a meaning is called a *block.*   A block consists of the symbol **begin,** followed by a sequence of declarations of identifiers, followed by a sequence of statements, followed by the symbol **end.**   The declarations are said to constitute the *blockhead,* and the statements are said to constitute the *block body.*   Identifiers can be used only within the block in whose head they are declared and are said to be *local* to the block in which they are declared.   The block in whose head a given identifier is declared is said to be the *scope* of that identifier.†

---

† In the following example, the semicolon of the statement which immediately precedes **end** is omitted.   In ALGOL, **end** fulfills the function of a semicolon.   A semicolon immediately preceding **end** is optional.   If there is a semicolon preceding **end** the language assumes that there is an empty statement with null effect between the semicolon and **end.**   Empty statements do not affect the result of a computation, so that the program executes correctly.

begin real K;   Execution of this block results in interchange of the
   K := X;   values of the variables X and Y. Its blockhead con-
   X := Y;   tains a declaration of a local variable K whose scope is
   Y := K   the given block. This local variable has meaning only
end   within the block and cannot be used outside the block.

A block is an example of a statement and can occur in any context in which statements may occur. A block may be thought of as a generalization of a compound statement which permits specification of local variables in its blockhead by means of declarations. Conversely a compound statement is a special case of a block where the number of declared variables is zero.

Since the body of a block consists of a sequence of statements and a block is an example of a statement, blocks may contain other blocks nested inside them to an arbitrary level.

A complete ALGOL program consists of a single block which may contain other blocks nested inside it. All identifiers used in an ALGOL program, apart from a special set of system identifiers initialized by the system,† must be declared in the blockhead of a block which encloses the point of use.

4.5.3 SCOPE RULES FOR IDENTIFIERS

The identifiers declared in a given blockhead are *bound variables* in the sense that replacement of all instances of a local identifier by a different identifier whose name does not conflict with other identifiers used in the block does not change the meaning of the program.

Making two declarations of an identifier with the same name in the same blockhead is illegal. However, two declarations of identifiers with the same name in different blockheads are permitted and result in the two names' denoting different information items in the different blockheads. The two identifiers will have different internal representations and may also be given different external representation by renaming all occurrences of one of the two identifiers. The following example illus-

---

† The system identifiers of ALGOL include the standard functions SIN, COS, LOG, and EXP. In an implementation library subroutines would also be initialized identifiers. System identifiers differ from other system symbols in that they can be redefined by a declaration to have a meaning different from the system interpretation. Pure system symbols are disjoint from the set of identifiers and have a fixed meaning. System identifiers are used also to specify system functions for input and output, and names of input and output media. The system functions *read* and *write* will be used below to denote input and output. The input medium can be thought of as a pushdown tape whose name is *read*, which is automatically popped up whenever the function read is executed. Similarly the output medium can be thought of as a pushdown tape whose name is *write*, which is automatically pushed down whenever the function write is executed.

trates occurrence of an identifier declaration for x in two blocks one of which is nested inside the other.

Example: Nomenclature rules for nested blocks are as follows:

B: **begin real** x,y;
    x := 3;
    y := 4;
  B1: **begin real** x,z;
      x := 5;
      y := 6;
      z := 7;
   end;
   print (x,y,z)
end

This sequence of ALGOL statements consists of a block $B1$ nested in a block B. The identifier y of the outer block can be used throughout the block B. However, the identifier x declared in the outer block cannot be used in the inner block because an identifier of the same name is declared in the inner block. The identifier x is bound in the inner block in the sense that if the two occurrences of the name x in the inner block were changed to another name, say u, then the computation defined by this program would be unaltered. The identifiers x, z of the inner block have meaning only in the inner block. In the print statement "print (x,y,z);" the identifiers x and y are associated with the declarations of x, y in the outer block and have the values $x = 3$, $y = 6$. The identifier z is undefined, so that this print statement would result in a diagnostic unless this program fragment were embedded in a block containing a declaration for the identifier z in its blockhead.

An identifier declared in the head of a block may be thought of as being created on entry to the block during execution and deleted on exit from the block. From a machine-oriented point of view entry to a block results in allocation of storage for identifiers declared in the blockhead, while exit from a block results in deallocation of storage for identifiers declared in the blockhead. Every time a block is entered, a new copy of the identifiers in the block is created. There is no carry-over of values from one instance of activation of a block to the next.

An identifier should be thought of as being a bound variable not merely of the static block but in a dynamic activation of the block. The identifiers associated with two different instances of execution of the block represent different bound variables and will have a different internal representation during execution even though they have the same external representation. Two instances of activation of a given block which do not overlap in time are said to be *dynamically disjoint*, while two instances of activation of a given block such that one is embedded in the time segment required for execution of the other are said to be *dynamically nested*. ALGOL does not permit activations of blocks to overlap in time unless they are dynamically nested.

ALGOL labels need not be declared in blockheads. However, they are always assumed to be declared in the head of the innermost block that encloses their occurrence as a label.   In the above example there is an implicit declaration of the form "**label** B1" in the head of the block labeled *B* and an implicit declaration of the form "**label** B" in the block that encloses the block *B*.

The above convention regarding labels automatically implies that a **go to** statement can never transfer from outside a block into the middle of a block, since a label can never be known in statements that occur physically outside the innermost block that encloses the label.†   However, labels are known in all inner blocks nested within the block in which they occur, so that transfer from an inner block to an outer block is permitted.

4.5.4   FUNCTION-TYPE AND STATEMENT-TYPE PROCEDURES

The identifiers declared in a blockhead include identifiers of the type **array** and identifiers of the type **procedure.**   Arrays declared in a blockhead come into existence on entry to the block during execution and are deleted on exit from the block.   The array dimensions associated with a given instance of execution of the block are determined by evaluating subscript expressions of the array declaration at the moment of entry to the block, so that an array may have different dimension bounds on different instances of execution although it has the same dimension bounds throughout a given instance of execution of the block.

There are two kinds of procedure declarations.   *Statement-type procedures* are like statements in that they have a null value and affect the computation by the side effect they produce during execution.   *Function-type procedures* are like expressions in that they produce a value; however, they may produce side effects.   The declaration and use of statement- and function-type procedures is illustrated by the following examples:

```
procedure ADD(A,N,SUM);
   real array A; integer N; real SUM;
   begin integer I;
   SUM := 0;
   for I := 1 step 1 until N do
   SUM := SUM + A[I];
end
```

This declaration is a statement-type procedure. The first line specifies the name and formal parameters of the procedure. The second line specifies the types of formal parameters. The first two lines together are said to constitute the *procedure heading*.   The remaining lines of the procedure constitute the *procedure body*, which in this case consists of a single block.   The effect of the procedure is to SUM *N* elements of the array which constitutes the first parameter and store the result as the value of the third parameter.

† Blocks in ALGOL must always be entered through their blockheads.

Statement-type procedures are *used* in procedure statements as in the following example:

ADD(X,15,S)   Add the first 15 elements of the array X and store the result as the value of S.

The above specification of a statement-type procedure will now be contrasted with a function-type procedure for the same purpose. The corresponding function-type procedure associates the function value with the procedure identifier and therefore uses one less procedure parameter. The *type* of the value produced by a function-type procedure is specified by a type specification preceding the symbol **procedure.**

real procedure SUM(A,N);
  real array A; **integer** N;
  begin integer I; **real** X;
    X := 0;
    for I := 1 **step** 1 **until** N **do**
    X := X + A[I];
    SUM := X;
  end

This function-type procedure has one parameter less than the corresponding statement-type procedure, since the value is identified with the name and does not have to be explicitly specified by a parameter. The quantity X is used in the procedure body for accumulating the sum since an occurrence of SUM on the right-hand side of an assignment statement would be interpreted as a reentrant call of the procedure.

Whereas statement-type procedures are called by a procedure statement, function-type procedures can be called in an expression in any place where a variable is permitted.

X := SUM(A,15) + 2 × SUM(B,20);   Form the sum of the first 15 elements of A, add twice the sum of the first 20 elements of B, and store the result in X.

Procedure identifiers are declared in the blockhead of some block just like other identifiers and can be called only within the block in whose head they are declared. However the convention is adopted that the identifiers declared in a given blockhead are known not only in the body of the block but also in the bodies of all procedures declared in the blockhead. This convention implies that two procedures declared in a given blockhead can call each other and in particular that a procedure has access to its own name and can call itself. A call within a given procedure of itself is known as a *reentrant* (recursive) procedure call, since the procedure may be thought of as reentering itself before it has completed execution of itself. The mechanism for reentrant procedure calls is discussed in the next section.

Statement-type procedures leave behind a null value when their execution is completed, so that their only effect on the environment is a side effect.   The statement-type procedure ADD above has the side effect of specifying a new value for its parameter SUM.

Function-type procedures leave behind a value which is used as an argument of a higher-level expression but may have side effects which set values of parameters or other nonlocal variables.   The procedure SUM above does not have any side effects.

Formal parameters of a procedure are bound variables of the procedure.   All occurrences of a given formal parameter may be changed to some other nonconflicting identifier without affecting the function represented by the procedure.

The types of formal parameters are indicated in the procedure heading, just as the types of local identifiers of a block are indicated in the blockhead, and procedure parameters play essentially the same role in the procedure heading that declarations play in a blockhead.   The principal difference lies in the mode of access to the information items represented by identifiers, as indicated in Sec. 4.6.

4.5.5 UNINITIALIZED AND INITIALIZED IDENTIFIERS

Identifiers of type **integer, real, Boolean,** and **array** declared in blockheads are *uninitialized* identifiers; their values must be assigned by assignment statements before they can be used and they can be reassigned during execution of the block in whose blockhead they are declared.   Labels and procedure declarations are *initialized declarations;* their values are defined at the moment of declaration, and they cannot be redefined during execution of the block in whose blockhead they are defined.

Procedure parameters may be regarded as initialized declarations that are initialized at the moment of procedure call to actual parameters which, in the case of parameters of type **integer, real,** and **Boolean** may be expressions.

4.5.6 INITIALIZATION BY VALUE AND INITIALIZATION BY NAME

There are two ways in ALGOL of initializing parameters whose values are expressions:

1.   Initialization by value.   This results in evaluation of the actual-parameter expression *at the moment of procedure call* and assignment of this value as the initial value of the parameter during execution of the procedure.
2.   Initialization by name.   This results in evaluation of the actual-parameter expression in the context of the point of call *every time the parameter is used during execution.*

Since the value of a parameter called by name is an expression, the corresponding formal parameter is effectively an identifier of type *expression*. The machinery for access to parameters called by name is therefore similar to that for access to expression-type procedures except that the expression is defined in the context of the point of call rather than in the context of an enclosing blockhead.

Initialization by value corresponds to argument evaluation *before* substitution into the function, while initialization by name corresponds to substitution of the unevaluated argument and evaluation every time the unevaluated argument is encountered during execution of the function.

Example: The difference in effect between initialization by value and initialization by name can be illustrated by considering the procedure declaration:

real procedure $P(A)$;   This procedure sets a nonlocal variable K to
    real A;   5 and then sets P to the value of A.
    begin
        $K := 5$;
        $P := A$;
    end

Let $P(K)$ be a call of the procedure P. Then if A is initialized by name, the value of $P(K)$ is always 5, while if A is initialized by value, the value of $P(K)$ is given by the value of K at the moment of entry to the procedure.

It was shown in the previous chapter that evaluation before and after substitution is identical in the absence of side effects except in the exceptional circumstances that there is an undefined argument with zero substitution instances. However, the effect of evaluation before and after substitution differs in the presence of side effects. The circumstances in which side effects can occur during expression evaluation, parameter evaluation, and function evaluation will be examined next.

4.5.7 SIDE EFFECTS OF PROCEDURES

It was pointed out that side effects could not occur in the evaluation of expressions whose arguments were simple variables of type **integer, real,** or **Boolean.** However, procedure calls for function-type procedures can occur in any position in an expression that a simple identifier can occur. Evaluation of function-type procedures can cause side effects and therefore results in side effects during expression evaluation.

A procedure is said to have a side effect if it modifies nonlocal identifiers in the environment during its execution. Side effects during the evaluation of procedures can occur in the following ways in ALGOL:

1. Assignment of a value to an identifier declared in an enclosing block of the procedure
2. Assignment of a value to an identifier initialized by name
3. Jump to a label in an enclosing block
4. Execution of a procedure call in an enclosing block having a side effect

If a given parameter is intended to have a side effect, it must be called by name. If a procedure has side effects, the side effect may affect the values of nonlocal identifiers during execution. The procedure P above has a side effect which assigns a value to an identifier in an enclosing block.

Exercise: Write a two-parameter procedure declaration and a procedure call of the declared procedure in which the first parameter is initialized by name and the result of the procedure call differs depending on whether the second parameter is initialized by value or by name.

Side effects in expression evaluation are a nuisance because they impose restraints upon the order in which arguments of an expression can be evaluated. In the absence of side effects, the expression "$a + b \times c$" can be evaluated by first forming the product of b and c and then adding a to the result. However, when side effects during argument evaluation may occur, then evaluation of "a" may result in a change of the values of "b" and "c" so that arguments must always be evaluated strictly in the order in which they occur in operands.

It has been advocated by a number of people that a class of expressions be defined in which side effects are not permitted,† so that optimization which involves interchange in the order of evaluation can be performed.

4.5.8 FUNCTION-TYPE BLOCKS

Whereas ALGOL procedures may be declared to be function-type procedures or statement-type procedures, ALGOL blocks must always occur in the context of a statement and never in the context of an expression. There is thus no facility in ALGOL for creating a new level of nomenclature during the evaluation of an expression except by defining a function-type procedure.

The principal problem in permitting expressions to create their own temporary nomenclature is that of devising a notation for identifying the

† See, for instance, [4].

value of the expression in the new level of nomenclature. A notation for this purpose, suggested by Landin and described by Strachey and Wilkes [4], consists of introducing the system symbol **result** as a name for the value of the expression in the new level of nomenclature. A second system symbol **result of** is used as a block prefix to distinguish expression-type blocks from statement-type blocks. The following example illustrates the use of this notation:

x := y + **result of**   The **result of** block in
     begin real p,q;   this assignment state-
         p := a + b;   ment declares two
         q := a − b;   local variables p, q
         result := p ↑ 2 + p × q + q ↑ 2;   and then uses them to
     end   compute the value of
                                  the system symbol

result.   This value is in turn used as a component of a higher-level expression.

   result of blocks are not part of the ALGOL language but have been introduced to emphasize the distinction between expressions and statements.

   The run-time representation of function modules which arise in an ALGOL program is discussed in the next section.

4.6 THE RUN-TIME REPRESENTATION OF ALGOL

4.6.1 CLASSIFICATION OF MODE OF ACCESS TO IDENTIFIERS

One of the principal problems encountered during the execution of ALGOL programs is that of keeping track of information items denoted by identifiers. Identifiers can be classified according to their mode of access to information items as follows:

   1.   System symbols, which access a *fixed* information item within the programming system

   2.   Local identifiers, which access information local to the innermost block currently being executed

   3.   Nonlocal identifiers in blocks, which dynamically enclose the innermost block currently being executed

   4.   Procedure parameters, which access information through the point of call of the procedure

   Any run-time representation of an ALGOL program must provide means of access for each of the above classes of identifiers and means of updating the run-time representation on entry to and exit from blocks and procedures so that correct access to identifiers is maintained.

When considering the mode of access to identifiers, it is convenient to choose as basic semantic units the executable program segments which result in changes in the set of accessible identifiers when entered and exited during execution.   In ALGOL these semantic units are the block and the procedure.   Entry to a block causes a new layer of identifiers local to the block to become accessible.   Call of a procedure causes certain identifiers to become temporarily inaccessible and initializes the procedure parameter identifiers.   Exit from a block or procedure reinstates the set of identifiers accessible prior to entry.

A procedure call at a given point of an ALGOL program normally calls a procedure declared in the block of the point of call or in an enclosing block.   However, if the procedure call corresponds to a parameter of type **procedure,** the procedure that is called need not be explicitly accessible and may in fact be declared in an inner block.   Access by a procedure to procedures and labels declared in an inner begin block enclosing the point of call is illustrated in the following example:

OB: **begin**
    procedure P(f,L);
    procedure f; **label** L;
    begin
      · · ·
      f;
      · · ·
      go to L;
      · · ·
    end P;
    · · ·
  IB: **begin**
      procedure Q;
        begin
          · · ·
        end Q;
      · · ·
    L1: · · ·
      · · ·
      P(Q,L1);
      · · ·
    end
  end

This ALGOL program contains a two-parameter procedure P in an outer block OB, and a parameterless procedure Q in an inner block IB.   The parameters of P are respectively of type **procedure** and of type **label.**   The procedure call of P in the inner block IB makes the procedure Q and the label $L1$ in IB accessible to the procedure P.   The procedure call "P(Q,L1)" results in a procedure call to Q when the statement "f;" is executed and in a jump to the label $L1$ of the block IB if the statement "**go to** L" in P is executed.   The jump "**go to** L1" automatically terminates the procedure call.

4.6.2 RUN-TIME REPRESENTATION OF FUNCTION MODULES

ALGOL blocks and procedures will be referred to as *function modules*, since they represent rules of correspondence between initial environments prior to entry to the module and terminal environments on exit from the module.   A complete ALGOL program consists of a single function module, which may have other function modules nested inside it.   Blocks are *explicitly* nested in the initial program representation, while procedures are *implicitly* nested at the point at which they are called.

In developing a run-time representation for ALGOL it will be assumed that function modules retain their identity in the run-time representation. It will be assumed also that function modules are represented *reentrantly* by means of a *fixed-program part*, which is in existence independently of instances of execution of the module, and an *activation record* for each instance of activation of the module, which is created on entry to the block during execution and destroyed on exit from the block.   These assumptions impose a structure on run-time representations of programs consisting of nested function modules with local nomenclature.   The characteristics of this structure will be examined below.

In execution of an ALGOL program, activation records are created on entry to blocks when interpreting their **begin** symbols and declarations and on entry to procedures by function calls.   ALGOL is carefully constructed so that execution of function modules is strictly in a last in, first out order; i.e., a block Q nested in a block or procedure P is always entered after P has been entered and exited before P is exited.   Similarly a procedure call Q occurring in a block P results in entry to the implicitly nested procedure Q *after* entry to the block P and in exit from the procedure *before* exit from the block.   This last in, first out execution of function modules ensures that activation records of function modules are always created and destroyed in a last in, first out order so that they can be stored in a stack.

The initial information in the activation record associated with a given function module can be classified into the following categories:

1.   Values of identifiers local to the function module.

2.   Pointers to values of identifiers nonlocal to the function module.

3.   Organizational information, such as the link to the previous function module in the activation-record stack, and an *instruction pointer* to the current point reached in interpretation of the fixed-program part of the function module.   The instruction pointer is stored in the processing unit of the computer when the module is being executed, but it is stored in the activation record when execution of the module is suspended in order to execute an inner function module.

On entry to a block or procedure, memory space is allocated for its activation record in the activation-record stack, and execution of the body of the function module is initiated.   During execution of the function module, working space might be required for temporary information during expression evaluation.   Expression evaluation is performed so that temporary information is always created and deleted in a last in, first out order, as indicated in Sec. 4.3.   This permits working space required during expression evaluation to be allocated at the top of the activation-record stack by extending the current activation record.

If during expression evaluation, a call of a function-type procedure is encountered, a new activation record is created during evaluation of the function.   When evaluation of the function is completed, the activation record is deleted, and the value of the expression is left at the top of the activation record of the calling module just as though a simple variable had been evaluated.

The activation record at the top of the activation-record stack is said to be the *current activation record*.   The fixed-program part corresponding to the current activation record is said to be the function module *currently being executed*.   When a given function module is being executed, access is permitted to information in activation records within the activation-record stack in a manner to be described below.   In the absence of side effects, access to information not in the current activation record is in a read-only mode.   Access which modifies values of nonlocal identifiers is referred to as a side effect.   Although side effects are permitted in ALGOL, no side effects which require storage allocation or deallocation are permitted.   All information structures other than temporary quantities created during expression evaluation are created on entry to a function module.   There is a basic dichotomy in ALGOL between creation of structures by declarations and assignment of values to primitive structures of the language.   However, the boundary between *structure specification* and *value specification* is in a sense arbitrary.   The distinction between structure and value specification is not inherent in programming languages but merely a feature of information structure-specification facilities of the ALGOL language.

The structure of activation records will be illustrated first for blocks with activation records containing only local variables of type **integer** and **real.**   In this case each local identifier has a storage register reserved for it on entry to the block which is initially empty (has an undefined value).   Assignments of values to the identifier within the block are stored in this register, and the value of the identifier is taken to be the current content of the register.   On exit from the block the register is deallocated, and subsequent entry to the block results in assignment of a new register having an undefined value.

Boolean identifiers have values which consist of one bit of information and can be stored several to a register. Arrays may require several registers for their storage. Labels and procedures are represented by pointers to a symbol in the fixed-program string together with some organizational information for distinguishing between labels and procedures.

4.6.3 RELATIVE ADDRESSING WITHIN ACTIVATION RECORDS

It is convenient to arrange for each local identifier to have a fixed address relative to the beginning of its activation record. This permits the identifier to be represented by its relative address in the fixed-program part of the function module and for access to local information to be accomplished by indexing relative to the initial address of the activation record.

The only identifier which may require different amounts of memory on different instances of execution is the array with dynamic bounds. Fixed relative addresses for identifiers in activation records which include arrays with dynamic bounds can be accomplished by representing the array by a pointer or set of pointers to array elements in an initial part of the activation record and storing array elements in a later part of the activation record following the basic information for all local identifiers. Thus fixed-length information is directly accessed in the activation record, while variable-length information or information with a complex structure is accessed indirectly through pointers in a fixed initial part of the activation record. In the case of arrays the pointers point to a later part of the activation record, while in the case of labels and procedures the pointers point to an information-storage area outside the activation record itself.

Example: Consider a block with the following sequence of declarations in its blockhead:

begin real x; **real array** A[1:10],B[m:n]; **real** y; . . . **end**

The declarations in this blockhead would give rise to the information structures shown in Fig. 4.8 in its activation record.

The complete activation record for a block contains additional linkage information to be described below. The pointer entries for arrays normally contain a group of entries for each array dimension and therefore vary in size for arrays of different dimensions. However, the number of dimensions of an ALGOL array is fixed by the initial program representation for all instances of activation.

The fixed-length array-pointer information is referred to as a *dope vector*. It usually includes the initial array address and lower and upper bounds for each array dimension. On access to an array element during execution the information in the dope vector together with the array-subscript expressions is used as a parameter by a program called an *address-mapping function,* which computes the actual array address.

Exercise: Develop a format for an array dope vector, and specify an address-mapping function which, given the information in the dope vector and a set of array subscripts, computes the address of the required array element relative to the beginning of the activation record.

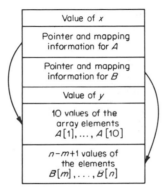

Figure 4.8 Activation-record data structure corresponding to the blockhead begin real x*;* **real array** $A[1:10]$, $B[m:n]$; **real** y;-

An array dope vector specifies *attributes* of the information structure denoted by the array identifier, and may be thought of as a special instance of a *description list* in the sense that this term is used in list processing [5]. Description lists may be thought of as mechanisms for specifying attributes of an information structure which remain fixed over a number of instances of access to the information structure. In ALGOL the information structure represented by identifiers of type **integer, real,** and **Boolean** are completely defined without requiring description lists. However, an array is a richer structure whose characterization is conveniently accomplished by a description list (dope vector) that specifies the *structure* as distinct from the *content.* In ALGOL, attributes of an object can be specified only on declaration and remain in force throughout the lifetime of the declared object. In list-processing languages attributes may be changed during the lifetime of the object. The property that structural characteristics cannot be changed during the lifetime of the object is essential in any language for which evaluation is implemented in a single stack and is another example of how characteristics of the source language are conditioned by the requirements of implementation.†

Whereas activation records of blocks contain information items and pointers for declared variables, activation records of procedures contain information items and pointers for parameters. Parameters called by value result on entry to the procedure in allocation of a register to hold the value of the parameter and in immediate computation of the value, so that a parameter called by value has the effect of an *initialized declaration*. Parameters called by name result on entry to the procedure in allocation of a register in which a pointer to the calling program is stored, pointing to the expression to be evaluated upon use of the parameter. The address relative to the beginning of the activation record of the register corresponding to a given parameter is fixed for all instances of activation and can therefore be specified by a relative address in the fixed-program part associated with the activation record.

This discussion indicates how local variables of a block and local parameters of a procedure are represented in activation records and accessed when interpreting the fixed-program part of the function module. We shall consider next how nonlocal identifiers and parameters of a function module can be represented and accessed during interpretation of the fixed-program part of the module.

4.6.4 REPRESENTATION OF IDENTIFIERS BY INTEGER PAIRS

Let the *level of nesting* of a given point of the fixed program be defined as the sum of the number of blockheads and procedure heads in which the point is physically enclosed. If k is the level of nesting of a given point of the fixed program, then there are presicely k activation records whose identifiers may be currently accessible.

It will be assumed that identifiers are represented by integer pairs (i,j), where i is the level of nesting of the declaration of the identifier, and j is the relative address of the identifier within its activation record. When execution is at level of nesting k, the set of accessible identifiers is precisely the set of identifiers declared in the heads of the k physically enclosing function modules.

It will be assumed that access to the k activation records accessible at nesting depth k is accomplished through a k-element vector whose ith element stores the initial address in the activation-record stack of the

---

† Note that if stacks are represented by list structures, it becomes technically feasible to insert information in the middle of a stack. However, the reason for having a stack in the first place is to make use of our knowledge of last in, first out creation and deletion to increase computational efficiency. Thus a list-structured stack is in a sense a contradiction in terms.

most recent instance of activation of the activation record associated with nesting depth i. Since this table defines the set of all accessible activation records at the current point of execution, it will be called the *current environment vector*. Access to an identifier at nesting depth i from a point at nesting depth $k \geq i$ is accomplished by indirect addressing through the ith entry of the current environment vector and relative addressing with respect to this entry.

Figure 4.9 illustrates the activation-record stack and current environment vector during execution of the statement S of the procedure P of the illustrative program.

When statement S in procedure P is being executed, the identifiers declared in blocks C and A are accessible, and the parameters of the

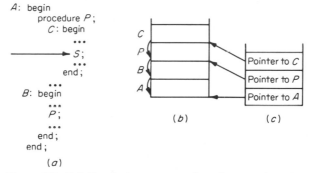

Figure 4.9 Relation between current environment vector and activation-record stack during execution. (a) **Program;** (b) **activation-record stack;** (c) **current environment vector.**

procedure P are accessible. The identifiers declared in the block B are inaccessible. However, indirect access to the parameters of the block B during the execution of P can be accomplished if P has parameters called by name. Evaluation of parameters called by name during execution of a procedure requires the current environment vector to be adjusted as further described below.

The activation-record stack of Fig. 4.9 contains a *back pointer* from each activation record to the dynamically preceding one. The back pointer is used principally during deletion of an activation record to adjust the stack pointer to point to the new top activation record. A back pointer is sometimes referred to as a *dynamic link*, since it links an activation record to the dynamically preceding one. The chain of back pointers is sometimes referred to as the *dynamic chain*.

The current environment vector could be replaced by a sequence of links which link each activation record to the most recent activation of the next textually enclosing one. Since this sequence of links is associated with nesting levels of the static program, it is sometimes referred to as the *static chain*. The relation between the static and dynamic chains for the above example is illustrated in Fig. 4.10.

In Figure 4.10, the current environment is effectively specified by the static chain of the current activation record. The n-element current environment vector at nesting level n is not needed, since the information contained in it is distributed over the n activation records corresponding to statically enclosing blocks. Access from level n to an identifier declared at level k can be accomplished by sequencing along $n - k$ links of the static chain followed by relative addressing within the resulting activation record. Since the number $n - k$ is known at translation time, it is convenient in this model to replace identifiers by integer pairs (r,j), where $r = n - k$.

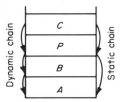

Figure 4.10 Static and dynamic chains.

An explicit current environment vector allows greater efficiency of accessing during execution. However, a static chain eliminates the need for updating the current environment vector on entry to and exit from function modules. Current environment vectors are more efficient if the number of identifier accesses is large compared with the number of times function-module boundaries are crossed, whereas static chains are more efficient when the frequency of crossing of function-module boundaries approaches the frequency of identifier access. We shall use the current-environment-vector model for purposes of exposition. However, the static chain model differs from the current-environment-vector model only by the method of storage of environment pointers.

Exercises: (*a*) Give a set of rules for constructing the static chain structure corresponding to a given run-time current environment structure and vice versa. (*b*) Describe the activation-record stack and the accessing mechanism for currently accessible activation records during the execution of the procedure Q in the example of subsection 4.6.1. Use both the current-environment-vector model and the static chain model.

(c) For both of the models above, construct a mechanism for avoiding indirect addressing during access to "local" identifiers declared in the currently executed function module.

Accessing by means of a current environment vector requires that all identifiers in the program be represented internally by integer pairs (i,j), where i is the nesting depth of the function module in whose head the identifier is declared and j is a relative address within the activation record of the function module.   Both the integers i and j associated with a given instance of use of an identifier are fixed throughout execution and may be specified at translation time.   This internal representation will in general associate the same internal representation (i,j) with identifiers denoting different information items.   The interpreter may access different physical addresses for identifiers with the same internal representation in the fixed-program part.

Having described the mode of representation and mode of access to different classes of identifiers, we shall next briefly describe the initial run-time representation of an ALGOL program and then describe how it is modified on entry to, and exit from, function modules while maintaining the ability to access all classes of identifiers in the proper fashion.

4.6.5 COMPILATION OF ALGOL PROGRAMS

It is assumed in the present model of run-time representation that prior to execution ALGOL programs are transformed by a compiling phase as follows:

1.   Explicit label declarations are introduced into blockheads for all labels.

2.   All identifiers of the program are specified by the integer pair (i,j), where i is the depth of nesting of the declaration for the identifier and j is the relative address of the identifier within activation records of the function module.

3.   Function heads of function modules are replaced by instruction sequences for storage allocation of activation records for the function module.

4.   Executable strings of symbols within function bodies are replaced by machine-language instruction sequences, assuming that working space is always allocated at the top of the run-time stack.

Items 3 and 4 above require many decisions to be made regarding details of machine-language representation of program segments.   However, we are not here concerned with the machine-language representation of segments of code but with the sequence in which code segments are executed, the techniques by which code segments access their data, and the data structures which are created by code segments during execution. These attributes of code segments can be considered independently of the details of representation of code segments. Moreover, segment-sequencing, data-accessing, and data-structure attributes of code segments tend to remain the same over a wide range of different representations. The present model is relatively inefficient if implemented literally but has the virtues of being clean and esthetic. A more efficient model for ALGOL is discussed in Sec. 4.7. Practical compilers contain many additional ad hoc features for improving efficiency.

4.6.6   STRUCTURE, CREATION, AND DELETION OF ACTIVATION RECORDS

Changes in the set of accessible names of a program occur at the following program points:

1. On entry to, and exit from, a block
2. On entry to, and exit from, a procedure
3. On evaluation of a parameter called by name within a procedure
4. On jump to a label

Since all identifiers other than system identifiers are in the activation-record stack and are accessed through the current-environment table, changes in the set of accessible identifiers are accomplished by changes in the activation-record stack and in the current environment, which will now be described for each of the above cases.

When execution is at nesting depth k, the current environment vector contains k pointers $d_1, d_2, \ldots, d_k$ to the accessible activation records. On entry to a new block the nesting depth becomes $k + 1$, a new activation record for the block which has just been entered is created, and a new pointer d_{k+1} to this activation record is added to the current environment vector. The new activation record consists of a sequence of entries (BP,IP,NL,DEC$_1$, . . . ,DEC$_m$,OTHER), where BP is the back pointer to the head of the previous activation record, IP is the register in which the instruction pointer associated with the activation record is stored when the block is interrupted, NL is the nesting level of the block, DEC$_1$, . . . , DEC$_m$ are entries for locally declared identifiers, and OTHER represents information structures which do not fit into the fixed initial part of the block and are pointed to by local identifiers.

On exit from a block at level $k + 1$ by execution of its **end** symbol, the block-activation record is deleted from the top of the activation-record stack, and the entry d_{k+1} in the current environment vector is deleted.

On a call from nesting level k of a procedure declared at nesting level $i \leq k$, only the environment pointed to by the initial part $d_1, \ldots, d_i$ of the current environment vector $d_1, \ldots, d_k$ will be accessible during execution of the procedure. However, the complete set of environment pointers $d_1, \ldots, d_k$ must be reinstated on return to the point of call. Thus on procedure call, the current environment vector must be pushed down and subsequently restored. This could be done in a separate *environment-vector stack*, but it can be accomplished more conveniently by storing the current environment vector in the current activation record prior to calling a procedure.

When the current environment vector is pushed down and an activation record for the procedure heading is created, the new environment vector becomes $d_1, \ldots, d_{i+1}$, where $d_1, \ldots, d_i$ are the first i pointers of the previous environment and d_{i+1} is a pointer to the new procedure activation record. If there are m parameters called by value and n parameters called by name, the activation record created for the procedure has the following form:

$$([F],BP,IP,NL,PV_1, \ldots ,PV_m,PN_1, \ldots ,PN_n,ENVSTK)$$

where [F] denotes a register for holding the function value of a function-type procedure and is absent in statement-type procedures, BP, IP, and NL are the back pointer, instruction pointer on descending to a lower level, and nesting level, as in block function modules, $PV_1, \ldots, PV_m$ are registers in which values of parameters called by value are stored on entry to the procedure, $PN_1, \ldots, PN_n$ are registers which hold pointers to parameters called by name, and ENVSTK holds the current environment vector at the point of call. On a call from level k to level $i \leq k$, ENVSTK needs store only the pointers $d_{i+1}, \ldots, d_k$ of the current environment vector at the point of call since the pointers $d_1, \ldots, d_i$ are given in the current environment vector of the procedure.

On entry to the procedure a sequence of instructions is executed which initializes the procedure activation record and creates the new current environment vector. If the procedure contains internal begin blocks, further pointers $d_{i+2}, \ldots$ will be added to the environment as these blocks are entered.

Note that in executing a procedure declared at level i, the pointer d_i, which points to the activation record in which the procedure is declared, is in the current environment vector. This permits the procedure to have access to all quantities declared in the same block in which it is declared, including other procedures declared in the same block and including the procedure currently being executed.

If during execution of a procedure it calls itself either directly or by means of a chain of calls through other procedures, the call is said to be a *recursive call* of the procedure. A recursive call of a given procedure results in more than one copy of the activation record of the procedure in the run-time stack. However the rules for setting up activation records during a recursive procedure call are precisely the same as those for a recursive call. A function module having a fixed-program part and activation records associated with instances of execution permits several higher-level interpreters to execute the module simultaneously.

On normal exit from a procedure by completing its last instruction, all blocks created during execution of the procedure will already have been deleted. Exit from a statement-type procedure causes deletion of the procedure-activation record and pop-up of the previous environment vector, while exit from a function-type procedure causes deletion of everything in the activation record other than the function value F. This in turn leaves the stack in exactly the same state in which it would have been left if the function call had been a constant or a variable.

Parameters PV_i called by value are implemented as references to the local register in the activation record in which the value of the parameter is placed on entry to the procedure. Parameters called by name PN_i are implemented as indirect references to the corresponding register and result in evaluation of the parameter in the environment of the *calling program*.

Evaluation of parameters called by name requires temporary pushdown of the current environment vector and reinstatement of the environment vector of the calling program during parameter evaluation. It is unnecessary to introduce a new activation record unless evaluation of the parameter called by name itself involves entry into a begin or a procedure block. If the parameter called by name in turn involves a parameter called by name, the environment vector is again pushed down. Eventually evaluation of the parameter called by name is completed, the value is transmitted back to the procedure, and the current environment vector of the procedure is reinstated (popped up).†

If the statement "**go to** L" is encountered during execution of a block or procedure, the label L must be a label in the same block or in an enclosing block of the **go to** statement, since labels are always local to the block in which they occur. If no block or procedure boundaries need be crossed to jump to the level L, the jump is implemented merely by a change of the instruction-location counter. If there are block or procedure boundaries between the **go to** statement and the labeled statement activation

---

† Note that it is not in general possible to determine how complex the actual parameter corresponding to a given formal parameter is going to be. It is therefore necessary to implement all parameter calls by name so that they work for complex actual-parameter expressions. The inefficiency introduced in this way can be avoided by introducing a third form of parameter calling known as call by reference, as indicated in subsection 4.6.8.

records must be deleted from the run-time stack until the activation record of the block in which the label is declared becomes the top activation record of the run-time stack. Because of the possibility of recursive procedures, the number of activation records to be deleted may be more than the number of static boundaries between the **go to** statement and the labeled statement. If the **go to** statement is at nesting level k and the label is at nesting level $i < k$, the process of deletion of activation records must be continued until the first activation record at nesting level i is encountered.

Exercise: Describe for the static chain model the process of entry to and exit from function modules and the evaluation of parameters called by name.

4.6.7 RECURSIVE PROCEDURES

The above mechanism for accessing identifiers will be illustrated by considering a simple recursive procedure for summation of a set of numbers.

real procedure SIGMA(i,L,M,f);
    value L,M; **integer** i,L,M; **real** f;
    begin i := L;
        SIGMA := **if** L > M **then** 0 **else**
        f + SIGMA(i,L+1,M,f)
    end

This recursive procedure computes the sum of a set of numbers using the formula $\sum_{L}^{M} f_i = f_L + \sum_{L+1}^{M} f_i$. Its body consists of a compound statement with two assignment statements. The second assignment statement contains a conditional expression on its right-hand side whose value is 0 when $L > M$ and whose evaluation involves a reentrant call of the procedure when $L \leq M$.

Use of the above procedure is illustrated by the following procedure call:

SIGMA(i,1,3,x[i])   This procedure call results in assignment to SIGMA of the value of the expression "x[1] + SIGMA(i,2,3,f)". The recursive call of SIGMA results in a value "x[2] + SIGMA(i,3,3,f)". This further recursive call results in a value "x[3] + SIGMA(i,4,3,f)". Evaluation of SIGMA(i,4,3,f) results in a value of zero, so that the value of this procedure call is $x[1] + x[2] + x[3] + 0 = \sum_{1}^{3} x[i]$.

Each recursive call of the procedure causes a new activation record for the procedure to be placed on the run-time stack. When the call

"SIGMA(i,4,3,x[i])" is being executed, there are four activation records for the procedure SIGMA on the run-time stack. Exit from this procedure with value 0 results in deletion of this activation record and return of control to the instruction following the point of call in the procedure "SIGMA(i,3,3,x[i])". Exit from the third level with the value $x[3]$ and from the second level with value $x[2] + x[3]$ proceeds in a similar fashion. On exit from the first level all activation records for SIGMA have been deleted from the stack, and $x[1] + x[2] + x[3]$ sits on top of the stack.

Both the formal parameters i and f in the above procedure declaration are called by name and are therefore accessed by pointers from the activation record to the point of call. The actual parameter i and the *real array* x must be declared in a block enclosing the point of call of the procedure. On execution of the procedure the nonlocal parameter i is first assigned a value and then used to index the actual parameter expression $x[i]$. Both i and $x[i]$ are evaluated in the context of the calling procedure. It is essential that i be declared by name rather than by value, since it must be available while $x[i]$ is being evaluated in the context of the point of call.

When a recursively called instance of the procedure SIGMA is being executed, the pointers for parameters called by name are pointers to the calling copy of the procedure. The values pointed to in the calling procedure are again parameters called by name in an outer copy, so that a parameter encountered at level n of a recursively entered procedure results in a chain of n pointers to the parameter in its environment. In order to access the parameter called by name, updating of the current environment will have to be performed n times, so that the process of accessing a parameter called by name in a recursive procedure may be quite lengthy.†

Exercises: (*a*) Describe the sequence of environment changes when accessing i in the procedure call "SIGMA(i,4,3,f)" above. (*b*) Modify the stack organization so that parameters called by name are initialized by direct links to their point of call.

4.6.8 CALL BY REFERENCE‡

Since the process of calling parameters by name involves relatively complex stack manipulations at execution time, a method of parameter calling

---

† The chain of links to be followed when accessing a parameter called by name can be collapsed into a single link by creating a direct link to the procedure and environment for computing the parameter at the time of initialization of the parameter on entry to the procedure.

‡ Call by reference is not available in ALGOL but is available in CPL [16], FORTRAN, and in PL/I. FORTRAN and PL/I do not have call by name and only have call by reference.

has been suggested which permits side effects to be produced at the point of call but which does not have the full substitutive generality of a call by name. This mode of call will be referred to as a *call by reference*.

In many instances access to the calling program for a parameter called by name is a simple indirect-address reference for either fetching or storing an item of information in the accessed register. A parameter which is called by reference has an *address reference* transmitted from the calling to the called program. Procedure parameters called by reference would be implemented by accessing the register specified by the address reference as though it were a data register, while parameters called by name are implemented by treating the address pointer supplied by the calling program as an entry point of a procedure.

The difference between call by value, call by reference, and call by name can be illustrated by considering the procedure call "P(A[i])", where P is the procedure name and $A[i]$ is a parameter. If $A[i]$ is called by value, the current value of $A[i]$ is stored in a local register of the activation record on entry to the procedure. If $A[i]$ is called by reference, the address of $A[i]$ for the current value of i is passed as a parameter to the procedure, and all references to $A[i]$ during execution will be to the fixed address determined at the time of call. If $A[i]$ is called by name, a pointer to a procedure for computing $A[i]$ is passed to P, and the register accessed during execution of the procedure will depend on the value of i at the instant of access rather than at the instant of call. Calls by reference do not necessarily preclude actual parameters which are expressions. For example, if it is known that the parameter of a procedure P is called by reference, a procedure call $P(a + b)$ can be implemented by computing the value of $a + b$ at the time of call, storing the value of the expression in a temporary register, and passing the address of this temporary register as a parameter to the procedure. However, in order to do this the system must know at the point of call that the parameter is called by reference. In FORTRAN all parameters are called by reference, and the above technique is automatically adopted for actual-parameter expressions. However, when parameters may be called either by name or by reference, it is necessary either to explicitly indicate whether an actual-parameter expression is to be implemented by name or by reference or to adopt the convention that calls by reference require actual parameters to be simple address references.

Although calls by reference are appealing because of their greater efficiency of implementation, calls by name are esthetically more appealing because they correspond to the notion of substitution of unevaluated parameters followed by evaluations on use of the parameter. Calls by reference constitute a hybrid form of substitution for which there is no clear theoretical substitutive model.

The difference between call by name and call by reference can be further illustrated by the following procedure for interchanging the values associated with two identifiers.

```
procedure swap (x,y);
  real x,y;
  begin real k;
    k := x;
    x := y;
    y := k
  end;
```

Assume that $i = 3$ and $A[3] = 5$ and consider the following two calls of the above procedure:

swap (i,A[i]);   This procedure call stores the value 3 in k, the value $A[3] = 5$ in i, and the value 3 in $A[i] = A[5]$.

swap (A[i],i)   This procedure call stores $A[i] = A(3) = 5$ in k, then stores $i = 3$ in $A[3]$, and then stores 5 in i.

The second procedure call has the intended effect of swapping i and $A[i]$, while the first does not.   However, if the parameters x, y of the above procedure were called by reference, the address reference to $A[i]$ would always be set up using the value of i at the time of entry to the procedure, and the two procedure calls would have an identical effect.

4.6.9   OWN VARIABLES

There is one exception in ALGOL to the above form of storage allocation, referred to as the **own** mode of storage allocation.   If an identifier declaration is preceded by the storage-allocation attribute **own**, it is said to be an **own** variable.   Storage for an own variable is not deleted on exit from the block in which it is declared but persists between successive activations of the block in which it is declared.   However, it is known only within the block in which it is declared and cannot be accessed from outside that block.

Own variables were introduced into ALGOL so as to allow preservation of local information between successive activations of a function module, as is the case in FORTRAN subroutines.   The concept of a single copy of storage for own variables which persists through time independently of activations of the activation record in which the variable is declared implies that there is only a single copy even when the function module is called reentrantly.   This interpretation may sometimes be contrary to the requirement that variables in each activation of a reentrant module be distinct, but it will nevertheless be adopted here.   With this interpretation **own** variables can be implemented by augmenting the fixed program by a fixed-data part for own variables.

This approach breaks down when own variables are declared whose storage requirements differ in different activations of the function module. This occurs in ALGOL only in the case of dynamic arrays. The breakdown arises because the concept of data which endures between activations is inapplicable when the information structure changes between activations.

The concept of an **own** variable was historically introduced into ALGOL to give it FORTRAN-like storage capabilities. At the time that **own** variables were introduced it was not realized that the concept leads to inconsistency when the data structure changes during execution. However, if the restriction is added that **own** variables imply an unchanging structure between activations, the concept is both acceptable and useful.

A better approach to storage allocation for information which endures between activations of blocks is that of declaring it independently of entry to, and exit from, blocks by means of a notation that is completely disjoint from the declarations used in blockheads. Such a notation is available for instance in PL/1, which contains the executable commands ALLOCATE and FREE for dynamically allocating and freeing storage for information at the time of execution of these commands. This approach is further discussed in the section on PL/I.

4.6.10 ALGOL MACHINES

In the previous sections the structure of the run-time stack during execution of an ALGOL program was carefully analyzed, and the effect on the stack of crossing boundaries between function modules was indicated. In the present section an ALGOL program will be thought of as giving rise to a sequence of instantaneous descriptions during its execution. Execution of the program is accomplished by scanning symbols of the source program and transforming instantaneous descriptions in a manner specified by the source symbol being scanned. The semantics of ALGOL can be specified by indicating the transformation of the instantaneous description for each of the possible combinations of source-program symbols that can be encountered. This approach is similar to that adopted for lambda-calculus machines and the SECD machine in the previous chapter. In the case of ALGOL, a machine which transforms instantaneous descriptions according to the rules specified by ALGOL will be called an ALGOL machine.

It will be assumed that, prior to execution, an ALGOL program goes through a compilation phase of the kind described in subsection 4.6.5. This compilation phase includes explicit introduction of label declarations, replacement of identifiers by integer pairs (i,j), replacement of function-module heads by corresponding storage-allocation and initialization programs, and replacement of expressions and statements in function bodies by machine-language instructions or by a prefix or postfix representation to be interpretively executed.

The initial instantaneous description prior to execution includes the compiled program and an initial environment E_I in which the meanings of all initialized symbols (free variables) are specified. The initialized symbols include numerical and logical constants, control and punctuation symbols **begin for** ; and so forth, operation symbols $+ :=$ and so forth, and initialized identifiers SIN, LOG, and so forth. The initial environment E_I specifies the meanings of all these symbols in the sense that it contains a prescription for the action to be taken when these symbols are encountered during execution of the program. All symbols other than the initialized identifiers are global in the sense that they are represented by the same information structure (or mechanical device) in the environment throughout execution of the program.

During execution of an ALGOL program it is convenient to classify the instantaneous description into the following four components:

1. The *program*, which will be referred to as the control string C.

2. An *environment* E, which consists of the initial environment E_I and a run-time stack R.

3. A *stateword SW* which contains a pointer P to the current point that is being scanned in the control string, and a current environment vector CE which consists of a vector of pointers to activation records in the run-time stack R that are accessible during execution of the current function module.

4. A set of input-output tapes IO which may include a number of read-only tapes, a number of write-only tapes, and a number of read-write tapes. We shall assume that there are functions in the initial environment E_I for reading and writing on tapes which change the instantaneous description by repositioning tapes, modifying the run-time stack on reading, and modifying an output tape on writing.

Execution of the program is accomplished by scanning successive symbols of the control string, looking up in the environment the action to be performed when the given symbol is scanned, and performing an action which in general changes one or more components of the instantaneous description.

The semantics of ALGOL can be defined by specifying the change of instantaneous description for every symbol that can be encountered during program execution. Since the instantaneous description has been split into four components (E,C,SW,IO), the semantics may be defined in terms of the change to these four components as successive symbols are encountered during program execution.

In the present section we shall not attempt to give a complete specification of the changes in instantaneous description for each of the possible symbols encountered during execution but merely give a qualitative description of the kinds of changes that are induced by various classes of symbols. A more detailed description of changes of the instantaneous description induced on execution is given earlier in this chapter.

During expression evaluation without side effects, the only changes in instantaneous description are in the stateword and at the top of the environment stack E. When a value is assigned to any identifier other than a parameter called by name, the state of E is changed by modifying one of the activation records pointed to by the current environment vector CE in the stateword SW. The state of E may be changed also by addition or deletion of temporary quantities at the top of the stack.

The most fundamental changes of the instantaneous description occur on entry to or exit from a function module. On entry to a function module a new layer of the environment E is created on top of the environment stack, containing values of or pointers to the set of identifiers declared or specified in the head of the function module. When the function module is a procedure, the stateword is updated by pushdown of part of the previous current environment in the environment E and replacement of the current environment by an initial part whose number of entries corresponds to the level of nesting of the newly entered procedure.

On exit from a function module a layer of the environment is removed. If the function module is a procedure, the current environment is restored.

On encountering an actual parameter called by name, the current environment is adjusted to the environment of the corresponding actual parameter during access to the parameter and subsequently restored.

On executing a jump to a label, a number of layers of the environment are peeled off until the one in which the label is declared is encountered, and the stateword is adjusted to continue execution beginning at the labeled statement.

This discussion indicates the principal kinds of changes of instantaneous description that must be considered when the semantics of ALGOL is described as an ALGOL machine. A more rigorous specification of the changes could be given by developing a "transform" function for ALGOL along the lines of the transform function for lambda expressions developed in Sec. 3.10. In the case of ALGOL, the transform function would have as its four parameters the four components of the instantaneous description (E,C,SW,IO). The function body would be specified as a conditional expression which tested the current symbol under the scan head for each of the alternative symbols that could appear under the scan head and specified the transformation on (E,C,SW,IO) for each of the possible cases.

Since the principal types of information structures created and deleted during execution are activation records, constructors such as the following ones would be required in specifying the transform function:

*constructbegin*AR(blockhead)   Construct an activation record (AR) for a begin block using its blockhead as a parameter.

*constructfunction*AR(P_1, . . . ,P_n)   Construct an activation record for a function-type procedure with n parameters.

*constructprocedure*AR(P_1, . . . ,P_n)   Construct an activation record for a statement-type procedure with n parameters.

A fragment of the transform function might appear as follows:

if C = **begin** *and* blockhead = (DEC$_1$, . . . ,DEC$_n$) **then** *constructbegin-*AR(DEC$_1$, . . . ,DEC$_n$); *and* **go to** bodypart;
else if C = assignmentstatement **then** execute(assignmentstatement) *and* **go to** next;
else if C = procedurecall **then** *constructprocedure*AR(P_1, . . . ,P_n) *and* **go to** procedurebody;
else if C = **end then** *deletebegin*AR

A specification along the above lines is essentially a specification of an ALGOL interpreter. Specification of an ALGOL interpreter in the above style of notation using high-level primitives such as those above is not too difficult. The high-level primitives can in turn be defined in terms of lower-level primitives. Primitives at any level may in turn be implemented as programs, and the interpreter may be used for the execution of ALGOL programs.

Exercises: (*a*) Design an ALGOL interpreter (ALGOL machine) using a suitable set of predicates, selectors, and constructors and using the style of specification indicated above.   (*b*) Implement your ALGOL interpreter by implementing your primitives as programs.

4.7   EFFICIENT ALGOL RUN-TIME ENVIRONMENTS

4.7.1   CLASSIFICATION OF PROGRAMS FOR RUN-TIME ALLOCATION

ALGOL variables vary over restricted domains whose elements all require the same amount of storage for their representation.   Storage requirements for activation records containing only fixed-size elements can be determined at translation time.   In the absence of procedures, the "dynamic predecessors" in the run-time stack of a given activation record are the same for every instance of activation and can therefore be predicted during translation.†   Even in the presence of procedures, certain predictions regarding the sequence in which activation records are created can be made at compile time.   In the present section we shall discuss the degree to which predictions about run-time storage allocation can be made at compile time and the way in which such predictions can be used to make execution of ALGOL programs more efficient.

Four increasingly complete subsets of ALGOL will be used for purposes of illustration:

1.   Programs with no identifiers of type **array** or **procedure.**
2.   Programs with no arrays and with nonrecursive procedures.
3.   Programs with arrays (including arrays with dynamic bounds) and nonrecursive procedures.
4.   Programs with arrays and recursive procedures, i.e., full ALGOL.

4.7.2   SIMULATED ALLOCATION WITH NO ARRAYS OR PROCEDURES

When no identifiers of type **array** or **procedure** are permitted, the program consists of a nest of begin blocks.   The size of the activation record for each begin block can be predicted at compile time, and the activation records already in the run-time stack on entry to a given nested block will always be the same.   The relative address of a given declared variable relative to the beginning of the run-time stack will be the same on every activation of the block.   Thus the integer-pair address (i,j) specified in the previous section can be dispensed with and replaced by a one-component address j relative to the beginning of the run-time stack.   This allows an indirect-addressing cycle to be saved in accessing a variable, allows back pointers and environment pointers to be dispensed with, and eliminates the requirement of initialization on passing through a block boundary during execution.

† The sequence in which function modules are entered and exited is determined by conditional and iteration statements and cannot be predicted during translation. However, in the absence of procedures, the activated function modules at a given point of execution of the static program are precisely those corresponding to physically enclosing blockheads.   Thus the activated function modules when a given point of the static program is executed are the same on every activation.

4.7.3 SIMULATED ALLOCATION WITH NO DYNAMIC ARRAYS OR RECURSIVE PROCEDURES

When nonrecursive procedures are introduced into the language, the size of individual activation records remains predictable during translation, but the set of activation records in the run-time stack on entry to a procedure-heading block or to a begin block within a procedure is no longer fixed.   A procedure may in general be called within any blocks enclosed by the block in which it is declared.   However, for nonrecursive procedures it is possible to compute the maximum number of storage registers that can ever be required in the run-time stack prior to call of the procedure and to allocate space for the procedure activation record at this point of the run-time stack.†   This strategy allows addresses relative to the beginning of the run-time stack to be fixed at translation time for nonrecursive procedures.   Although the strategy sometimes results in activation records' being allocated further from the beginning of the run-time stack than is strictly necessary, the maximum size of the run-time stack does not exceed the maximum size of the run-time stack using the strategy of the previous section.   Indeed, the stack size will be slightly less because back pointers, environment pointers, etc., are not needed; i.e., accessing is performed by direct relative addressing rather than through environment pointers in an environment stack.

4.7.4 SIMULATED ALLOCATION WITH NO RECURSIVE PROCEDURES

When variables of type **array** are declared in an ALGOL program, they are usually handled by means of a fixed-length dope vector [6] containing one entry per array dimension, which allows an address to be computed for a given set of subscripts by means of an address-mapping function stored in the fixed-program part.   The array itself is normally stored following the declared variables of the block.   If the array has dynamic bounds, the activation record may have a different size on different activations, but the set of declared variables and the dope vector can be accessed through fixed addresses relative to the beginning of the block.

In the absence of recursive procedures, fixed-length information items and dope vectors of all variable-length information items can be assigned fixed addresses relative to the beginning of the activation-record stack.   All variable-length information, including arrays with dynamic bounds, can be stored in the activation-record stack beyond the fixed-length segment which stores fixed-length information.   When a block is entered which contains a declaration for an information structure stored

---

† This may be done by considering all possible flow paths through the program to this procedure, computing the storage required for activation records along each flow path, and choosing the maximum required storage over all flow paths as the origin of the procedure activation record in the run-time stack.

beyond the end of the fixed-length stack, dynamic allocation for that information structure must be performed by initializing its dope vector.   References to components of the information structure will use the information in the initialized dope vector to compute the required address.

The activation-record stack can be thought of as having a single fixed-length activation record for all fixed-length information and dope vectors and a variable-length portion in which variable information items are allocated in a last in, first out order.   Temporary information items such as operands during expression evaluation can be stored at the current top of the variable-length portion of the activation-record stack.

When the stack is organized as above, fixed-length information items can be directly addressed, so that the indirect-addressing cycle required when accessing through a current environment vector can be saved.   The saving is even greater when accessing parameters called by name of a (nonrecursive) procedure; i.e., the identifiers encountered in the evaluation of a parameter called by name always have a fixed address in the activation-record stack, and it is unnecessary to redefine the accessible environment during the evaluation of parameters called by name.

This technique for accessing variable-length information through fixed-length dope vectors is a powerful one and is used in many applications for separating out intrinsic problems of information organization from problems which arise because the information has variable storage requirements.   In subsection 4.7.5 we shall be concerned with multiple occurrences of activation records due to recursive activation or procedures. It is convenient to separate the problem of multiple occurrences from the problem of variability of length.   We shall therefore assume that groups of activation records in which no multiple occurrences are permitted have a fixed total length and that the problem of variability of length is dealt with as in the present section by placing variable-length information beyond the fixed-length information for all activation records that form a single unit for purposes of relative addressing.

4.7.5 SIMULATED ALLOCATION FOR FULL ALGOL

When full ALGOL, including recursive procedures, is permitted, a given recursive procedure gives rise to multiple activation records.   An identifier in a recursive procedure has a different address relative to the beginning of the run-time stack for each recursive instance of activation. It is clearly impossible to specify a unique address relative to the beginning of the run-time stack for such an identifier.

The problem of allocation for recursive procedures is illustrated by the following ALGOL program which contains two recursive procedures P and Q nested in the block B, and a recursive procedure R nested in the recursive procedure P.

A: **begin**
   procedure P;
  B: **begin**
      procedure R;
    D: **begin**
       · · ·
       R;
      end;
     · · ·
     P;
     R;
   end;
  procedure Q;
  C: **begin**
    · · ·
    Q;
    P;
   end;
  · · ·
  P;
  Q;
  · · ·
end A;

On entering the block A an activation record of A is created, including procedure references to procedures P and Q. Control then passes to the first executable statement of the block body and eventually reaches the procedure calls for P and Q. A call of procedure P creates an activation record for P and results in entry to the block B which contains a procedure declaration for the procedure R and inner calls of the procedures P and R. A call of the procedure Q results in entry to the block C which contains calls of Q and P.

Figure 4.11 illustrates the activations in the activation-record stack when execution is in the block D after the indicated sequence of procedure calls.

The relative-addressing problems in the above structure include the following: (1) the address of identifiers within the procedures P and Q

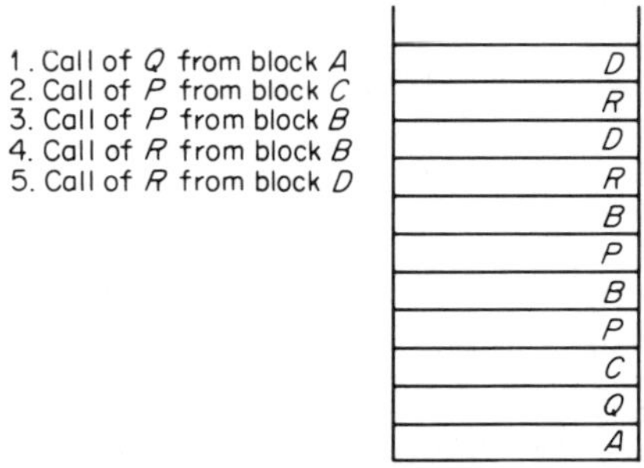

1. Call of Q from block A
2. Call of P from block C
3. Call of P from block B
4. Call of R from block B
5. Call of R from block D

D
R
D
R
B
P
B
P
C
Q
A

Figure 4.11 Activation-record stack resulting from the indicated sequence of procedure calls.

relative to the beginning of the run-time stack cannot be predicted, and (2) the address of identifiers within the procedure R relative to the beginning of the activation record of P in which R is called cannot be predicted. However, identifiers in the activation records for P and B have a fixed address relative to the beginning of the activation record of P, and identifiers in the activation records for Q and C have a fixed address relative to the beginning of the activation record of Q.

From the above example it is a short step to formulation of the following general rule.

The relative distance in the activation-record stack between an identifier I_1 at nesting level k_1 and an inner identifier I_2 at nesting level $k_2 \geq k_1$ can be predicted if and only if none of the $k_2 - k_1$ function modules that enclose I_2 but not I_1 is a potentially recursive procedure.

The above rule in turn leads to the notion that activation records of function modules corresponding to potentially recursive procedures serve as a new origin for relative addressing in the run-time stack, while addresses within function modules not corresponding to potentially recursive procedures can be specified relative to the most recent activation of the next enclosing potentially recursive procedure. If there is no enclosing potentially recursive procedure, the address can be specified relative to the beginning of the run-time stack.

A group of function modules which forms a single unit for relative addressing in the above stack organization has been referred to as a *program level* [7]. Program levels are associated with the static program structure as follows: the *outer program level* starts with the first **begin** symbol and includes all points of the program that can be dynamically reached without entering a potentially recursive procedure; *inner program levels* start with a potentially recursive procedure heading and include all inner points of the procedure declaration which can be reached without entering a potentially recursive procedure.

A level of nesting will be associated with each program level. The outer program level is defined to have nesting level 1, and inner program levels are defined to have a nesting level which is 1 greater than the minimum number of potentially recursive procedures which must be called to enter that program level.

An ALGOL compiler which uses program levels rather than function modules as the unit of relative addressing can be implemented using precisely the same techniques as those developed in Sec. 4.6, except that changes in the current environment are associated with crossing boundaries between program levels. Identifiers of the program have internal names (i,j) just as in Sec. 4.6, but the integer i refers to the level of nesting of the program level and the integer j refers to a relative address within the program level. The concept of a local identifier refers to an identifier local to the program level rather than to an identifier local to the function module.

During execution, the current environment is specified by a current environment vector whose number of entries corresponds to the level of nesting of the program level currently being executed. The current environment vector specifies all program levels that are currently accessible. The current environment vector need be changed only when a program-level boundary is crossed during execution or when a parameter called by name in an environment outside the current program level is evaluated.

The use of the program level rather than the function module as the unit for purposes of relative addressing is more efficient for the following reasons:

1. Storage allocation is performed less frequently and in larger units for program levels than for function modules.

2. Changes of environment for repetitive crossing of function-module boundaries within a program level are altogether avoided.

3. The set of quantities local to a program level is much larger than the set of quantities local to a function module, so that efficient accessing without the use of indirect addressing occurs a greater proportion of the time. In particular, many programs contain no potentially recursive procedures, so that all quantities are local to the outer program level and can be accessed by relative rather than indirect addressing.

Thus the use of program levels introduces efficiencies both in the overhead of dynamic storage allocation and in accessing during execution.

4.7.6 DETECTING RECURSIVE PROCEDURES

In order to implement an efficient run-time system such as that described above, it is necessary to distinguish prior to execution between recursive and nonrecursive procedures. This could be accomplished by explicitly requiring an additional type specification for procedures stating whether or not the procedure is potentially recursive. Alternatively, in the absence of such type specifications, it is possible to determine whether a procedure is potentially recursive by flow analysis using simple graph-theoretical techniques.

By examining a static program with n procedure declarations $P_1, \ldots, P_n$, an $n \times n$ incidence matrix M can be constructed whose ijth position p_{ij} is a 1 if and only if procedure P_i calls procedure P_j. From this matrix a matrix M' can be constructed whose ijth position p'_{ij} is a 1 if and only if procedure P_i can call procedure P_j by a sequence of two procedure calls. The matrix M' is constructed as follows:

The procedure P_i can access the procedure P_j by a sequence of two procedure calls if and only if there is an intermediate procedure P_k such that P_i calls P_k and P_k calls P_j. This condition obtains if $\sum_{k=1}^{n} p_{ik}p_{kj} \neq 0$. Since $\Sigma p_{ik}p_{kj}$ is precisely the ijth element of the matrix P^2, the matrix M' can be obtained from P^2 by replacing its nonzero elements by 1, or by performing an equivalent Boolean matrix "product" $\bigcup_{k=1}^{n} p_{ih} \wedge p_{hj}$.

It can be shown by induction that the nonzero elements p_{ij}^3 of P^3 correspond precisely to procedure pairs P_i, P_j for which P_j can be reached by a sequence of two intermediate procedure calls from P_i. Similarly the nonzero elements p_{ij}^n of P^n correspond to procedure pairs P_i, P_j for which P_j can be reached from P_i through a sequence of $n - 1$ intermediate procedures. The matrix which has 1s in nonzero positions of P^n and zeros elsewhere will be denoted by M^n.

If there are n procedures altogether, it can be shown that P_j can be reached from P_i if and only if there is a path with $n - 1$ or fewer intermediate procedure calls from P_i to P_j. Thus there is a path from P_i to P_j if and only if the ijth element of the matrix $P + P^2 + \ldots + P^n$ is nonzero, i.e., if and only if there is a one-step path, a two-step path, $\ldots$, or an n-step path.

Determination of whether there is a chain of procedure calls from P_i to P_j can be determined from the static program by construction of the incidence matrix for the program, computation of all powers of the matrix up to the nth power, where n is the total number of procedures in the program, and summation of the resulting matrices. The reentrant procedures are those which have a 1 on the diagonal of the resulting matrix.

Example: Consider a set of four procedures A, B, C, D with direct procedure calls as indicated in Fig. 4.12. This pattern of procedure calls gives rise to the following matrix P:

$$M = P = \begin{array}{c} \\ A \\ B \\ C \\ D \end{array} \begin{array}{c} \begin{array}{cccc} A & B & C & D \end{array} \\ \left[\begin{array}{cccc} 0 & 1 & 0 & 1 \\ 0 & 1 & 1 & 0 \\ 1 & 0 & 0 & 0 \\ 0 & 0 & 0 & 0 \end{array} \right] \end{array}$$

That is, procedure A calls procedures B and D, procedure B calls procedures B and C, procedure C calls procedure A, and procedure D does not call any procedures. M^2, M^3, and M^4 respectively denote the set of

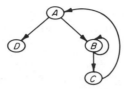

**Figure 4.12   Intercon-
nection graph for four
procedures.**

all two-, three-, and four-stage procedure-calling chains. These can be
obtained either by matrix multiplication or by inspection.

$$M^2 = \begin{array}{c} \\ A \\ B \\ C \\ D \end{array} \begin{array}{cccc} A & B & C & D \\ \left[\begin{matrix} 0 & 1 & 1 & 0 \\ 1 & 1 & 1 & 0 \\ 0 & 1 & 0 & 1 \\ 0 & 0 & 0 & 0 \end{matrix}\right] \end{array} \qquad M^3 = \begin{array}{c} \\ A \\ B \\ C \\ D \end{array} \begin{array}{cccc} A & B & C & D \\ \left[\begin{matrix} 1 & 1 & 1 & 0 \\ 1 & 1 & 1 & 1 \\ 0 & 1 & 1 & 0 \\ 0 & 0 & 0 & 0 \end{matrix}\right] \end{array}$$

$$M^4 = \begin{array}{c} \\ A \\ B \\ C \\ D \end{array} \begin{array}{cccc} A & B & C & D \\ \left[\begin{matrix} 1 & 1 & 1 & 1 \\ 1 & 1 & 1 & 1 \\ 1 & 1 & 1 & 0 \\ 0 & 0 & 0 & 0 \end{matrix}\right] \end{array}$$

The nonzero positions of the matrix $M \vee M^2 \vee M^3 \vee M^4$ are as
follows:

$$M \vee M^2 \vee M^3 \vee M^4 = \begin{array}{c} \\ A \\ B \\ C \\ D \end{array} \begin{array}{cccc} A & B & C & D \\ \left[\begin{matrix} 1 & 1 & 1 & 1 \\ 1 & 1 & 1 & 1 \\ 1 & 1 & 1 & 1 \\ 0 & 0 & 0 & 0 \end{matrix}\right] \end{array}$$

Thus procedures A, B, and C are potentially recursive, since they
have nonzero diagonal entries.

Exercise: Draw the interconnection graph and compute the nonzero
entries of $M \vee M^2 \vee M^3 \vee M^4 \vee M^5$ for the following P.

$$M = P = \begin{array}{c} \\ A \\ B \\ C \\ D \\ E \end{array} \begin{array}{ccccc} A & B & C & D & E \\ \left[\begin{matrix} 0 & 1 & 1 & 0 & 0 \\ 0 & 0 & 1 & 0 & 0 \\ 0 & 0 & 0 & 1 & 0 \\ 0 & 0 & 0 & 0 & 1 \\ 0 & 1 & 0 & 0 & 1 \end{matrix}\right] \end{array}$$

The matrix $\bigcup\limits_{i=1}^{n} M^i$ obtained from a matrix M in the manner described above is sometimes referred to as the *transitive closure* of M.

Exercise: Write an ALGOL procedure which, given a matrix M of zeros and 1s together with its order n, computes the transitive closure of M.

4.8 PROGRAMMER-DEFINED INFORMATION STRUCTURES

4.8.1 INFORMATION STRUCTURES IN ALGOL

Among the more important features of a programming language are the facilities for associating information structures with identifiers and the facilities for creating and deleting information structures.   In the present section the facilities available in ALGOL for both these purposes will be summarized, and a number of suggestions for providing more general data structures and more general creation and deletion facilities will be considered.   The possibility of introducing new syntactic forms (program structures) into the language by means of syntax macros will also be considered.   The purpose of this section is not to provide a complete specification for an extension of ALGOL but rather to develop an insight into the kinds of extensions that are possible in this direction.

In ALGOL the only way of creating an information structure is by entry to a function module, and the only way of deleting an information structure is by exit from a function module.   ALGOL permits (1) the three basic data types **integer, real,** and **Boolean,** (2) homogeneous arrays of elements for each of these data types, and (3) identifiers to be associated with executable information structures by means of **procedure** declarations and implicit **label** declarations.

Since all information structures associated with declarations in the head of a function module are created and deleted simultaneously, we may think of the set of information structures in the head of a given function module as a single information structure which is more general than a vector, in that it includes constituents of a number of different types, but less general than a tree structure, in that multiple levels are not permitted.

In ALGOL, composite information structures can be created and deleted only by entry to, and exit from, function modules.   ALGOL-based programming languages which require dynamic creation and deletion of composite information structures make heavy use of function-module nesting for precisely this purpose.   SIMULA (see Sec. 4.11), which requires creation and deletion of simulated entities during execution, is an example of such a language.

However, creation and deletion of composite information structures by entry to, and exit from, function modules is both cumbersome and artificial. It is cumbersome because the function modules that contain the required information structures must physically enclose all function modules in which they are used. It is artificial because creation and deletion of information structures is more naturally accomplished by explicit commands such as CREATE and DESTROY or ALLOCATE and FREE than by entry to, and exit from, function modules.

In ALGOL a declaration such as "**real array** A[m:n];" contains the complete structure specification of the identifier A. An instance of the information structure denoted by A is created whenever the block in which this declaration occurs is entered during execution.

There is no need in ALGOL to distinguish between the structure specification for the identifier A and the declaration which creates an instance of the information structure when it is executed, since every declaration carries with it a complete specification of the structure of the declared identifier. However, when more flexible facilities for the specification and creation of data structures are introduced, it is convenient to separate the structure specification from declaration of individual instances of the identifier. The structure specification can be thought of as a *template*. Creation of individual information structures having the form specified by the template can be thought of as macro calls which create an instance of the structure defined by the template, associate a name with it, and make the structure available for further manipulation. In ALGOL further manipulation is confined to the assignment of **integer, real,** or **Boolean** values to certain fields of the structure. However, in general, manipulation of created structures may allow tampering with the structure as well as with data fields. List- and string-manipulation languages are specifically designed to manipulate structures having the forms of lists and strings. Formula languages are designed to manipulate formulas. General-purpose languages should contain facilities not only for the definition of structures belonging to a number of predefined types but also for building new structures out of previously defined structures by composition.

Templates which constitute a structure specification may consist either of a direct specification of a structure in terms of component substructures or of a structure-valued procedure which, when it is executed, produces an instance of the desired structure. Structure-valued procedures permit a class of information structures to be specified by the same structure definition and permit selection of a member of the class by appropriate specification of parameters. This approach to structure specification has been developed by Standish [14] and is further discussed below.

4.8.2 DATA TEMPLATES AND PROGRAMMER-DEFINED DATA STRUCTURES

A number of alternative notations for the specification of data templates in procedure-oriented languages will now be given.   The first notation, due to Wirth [17], introduces new structures by means of a new kind of declaration referred to as a **type** declaration.†

type identifier template   This type declaration specifies that the identifier following the symbol **type** has as its structure specification the template which follows the identifier.

For example,

type complex[realpart:**real**,cpart:**real**]   This type declaration declares the identifier complex to have a template consisting of a component realpart of type **real** followed by a component cpart of type **real.**

An alternative notation, suggested originally by Perlis and developed more recently by Standish [14], separates the declaration of template-valued identifiers from the assignment of values to template-valued identifiers.   Template-valued identifiers are declared by a *descriptor declaration* and have values assigned by *template-type assignment statements*.

descriptor A;   The descriptor declaration declares A to be an identi-
$A :=$ template;   fier of type descriptor.   The template-type assign-
        ment statement assigns a template as the value of A.

The right-hand side of a template-type assignment statement is a *template-type expression*.   Template-type expressions contain concatenation operators and other operators that are useful in structure definition. The comma will be used to denote concatenation.   Names of subfields of the template will be followed by a colon and by a specification of the subfield structure.   Complete template-type expressions will be enclosed in square brackets.

For example,

descriptor complex;   This   descriptor   declaration
complex := [realpart:**real**,cpart:**real**];   declares "complex" to be of the type **descriptor.**   The assignment statement specifies that the template for complex has two information fields of type **real,** respectively called realpart and cpart.

---

† Data-structure definition facilities similar to the above were suggested by McCarthy [18], who uses the reserved symbol **cartesian** instead of the reserved symbol **type** in order to emphasize that the domain of newly defined structures is the cartesian product set of the domains of components.

A third form of template specification is that used in PL/I, where storage for declared structures may be allocated "statically" at translation time, "automatically" on entry to the function module in which the structure is declared, or by explicit "controlled" allocation for structures associated with template-valued variables. Template-valued identifiers are thought of as being subject to *controlled storage allocation*. A template in PL/I is referred to as a *structure*. A structure (template) may be associated with an identifier by the following declaration:

DECLARE 1 A BASED(P);   This declaration specifies that the
structure specification   identifier A has the storage-allocation
                                attribute BASED and that it has the
structure specified by the structure specification which follows. The 1 preceding the A is a level count associated with A. The P following the attribute BASED specifies the name of an identifier of type "pointer" which points to the most recently created instance of the structure A, so that components of the most recently created instance of the structure can be accessed through the pointer P. Further details are given in subsection 4.9.11.

A number of notations for the creation of instances of structures from template definitions will now be considered. The first notation is due to Wirth [17] and may be used with both the first and second form of template-definition conventions above:

new $A(a)$ Create a new instance of the structure associated with the
                template A and name it "a". Subsequent references to
"a" will refer to the newly created information structure.

For example,

new complex(C) Create a new instance of the structure complex and
                      call it C.

Access to components of C requires the introduction of conventions for component referencing. For example,

realpart $(C) := S$;   These two assignment statements adopt different
$C[\text{realpart}] := S$;   conventions for accessing the component realpart
                      of the information structure C.

The notation for creating instances of a template adopted in PL/I is the following:

ALLOCATE A SET(P);   Create an instance of the structure A and
                      set a pointer P to point to the newly
created instance of the structure.

Note that the pointer-valued identifier P is effectively the name of this instance of the structure A. A second instance of the structure named Q would be created by the statement "ALLOCATE A SET(Q);".

Information structures can be deleted by a statement of the following form:

FREE P;   Delete the information structure having the name P.

This convention for deletion can be used with all three styles of creation conventions discussed above.

Exercise: Indicate how template specification, creation, and deletion might be implemented.

A template may in general have an arbitrarily complex internal structure, and notations are required for *selecting* components of created instances of templates so that they can be manipulated. Probably the most common notation for selection of components of a structure is the notation $a[i]$ for selecting the ith component of a vector "a". Alternative notations for selection of the ith component of a vector are "select field i of a" or "$i(a)$".

An n-dimensional array requires n selection subscripts to select a component. When the structures being considered are trees, the sequence of selectors selecting alternatives at successive levels of the tree structure is sometimes referred to as the *tree name*. A further discussion of tree names is given in Sec. 4.9.

4.8.3 PARAMETERIZED TEMPLATES AND PROCEDURES

It has already been noted that a template specification is like a macro definition and that creation of an instance of a template is like a macro call. Since macro definitions may have parameters that vary on successive instances of call, it is natural to introduce the notion of parameterized template specifications.

type typename (parameters)   This style of template specification could
template body   be used to specify a parameterized template with the given typename, parameters, and template body.

new typename (actual parameters)   This style of declaration could be
name   used to specify the creation of a named instance of the template with the given typename with the given actual parameters substituted for the formal parameters of the template.

It was assumed above that the template was a static structure description and that a given created instance of an information structure was obtained by physical substitution of actual for formal parameters in the template. However, templates may also be thought of as structure-valued procedures which, when called by a declaration, compute the structure that is to be assigned to this instance of the identifier. This approach has been further developed by Standish [14].

Example: The following structure-valued procedure creates a structure that consists of a sequence of n structures of the kind specified by the second parameter.†

structure procedure sequence (n,t); **value** n,t;
        integer n; **structure** t;
        begin structure temp; **integer** i;
          temp := nil;
          for i := 1 **step** 1 **until** n **do** temp := [t,temp];
          sequence := temp;
        end

The call "sequence(3,**integer**)" would create the structure "[integer, integer,integer]". The declaration "**new**(sequence(3,**integer**))a" would assign the name a to the structure computed by evaluation of the structure-type procedure.

    Facilities for the specification of data templates allow the programmer to build up his own data types from a set of primitive data types supplied within the system. In order to allow flexible specification of structures and structure-valued procedures, a programming language must be available which allows the specification of structures, operations on structures, and structure-valued procedures. Formula ALGOL [15] is an example of a language which extends ALGOL to permit structure manipulation. PL/I also permits structure manipulation. However, neither of the above languages permits structure-valued procedures.

Exercise: Compare the concepts and techniques for structure specification in procedure-oriented languages with those for structure manipulation in list and string languages.

4.8.4 LEVELS OF INFORMATION-STRUCTURE SPECIFICATION

In the above discussion, the specification of information structures has been split into a number of phases:

    1.   Type specification of a class of structures
    2.   Creation and deletion of instances of a structure
    3.   Value specification for components of a structure

    † In this example, "nil" is assumed to be a constant which has the property of being an identity under string concatenation.

In ALGOL the type of structure is specified at the moment of creation or deletion, and phases 1 and 2 are combined. Moreover, a created information structure can be manipulated only by assignment of values to data fields and not by structural transformation. Thus structural characteristics of ALGOL cannot vary once they have been created except by being deleted.

The distinction between the structure and value components of an information structure becomes less definite when the language contains operations for structure transformations as well as for value assignment. However, even in this case we can still distinguish between fields containing pointers and fields containing values.

Exercise: Contrast the facilities for structure and value manipulation in ALGOL with those for LISP described in Sec. 3.9.

In ALGOL the creation and deletion of primitive data items is rigidly separated from value assignment to those data items, and all created primitive data items initially have undefined values. However, there is no reason why initialization of a data item should not be combined with their creation. The following notation illustrates combined declaration and initialization.

new A(a) initial value 3;   Initialize instance a of the structure A to the value 3.

new integer I **initial** 3;   Initialize the integer I to the value 3.

4.8.5 SPECIFICATION, RECOGNITION, AND CONSTRUCTION OF SETS OF STRUCTURES

The notion of a structure specification can be generalized to the case when a given structure name may be associated with a number of alternative templates. Such specifications are useful, for example, in the syntactic specification of programming languages (see Appendix 1), where a given syntactic category, such as a statement, may be associated with a number of different syntactic forms each of which is specified by a template. As an example of a specification of a syntactic structure with two alternative templates, consider the following syntactic specification of a list:

type list (**null** ∨ [head tail])   This set of four template defini-
type head (list ∨ data)   tions specifies that a list is
type tail (list)   either null or consists of a head
type data (**integer** ∨ **real** ∨ **Boolean**)   which is a list or a data item
                                             followed by a tail which is a list.

In the above example, the type "list" is specified in terms of other types which may in turn be of the type "list". This recursive specification results in an infinite set of alternative structure templates which are of the type "list".

The above set of template definitions defines a class of structures, and it no longer makes sense to ask for a definition of a list since the specification of "**new** list(L)" does not specify which of the alternative templates to use. However, the convention may be adopted that the use of a template in a data-creation operation results in creation of the data structure denoted by the first alternative.† In the above example this convention would yield the data structure **null.**

The most common use of a type which denotes a set of alternative template definitions is as a *predicate* for testing whether a given structure belongs to the set specified by the template definitions. Thus if "list" is defined as above, then "list(X)" would be **true** if X were a member of the class of lists and **false** otherwise.

Given a set of structures, it is sometimes desirable to introduce construction operations for building up instances of the structure. For example, if we are given the above definition of list, the following two primitive constructors would be sufficient for constructing any instance of the list structure:

constructnulllist   This constructor has no arguments and constructs the element **null.**

constructlist   This constructor has two arguments, say h and t, where h is a nonnull list or one of the primitives **integer, real, Boolean** and t is a list. The result of constructlist(h,t) is to construct a list whose head is h and whose tail is t.

The notion of a structure definition and the use of constructors, selectors, and predicates in manipulating structure definitions has already been introduced in Sec. 3.10. It is brought up again here to emphasize that these concepts apply at the level of procedure-oriented languages and to gain an insight into the kinds of operations that must be introduced into procedure-oriented languages in order to permit the manipulation of structures. A deeper development of these concepts can be found in the work of Landin [13].

4.8.6 PROGRAM STRUCTURES AND SYNTAX MACROS

In addition to facilities for the creation and manipulation of new data, it is desirable also to have facilities for the creation and execution of program structures. The basic facility for this purpose is the procedure declara-

---

† If the first alternative is not a primitive data type, the convention is extended to repeated taking of the first alternative.

tion, which is available in its full generality even in ALGOL.† However, it is sometimes desirable to introduce new syntactic forms into the language which represent executable program segments to be executed in line.

In any universal programming language (Sec. 3.11) any executable program segment can be represented by an executable sequence of instructions within the *basic language* into which the new syntactic form is being introduced. Thus a new syntactic form can be introduced into the language as a macro whose template is given by the new syntactic form and whose body is given by a corresponding base-language program. Macros of this kind, known as syntax macros, were discussed in detail in Sec. 3.4. They are discussed also in Appendix 1.

New syntactic forms are introduced into a universal base language by macros executed during translation in precisely the same way that macro operations denoting component machine-language instruction sequences are introduced into machine language.

New data structures may also be thought of as being introduced by macros. The macros corresponding to new data structures are defined during execution at the point where the **type** declaration is encountered and called at points where a **new** declaration for the named type occurs.

Exercise: Compare the structure-specification facilities of Sec. 4.8 with those of subsection 3.10.2 and with the macro specification facilities of Secs. 3.2 and 3.3. Consider especially the facilities for performing operations on structures once they have been created.

4.9 THE STRUCTURE OF PL/I

4.9.1 STATEMENT PREFIXES

The source-language characteristics and run-time representation of ALGOL described above constitute a prototype for procedure-oriented languages whose function modules are both statically and dynamically nested. PL/I is a language whose basic structure is similar to that of ALGOL but which permits richer classes of attributes to be associated with identifiers than in the case of ALGOL. In the present section the basic characteristics of PL/I will be developed, emphasizing the similarities and differences between ALGOL and PL/I.

The present discussion of PL/I is not intended to be complete. It is intended to emphasize the structure of the language rather than nota-

† ALGOL is not called a procedure-oriented language for nothing.

tional details. The discussion of structure is related to concepts of structure developed in previous sections. The present section should be understandable without reference to a PL/I manual to those who have read previous sections of the chapter. It is useful also as supplementary reading for students learning PL/I as an applications language.

PL/I is a language which aims to stay syntactically close to FORTRAN while adopting the basic structural form of ALGOL and including many new structures and facilities. The basic executable module in PL/I is the *statement*. All statements other than the assignment statement start with an initial keyword such as IF, DO, ON, or BEGIN and terminate with a semicolon. The keyword corresponding to the assignment statement is the = sign and occurs in the middle rather than at the beginning of the statement. Statements may be labeled by one or more labels, as in ALGOL. Labels are referred to as *statement prefixes*. PL/I permits a second form of prefix called a *condition prefix*, which specifies whether or not an interrupt is to occur when certain abnormal conditions (such as overflow) arise during execution of a statement.

The following eight system-defined condition prefixes are defined in PL/I:

CHECK (identifier list)   Prints tracing information when values of the listed identifiers are changed.

CONVERSION   Diagnostic when illegal conversion is attempted.

FIXEDOVERFLOW   Diagnostic on overflow in fixed-point arithmetic.

OVERFLOW   Diagnostic on floating-point overflow.

SIZE   Diagnostic on loss of significant digits.

SUBSCRIPTRANGE   Diagnostic when array subscript exceeds bounds.

UNDERFLOW   Diagnostic on floating-point underflow.

ZERODIVIDE   Diagnostic on division by zero.

The appearance of one or more of these conditions as a statement prefix specifies that an interrupt with a predefined effect is to occur if the condition occurs during execution of the statement.

(ZERODIVIDE): L: X = A/B;   This assignment statement has the condition prefix ZERODIVIDE and the label prefix *L*. The condition prefix specifies that an interrupt is to occur if division by zero is attempted during execution of the statement.

Condition prefixes effectively permit a local mode of execution to be associated with each statement. In the absence of explicit condition prefixes, there is a set of "default"† condition prefixes in effect during statement execution, representing a standard mode of execution. For example, interruption on division by zero would normally be performed in the standard mode, so that the above condition prefix is unnecessary. If interruption on division by zero is to be inhibited,the condition prefix NOZERODIVIDE can be used. The prefix NO can be used with each of the above conditions to inhibit interruption when the condition occurs.

4.9.2 THE ON STATEMENT AND INTERRUPT-MODE FUNCTION MODULES

The PL/I conditional statement is similar to the ALGOL conditional statement and has the following form:

IF B THEN S1 ELSE S2   If the Boolean expression B has the value
                          TRUE, then execute the statement $S1$;
    otherwise execute the statement $S2$.‡

In addition to conditional branching by in-line testing of a condition, PL/I permits an *interrupt form* of conditional branching. This is accomplished by an interrupt specification statement, called an ON statement, which can be used to define interrupt actions for a set of predefined interrupt conditions. The form of the ON statement is as follows:

ON condition-specification action-specification.   If after executing this
                                    statement the con-
    dition specified in the condition field occurs, execution will be interrupted, and the action in the instruction sequence specified in the action field will be executed. A subsequently executed ON statement for the given condition will cause a new action to be associated with occurrence of that condition.

The ON statement is a declarative statement and effectively declares a procedure in the action-specification field. However, the procedure is not called by an explicit procedure call but implicitly by occurrence of the

---

† The concept of default conditions in the absence of explicit specification is an important one in PL/I. PL/I has an overwhelming number of options that can be associated with identifiers and statements, and it would place an intolerable burden on the user if options had to be specified explicitly in every case. Provision of a default (normal) alternative for each option allows the user to avoid explicit specification of options as long as the default option obtains. If nondefault alternatives of a given option are never used, the programmer is in fact programming in a subset of PL/I. PL/I was designed with the intention of allowing programmers to use simple subsets by merely being ignorant of certain options.

‡ PL/I explicitly specifies that the logical values TRUE and FALSE are represented by the Boolean literals 1 ('1'B) and 0 ('0'B).

interrupt condition. In contrast to other declarations which come into effect on entry to the block in which they are declared, the procedure declared by an ON statement comes into effect at the moment of in-line execution of the ON statement; i.e., the ON statement is a "dynamic declaration."

The system conditions which can be specified as conditions in an ON statement can be classified as follows:

1. *Computational conditions*, which occur during compilation
2. *Input-output conditions*, which occur during data transmission
3. *Program-checkout conditions*, which facilitate debugging and tracing of programs
4. *List-processing conditions*, which occur in connection with storage allocation

The condition prefixes CONVERSION, FIXEDOVERFLOW, OVERFLOW, SIZE UNDERFLOW, and ZERODIVIDE are examples of computational conditions; whereas CHECK and SUBSCRIPTRANGE are examples of program-checkout conditions. A complete list of conditions, together with their detailed specifications, is given in [9].

All PL/I conditions are initialized to a standard (default) action, which is automatically performed when no ON statement or condition prefix for that condition is in effect. ON statements permit nonstandard interrupts to be specified for conditions.

The interrupt action for a condition determined by a given ON statement can be suspended or terminated in three ways:

1. By exit from the block in which the ON statement occurs
2. By execution of a further ON statement for the given condition
3. By execution of a REVERT statement for the given condition

The rules for determining the dynamic sequence of statements during which a given ON statement is effective can best be understood by considering how ON statements would be implemented in the framework of an ALGOL-like block structure.

ON statements are implemented with the aid of an *interrupt cell* in the activation record of the immediately enclosing block, which is initialized when the ON statement is executed to point to the function module specified in the action field. When this ON condition occurs during execution, control is automatically transferred to this interrupt cell, and the interrupt function module is triggered after storing information of the interrupted procedure.

The function modules of PL/I may be thought of as being reentrant, just as in the case of ALGOL. PL/I function modules consist of a fixed-program part, together with an activation record associated with each instance of execution of the function module. PL/I function modules are dynamically nested in the sense that entry to, and exit from, function modules is always in a last in, first out order.

The ON statement is one of the kinds of function modules of PL/I. It differs from other function modules principally in the way in which its execution is initiated; i.e., begin function modules of ALGOL or PL/I are initiated when their first symbol is encountered during program execution, procedure function modules are initiated by explicit procedure call, while ON function modules are initiated implicitly and less predictably at any point where the interrupt condition specified in the ON statement occurs.

Although the mode of call of ON function modules differs from that of other function modules, execution of ON statements does not violate the last in, first out rules with regard to execution of function modules. When execution of an ON statement is completed, control is returned unless a jump to a level known in the ON statement is executed. Note that termination of the program may be thought of as a jump to a globally known label.

Since execution of ON function modules is dynamically nested with other function modules, their activation records can be stored in the activation-record stack on entry to the function module and deleted from the activation-record stack on exit in the normal manner described for ALGOL programs.

There is one respect in which the facilities of the ON statement do not match up to those of a procedure call. In a procedure call, actual parameters can be used to transmit information from the point of call to the point of execution. The PL/I ON statement has no such facility. When execution of an ON statement is initiated, the return link must clearly be stored in order to allow return to the interrupted program. Provision is made for allowing the programmer to explicitly examine other selected information from the environment at the time of interruption by means of a special set of condition built-in functions (see PL/I manual). However, systematic conventions for communicating between an ON module and its point of call would be better than the present somewhat ad hoc facilities.

Since call of an ON module is normally implicit rather than explicit, it is not possible to explicitly designate actual parameters at the point of call, as in the case of procedures.† Probably the most convenient way

† PL/I does in fact allow interrupt function modules to be explicitly called by means of the SIGNAL statement [9]. A statement of the form "SIGNAL C;", where C is a condition, is similar in its effect to a call to a parameterless procedure named C.

to introduce a parameter facility for ON statements is to allow ON statements with formal parameters and to adopt a convention for marking selected declarations in the scope of the ON statement so that they can be matched with the ON statement when the interrupt occurs.

Exercise: Design a consistent extension of PL/I which allows interrupt function modules with parameters.   Consider the difference between initialization by value and initialization by name for parameters of interrupt function modules.

Since one of the principal reasons for the execution of interrupt function modules is to print out messages when abnormal conditions obtain, it is likely that character strings representing messages would be one of the principal parameters to be passed to the module.   Note that a given interrupt module may in general result in potential interruption in a number of different contexts each of which requires a different message to be printed out, so that such a facility is genuinely useful.

Interrupts associated with ON conditions may be caused directly by the hardware or simulated by interpretive code.   For example, the ZERODIVIDE interrupt normally corresponds to a direct hardware interrupt, while an interrupt caused by an array subscript's exceeding its lower or upper bounds would normally be executed interpretively.

From the above discussion of implementation of ON statements, it is evident that the effect of a given ON statement is terminated on exit from the immediately enclosing block in which it occurs, since the activation record which stores the interrupt cell is deleted from the run-time stack.

The rules for multiple ON statements associated with a given condition may similarly be deduced from the discussion of implementation. If for a given condition C an ON statement S_1 is executed, followed by execution of an ON statement S_2 in an inner block, then the activation record for the inner block contains the interrupt cell for the inner ON statement.   When the inner ON statement is executed, the outer ON statement is pushed down and is popped up on exit from the inner block. The above argument applies in the case of both statically and dynamically nested blocks.   In particular it applies to recursively executed ON statements in recursive procedures.

When two ON statements for a condition C are in the same immediately enclosing block, they may be assigned separate interrupt cells in the same activation record or a common interrupt cell.   If they are assigned a common interrupt cell, execution of any one of the ON statements will destroy rather than merely push down the action specification of the other.   If they are assigned separate interrupt cells, it would in principle be possible to push down the first executed ON statement when the second is executed. However, problems would arise on iterative execution of multiple ON statements. The convention is adopted in PL/I that execution of an ON statement for a given condition C is destructive of any previously executed ON statements for condition C in the same immediately enclosing block; i.e., the effect is as though all ON statements for a given condition in a given immediately enclosing block shared the same interrupt cell.†

The statement "REVERT C;" results in pop up of the stack associated with condition C and reinstatement of the most recently pushed-down action specification. If there are no pushed-down action specifications, the standard system action specification is reinstated.

4.9.3 STATEMENT GROUPING AND ITERATION

Grouping of statements into a single statement is performed in PL/I by the DO statement or by a begin block.

DO; The DO-END statement parentheses result in treatment of
X = 5; the statements inside the statement parentheses as a single
Y = 3; statement. The effect of the DO-END parentheses is the
END; same as that of the **begin-end** parentheses of ALGOL when
     used only for purposes of grouping and not for purposes of
defining the scope of nomenclature.

Although DO-END parentheses perform the same function as ALGOL **begin-end** parentheses for simple grouping of statements, they differ from them in that (1) DO-END parentheses cannot be used for defining the scope of names. This function is accomplished by PL/I BEGIN-END parentheses (see below) and (2) DO-END parentheses are used to define statement groupings for purposes of iteration and in this respect fulfill the role of the ALGOL **for** clause and FORTRAN DO statement.

DO I = 1 BY 1 TO N; This group of statements adds the value of
SUM = SUM + A[I]; the N array elements $A[I]$ through $A[N]$ to
END;   the value of SUM.

A DO statement consists of the keyword DO followed optionally by an iteration specification and terminated by a semicolon. The iteration specification consists of a list of specifications each of which may specify

---

† The effect of an ON statement can be locally suspended by a condition prefix. A condition prefix effectively corresponds to an ON statement with a local effect.

execution of the sequence of statements in the DO group (1) for a single value of a variable, (2) for a sequence of values of a variable, (3) while a certain condition holds, or (4) for a combination of the above conditions. A detailed specification of the DO statement is given in the PL/I manual. For the present purpose it is sufficient to note that the PL/I DO statement combines ALGOL compound facilities and iteration facilities.†

4.9.4 BEGIN AND PROCEDURE BLOCKS

Creation and deletion of sets of identifiers is accomplished in PL/I by means of *begin blocks* and *procedure blocks*.   Begin blocks are the counterpart of the ALGOL block, and procedure blocks are the counterpart of the ALGOL procedure declaration.   However, there are significant syntactic differences between the PL/I structures and the corresponding ALGOL structures.

A PL/I begin block consists of the keyword BEGIN followed by a sequence of statements and declarations followed by the keyword END. Its syntax differs from that of the ALGOL block principally in that declarations need not precede executable statements but may be intermixed with executable statements.   However, the effect of a given AUTOMATIC declaration‡ in a PL/I begin block is to create the declared quantity on entry to the block and to delete it on exit from the block. The point at which the declaration occurs within the block is irrelevant in determining its effect.   The ability to specify declarations in the middle of a block is therefore a purely syntactic device to allow greater flexibility for the user.§

PL/I begin blocks are entered during execution of a PL/I program when sequential execution of program elements causes the keyword

---

† In addition to syntactic differences between an ALGOL **for** clause and PL/I DO statement, there is the difference that in the ALGOL **for** clause "**for** $i = \mathrm{E}_1$ **step** E_2 **until** E_3 **do**" E_2 and E_3 are in principle dynamically evaluated on every iteration, while in the PL/I DO statement "DO I = E_1 BY E_2 TO E_3;" E_2 and E_3 are initialized by value prior to iteration.

‡ PL/I permits declarations within a block such that the lifetimes of declared quantities are not restricted to the execution time of the block.   However, the default attribute for declarations within a block is AUTOMATIC.   Storage-allocation attributes are further discussed in subsection 4.9.10.

§ This is true for "static" declarations to be executed on entry to the block but not true for dynamic declarations, like the ON statement, which are executed when they are encountered during execution.   In ALGOL and PL/I, storage allocation is performed on entry to a block prior to execution, so that declarative information relating to storage allocation is static in the above sense.   However, languages in which all declarations are dynamically executed are also feasible.   This approach is adopted, for example, in list-processing languages.   CPL [16] allows a time sequence to be specified for the order of execution of declarations in a blockhead and therefore has a rudimentary facility for dynamic declarations.

BEGIN of the begin block to be executed. Begin blocks may be optionally labeled, and if labeled, may be entered by a jump to the label of the block from a point at which the label is known.

The variables declared within a given block are normally created on entry to the block and deleted on exit from the block, just as in ALGOL. However, PL/I permits creation and deletion of information structures not exclusively tied to the creation and deletion of blocks, as further described below.

Procedure blocks consist of a procedure statement followed by a sequence of statements and declarations and terminated by an END statement. Procedure statements consist of the keyword PROCEDURE preceded by one or more labels and followed by optional specifications regarding the mode of calling of the procedure and the class of values produced by the procedure. The declarations within a procedure include specifications of attributes for formal parameters and for local variables of the procedure. Thus PL/I procedure blocks differ from ALGOL procedure declarations in that declarations for formal parameters and for local variables occur on an equal footing. Since both local variables and formal parameters are created on entry to the procedure and deleted on exit from the procedure, it is quite natural that these two classes of identifiers be on an equal footing.

The label associated with a procedure statement is said to be the *principal entry name* of the procedure. However, a procedure may in general have an arbitrary number of entry points each of which is characterized by a labeled ENTRY statement. The number and names of formal parameters specified at each of the entry points and the attributes of the returned value may in general be different. Specifications of the parameters at each of the entry points may occur at any point in the body of a procedure. The label associated with an entry point is called the *entry name* associated with that entry point. A procedure can be entered at any of its entry points by a call to the entry name. A call to a given entry name causes execution of the procedure starting at the first executable statement following the entry name.

When a procedure is a function-type procedure, the type specification for the value may be specified at each entry point. Control is returned to the calling procedure by executing the statement "RETURN". In the case of function-type procedures the value to be returned is specified in parentheses in a "RETURN" statement.

Example: "RETURN(X)" specifies a return to the calling procedure with a value given by the value of X.

In PL/I begin blocks and procedure blocks constitute the basic function modules within which nomenclature can be created. The principal difference between begin and procedure blocks is in the method by which execution of the function module is initiated.   Begin blocks are activated by normal sequential flow, while procedures are activated by procedure calls to the procedure block from program points within the scope of the procedure identifier.

Whereas labels are optional in the case of begin blocks, they are obligatory in the case of procedure blocks, since the procedure label is one of the procedure identifiers used in procedure calling.   Although the procedure label has some of the properties of a label identifier, it differs from an identifier of the type label because it results in a different kind of branching than a label identifier.   As indicated in the discussion of ALGOL, branching to a procedure requires pushdown of the state of the current function module for subsequent return, while branching to a label does not require any provision for return.

4.9.5   DECLARATIONS AND CLASSIFICATION OF IDENTIFIER ATTRIBUTES

The above discussion has revealed a number of relatively superficial syntactic differences in block structure between ALGOL and PL/I and one significantly new form of interrupt transfer of control determined by the ON statement.   However, the really significant differences between ALGOL and PL/I arise because of the richer set of attributes which can be associated with identifiers in PL/I.

Attributes are associated with identifiers at the time of their declaration by means of a DECLARE statement.   The basic DECLARE statement in PL/I has one of the following forms:

DECLARE name attribute list;   Declare an identifier with the given name having the attributes specified in the attribute list.

DECLARE (N1, . . . ,NK)AL;   Declare the names $N1, . . . , NK$ to have the attributes specified in the attribute list AL.

DECLARE(N1 AL1, . . . ,NK ALK)AL;   Declare   the   attribute AL to be common to all names $N1, . . . , NK$ and declare successive attribute lists $AL1, . . . ,$ ALK to be respectively associated with the names $N1, . . . , NK$. More complex uses of parentheses are permitted to allow association of common attributes with a subgroup of the names of a single declaration. The use of parentheses to associate attributes with more than one name is referred to as *factoring of attributes*.

The attributes which may be associated with identifiers can be classified into the following categories:

1.   Type specifications, which specify the range and nature of values of the identifier

2.   Structure specifications, which specify the substructure of the information structure denoted by the identifier

3.   Scope specifications, which specify the range of statements of the static source program over which the identifier has meaning

4.   Storage-allocation specifications, which specify the dynamic duration of storage allocated for the information structure named by a given identifier

These categories are not mutually exclusive, since structure specifications influence the range of values of the identifier and scope and storage attributes may be thought of as characteristics of the value of the identifier.   However, these categories nevertheless form a convenient framework for classifying attributes.

In ALGOL the type specification specifies the range of values which an identifier can assume.   Identifiers of type **integer, real,** and **Boolean** have a fixed structure which need not be explicitly specified by a structure specification.   Identifiers of type **array** have a structure specification which gives the dimension sizes.   Procedures may be thought of as having a structure specification consisting of both the procedure heading and the procedure body.

ALGOL has fixed rules for determining scope and therefore does not require scope specifications.   The duration of storage allocation for an ALGOL identifier is normally tied to entry to, and exit from, the block in which it is declared and need not therefore be specified as an explicit attribute.   However ALGOL permits identifiers with local scope and a permanent existence to be specified by an **own** declaration.

PL/I permits a richer attribute structure than ALGOL in all four of the above attribute classes.   The attributes permitted in each of the classes will be examined in turn.

The basic PL/I data attributes permit identifiers corresponding to the ALGOL types **integer, real,** and **Boolean** to be defined but use a different scheme of classification.   The basic data attributes of PL/I are described below.

4.9.6 DATA ATTRIBUTES

Arithmetic data attributes include *base* attributes, which specify the number base of the representation, *scale* attributes, which specify whether the number is fixed or floating point, *mode* attributes, which specify whether the data are real or complex, and *precision* attributes, which specify the precision of the arithmetic data.

The two alternative base attributes are DECIMAL and BINARY. The two alternative scale attributes are FLOAT and FIXED. The two alternative mode attributes are REAL and COMPLEX. Precision attributes consist of integers enclosed in parentheses giving the precision of each data component, for example,

DECLARE A DECIMAL FIXED (3,2);   This declaration specifies that A is a fixed-point decimal number with three significant figures preceding the decimal point and two significant figures following the decimal point.

It is unnecessary to specify every attribute of a data item in the declaration, since *default attributes* are automatically supplied for unspecified attributes by the system. The default attributes supplied by the PL/I system when no attributes are specified in the declaration are related to original FORTRAN nomenclature conventions. For identifiers starting with I through N, base, scale, and mode default attributes are assumed to be BINARY, FIXED, and REAL, while for all other identifiers, base, scale, and mode default attributes are assumed to be DECIMAL, FLOAT, and REAL. The default precision attribute is assumed to be implementation-defined.

Logical identifiers of PL/I have the type attribute BIT. Identifiers of type BIT are assumed to represent bit strings and normally have their length specified as a length attribute if the bit string is of fixed length. If the bit string is of varying length, the attribute VARYING is associated with the bit string, but a maximum length must be defined.

PL/I also permits identifiers of type CHARACTER, whose values are character strings. Here again fixed-length strings have a length attribute, and variable-length strings have the attribute VARYING, together with a specification of maximum length. The ability to declare and manipulate character strings of variable length is a useful facility that is currently not available in other arithmetically oriented languages.

DECLARE S(10) CHAR(8);   Here S is an array of 10 elements each of which consists of 8 characters.

4.9.7 LABEL IDENTIFIERS

PL/I permits label identifiers to be explicitly declared by a LABEL declaration. Label identifiers have labels as their values, and assignments of label constants to label variables can be performed by assignment statements. However, assignment of label constants to label variables must be performed within a block in which the label is known.

A label prefix used within a given block is normally assumed to be declared in the innermost block enclosing its point of use and therefore to be inaccessible outside the block in which it is declared.

Procedure identifiers in PL/I may be thought of as identifiers which have some of the properties of labels but not others. Label and procedure identifiers represent two alternative modes of transfer of control between procedures. PL/I has still other modes of transfer of control which are specified by the TASK or EVENT attribute. Still other methods of transfer of control have been developed and are discussed in Sec. 4.10. Each mode of transfer of control may be thought of as giving rise to a different class of labels.

Whereas the value class of numerical and logical identifiers may be thought of as a class of strings, the value class of label identifiers may be thought of as a class of functions. The difference between the alternative classes of labels above is not so much a difference between alternative classes of functions as a difference between the modes of sequencing. A label is essentially a parameterless procedure which makes no provision for return to its point of call.

4.9.8 VARIABLES OF TYPE POINTER

An important type of identifier not available in ALGOL is the type POINTER. The value set of identifiers of type POINTER is the set of names of data. In the static source language the value of a pointer may be thought of as an identifier, while in the run-time representation the value of a variable of type POINTER is a pointer to a data item.

The one-argument system function ADDR has identifiers as arguments and produces the pointer to the object denoted by the identifier as its value.

Example: If P is an identifier of type POINTER and A is an identifier of any type whatsoever, the assignment statement "P = ADDR(A);" assigns to the pointer-value variable P a pointer which points to the object denoted by A.

Variables of type POINTER allow list structures to be specified in the language. The use of pointer variables will be further discussed below.

The set of PL/I *type attributes* is richer than that of ALGOL principally in that it allow identifiers of type POINTER and CHARACTER. The primitive data types of PL/I may in turn be built up into *data structures* in a more flexible way than is possible in ALGOL. This is accomplished in PL/I by *structure attributes*.

4.9.9   STRUCTURE ATTRIBUTES

The *structure attributes* of PL/I are considerably richer than those of ALGOL.   The principal class of data structures permitted in ALGOL is that of rectangular arrays with a fixed number of dimensions specified during translation and a number of elements in each dimension which can be respecified every time the block in which the array is declared is entered during execution.

Arrays in PL/I do not require an explicit *array* attribute but merely a *length* attribute, which specifies that the identifier is to be replicated. In the absence of length attributes, a default length attribute is supplied, specifying that only one instance of the structure is to be created.

PL/I length specifications may consist of simple integer expressions or lower- and upper-bound expressions.   When only a single integer expression is supplied, the lower bound is taken to be 1.

DECLARE A(I,5:10);   This declaration declares A to be a two-dimensional array whose first dimension varies from 1 through I and whose second dimension can take the values 5 through 10.

Dimensions can be left unspecified in the declaration by using the symbol * in place of an integer expression:†

DECLARE MATRIX(*,*);   Matrix is a two-dimensional array whose bounds are to be taken from a previous allocation for MATRIX or from a subsequent ALLOCATE statement.   If MATRIX is a procedure parameter, the bounds are taken from the corresponding actual parameter.

A rectangular array is a very specialized form of structure in that it is rectangular and all its elements are of the same type.   PL/I permits the declaration of structures in which both these requirements are relaxed. The more general form of structure is appropriately referred to as a STRUCTURE.

A PL/I structure may be defined reentrantly as a hierarchical collection of structures.   A structure may be thought of as a tree whose nonterminal vertices are associated with names and whose terminal vertices have data values.   The root vertex is said to have level 1, and vertices which can be reached by a path of length $i - 1$ from the root

---

† PL/I declarations with arbitrary bounds cannot occur where execution of the declaration creates an instance of the structure but only where the declaration specifies the structural form without creating an instance of the structure.   Parameter specifications of ALGOL procedures fall into precisely this category.

vertex are said to have level i. The following example illustrates a three-level structure declaration which might be used in a payroll computation:

DECLARE 1 PAYROLL,   This structure has the name PAY-
   2 NAME,   ROLL, three vertices at level 2
   2 HOURS,   named NAME, HOURS, and
    3 REGULAR,   RATE, and two vertices associated
    3 OVERTIME,   with HOURS at level 3.
   2 RATE;

  The tree associated with the above structure has two terminal vertices NAME and RATE at level 2 and two terminal vertices REGULAR and OVERTIME at level 3. Each of these vertices may have an associated value. The nonterminal vertices PAYROLL and HOURS may be thought of as denoting the subtree having the given name as the root.

  Whereas an element of an array is referred to by specifying its subscripts, an element of a structure is referred to by specifying the sequence of names (separated by periods) of the vertices leading from the root vertex to the vertex to be accessed. The sequence of identifiers required to name a given vertex is referred to as its *tree name*.

PAYROLL.HOURS.REGULAR   This is the tree name of the
             information item REGULAR in
the structure PAYROLL above.

  In PL/I all components other than the lowest level component of a tree name can be omitted if the resulting name is unique. If in the scope of the above structure there are no other identifiers named REGULAR, this identifier can be used in place of the tree name. Equally, the partial tree names PAYROLL.REGULAR or HOURS.REGULAR can be used to name this element of the structure if they are unique.

  As complex data structures are introduced into a programming language, the names used to reference the data structures inevitably become more complex. An element in a complex data structure can be accessed (1) by a program which sequences through the structure and then accesses the element by a simple name relative to a sequencing pointer pointing at or "near" the data item or (2) by a direct name which names substructure components. A tree name is a means of direct naming of elements within a complex structure.

  The elements of a PL/I structure may in turn have attributes associated with them. For example, the elements of the above structure may have the following associated attributes:

DECLARE 1 PAYROLL,   This structure declara-
    2 NAME CHARACTER(50)   tion declares NAME to
      VARYING,   be a 50-element char-
    2 HOURS,   acter array, REGULAR
      3 REGULAR FIXED,   and OVERTIME to be
      3 OVERTIME FIXED,   of type FIXED, and
    2 RATE FLOAT;   RATE to be a floating-
                             point number.

Every tree vertex may have length attributes associated with it. Type attributes may be associated only with terminal vertices of the structure. Dimension attributes associated with a vertex will cause replication of the substructure associated with that vertex.

4.9.10 SCOPE AND STORAGE-ALLOCATION ATTRIBUTES

Scope attributes of an identifier specify the range of statements over which the identifier is known, while storage-allocation attributes specify the dynamic span of execution over which the identifier remains in existence. In PL/I, an identifier may be in existence without being known (accessible), and an identifier may be known without the structure to which it corresponds being in existence. Scope and storage-allocation attributes of an identifier are therefore independent of each other.

Scope and storage-allocation attributes may be associated only with the structure as a whole; i.e., all elements of a structure come into existence and are destroyed together, and access to one element of a structure implies access to all elements of the structure.

The *scope* of an identifier may be either INTERNAL or EXTERNAL. An identifier with the scope attribute INTERNAL is known only within the block in which it is declared, using the same scope rules as in ALGOL. An identifier with the scope attribute EXTERNAL has the same meaning in all blocks in which it is declared to be external and can be used for purposes of communication between blocks. *Data* having the attribute EXTERNAL fulfill somewhat the same function as COMMON data in FORTRAN.

Identifiers for which no scope attribute is specified are normally assumed to have the default attribute INTERNAL. However procedures which constitute complete PL/I programs and are not therefore declared in any enclosing block are assumed to have the attribute EXTERNAL. Alternatively procedure identifiers of complete PL/I programs may be thought of as being implicitly declared in an outer system block.

Identifiers in PL/I have one of the three storage-allocation attributes STATIC, AUTOMATIC, or CONTROLLED. Storage for identifiers whose storage-allocation attribute is STATIC is assigned prior to execution and remains in existence throughout execution of the program in which the declaration occurs.   STATIC storage allocation corresponds to the form of storage allocation used for FORTRAN variables or for ALGOL **own** identifiers.

PL/I specifies that identifiers having the scope attribute EXTERNAL have the default storage-allocation attribute STATIC.   Identifiers having the scope attribute INTERNAL have the default storage-allocation attribute AUTOMATIC.   Identifiers with no scope or storage-allocation attributes have the default attributes INTERNAL AUTOMATIC.

Storage for identifiers whose storage-allocation attribute is AUTOMATIC is assigned during execution on entry to the block in which the identifier is declared and destroyed on exit from the block in which the identifier is declared, just as in ALGOL.   Identifiers whose storage-allocation attribute is AUTOMATIC must have INTERNAL as their scope attribute.

4.9.11 CONTROLLED STORAGE ALLOCATION

The storage-allocation attribute CONTROLLED allows storage for information structures to be assigned and destroyed during execution in a manner similar to the assignment of values to variables.   The commands for assignment and deletion of storage during execution are ALLOCATE and FREE.   Identifiers with the storage-allocation attribute CONTROLLED have the default scope attribute INTERNAL.

Whereas an identifier with the storage-allocation attribute AUTOMATIC has storage automatically allocated on entry to the block in which it is declared, an internal identifier with the storage-allocation attribute CONTROLLED merely becomes known on entry to the block in which it is declared and has no storage allocated for it.   The declaration of a CONTROLLED variable is a *template definition* which allows instances to be created by means of ALLOCATE commands.

If an identifier A having the storage-allocation attribute CONTROLLED is known at a given point of the program, the command "ALLOCATE A" will allocate an instance of the structure denoted by the identifier A.   If A is a simple variable, just a single data location for holding the value of the variable will be allocated.   If A is an array, an instance of the array will be allocated, while if A is a structure, an instance of the structure will be allocated.

The command "FREE A" following an "ALLOCATE A" command will cause the memory registers allocated to A to be released.   A second "ALLOCATE A" command without an intervening "FREE A" command will cause a second copy of the structure A to be created and result in all references to A or elements of A to refer to the most recently created instance of the structure. Previously created instances of A are pushed down in a stack and are popped up again when a "FREE A" command is executed.

When storage is allocated for a CONTROLLED identifier by an ALLOCATE command, a facility is available for simultaneously setting an identifier of type POINTER to point to this structure.

ALLOCATE A SET(P);   This command allocates an instance of the CONTROLLED structure A and sets a pointer variable P to point to the structure.

Pointers can be used to distinguish between different instances of a created structure. Thus "$P \rightarrow A$" denotes the instance of A pointed to by the pointer P, and "$Q \rightarrow A$" denotes the instance of A pointed to by the pointer Q.

$P \rightarrow A$ and $Q \rightarrow A$ can be thought of as compound names consisting of a pointer followed by an identifier. A name in PL/I may be quite complex and can consist of a sequence of pointers and structure components intermixed in arbitrary order.

PL/I has an alternative form of storage allocation, referred to as BASED storage allocation. Identifiers with the storage-allocation attribute BASED are declared as templates and have instances of the structure created by ALLOCATE commands, just as in the case of CONTROLLED allocation. However, BASED structures are associated with a pointer-valued variable specified in the declaration which is always set to point to a new instance of the structure at the moment that it is created.

DECLARE A BASED(P);   This declaration declares P to be a pointer associated with the structure A. An instance of the command "ALLOCATE A" in the scope of this declaration would create an instance of the structure A and would set the pointer P to point to the most recently created instance of the structure; i.e., every instance of "ALLOCATE A" would be equivalent to "ALLOCATE A SET(P);".

The identifier A above is referred to as a *based variable* based on the pointer P. The occurrence of P in the above declaration is assumed to constitute a declaration for P with a contextual default type attribute POINTER and contextual default attributes INTERNAL and AUTO-MATIC. However, additional attributes of P may be declared in a separate declaration.

Whereas successive ALLOCATE instructions for a CONTROLLED identifier lead to a stack of structures associated with the identifier, successive AI LOCATE instructions for a BASED variable merely reset the pointer P to point to the most recent instance of the structure.

However, it will be shown below that sequences of structures allocated by BASED allocation can be organized into lists by judicious manipulation of pointer-valued variables.

Both CONTROLLED and BASED storage allocation will be referred to as instances of *controlled* storage allocation.

Another difference between CONTROLLED and BASED storage allocation is that CONTROLLED allocation of a structure results in allocation of a copy of the dope vector (description list) for the given instance of the structure, while BASED allocation results in allocation of the structure only. All instances of a BASED structure are assumed to share a single dope vector which is created at the time that the template for the based structure is created.

DECLARE A(M;N) BASED(P);   This declaration creates a template for the array A, creates a dope vector, and initializes the dope vector to the current values of M and N. Subsequent allocation of instances of A will result in allocation of $M \times N$ arrays where M and N are determined at the time this declaration is executed.

DECLARE A(M;N) CONTROLLED(P);   This declaration creates a template for the array A. Successive allocations of A will create an instance of A and a dope vector that is initialized to the values of M and N at the time the ALLOCATE command is executed.

Exercises: (*a*) Discuss the difference between CONTROLLED and BASED allocation in terms of the concept of binding time. (*b*) Compare the techniques of implementation and the techniques of accessing during execution for CONTROLLED and BASED storage allocation.

4.9.12 LISTS OF STRUCTURES

The above facilities can be used to create lists of structures by allowing one or more components within the allocated structure to be of the type POINTER. Consider, for instance, the following structure containing a value field and a pointer field:

DECLARE 1 ELEMENT BASED(P),   The identifier ELEMENT is
        2 A FIXED,   declared to be of storage class
        2 B POINTER;   BASED, to be based on P, and to contain a field named
A of type FIXED and a field named B of type POINTER.

A pointer field in a structure can be used to point to some other structure. The following example chains together three instances of the structure ELEMENT into a list:

DECLARE (Q,HEAD) POINTER;
DECLARE 1 ELEMENT BASED(P),
    2 A FIXED,
    2 B POINTER;
ALLOCATE ELEMENT;
HEAD = P;
Q = P;
ALLOCATE ELEMENT;
Q → B = P;
Q = P;
ALLOCATE ELEMENT;
Q → B = P;
B = NULL;

This program declares Q and HEAD to be of type POINTER and ELEMENT to be a structure based on P. The instruction "ALLOCATE ELEMENT" automatically sets P to the most recent instance of ELEMENT. The assignment statements "HEAD = P; Q = P;" assign the value of the pointer P to the pointers Q, HEAD. When the second instance of ELEMENT has been created, Q points to the first instance, and "$Q → B = P$" sets the pointer B of the first instance to point to the second instance. Similarly after creation of the third instance of ELEMENT, "$Q → B = P$" sets the pointer B in the second instance to point to the third instance. Finally "B = NULL", which is equivalent to "$P → B = $ NULL" sets the current instance of B to the special pointer value NULL, which indicates the end of the list.

The three-element list created by the above program has the form indicated in Fig. 4.13.

Figure 4.13   Three-element list created by the previous program.

This example illustrates how a sequence of structures can be chained together into a list. Once a chain of structures has been created, access to individual structures can be accomplished by pointer manipulation.

In this example a chain of structures was created each consisting of one value field and one pointer field. In general, structures can be defined with several value fields and several pointer fields. These structures can be linked together in arbitrarily complex ways.

4.9.13   SPECIFICATION OF LIST-PROCESSING OPERATIONS

Individual list-processing languages such as LISP [8] and SLIP [5] permit linked structures to be built up from one basic modular component referred to as a *list element*. The basic modular component of LISP consists of two pointer fields and a mode field, as illustrated by the following PL/I declaration:

DECLARE 1 LISPCELL BASED(P),   This declaration specifies the
    2 CAR POINTER,   basic format of a list cell in
    2 CDR POINTER,   LISP to consist of two pointer
    2 MODE BIT(6);   fields named CAR and CDR
                                   and a 6-bit mode field.

The basic modular component of SLIP consists of two pointer fields, a mode field, and a value field, as illustrated by the following declaration:

DECLARE 1 SLIPCELL BASED(P),   This declaration declares a
    2 LINKL POINTER,   SLIPCELL to contain two
    2 LINKR POINTER,   fields LINKL, LINKR of
    2 MODE BIT(2),   type POINTER, a 2-bit mode
    2 VALUE FIXED;   field, and a value field. In
                                   SLIP the type of the value
in the value field is determined by the mode field. PL/I has no direct method of specifying that the attributes of a given data field may vary according to some parameter (in this case the mode field). In the present case a number of different SLIP cells each with different attributes associated with the value field could be defined.

Basic list-processing operations can be performed by relatively simple PL/I procedures. The basic LISP operations of accessing the first list element and accessing the rest of the list can be performed by the following PL/I procedure with two entry points HEAD and TAIL:

HEAD: PROCEDURE(P) POINTER;   This pointer-valued proce-
    DECLARE 1 ELEMENT   dure has two entry points,
              BASED(P),   HEAD and TAIL. The
        2 CAR   declaration of ELEMENT
          POINTER,   specifies   the   structure
        2 CDR   pointed to by the procedure
          POINTER;   parameter P. The struc-
    RETURN(CAR);   ture itself is assumed to
TAIL: ENTRY(P);   have been created outside
    RETURN(CDR);   the procedure and to be an
    END HEAD;   element of a list of structures
                                   of the kind arising in LISP.
The call HEAD(P) returns with a value given by the pointer in the first field of the structure pointed to by P while the call TAIL(P) returns with a value given by the second field of the structure pointed to by P.

The LISP operation CONS or JOIN, which forms a single list out of two sublists, can be specified by the following operation:

CONS: PROCEDURE(P,Q) POINTER;
      DECLARE 1 ELEMENT
             BASED(X),
          2 LEFT
             POINTER,
          2 RIGHT
             POINTER;
      ALLOCATE ELEMENT;
      LEFT = P;
      RIGHT = Q;
      RETURN(X);
      END CONS;

This pointer-valued procedure has two pointer-valued parameters, P and Q. It allocates an instance of the structure ELEMENT, stores the pointers P and Q in the first and second registers of the newly created structure, and delivers a pointer to the newly created structure as its value.

4.9.14 IMPLEMENTATION OF CONTROLLED STORAGE ALLOCATION

Controlled storage is allocated independently of entry to, and exit from, function modules and cannot therefore be allocated at the top of the run-time stack. Controlled storage is normally allocated in an independent area of memory, referred to as the *free-storage area*. When an "ALLO-CATE A" command is executed, it calls on a system storage-allocation program to allocate a segment of free storage for A, and when a "FREE A" command is encountered, the storage space occupied by A is returned to free storage. A mechanism must be provided for distinguishing between free and occupied portions of the free-storage area.

If an attempt is made to allocate more storage than is actually available, a diagnostic "SIGNAL AREA" will occur, indicating that the program has run out of storage. However, a situation may arise where storage is available but is so fragmented that there is no contiguous portion sufficiently large to accommodate the item for which storage has been requested. In this case the storage allocator should have facilities for the reallocation of storage for currently allocated information structures by physically moving them in free storage, adjusting pointers which point to the moved structures, and thereby providing a contiguous portion of free storage that is as large as possible.

Since all structures stored in free storage are explicitly allocated and freed, the question of "garbage collection" of storage that is implicitly freed during execution does not arise in PL/I. However, the problems of accounting, efficient allocation, and compactifying of free storage are nevertheless formidable.

Allocation of structures can be implemented by means of a generalized dope vector residing in the activation record of the function module in which the structure is declared.   The dope vector contains information about the number and type of vertices at each level of the tree associated with the information structure and can be stored in a fixed number of storage registers.   If the structure has the storage-allocation attribute AUTOMATIC, storage for the structure is allocated on creation of the activation record, just as for arrays.   The number of replications of dimensioned substructures with dynamic bounds may vary between activations, so that storage for structures is conveniently allocated in a variable-length final part of the activation record to permit all declared identifers of the structure to be represented by fixed addresses relative to the beginning of the structure.

If the structure has the storage-allocation attribute BASED, only the dope vector is created on entry to the block, and instances of the structure are created and destroyed by ALLOCATE and FREE commands.   Access to the structure during execution is performed by a storage-mapping function, which uses the information in the dope vector together with an initial-address parameter to compute the register to be accessed.   When storage allocation is AUTOMATIC, the initial-address parameter remains fixed throughout the lifetime of the activation record in which the structure is declared.   When storage allocation is controlled, the initial address is supplied by a pointer-valued variable. Composite names such as "P → A" are translated into calls of the storage-mapping function for the structure A using the value of the pointer P as the initial-address parameter.   If P is omitted, the based variable P mentioned in the structure declaration is taken to be the initial-address parameter.

The ability of a programmer using PL/I to create and manipulate list structures rests specifically on the following features of PL/I:

1.   Identifiers of type POINTER, which allow links between information structures to be explicitly specified and manipulated
2.   Structure declarations, which allow list elements containing several pointer and value fields of different types to be explicitly declared
3.   Controlled storage allocation, which allows structures to be dynamically nested and deleted as they are required

In actual list-processing languages the data structures and list-processing operations are sometimes specified in a problem-oriented form which disguises the internal manipulation required in performing the operation.   However, the above features are present in all list-processing languages to some degree.   Given list-processing languages, such as LISP or SLIP, allow only one kind of structure, corresponding to the list element structure, and contain primitives at the level of the procedures introduced above for simulating LISP operation.   PL/I contains basic list-processing primitives that are more basic than those of actual list-processing languages.   The primitives of actual list-processing languages can be built up from PL/I primitives by means of procedures indicated above.

In the present section the basic features of PL/I have been introduced, and it was shown that PL/I is a richer language then ALGOL principally because it allows identifiers to have a richer attribute structure than ALGOL.   An attempt was made to classify attributes into categories and to indicate some of the more important attributes that may be possessed by data in PL/I.   However, no attempt was made to discuss the complete list of data attributes.

Not discussed above are the TASK and EVENT attributes, which allow parallel computations to be specified in PL/I.† This important class of attributes will be discussed in the next section in the context of techniques for controlling the sequence in which function modules of a program are to be executed.

4.9.15 STATEMENT GROUPING IN FORTRAN, ALGOL, AND PL/I

In the present section the term "lower-level program structure" will refer to the structure of statements and expressions of the programming language while the term "higher-level program structure" will refer to the structure of a program in terms of its function modules and other facilities for statement grouping.   The higher-level program structure of FORTRAN, ALGOL, and PL/I will be compared, in order to gain an insight into some of the parameters that should be used when making comparisons between programming languages.

In characterizing higher-level program structures of a language it is necessary to examine the facilities for statement grouping in the language. The functions that are served by statement grouping can be classified as follows:

1.   To delimit a procedure which may be called in several places
2.   To delimit the scope of names
3.   To group statements for control purposes
4.   To specify the lifetime (duration of allocation of storage) of an information item

In FORTRAN there are two principal facilities for grouping statements, which we shall refer to as the DO loop and the program unit.‡

---

† The TASK facility has not been implemented in any current implementation of PL/I.

‡ A DO loop consists of the sequence of statements between the DO statement and the label specified in the DO statement.   A program unit is the term used to denote either a subroutine or the main program.

The function of the DO loop is to group statements for control purposes, and the program unit serves to delimit procedures and to delimit the scope of names.   In FORTRAN there is no dynamic storage allocation. All information structures associated with identifiers come into existence prior to execution and remain in existence throughout execution of the program.   FORTRAN does not therefore require facilities to specify the lifetimes of information structures associated with identifiers.

In ALGOL the principal facilities for statement grouping are the block and the procedure.   Grouping for iteration and other control purposes is accomplished by blocks.   All statement grouping in ALGOL is uniformly performed by **begin-end** parentheses.   These parentheses are qualified by a procedure heading when used to delimit the scope of

Purpose	FORTRAN	ALGOL	PL/I
1. Delimit procedures	Program unit	begin-end (procedure heading)	PROCEDURE-END
2. Scope of nomenclature	Program unit	begin-end	PROCEDURE-END BEGIN-END (INTERNAL EXTERNAL)
3. Unit for control purposes	DO-loop	begin-end (for clause)	BEGIN-END DO-END (DO-statement)
4. Lifetime of information	not needed	begin-end (own)	BEGIN-END for AUTOMATIC (STATIC AUTOMATIC CONTROLLED)

Figure 4.14 Comparison of statement-grouping facilities in FORTRAN, ALGOL, and PL/I.

identifiers declared in a blockhead.   The information structures associated with a block are normally created on entry to the block and deleted on exit from the block.   However, information structures may be given a permanent (FORTRAN-like) existence by qualifying the identifier which denotes them by the qualifier **own.**

PL/I has more flexible statement grouping facilities than ALGOL or FORTRAN.   There are three kinds of statement-grouping parentheses, represented respectively by PROCEDURE-END, BEGIN-END, and DO-END.   PROCEDURE-END parentheses serve to delimit procedures and to define the scope of nomenclature defined in the procedure heading. BEGIN-END parentheses serve to denote the scope of nomenclature and may also be used for control purposes.   The scope attributes INTERNAL and EXTERNAL may be used to qualify the scope specified by BEGIN-END parentheses.   DO-END parentheses are used for control purposes. They permit iteration to be specified but cannot serve as scope delimiters for identifiers.   When the storage class is AUTOMATIC, the lifetimes of identifiers are determined by the lifetimes of activations of statement groupings in which they occur.   When the storage class is STATIC, identifiers have a permanent existence.   When the storage class is CONTROLLED, identifiers have lifetimes which can be dynamically specified independently of block activations.

The table in Fig. 4.14 summarizes the respective techniques used in FORTRAN, ALGOL, and PL/I to accomplish statement grouping for each of the purposes indicated above.

4.10   COROUTINES, EVENT NOTICES, AND TASKS

4.10.1   CLASSIFICATION OF FUNCTION MODULES BY MODE OF EXECUTION

In the present section function modules will be classified according to the mode of access to them during execution.   The basic function modules of ALGOL are *blocks* and *procedures*.   Blocks are entered on encountering their first symbol during sequential execution and exited on encountering their last symbol.   Procedures are entered by a procedure call and may involve transmission of parameters from the environment of the point of call to the environment of the procedure declaration.

In addition to blocks and procedures, a label may be thought of as a function module that is entered by a **go to** statement and exited only on completion of the program as a whole.

PL/I introduces a new type of function module which is called an *interrupt function module*.   It is entered when a condition associated with the module occurs dynamically during execution and exited by return to the point of call, just like a procedure.

In the present section three additional modes of accessing of function modules will be considered.   The function modules corresponding to these modes of accessing are respectively referred to as *coroutines, event notices,* and *tasks.*†   However, before discussing these classes of function modules, the mode of accessing during procedure calling will be briefly reviewed.

4.10.2   ASYMMETRIC FUNCTION CALLS—PROCEDURES

In ALGOL there are two distinct restrictions on the order of execution of function modules:

---

† This classification of function modules by mode of access and control is not intended to be complete.   For example, the nondeterministic modules suggested by Floyd [19] for use in nondeterministic algorithms are an interesting form of function module whose form of scheduling differs from those discussed in the present text. The study of forms of control and scheduling in languages and computer systems has not received the attention it deserves.

1.   Function modules are dynamically nested, so that a call by a function module A of a function module B requires execution of B to be completed before control is returned to A.†

2.   Execution is performed by a single interpreter, so that the sequence of instructions actually executed can be thought of as a unique one-dimensional string.

In the present section we shall first relax the requirement that function modules be executed in a last in, first out order and then relax the requirement that the program be executed by a single interpreter.

The requirement that interrupted function modules always be resumed in a last in, first out order imposes an asymmetry between the calling procedure and the called procedure.   When a procedure is called, it is always entered at one of a number of fixed entry points, and an activation record for the procedure is created.   On exit from the procedure, the procedure activation record is destroyed.   When a procedure B called by a procedure A is being executed, there are two ways of returning control to the procedure A : (1) by a return of control to the point of call, which destroys the activation record of procedure B and (2) by a reentrant call of A, which pushes down the activation record of B and creates an activation record for a new activation of A.

4.10.3   SYMMETRIC FUNCTION CALLS—COROUTINES

It is convenient in certain applications to permit a third form of procedure call that is symmetric in the sense that it does not create or destroy activation records.   This form of procedure call will be called a **resume** *call*, and procedures which can be called by a resume call will be called *coroutines*.

A resume call allows execution of a coroutine to be resumed at the point where it was interrupted when previously exited, without destroying the activation record of the calling block.   The resume command for transfer of control between coroutines has the following form:

resume $P(a_1, \ . \ . \ . \ ,a_n);$ Resume execution of coroutine P with reentry parameters $a_1, \ . \ . \ . \ , a_n$.   These parameters can be omitted if they are already initialized by a previous call.

Resume calls allow the reentry point of a coroutine to be variable, depending on the last point of exit.   In order to implement coroutines it

† B is considered to be completed both on normal exit and on exit by a transfer-of-control statement.   Both of these forms of exit are assumed to result in deletion of the activation record of B, so that return to the given activation of B becomes impossible.

is necessary to store the restart point of the coroutine explicitly as part of the activation record of the coroutine.

Whereas a procedure call to a procedure creates an activation record for the procedure and then enters the procedure, a resume call to a coroutine does not create an activation record for the coroutine but merely enters the coroutine at its current restart point.

The coroutine mode of transfer of control is useful when it is desired to simulate execution of a number of procedures in parallel. For example, if X, Y, Z are three procedures whose parallel execution is to be simulated, specification of the procedures as coroutines allows execution of part of X followed by a resume call to Y followed by execution of part of Y followed by a resume call to Z followed by execution of part of Z followed by a resume call to X.

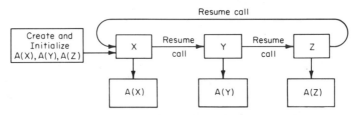

Figure 4.15 Interleaved execution of three coroutines.

In order to execute the three coroutines X, Y, Z in parallel it is necessary first to initialize an activation of each of the coroutines by creating activation records $A(X)$, $A(Y)$, $A(Z)$ for each of the coroutines. Interleaving the execution of the coroutines can then be accomplished by resume calls, as indicated in Fig. 4.15.

Such parallel execution is essential, for example, in tree-searching programs, where success along any one branch of the tree results in termination of the program but some of the branches may be infinite. If X, Y, Z are programs to search individual regions of a tree, each program by itself may be nonterminating, and it is essential to alternate between the programs.

Another use of coroutines occurs in simulation languages, where simulation of a number of processes being executed in parallel is required. Coroutines are used, for instance, in the SIMULA language, as described in the next section.

It will be assumed that coroutines are implemented as reentrant blocks, just like procedure and begin blocks, and that they are declared just like begin blocks except that the symbol **coroutine** is used instead of the symbol **procedure.** It will be assumed also that coroutines, procedures, and blocks can be freely nested in each other.

Two different kinds of calls must be provided for coroutines, corresponding to an initial call, in which the activation record is created, and a resume call, in which execution of a previously created and partially executed activation record is resumed.   The initial call can be thought of as a "passive" call which merely creates and initializes the activation record for a coroutine without actually performing any execution.   In this way creation of the activation record of a function module can be separated from execution of the function module.   Allocation of the activation record of a coroutine can be accomplished by the following allocate command:

allocate $P(a_1, \ldots , a_n)$;   Allocate an initial activation record for the coroutine P. The actualp arameters of the coroutine can be created either on allocation of the first activation record or on entry to the coroutine by the first **resume** command.

Deletion of a coroutine activation record can be accomplished either implicitly by executing the last coroutine instruction or explicitly by execution of the following command:

free P;   Delete the coroutine activation record and all activation records of inner blocks and procedures of the coroutine.

Creation of activation records on entry to a block during execution will be referred to as *automatic* storage allocation, while creation of an activation record by an **allocate** command will be referred to as *controlled* storage allocation.   The **allocate** and **free** commands above are specializations of the controlled storage-allocation facilities of PL/I to the case when the information item being allocated is an activation record whose structure is declared by a procedure declaration.

Coroutine activation records can be created and deleted dynamically by explicit instructions.   If a coroutine enters inner blocks and procedures during execution, they are created and deleted in a last in, first out order and can therefore be stored in an activation-record stack associated with the coroutine.   However, the activation-record stack of each coroutine can grow and contract independently, so that an independent stack is required for each coroutine.

Whereas the instantaneous description of an ALGOL-like program with blocks and procedures requires only a single stack to represent its data part, a process that permits coroutines requires multiple stacks. An ALLOCATE command must allocate an activation record which is the potential beginning of an independent stack.

A coroutine is said to be *active* if the function module currently being executed has its activation record in the activation-record stack of the coroutine. A coroutine which is not currently being executed is said to be in the *passive* state. When a coroutine X transfers control to a coroutine Y by a resume call, the coroutine X switches from the active to the passive state, and the coroutine Y switches from the passive to the active state. During the lifetime of the coroutine within the system it alternates between active and passive states. The individual periods of activity of the coroutine will be referred to as *active phases*.

Exercise: Define the notion of a recursive coroutine. Show that two recursive coroutines cannot be implemented in a single stack even if their storage requirements can be predicted.

4.10.4   SCHEDULED FUNCTION CALLS—EVENT NOTICES

Coroutines permit simulation of parallel execution of procedures. However, coroutines do not permit true parallelism, since control resides in precisely one coroutine at any given point of the computation. When a coroutine X gives control to the coroutine Y, it dies at precisely the point the Y becomes active. The sequence of instructions actually executed is strictly one-dimensional, although active phases of different coroutines may alternate in this one-dimensional sequence.

The possibility of performing parallel processing of function modules will be introduced into the system in two stages: (1) the concept of scheduling function modules by a higher-level interpreter rather than by explicit transfers of control will be introduced within the framework of strictly one-dimensional control sequencing, and (2) the scheduling performed by the higher-level interpreter will be broadened to allow scheduling of several streams of interpretation simultaneously.

When an explicit scheduler is introduced for function modules, explicit transfers of control which cause immediate transfer to a function module can be replaced by *scheduling commands*, which specify the name of the module to be scheduled, and *scheduling parameters*, which are used by the scheduler in scheduling the function modules. Function parameters which specify information to be transmitted to the scheduled process on execution may also be specified as part of the scheduling command.

Function modules which are scheduled by a scheduler will be referred to as *events*. When an event is scheduled, the scheduling parameters are stored in an information module called an *event notice*. When execution of a given event is completed or interrupted, control is returned to the scheduler, which examines the event notices of all currently scheduled events in order to determine the next event to be executed. The scheduler may be thought of as an interpretive computer whose primitive instructions are events and whose execution cycle consists of a scheduling phase followed by an execution phase.

When a scheduler is superimposed on a language with coroutines, events correspond to active phases of the coroutine.   A resume call is interpreted not as a direct transfer of control to a coroutine but as a call which creates an event notice for the called coroutine and then transfers control to the scheduler, which may schedule the called coroutine immediately or schedule some other function module.

Resume calls may be thought of as deleting the event notice of the currently active coroutine and creating an event notice for the called coroutine.   It is necessary also to have a command which creates a new event notice without deleting the current event notice.   This can be accomplished by the following command:

cause E scheduling parameters function parameters   Create an event notice for the coroutine E with the listed scheduling parameters and function parameters.   Then continue execution of the next instruction of the current function module.

The **cause** instruction allows multiple event notices to be scheduled within the system.   When a given event is completed, the scheduler determines the next event to be executed by examining the scheduling parameters of event notices.   Alternatively, scheduling parameters of event notices can be examined when the event notice is created, and the event notice can be placed in a queue of scheduled events from which the scheduler always selects the first element.

The choice of scheduling parameters depends on the application. In time-sharing programming systems the principal scheduling parameter is a priority specification, which may in turn be determined by the length of time permitted for computation.   In other applications, such as simulation, there are inherent constraints on the order in which processes are to be executed.   Simulation systems contain a system variable, which keeps track of the time scale of the system being simulated, and the principal scheduling parameter is the point of system time at which the event is to be executed.   Some additional rules are required for scheduling events scheduled at the same system time.

4.10.5 CONCURRENTLY EXECUTED FUNCTION CALLS—TASKS

When there is more than one function module within the system waiting to be executed, it becomes meaningful to consider the possibility of scheduling them in parallel on more than one interpreter.   Since PL/I has facilities for specifying that two modules are to be executed in parallel, the PL/I notation for specification of parallel execution will be used below.   In PL/I a function module that can be executed in parallel with other function modules is referred to as a *task*.

The basic PL/I statement for the creation of tasks is the CALL statement.   A CALL statement is recognized to be a call for a task by the presence of one or more task attributes.   The general form of the CALL statement is as follows:

CALL P(a$_1$,a$_2$, . . . ,a$_n$), TASK(task name), EVENT(event name), PRIORITY(N);

> TASK, EVENT, and PRIORITY attributes are optional.   If none occur, the call is treated as an ordinary procedure call.   If at least one occurs, the call results in the creation of a task to be executed in parallel with the instruction sequence following the call statement.   The task name, if present, associates a name with the task.   The priority, if present, determines the priority of this task as compared with other tasks.   The sequence of instructions within which a call statement of a task is embedded is referred to as an *attaching* task, while the sequence of instructions of the called task is referred to as the *attached* task.

A call of a task in PL/I results in the creation of an activation record for the procedure P and of a stateword which can be loaded into a processor for execution of the procedure P.   The stateword corresponds in the case of tasks to the event notice in the case of coroutines.   The scheduling parameters of an event notice are represented in the case of PL/I tasks by the priority specification.

If the computer on which tasks are implemented has only one processing unit, execution of tasks will be interleaved with each other, just as in the case of coroutines.   However, the sequence of execution of coroutine segments or of event notices is explicitly specified by transfers of control or by the scheduling algorithm, while the sequence of instruction execution for parallel tasks is unspecified.   The result of executing two tasks in parallel is assumed to be the same for all possible ways of interleaving active phases of the two tasks into a linear sequence.   Whereas the action of a scheduler for coroutines must be specified as part of the programming language, the action of a scheduler for tasks need not be specified as part of the language.   The scheduling algorithm for parallel tasks is normally chosen by the system programmer to optimize an index of execution-time efficiency.

When a task A creates an attached task P, the tasks A and P have as their common environment the part of the stack of A in existence when P is created.   As A and P continue execution, each may create additional local activation records.   From the point of view of storage allocation, a point at which a task is created may be thought of as a point at which the stack forks into two components.

However, in addition to local variables created on entry to function modules of the task there are certain additional *task-dependent* quantities for which storage must be allocated on entry to the task and relinquished on exit from the task. This information includes task parameters, such as the priority information, and also a private set of interrupt cells for system- and programmer-defined interrupts. The interrupt cells are initialized to the state specified within the attaching program A. If an interrupt in encountered for which an action is defined by an ON statement in the attaching task A, the action specified by this ON statement is executed in the normal manner. Interrupts which require execution of such an ON statement may occur in the attaching and the attached task in such a way that they overlap in real time.

An attached task P may have an event name associated with its completion as indicated in the call statement. This event name may in turn be used within the attaching task A to synchronize execution following completion of the attached task. The PL/I instruction for synchronizing asynchronously executed instructions is the WAIT instruction, which has the following form:

WAIT(EI,E2, . . . ,EN)K   Wait until K of the event names
$E1, \ldots , EN$ associated with the completion of attached tasks have occurred before continuing with the next instruction. If K is unspecified, wait until all the specified tasks have been completed.

A task which accesses its nonlocal environment only in a read-only mode is said not to have any side effects, while a task which writes into its nonlocal environment is said to have side effects. When both the attaching and the attached task have no side effects, the result of parallel execution of the tasks is always independent of the relative time sequence in which components of each task are executed. However, if one or both of the two parallel tasks have side effects, the order of execution may affect the final state of the environment when both tasks have been executed.

The register which contains the event associated with termination of a task must be accessible both to the attaching and the attached task and is therefore part of the common environment. Storage of an indicator into this register to indicate that the attached task has been completed is therefore a side effect. The WAIT instruction capitalizes on this particular side effect to perform task synchronization.

Coroutines and tasks represent two different ways of specifying parallelism in programs. Coroutines may be thought of as specifying *scheduled parallelism*, while tasks may be thought of as specifying *unscheduled parallelism*. From the point of view of implementation, coroutines are associated with *independent stacks*, while tasks are associated with *forked stacks*.

In the next section languages for scheduled execution of function modules will be further explored.

Exercises: (*a*) Discuss the following statement: "The *coroutine* control mechanism is a specialization of the *task* control mechanism.   The distinction is useful because coroutines can be implemented more efficiently and more simply than tasks.   However, a task facility allows coroutines to be implemented relatively simply in terms of task primitives."   (*b*) Compare implementation techniques for coroutines with implementation techniques for tasks, emphasizing the information structures to which they give rise during execution.

4.10.6   APPLICATION TO MULTIPROGRAMMING

The general-purpose multiprogramming systems discussed in Chap. 1 constitute an area of application which makes use of all the control mechanisms discussed above.   Nested block structure and procedure calls occur within both user programs and system programs.   Interrupt modules are defined within the system and occur when certain conditions occur during the execution of user programs.   Individual user programs may be regarded as coroutines which transfer control to each other through the system without being pushed down in a stack and with preservation of the current state of execution.   The transfer of control may be explicit or by an interrupt, so that an interrupt control mechanism must be embedded in the coroutine control mechanism.   Since scheduling is performed by the system to determine the next process to be executed, an information module corresponding to an event notice must be available for each process.   Finally, the control mechanism for processes in a multiprogramming system has tasklike characteristics because interprocess sequencing is not subject to time constraints.

Exercise: Classify the forms of control between user and system programs of a multiprogramming system.   Indicate how the forms of control may interact.   Suggest an implementation of the control mechanisms, emphasizing the run-time information structures to which the implementations give rise.

4.11   SIMULATION LANGUAGES†

4.11.1   SCHEDULING OF FUNCTION MODULES

Simulation languages are concerned with the simulation of systems which involve the interaction in time of a number of interrelated processes. Processes in a system are modeled by a sequence of discrete *events*, each of which is assumed to occur instantaneously in the time scale of the system being simulated.   The effect of an event is to change the *state*

---

† Only languages for the simulation of discrete systems are considered.

of the system.† The state of the system can be changed by changing values of data items known to the system, by creating new data items or destroying data items, or by causing or canceling future events. The effect of a process is the sum of the effects of the sequence of events by which it is characterized.

Since the different processes within the system being simulated may interact, the sequence of events associated with the set of all processes of the simulated system must be executed in the order in which it occurs in the time scale of the simulated system. This is accomplished by means of a scheduling algorithm, which determines the event with the earliest system execution time from a list of events which have been scheduled and causes execution of that event.

Events can be classified into two categories according to the mechanism by which they are scheduled. *Exogenous events* are scheduled by a mechanism outside the system being simulated, while *endogenous events* are scheduled during the execution of other events. When execution of a given event has been completed, control is turned over to the scheduler, which examines the list of exogenous and currently scheduled endogenous events to determine the next event to be executed and updates system time. When two events scheduled to be executed at the same instant of system time are encountered within the system, they can in the absence of side effects notionally be executed in parallel as independent tasks. However, if they are to be executed on a single processor, the scheduling algorithm must have a rule for breaking ties and scheduling simultaneously occurring events in sequence. Simulation algorithms allow the user to have explicit control over the order in which simultaneous events are to be scheduled and to specify explicitly the sequential order in which the system schedules simultaneous events. Such specification is an essential part of the language, since simultaneously occurring events may in general have side effects on mutually accessible data, and different orders of execution of notionally simultaneous events may therefore lead to different results.

4.11.2 CREATION AND DELETION OF INFORMATION STRUCTURES

The information structures on which events operate will be referred to as *entities*. Entities have properties similar to PL/I structures in that an entity forms a single unit with respect to creation or deletion but may

---

† The notion of a state of a system corresponds to the notion of an instantaneous description of the information structure representing the system. Events of a system are simulated by the execution of function modules. Since events are assumed to occur instantaneously in the time scale of the simulated system, function modules which correspond to events are assumed to be executed instantaneously in system time.

have a number of data fields of different value types. The entities manipulated by event subroutines of a simulation language include both *data entities*, which specify data attributes of the processes being simulated, and *event-notice entities*, which specify information about events which have been scheduled for execution at a point in system time but not yet executed.

The principal features of simulation languages will be illustrated and compared by considering the two simulation languages SIMSCRIPT and SIMULA. SIMSCRIPT is based on FORTRAN, while SIMULA is based on ALGOL. It will be seen below that the difference in approach of SIMSCRIPT and SIMULA is largely due to the difference in the structure of function modules in ALGOL and FORTRAN.

Both the SIMSCRIPT and the SIMULA languages are concerned with scheduling events that may change data values of entities, create and delete entities, and schedule further events by means of event notices. The principal difference between SIMSCRIPT and SIMULA lies in the mechanisms for creation and deletion of entities and for representation of the successive stages of processes being simulated as they pass through the system.

SIMSCRIPT has explicit mechanisms for the creation and deletion of entities during its execution by means of the commands CREATE and DESTROY, which are analogous to the PL/I commands ALLOCATE and FREE. A process in SIMSCRIPT is initially triggered by an exogenous event which normally creates a number of entities associated with the process and schedules endogenous events at later points of time, which may in turn generate endogenous events. The endogenous events associated with a process may create or delete entities, schedule further events, modify values associated with the process, and modify data values associated with a group of processes or with the system as a whole. A process is therefore characterized by a sequence of events linked together by operating on a common data base and by the fact that an event earlier in system time may schedule a later event associated with the process.

SIMULA is an ALGOL-based language which does not have explicit commands for the creation and deletion of entities. The only means by which entities can be created in SIMULA is by entry to a block during execution.

A process is represented in SIMULA by means of a special kind of procedure called an *activity*. An activity is declared in SIMULA by means of an *activity declaration*. Activity declarations have the same format as procedure declarations except that the type specification **procedure** is replaced by the type specification **activity.**

Whereas ALGOL procedures must be explicitly called by a procedure call, SIMULA activities may be scheduled to occur at a point in system time by means of a special class of system functions referred to as *scheduling statements.* Scheduling statements may be used both to schedule activities at a point in system time and to suspend an activity that is being executed and schedule its continuation at a later point in system time. Execution of an activity is normally accomplished by a sequence of active phases each of which is executed instantaneously in system time. The active phases alternate with suspended phases, during which the activity is dormant, waiting to be rescheduled by the scheduler. The different active phases may correspond to different points of system time.

Entities specifically associated with the activity must be declared in inner blockheads of the activity, while nonlocal entities to which the activity has access must be declared in the head of a block enclosing the activity declaration. Entities in SIMULA can be created only on entry to, and exit from, a block.

Since entry to an ALGOL or SIMULA block has the effect of creating information structures corresponding to local identifiers, while exit from a block has the effect of deleting local identifiers, it is appropriate that these mechanisms be used for dynamic creation and deletion of data structures. However, it is nevertheless artificial to tie creation and deletion of data structures to entry to, and exit from, function modules. Explicit creation and deletion of data structures by some form of controlled storage allocation, as in SIMSCRIPT, is on the whole cleaner.

4.11.3 THE JOB-SHOP MODEL

The SIMSCRIPT and SIMULA languages will be illustrated in detail by considering how the basic features of the *job-shop scheduling problem* can be programmed in the two languages. The system to be simulated is a *job shop*, which consists of a number of *machine groups* NMG, each containing a number of identical machines. The purpose of the job shop is to process a sequence of *orders*, where each order requires processing for a specified time on each of a sequence of machine groups. The order is characterized by the number N of machine groups on which it is to be processed, and by the machine-group identification MGROUP(I) and processing time PTIME(I) for $I = 1, 2, \ldots, N$. The sequence of machine groups MGROUP(1), . . . , MGROUP(N) on which the order is to be processed is referred to as the ROUTE of the order.

The system to be simulated initially has NOAVL(J) machines available in the Jth machine group. As orders enter the system, they are scheduled on the first machine MGROUP(1) in their route for a processing time PTIME(1) provided a machine in that machine group is available. When a system time PTIME(1) has elapsed, they can be scheduled on the next machine in their route. The order is completed when it has used a time PTIME(I) on each of the machine groups MGROUP(I) in the sequence specified by the route.

If when an order reaches a machine group in its route no machines are available, the order is placed in a queue associated with the machine group and must wait its turn in the queue until a machine in the machine group becomes available. We shall assume that orders waiting in the queue of a particular machine group are processed in a first come, first served order as machines in that machine group become available.

The principal type of exogenous event of the simulation is the arrival of an order in the job shop. On arrival of an order the routing and the processing times for each order must be stored within the system, and processing of the order by the first machine group in its route is initiated. The principal endogenous event of the simulation is the termination of processing of an order by a machine in a given machine group. This endogenous event triggers processing of the given order at the next machine group in its route or deletion of the order if processing has been completed. It also frees a machine in the given machine group for processing some other order.

Following this description of the overall features of the job-shop simulation problem the details of programming this problem in SIM-SCRIPT and in SIMULA will be considered.

4.11.4 JOB-SHOP SIMULATION IN SIMSCRIPT

SIMSCRIPT distinguishes between permanent entities, which are created at translation time, and temporary entities, whose storage is allocated during execution by create and destroy operations. Permanent entities are used to specify information structures of the system being simulated which do not change during execution, such as the number of machine groups in a job shop. Temporary entities are used to specify information structures associated with processes that enter and leave the system, such as orders processed in the job shop.

It is convenient to adopt the convention that the number of information fields in an entity is fixed at translation time. However, the number of data fields required to represent the data associated with a given process may be variable. For example, an order in a job shop requires $2N$ data fields to store the routing and processing-time information for each of its machine groups, where N varies for different orders. Similarly the queue associated with a machine group has a variable number of information fields depending on the number of elements in the queue.

Structures with a variable number of attributes are introduced into SIMSCRIPT by means of a SET. A SET is an ordered sequence of entities having a first and last element. Sets may in turn be pointed to by entities. SIMSCRIPT contains commands for sequencing through elements of an ordered set pointed to by an entity and for creation, deletion, and modification of entities that are elements of the set. An entity which points to a set normally contains a pointer to both the first and last element of the set. In this way it is possible to implicitly introduce a variable number of attributes for the entity within the set while at the same time specifying the entity itself by means of a fixed number of attributes including two pointers to the set. The ordered set is effectively a single-level list and is manipulated by SIMSCRIPT commands that are effectively list-processing operations. Since the entities which constitute elements of a set may themselves point to sets, multiple-level lists can effectively be defined in SIMSCRIPT. Thus the ENTITY and SET specification facilities of SIMSCRIPT require all the machinery for generalized list processing, although the notations and permitted operations differ from those normally available in actual list-processing languages.

In order to specify the job-shop scheduling problem in SIMSCRIPT it is convenient to specify two kinds of sets, referred to respectively as ROUTE sets and QUEUE sets. The elements of a ROUTE set consist of entities which specify the machine group and processing time of the sequence of machine groups in the route of an order. The entities of the QUEUE set consist of pointers to the entities that represent orders. The two basic temporary entities required to characterize a job shop in SIMSCRIPT are the entities ORDER, for characterizing an order, and DESTN, which specifies the machine group and processing time in the ROUTE set of an order. The tree structure of these entities is as follows:

The entity ORDER points to the first and last elements FROUTE, LROUTE of the set ROUTE, and the successor SQUEUE of the set QUEUE if it is currently in the queue of a machine group. This entity completely characterizes the current state of the order in its passage through the machine shop. The entity DESTN specifies the machine group, processing time, and the successor in the ROUTE set to which it belongs.

The basic permanent entity of the system is the machine group MG, which has the following structure:

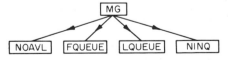

For each machine group there is a permanent entity specifying the number of machines currently available, the first and last elements in the queue of this machine, and the number of elements currently available.

One further type of temporary entity which is created and destroyed during the simulation is the event-notice entity ENDPROC, which causes scheduling of the endogenous event associated with completion of an order at a given machine group.   The event-notice entity has the following structure:

Each ENDPROC entity specifies a machine group, an order being processed on the machine group, and the time at which processing of the order on this machine group will be completed.

A flow diagram for the events which occur in the simulation and the subroutines which they call is as follows:

EXOGENOUS EVENT ORDRIN
Create an order entity and the ROUTE set for the order entity. Read in the 2N order parameters and create destination entities for each machine group on the route, attaching them to the ROUTE set for the order. Call the subroutine which schedules arrival of the order at the first machine group.

ENDOGENOUS EVENT ENDPROC
After storing the attributes of the event notice by which it is triggered, this event deals with the order whose processing has been completed and then reallocates the freed machine. The completed order is routed to the next machine group in its route if there is one or else removed from the system. The freed machine is allocated to the next order in the queue if there is one or else returned to the pool of idle machines.

SUBROUTINE ARRIVAL
If a machine is available, reduce the number of available machines by 1 and call a subroutine for allocating the machine to process the order. Otherwise file the order in the queue for this machine group.

SUBROUTINE ALLOCATE
Create an event notice ENDPROC which will cause an endogenous event when processing of the order is completed.   Store the attributes in the event notice.   Delete the first destination entity from the ROUTE set of the order being allocated.

There are essentially three kinds of subroutines in SIMSCRIPT, referred to respectively as EXOGENOUS-EVENT subroutines, ENDOG-ENOUS-EVENT subroutines, and regular subroutines. These three kinds of subroutines differ principally in the mode by which they are called. Exogenous- and endogenous-event subroutines are scheduled by the scheduler at the system time at which they are intended to occur, while subroutines are explicitly called by subroutine calls.

The SIMSCRIPT programs for each of the above subroutines will now be given.

```
EXOGENOUS EVENT ORDRIN
CREATE ORDER
LET DATE(ORDER) = TIME
READ N
DO TO 10, FOR I = (1)(N)
CREATE DESTN
READ MGROUP(DESTN), PTIME(DESTN)
FILE DESTN IN ROUTE(ORDER)
10 LOOP
CALL ARRIVAL(ORDER)
RETURN
END
```

This event creates an instance of the entity ORDER with an initially empty ROUTE set and sets the DATE attribute of the order to the current system time. Successive destinations are then created, have their MGROUP and PTIME attributes specified from the input medium, and are then filed in the ROUTE set for the order. The FILE command automatically sets the successor attribute of successive destinations so that they form an ordered set. When all destinations for the order have been filed in the ROUTE set, the ARRIVAL subroutine is called with the parameter ORDER.

The subroutine ARRIVAL is specified as follows:

```
SUBROUTINE ARRIVAL(ORDER)
LET MG = MGROUP(FROUTE(ORDER))
IF (NOAVL(MG)) EQ(O), GO TO 10
LET NOAVL(MG) = NOAVL(MG) − 1
CALL ALLOCATE (MG,ORDER)
RETURN
10 FILE ORDER IN QUEUE(MG)
RETURN
END
```

This subroutine sets MG to the machine group of the next order to be processed.   If the number of idle machines in this machine group is non-zero, this number is reduced by 1, and the ALLOCATE subroutine is called.   Otherwise the order is filed in the QUEUE for that machine group.

The subroutine ALLOCATE is specified as follows:

```
SUBROUTINE ALLOCATE(MG,JOB)
CREATE ENDPROC
LET MGROUP(ENDPROC) = MG
LET ORDER(ENDPROC) = JOB
CAUSE ENDPROC AT TIME + PTIME(FROUTE(JOB))
REMOVE FIRST DESTN FROM ROUTE(JOB)
DESTROY DESTN
RETURN
END
```

This subroutine creates an ENDPROC event notice, assigns the attributes MGROUP and ORDER for the newly created entity, and then schedules the event associated with termination of processing of this order on the machine group.   The allocated destination is then removed from the ROUTE set, and the destination entity is destroyed.

The endogenous event ENDPROC is specified as follows:

```
ENDOGENOUS EVENT ENDPROC
LET JOB = ORDER(ENDPROC)
LET MG = MGROUP(ENDPROC)
DESTROY ENDPROC
IF ROUTE(JOB) IS EMPTY, GO TO 10
CALL ARRIVAL(JOB)
GO TO 20
10 DESTROY JOB
20 IF QUEUE(MG) IS EMPTY, GO TO 30
REMOVE FIRST ORDER FROM QUEUE(MG)
CALL ALLOCATE(MG,JOB)
RETURN
30 LET NOAVL(MG) = NOAVL(MG) + 1
RETURN
END
```

This event stores the ORDER and MGROUP attributes of the event notice and destroys the event-notice entity.   If the ROUTE set associated with the ORDER parameter of the event notice is empty, the order has been completed, and the ORDER entity is destroyed.   Otherwise the ARRIVAL subroutine is called to schedule the order at the next machine group.   Having dealt with the order whose processing has been completed, the queue for the machine group is tested.   If the queue is nonempty, the next order in the queue is allocated, while if the queue is empty, the number of available machines is increased by 1.

Initially, the system starts with a sequence of orders queued up on the input tape.   It is assumed that there is a mechanism for determining automatically the time at which successive orders are to be read in. When successive orders are read in, entities are created, and a sequence of endogenous events for each order is triggered, associated with processing of orders on successive machine groups.

The event notices which serve to trigger endogenous events contain both the system time of the endogenous event and the set of parameters to be transmitted to the endogenous-event routine when it is executed. Whereas the set of actual parameters of a FORTRAN subroutine are stored in a set of registers relative to the point of call, the set of actual parameters of an event are stored as an independent data entity.   This allows several event notices to be simultaneously within the system and breaks away from the one-to-one correspondence between programs and data that is normally associated with FORTRAN subroutines.   The time component of an event notice may be regarded as an additional subprogram parameter that has a default interpretation of immediate execution in the case of regular subroutines.

When a simulation such as the above job-shop simulation is performed, the object is normally to accumulate certain statistics about the behavior of the simulated system, such as the average length of queue, average waiting time of an order in queues, and maximum waiting time of an order in queues.   This can be done by associating statistical attributes with both permanent and temporary attributes of the simulated system.   Events will in general include commands for updating these statistical attributes, and certain additional events can be introduced into the system which are concerned solely with statistical or accounting functions.   Statistical features have been omitted from the example in order to keep it as simple as possible, but a version which includes statistical updating is given in the SIMSCRIPT manual [11].

A system simulation can be thought of as a program executed by an interpreter, called a *scheduler*, whose basic function modules are events whose sequencing is performed by a scheduling algorithm.   It is convenient to think of events as generalized instructions and of the event interpreter as a generalized instruction-processing unit.   The basic execution cycle consists of a scheduling phase, in which the next event (instruction) to be executed is determined, followed by an execution phase, which may change the state of the system both by changing data entities and by rescheduling the order of subsequent events (instructions). When viewed from this point of view, simulation languages differ from other languages principally in that flexible facilities are provided for determining the order in which function modules are to be executed; i.e., the order of execution of function modules is determined by a scheduler rather than by explicit transfers of control.

Both SIMSCRIPT and SIMULA have basically similar scheduling algorithms which cause execution of the earliest scheduled event in system time and resolve conflicts for events scheduled simultaneously in system time. However, the method of defining events within the program structure is completely different for SIMSCRIPT and SIMULA.

4.11.5 JOB-SHOP SIMULATION IN SIMULA

SIMULA is an ALGOL-based language which builds on ALGOL by introducing a number of new syntactic constructs and a number of built-in system functions. Two new kinds of function modules are introduced, referred to respectively as SIMULA *blocks* and *activities*.

A SIMULA program consists of a single ALGOL block with a single SIMULA block nested inside it. The simulation facilities of SIMULA become dynamically available on entry to the SIMULA block during execution. All internal tables and explicit structures created during the simulation are destroyed on exit from the SIMULA block so that a system simulation is effectively accomplished, while control resides within a single SIMULA block. On initial entry to a SIMULA block the system time is set to zero, an empty sequencing set SQS is created, a number of additional simulation variables are initialized, and a set of system identifiers which can be used only within SIMULA blocks is given meaning. Once the system has been initialized for simulation, an activation record for the SIMULA block is created which holds values of identifiers declared in the blockhead of the SIMULA block.

The most important system functions available within a SIMULA block that are not available in an ALGOL block are described below. The principal notion present in SIMULA but not in ALGOL is the *activity*. An activity is essentially ac oroutine in the sense discussed in the previous section. However, the notations for declaration and call of activities differ from those used in the previous section.

An activity declaration is a function module which is specified syntactically like a procedure declaration except that the system symbol **procedure** is replaced by the system symbol **activity.** Activity declarations may occur only within SIMULA blocks and may therefore contain syntactic constructs and system functions of SIMULA blocks.

The principal semantic difference between ALGOL procedures and SIMULA activities lies in the mode of call of the function modules. Procedure calls in ALGOL must be dynamically nested, so that a call by procedure A of procedure B requires execution of B to be completed before control is returned to A. Activity calls in SIMULA result in execution of only part of the activity rather than the whole of the activity. Moreover, activity calls normally do not result in direct transfer of control to an activity but in scheduling the activity at some future point of system time by means of an event notice.

An activity in SIMULA is dynamically partitioned into a number of active phases, corresponding to events that occur instantaneously in system time, separated by inactive phases, during which system time may elapse. Active phases of an activity are initiated by the scheduler when the event notice for the activity reaches the top of the sequencing set SQS. The transition from an active to an inactive phase is accomplished by executing a scheduling command within the activity itself that causes the activity to become temporarily or permanently inactive. On reentry to the activity after an inactive phase, execution is normally continued with the command following the one which caused the activity to become inactive. Since the restart point of an activity may vary for successive calls of the activity, it must be explicitly stored as part of the activation record associated with each instance of activation of the activity.

It is convenient to distinguish three kinds of inactive activities:

1. *Suspended Activities.* A suspended activity is one whose execution has been scheduled for some future point of system time, but which is not currently being executed; i.e., there is an event notice for the activity in the sequencing set SQS.

2. *Passive Activities.* A passive activity is one which is neither currently scheduled nor being executed. However, an activation record for the activity exists, and a restart point is specified within the activation record, so that the activity may meaningfully be scheduled.

3. *Terminated Activities.* Terminated activities are activities for which no restart point is defined, so that it is not meaningful for terminated activities to be scheduled.

SIMULA has facilities for handling ordered sets of activities which parallel the SIMSCRIPT facilities for handling ordered sets of entities. In order to handle ordered sets of processes a special data module called an *element* is defined. An element consists of a pointer to predecessor and successor elements of the set to which it belongs and a pointer to the activity with which it is associated. In a simulation language there are many operations on activities that are independent of the internal structure of the activity.   When performing such operations it is convenient to represent the process in a uniform manner.   The uniform representation chosen in SIMULA consists of an activity pointer together with list pointers which allow activities to be members of an ordered set.

SIMULA allows identifiers to be of type *element* and of type *set.* Identifiers which represent arrays of elements or sets are respectively introduced by the declaration **element array** and **set array.**   SIMULA has facilities for placing elements in sets, removing elements from sets, sequencing through sets, and testing whether a set is empty.   The system functions first(S) and last(S) refer to the first and last elements of a set, the function empty(S) tests whether S is empty.   The function include(A,S) adds activity A at the end of the set S and the function remove(S) deletes the first element of the set S.

The scheduling commands of SIMULA are implemented partially by additional syntax and partly by system functions.   The basic syntactic scheduling commands are **activate** and **reactivate.**   The **activate** command has the following form:

activate element-expression scheduling clause   The **activate** command creates an event notice for the passive activity specified by the element expression at the time specified by the scheduling clause and continues execution of the active phase of the activity currently being executed.   It is equivalent to the CAUSE command of SIMSCRIPT.

The **activate** command is used when calling a new activity:

activate new element-expression scheduling clause   This command creates an activation record for the activity specified by the element expression and schedules it at the time specified by the scheduling clause.

Both instances of the activate command above schedule a new activity while allowing the active phase of the current activity to continue and thereby increase the total number of activities scheduled within the system.   If there is no scheduling clause, the event notice for the activity is placed in the sequencing set at the end of the activities scheduled for the current system time.   However, the activity can be placed at the head of the sequencing set by adding the word **prior.**

activate new element expression **prior;**   Place the event notice for the activity specified by the element expression at the head of the sequencing set; i.e., place it prior to all other events scheduled at the current system time.

Whereas the **activate** command increases the number of scheduled activities in the system, the **reactivate** command leaves this number unchanged.

The **reactivate** command has the following form:

reactivate element expression scheduling clause   The **reactivate** command is used to reschedule an active or suspended process.   It deletes the event notice of the process associated with the element expression and creates a new one.

reactivate current **delay** T;   This command causes the currently active activity to become suspended and places an event notice for the process in the sequencing set at the end of the list of processes scheduled at current system time $+ T$.   The event notice could be placed at the beginning of the list of activities scheduled at system time $+ T$ by the command "**reactivate** current **delay** T **prior**".

The system scheduling functions available in SIMULA include the following:

hold(T);   Suspend the current process and reschedule it at system time $+ T$.   This function is equivalent to "**reactivate** current **delay** T".

cancel(A);   Delete the event notice for the activity A; that is, make the activity A passive.   The command "cancel (current)" causes the currently active process to become passive.

terminate(A);   Delete both the event notice and the restart point of the activity A.   For practical purposes this is equivalent to deleting the activation record of the activity A.   The effect of termination is achieved also by exiting through its **end** statement.

wait(S);   **wait** is a system command that combines set manipulation with scheduling.   It causes the current activity to be included as a new last element of the set S and then causes the current activity to become passive; i.e., it is equivalent to the sequence of commands "include (current,S); cancel(S)".

The following example illustrates how an activity for writing reports at regular intervals could be specified in SIMULA.

activity report(t); real t;   If this activity is entered
    begin L: write(· ·); hold(t); **go to** L **end**   by the command "**activate** new report(t)", it will execute itself repeatedly at intervals of time t, writing out the items specified in the write statement.

These features of SIMULA will now be illustrated by showing how SIMULA can be used to program the job-shop scheduling problem. This example will at the same time underline the similarities and differences between the SIMULA and SIMSCRIPT simulation languages.

It will be assumed that the input tape initially contains the job-shop specification followed by a sequence of orders. The job-shop specification consists of an integer specifying the number of machine groups NMG followed by a vector with NMG elements specifying the number NOAVL(I) of machines available in each machine group $I = 1, 2, \ldots$, NMG.

Each order is assumed to contain the number N of machine groups in its route, the time T of its arrival at the machine group, the vector MGROUP of machines in its route, and the vector PTIME of processing at each machine group. The sequence of orders is terminated by a dummy order with $N = 0$.

The SIMULA program for the job-shop simulation is as follows:

```
          begin integer NMG; read(NMG);
SIMULA    begin integer array NOAVL[1:NMG];
          set array QUEUE [1:NMG];
          integer N; real T;
          activity ORDER(N);
            integer N
            begin integer I, MG;
              integer array MGROUP [1:N]
              real array PTIME [1:N]
              read (MGROUP, PTIME)
              for I : = 1 step 1 until N do
              begin MG := MGROUP [I];
                if NOAVL [MG] = 0 then
                begin wait (QUEUE[MG]); remove(current) end
                else NOAVL[MG] := NOAVL[MG] − 1;
                hold (PTIME[I]);
                if empty (QUEUE[MG]) then
                NOAVL[MG] := NOAVL[MG] + 1;
                else activate first (QUEUE[MG])
              end path through shop
            end activity ORDER
            comment main program of SIMULA block;
            read (NOAVL);
      NEXT: read (N,T); reactivate current at T;
            if N > 0 then
            begin activate new ORDER(N); go to NEXT end
```

end SIMULA block
end program

This SIMULA program consists of a single ALGOL block containing a single enclosed SIMULA block. The number of machine groups NMG is declared and read in, in the outer ALGOL block. The SIMULA block contains declarations for the availability array NOAVL, the *set array* QUEUE, whose elements are sets (queues), the order parameters N and T, and the activity declaration for the activity ORDER, which represents the successive stages of processing of an order through the job shop. The main program, which starts following the **comment** statement, reads in the array NOAVL and then goes into a loop for processing successive orders. The order parameters N, T are read in for successive orders and the SIMULA block (which is an anonymous activity) is suspended till system time T. When system time T is reached, if $N > 0$, a new instance of the activity ORDER is activated in parallel with the process currently being executed, and control is returned to NEXT, so that the order parameters for the next order can be read in. The **activate** command puts the activity call for the new instance of ORDER into the sequencing set SQS at the end of the sequence of processes to be executed at the current point of system time and continues with execution of the current process until a point of interruption is reached. When the activated process **new** ORDER(N) is executed, a new activation record for this instance of execution of the activity is created, and execution of the first active phase of this activity is initiated. This causes input of the two N-element arrays MGROUP and PTIME and execution of the **for** statement. Each iteration of the **for** statement represents processing of the order at one machine group. If there are no machines available at the machine group, the order is placed at the end of the queue for the machine group by the wait function. The wait function also causes the active phase of the activity to be terminated and causes the activity to become passive. The activity is reawakened from its passive state when it becomes the first activity in the queue of the machine group by the command "**activate** first (QUEUE[MG])". When this occurs, the next command "remove (current)" is executed, which removes the activity from the queue for the machine group. The activity is then scheduled on a machine of the machine group by the command "hold (PTIME[I])". If a machine in the machine group MG is immediately available, the **else** branch of the **if** statement is taken, the number of available machines is reduced by 1, and the order is scheduled on the machine group by the hold statement. The hold statement terminates an active phase of the activity by throwing it into a suspended state from which it is automatically re-reactivated by the scheduler at a specified system time. On reactivation a machine in the machine group becomes freed and is used for the next order of the queue of the machine group if there is one or returned to the pool of available machines if the queue is empty. The next iteration, if there is one, is then started for the given order. If there is no next iteration, the order has been completed and drops out of the system. The simulation terminates when an order with order parameter $N = 0$ is encountered.

The above discussion of simulation language illustrates how arithmetically oriented languages can be augmented by a set of special-purpose primitives for handling a specific class of problems. Simulation languages require a set of scheduling primitives including facilities for coroutines and tasks, dynamic data-creation and -deletion facilities, and facilities for handling sets (lists) of data. It is not at present clear whether such special-purpose languages will be rendered obsolete by general-purpose "shell languages" such as PL/I with carefully thought-out primitives for handling a wide spectrum of special-purpose applications, whether they will be rendered obsolete by "core languages" with powerful definitional facilities for defining special-purpose primitives, or whether such special-purpose languages will prove to be the best long-run solution for efficient handling of special classes of computation. The author feels that general-purpose languages are not yet sufficiently well understood to take over from special-purpose languages and that special-purpose languages will continue to play a useful role for at least another twenty years. The situation in the language field is somewhat similar to that in the system field, where attempts to take large steps forward in system design frequently fail. Just as large-scale programming systems do not always live up to their expected performance, so large-scale programming languages such as PL/I are not always as useful as would be expected from the facilities they contain. However, it is likely that the programming community will eventually learn how to design large languages and systems. This book is an attempt to further the development of such an understanding.

REFERENCES

1. Naur, P., et al.: ALGOL 60 Report, *Commun. ACM*, May, 1960.
2. Naur, P., et al.: Revised ALGOL Report, *Commun. ACM*, January, 1963.
3. Wirth, N., and H. Weber: EULER—A Generalization of ALGOL and Its Formal Definition, *Commun. ACM*, January and February, 1966.
4. Strachey, C., and M. V. Wilkes: Some Proposals for Improving the Efficiency of ALGOL 60, *Commun. ACM*, November, 1961.
5. Weizenbaum, J.: Symmetric List Processor, *Commun. ACM*, September, 1963.

6. Randell, B., and L. J. Russell: "ALGOL 60 Implementation," Academic Press Inc., New York, 1964.

7. Huxtable, D. H. R.: On Writing an Optimizing Translator for ALGOL 60, in P. Wegner (ed.), "Introduction to System Programming," Academic Press Inc., New York, 1964.

8. McCarthy, J., et al.: "LISP 1.5 Programmer's Manual," The MIT Press, Cambridge, Mass., 1962.

9. PL/I Language Specification, IBM System Reference Library, File 5360-29, Form C28-6571-4.

10. Conway, M. E.: Design of a Separable Transition Diagram Compiler, *Commun. ACM*, July, 1963.

11. Markowitz, H., et al.: "SIMSCRIPT Manual," Prentice-Hall, Inc., Englewood Cliffs, N.J., 1963.

12. Dahl, D., and K. Nygaard: SIMULA—An ALGOL-based Simulation Language, *Commun. ACM*, September, 1966.

13. Landin, P.: The Mechanical Evaluation of Expressions, *Computer J.*, January, 1964.

14. Standish, T.: A Data Definition Facility for Programming Languages, Ph.D. thesis, *Carnegie Tech. Rept.*, May, 1967.

15. Perlis, A., et al.: Formula ALGOL Manual, *Carnegie Tech. Rept.*, 1966.

16. Barron, D., et al.: The Main Features of CPL, *Computer J.*, July, 1963.

17. Wirth, N.: On Certain Basic Concepts of Programming Languages, *Stanford Univ., Computer Science Dept. Tech. Rept.* CS65, May 1, 1967.

18. McCarthy, J.: Definition of New Data Types in ALGOL X, *ALGOL Bull.* 18, October, 1964.

19. Floyd, R. W.: Non-deterministic Algorithms, *Carnegie Tech. Rept.*, November, 1966.

20. Knuth, D. E.: The Remaining Trouble Spots in ALGOL 60, *Commun. ACM*, October, 1967.

APPENDIX 1

SYNTACTIC SPECIFICATION
AND SYNTACTIC ANALYSIS

A1.1 INTRODUCTION

In this appendix a notation for the syntactic specification of programming languages is developed, and techniques for the structural analysis and compilation of programs by use of a syntactic notation are surveyed. A notation similar to that developed here is used in Appendix 2 to develop the syntax of ALGOL as given in the ALGOL report [2].

A *syntax*, or *grammar*, for a programming language is a set of rules for specifying the set of valid programs of the language, while a *semantics* for a language is a set of rules for determining the transformations to which expressions give rise when they are scanned during evaluation (see subsection 1.1.8). There are many different notations for specifying the set of valid programs of a given language. One class of notations will be developed in some detail below.

The programs of a given programming language (or sentences of a given natural language) are usually represented by strings of characters over a finite alphabet, which normally includes the 26 alphabetic characters, the 10 digits, and a number of punctuation and operation symbols. The set of all characters which may occur in strings of a given language L will be denoted by T and will be referred to as the *alphabet* of the language. The set of all finite strings over the alphabet T of a language L will be denoted by T^*. The purpose of a syntactic specification is to distinguish the strings of T^* which belong to the language L from strings of T^* which do not belong to the language L.

Example: Consider a language which consists precisely of all possible combinations of single-letter variables connected by + signs. The alphabet T in this case contains 27 characters consisting of the 26 letters and the symbol +. Expressions like "$a + b$", "$a + b + a$", and "$a + a + a$" are *valid expressions* of the language. However, expressions like "$ab+$" or "$++c$" are not valid expressions although they belong to the set T^* of strings over the alphabet T.

A grammar G for a language L is required to specify the language $L(G)$ in a *constructive* (*effective*) manner; i.e., it is important that given the grammar G, it can be determined for an arbitrary string t of T^* whether or not t is a valid string of the language $L(G)$. The algorithm for determining whether a given string belongs to the language generated by a given grammar is called a *syntactic recognition algorithm*.

Syntactic specification of a language allows mechanical recognition algorithms to be developed for recognizing and for use in transforming programs of a programming language. However, the number of recognition steps may easily become combinatorially explosive. The present appendix considers both the *feasibility* and the *efficiency* of a number of classes of syntactic recognition algorithms.

The semantics associated with a program which represents a function f is usually thought of as the set of rules which specify, for every element x of the input domain, the corresponding value $y = f(x)$ in the range of the function. However, a function may be transformed for other purposes than application to an argument x in its domain. For example, if the function is being translated from a source to a target language, the transformation associated with the function is a translation of the function into a target language. The semantics associated with the function must be adjusted accordingly to represent transformations associated with translation. Whereas a syntax of a programming language is a specification of a fixed set of programs, a semantics is not completely specified by the set of programs of the language but requires additional information as to the kind of transformation to be performed. Failure to recognize that semantics cannot be associated with languages unless specific assumptions are made regarding the class of computations has led to a good deal of confusion regarding the concept of semantics. A number of illustrations of different semantics for a fixed language are given below (Sec. A1.8).

The syntactic approach to language specification is not emphasized in the body of the present text because the text is concerned principally with transformations of programs during their execution. The technical details that arise in any attempt at a complete formal specification of a programming language are avoided wherever possible. However, the notion of how the set of strings which constitutes a programming language may be rigorously specified is an important notion which should be understood by the time the reader reaches Chap. 3.

A1.2   SPECIFICATION OF SETS

A grammar is a notation for specifying sets of strings. The standard notation for specifying a set consisting of a small number of elements is to list the elements. Thus the set S consisting of three elements a, b, c would normally be specified as $S = \{a,b,c\}$. We shall adopt a variant of this notation and write $S \rightarrow a|b|c$ to denote this three-element set.

Explicit listing becomes unwieldy for sets consisting of a large or infinite number of elements. However, such sets can sometimes be conveniently specified in terms of other sets. Thus the four-element set $\{ab,bc,cd,de\}$ can be specified by the sequence of definitions "$S \rightarrow X|Y$, $X \rightarrow ab|bc$, $Y \rightarrow cd|de$".

Sets with an infinite number of elements can sometimes be specified by a *recursive definition* in which the name of the set being defined appears also on the right-hand side of the definition.

$S \rightarrow a|Saa$ The recursively defined set S is defined to be either a or S followed by aa. Successive application of the definition results in set elements "aaa", "$aaaaa$", and all strings with an odd number of instances of a.

The notation x^n will be used to denote n occurrences of the symbol x. Using this notation, the recursively defined set S above can be defined as $S = \{a^{2m+1}|m = 0, 1, 2, \ldots\}$.

If X and Y are sets, the notation XY is used to denote any element of the set X followed by any element of the set Y. Thus if $X \rightarrow a|b$ and $Y \rightarrow c|d$, then $XY = \{ac|ad|bc|bd\}$. More generally if U is a string of symbols consisting of set variables X, Y interspersed with constants, it may be thought of as representing the set of all strings of constants that can be obtained by substitution of set elements for set variables.

A1.3 FORMAL GRAMMARS

A specification such as "$S \rightarrow a|Saa$" can be regarded as an abbreviation for the specification "$S \rightarrow a$, $S \rightarrow Saa$". Specifications of the form $S \rightarrow a$ with only one alternative on the right-hand side are referred to as *productions*. The symbol on the left-hand side is referred to as the *defined symbol* associated with the production. The symbols which appear on the right-hand side of a production may be classified into *terminal symbols*, which are symbols of the language being specified, and *nonterminal symbols*, which are names of sets used in specifying the language. One of the nonterminal symbols specifies the set which constitutes the complete language, while other nonterminal symbols constitute sets that are used in building up the set that constitutes the complete language.

A grammar G may be thought of as being specified by four components:

    1. An alphabet N of nonterminal characters which specify sets used in building up the language

    2. An alphabet T of terminal characters which occur in the language

    3. A distinguished nonterminal S which is the set that constitutes the whole language

    4. A set of productions P of the form "$X \rightarrow U$", where X is a single nonterminal and U is a string of terminals and nonterminals

Thus we can write $G = (N,T,S,P)$, where N, T, S, P are defined as above. Grammars of the form specified above are usually called *context-free grammars.*†

Example: In the grammar "$S \rightarrow XY, X \rightarrow a|b, Y \rightarrow c|d$" $N = \{S,X,Y\}$, $T = \{a,b,c,d\}$, $S = S$, and P is the above set of productions.

The language associated with a given context-free grammar G is the set of all strings of terminals which can be generated from S by sequences of productions; i.e., if $X \Rightarrow U$ denotes that U can be generated from X by a sequence of productions, then the language $\mathcal{L}(G)$ associated with a grammar G can be defined as follows:

$$\mathcal{L}(G) = \{x|S \Rightarrow x \land x \in T^*\}$$

A1.4 SYNTACTIC CHARTS

A context-free grammar can be represented pictorially by a syntactic chart. For example, the grammar "$S \rightarrow a|Saa$" can be represented by the following syntactic chart:

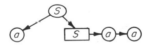

In a syntactic chart ovals represent points of *definition* of the enclosed nonterminal. Rectangles represent points of *use* of the enclosed nonterminal and may be thought of as subroutine calls to the point of definition. Circles represent points of use of the enclosed terminal. Horizontal lines represent concatenation of symbols on the right-hand

† The above class of grammars is called context-free because if "$X \rightarrow U$" is a production of the grammar, then any occurrence of X in a partially expanded string can be replaced by U regardless of the context in which X occurs. Context-free grammars are contrasted with *context-sensitive grammars*, in which productions of the form "$AXB \rightarrow AUB$" are permitted. A production of the form "$AXB \rightarrow AUB$" specifies that X can be replaced by U if and only if the occurrence of X is preceded by the symbol string A and followed by the symbol string B, i.e., if and only if X occurs in the context $A \cdots B$.

side of a production, while lines with a vertical component imply that the higher-level nonterminal is associated with a production whose right-hand side is the sequence of horizontally connected lower-level components.   The convention is usually adopted that all productions associated with a given nonterminal emanate from a single oval instance of definition of that nonterminal.

In the above example the nonterminal S is defined by its oval instance and is seen to give rise to two productions, one of which involves a recursive instance of use of S.

A syntactic chart is a specification of a grammar and therefore of a set of strings.   The set of all strings associated with a given grammar may be thought of as being generated by plugging in instances of definition of nonterminals for instances of their use in all possible ways.   For example, if in the above syntactic chart the oval instance of S is plugged in for the rectangular instance, the following figure is obtained.

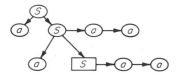

An oval instance of S may in turn be plugged in for the new rectangular instance of S.   Iteration of this process yields trees of arbitrary depth.

Terminal strings can be generated from figures derived in this way, by the rule that exactly one downward path be followed from any oval vertex.   When the lower-level string reached on descending does not contain any terminals, it can be substituted for the higher-level vertex. Substitution of terminals for nonterminals at successively higher levels will eventually associate a string of terminals with the highest-level vertex.   This string represents the string of terminals generated by this particular path through the syntactic chart.

A1.5 PHRASE STRUCTURE IMPOSED ON STRINGS BY A GRAMMAR

A given language may in general be specified by a large number of different grammars.   For example, the language consisting of all strings with an odd number of a's can be represented by any one of the following context-free grammars:

1. $S \rightarrow a|Saa$
2. $S \rightarrow a|aSa$
3. $S \rightarrow a|aaS$

Although these three grammars generate the same language, there is a difference in the order in which terminal characters are generated for given strings of the object language. This difference will be illustrated for the string consisting of five a's.

1. $S \rightarrow Saa \rightarrow Saaaa \rightarrow aaaaa$
2. $S \rightarrow aSa \rightarrow aaSaa \rightarrow aaaaa$
3. $S \rightarrow aaS \rightarrow aaaaS \rightarrow aaaaa$

The difference between these three orders of generation can be illustrated by the use of parentheses as follows:

1. $(((a)aa)aa)$
2. $(a(a(a)a)a)$
3. $(aa(aa(a)))$

The groups of characters grouped together by parentheses are sometimes referred to as *phrases*, and the grouping into phrases imposed on strings of a language by a grammar is referred to as *phrase structure*. Different grammars impose a different phrase structure on strings of a given language.

The difference between the three modes of generation can also be illustrated by the tree structures in Fig. A1.1, which are obtained by

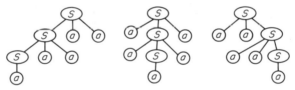

Figure A1.1 Trees representing the derivation of $aaaaa$
in three different grammars.

replacing every production of the form $X \rightarrow U_1U_2 \cdots U_k$ by a *derivation subtree* having X as the root and $U_1U_2 \cdots U_k$ as the terminal vertices. Those U_i which are nonterminals will in turn be the root of a derivation subtree, leading to a multilevel tree.†

The order in which characters of the terminal string are generated is irrelevant as far as defining the set of strings is concerned, but it may become significant when semantics is associated with strings of the language being generated. In particular, it is convenient if the nonterminals associated with partially recognized strings during successive recognition steps correspond to semantically meaningful constructs. The

† Since the generation process for an individual string may be represented by a tree, the grammar as a whole or its syntactic chart may be thought of as a representation of a set of trees, where each tree represents the derivation process of the string determined by the left-to-right sequence of terminal vertices of the tree.

successive sets of strings associated with nonterminals for the above three grammars can be seen both in the parenthesized expressions and in the tree structures. It is evident that grammar 1 assumes that the meaningful constructs are the successive initial substrings a^{2i+1}. Grammar 2 assumes that the meaningful substrings are obtained by working outward from the center. Grammar 3 assumes that the meaningful substrings are successive final substrings of the form a^{2i+1}.

A context-free grammar G determines a set of trees which specifies the syntactic structure of terminal strings of the language $L(G)$. The tree associated with a given terminal string of a grammar G may be thought of as being generated by a sequence of *elementary generation steps* or *derivations*, corresponding to the application of individual productions. If X is one of the terminal vertices of a partially expanded tree, then application of the production $X \to U_1 U_2 \cdots U_k$ corresponds to augmenting the tree with an ordered set of k new vertices labeled $U_1, U_2, \ldots, U_k$ at the vertex.

In generating a given tree from the grammar there is generally a choice of the order in which derivations are applied. In particular the final string of terminals is independent of the order in which nonterminals of a partially expanded string are expanded into terminals. However, a *unique* generating sequence can be associated with any given tree by requiring that for every partially expanded string the *leftmost* nonterminal is always expanded before subsequent nonterminals. This generating sequence is referred to as the *canonical generating sequence* or the *canonical parse* for the given string.

A grammar G is said to be *unambiguous* if it has precisely one canonical generating sequence for every string which it generates. It is said to be *ambiguous* if there is at least one terminal string of the language for which there is more than one canonical generating sequence. A language is said to be *inherently ambiguous* if all context-free grammars generating the language are ambiguous.

The notion of ambiguity is important in syntactic analysis since derivations generally have semantic actions associated with them. If a given terminal string of a language $L(G)$ has two canonical generating sequences, it will be associated with two different sets of semantic actions and will therefore be semantically ambiguous.†

The concept of ambiguity can be characterized more precisely by introducing the concepts of *lexicographic ordering* and *characteristic sequences* for grammars over a given alphabet. A *lexicographic ordering* of the set of all strings T^* over a finite alphabet T is obtained by specify-

---

† Note that even two generation sequences having the same canonical parse may be semantically different if the semantic actions associated with individual generation steps have side effects.

ing an alphabetic ordering for characters of T, ordering sets of strings over T^* by increasing length, and ordering all strings of a given length in dictionary order, using the alphabetic ordering over T.

The *characteristic sequence* determined over T^* by a grammar $G = (N,T,S,P)$ is a sequence of integers $(i_0, i_1 \cdots)$ such that the jth element of the sequence specifies the number of different canonical derivations in the grammar G of the jth word in the lexicographic ordering over T^*. The set of positions in the characteristic sequence of G with nonzero coefficients will be called the *support* of G. The set of positions in the characteristic sequence of G with coefficients greater than 1 will be called the *ambiguity set* of G. An unambiguous language has a characteristic sequence such that no coefficient is greater than 1 and hence an empty ambiguity set.

A number of alternative definitions of the *equivalence* of context-free grammars will now be given. Two context-free grammars G_1, G_2 are said to be *weakly equivalent* if their characteristic sequences have the same support, i.e., if they generate the same language. Two weakly equivalent grammars may differ radically in the way that words of the language are generated and in the number of canonical derivations of words of the language. It is convenient to introduce definitions of the equivalence of grammars which determine an equivalence between derivations and not merely between words of the language.

Two context-free grammars G_1, G_2 are said to be *derivation equivalent* if they have the same characteristic sequences, i.e., if there is a one-to-one correspondence between canonical derivations of the two grammars. Two grammars G_1, G_2 are said to be *equivalent with preservation of ambiguity* if their characteristic sequences have the same ambiguity set, i.e., if the sets of ambiguous words in the two languages are the same.†

Characteristic sequences distinguish between grammars on the basis of the number of alternative canonical derivation sequences of words of the grammar. However, there may be structural differences between derivation-equivalent grammars which make a considerable difference for purposes of recognition but which cannot be distinguished on the basis of characteristic sequences.

Two context-free grammars G_1, G_2 are said to be *structurally equivalent* if they are derivation equivalent and if corresponding labeled trees of G_1 and G_2 are structurally identical.‡ Two context-free grammars are said to be *isomorphic* if they differ merely in the labels used for nonterminals.

† Note that a hierarchy of ambiguity-preserving grammars can be defined such that the kth class of the hierarchy preserves k-fold ambiguity. For practical purposes we are interested principally in preserving the set of words having unique derivations.

‡ Two labeled trees are *structurally identical* if there is a one-to-one correspondence between vertices which preserves successor relations and the left-to-right ordering of successors of a given vertex.

Example: "$S \rightarrow XY, \ X \rightarrow a, \ Y \rightarrow b$" and "$S \rightarrow Xb, \ X \rightarrow a$" are derivation equivalent but not structurally equivalent. "$S \rightarrow XY, \ X \rightarrow a, \ Y \rightarrow a$" and "$S \rightarrow XX, \ X \rightarrow a$" are structurally equivalent but not isomorphic.

A grammar is said to be *nondecreasing* if there are no productions of the form $X \rightarrow \wedge$ where X is a nonterminal and $\wedge$ is the null string. A grammar is said to be *increasing* if all productions are of the form $X \rightarrow U$, where X is a nonterminal and the number of symbols in U is at least 2. A grammar is said to be in *Chomsky normal form* if all productions are of the form $X \rightarrow a$ or $X \rightarrow YZ$, where a is a terminal and X, Y, Z are nonterminals. A grammar is said to be in *Greibach normal form* if all productions are of the form $X \rightarrow a$ or $X \rightarrow aY_1 \cdots Y_m$ where a is a terminal and $X, Y_1, \ldots , Y_m$ are nonterminals.

It can be shown that for any context-free language L, $L - \wedge$ can be generated by a nondecreasing grammar, $L - T - \wedge$ can be generated by an increasing grammar, and $L - \wedge$ can be generated by a Chomsky normal-form grammar or a Greibach normal-form grammar. The normal-form grammars can be chosen to be derivation equivalent but not necessarily structurally equivalent or isomorphic to the original grammars. In particular, a normal-form grammar may result in a number of nonterminals that is greater by an exponential factor from the grammar for that language having the smallest number of nonterminals.

Given a grammar G_1 whose language $L(G_1)$ is smaller by a finite number of strings $\{s_1, s_2, \ldots , s_k\}$ than the language $L(G)$ generated by a grammar G, the language $L(G)$ may be generated by augmenting G_1 by a new nonterminal, say S', and adding the productions "$S' \rightarrow S, S' \rightarrow s_1 \ldots , S' \rightarrow s_k$". The resulting grammar G_1' generates $L(G)$, associates derivation sequences determined by G_1 with strings of $L(G)$ generated by G_1, and associates trivial derivation sequences with the finite set of strings of $L(G)$ not generated by G_1.

The above procedure may be used to augment a grammar generating $L - \wedge$ or $L - T - \wedge$ in a trivial manner so that it generates L.

Although the results above indicate that it is possible to choose the grammar for describing a given context-free language in a wide variety of ways, there is usually a natural grammar for a language, whose generation steps reflect the semantics of the language more adequately than other grammars. The notion of a natural grammar is further illustrated in developing a grammar for arithmetic expressions in the next section.

A1.6   SPECIFICATION OF PRECEDENCE IN FORMAL GRAMMARS

In evaluating expressions that consist of sequences of operands separated by infixed operators, certain operators may take precedence over others for purposes of evaluation. For example, expressions that contain addition and multiplication operators are evaluated by first performing all multiplications in a left-to-right order, leaving a sequence of numbers separated by addition symbols, and then performing all additions in a left-to-right order. This order of evaluation is conveniently reflected in the syntax by specifying a term to be a sequence of factors separated by multiplication signs and an expression to be a sequence of terms separated by addition signs.

A-expression → term|A-expression + term
term → factor|term × factor

These two productions mirror the fact that, in evaluation of arithmetic expressions, the application of multiplication signs to their operands takes precedence over the application of addition signs to their operands.

Note that the above effect could be obtained by the following simpler set of productions:

op → +| ×
A-expression → factor|A-expression op factor

These productions generate the same set of substrings as the previous productions but do not reflect the precedence of multiplication over addition.

The precedence of exponentiation over both multiplication and addition can be reflected in the syntax by adding the following production:

factor → primary|factor ↑ primary

This production specifies a primary as a sequence of factors connected by exponentiation signs. It implies that within a primary, exponentiation signs are applied to their arguments in a left-to-right order. Taken together with previous productions, this production implies that exponentiation takes precedence over multiplication and addition.

In order to complete the specification of an arithmetic expression, the form of a primary must be specified in terms of terminal characters of the language. The following production set specifies the structure of a primary in terms of lower-level constructs but not yet in terms of terminals.

primary → number|variable|(A-expression)

This production set specifies that a primary is either a number or a variable or an arithmetic expression in parentheses. The first two right-hand-side components specify the structure of a primary in terms of lower-level constituents, while the third right-hand-side component implies that evaluation of expressions in parentheses takes precedence even over exponentiation.

Decimal numbers may in general be written in a number of alternative notations and have a relatively complex syntax. However, if we restrict numbers to be unsigned integers, the syntax can be specified as follows:

number → *unsigned-integer*
unsigned-integer → *digit*|*unsigned-integer   digit*
digit → 0|1|2|3|4|5|6|7|8|9

These productions specify the format of a number in terms of digits. The 10 digits 0 to 9 are assumed to be terminals of the language.

A variable can be specified as a letter followed by an arbitrary number of letters or digits.

variable → *letter*|*variable   letter*|*variable   digit*

The form of the nonterminal *digit* has already been specified in terms of its nonterminals. The nonterminal letter can be chosen to be either the set of 26 capital roman letters or the set of 52 capital and small roman letters.

From the point of view of recognition of character strings as programs, a terminal can be thought of as any character or character string that can be directly recognized. When this point of view is adopted, terminals need no longer be restricted to individual characters. The concept of terminal can be extended to denote any class of strings for which a recognition subroutine is available. Thus it is convenient in most programs for scanning, compiling, or interpretively evaluating arithmetic expressions to have recognition subroutines for directly recognizing variables and numbers and effectively treating variables and numbers as terminals of the language.

Using this approach, we can specify a grammar $G = (N,T,S,P)$ for a subclass of arithmetic expressions as follows:

$N = \{$*A-expression, term, factor, primary, number, variable*$\}$
$T = \{+,\times,\uparrow,(,),N,V\}$
$S = $ A-expression

and P is the following set of productions:

A-expression → *term*|*A-expression* + *term*
term → *factor*|*term* × *factor*
factor → *primary*|*factor* ↑ *primary*
primary → *number*|*variable*|(A-expression)
number → N
variable → V

A1.7 THE USE OF GRAMMARS FOR RECOGNITION

A syntactic specification of a language by a context-free grammar is said to be a *generative* specification of a grammar, since it specifies how strings of the language can be generated from the initial symbol S. However, context-free grammars can be used also as a basis for *recognition* of strings in the language. In translating or executing the symbol strings of a given programming language, it is necessary first to *recognize* the symbol strings being scanned, so that the use of grammars for purposes of recognition is far more widespread than their use for generation of program elements.

In order to recognize that a string such as "$a + 3.5 \times b$" belongs to the arithmetic-expression grammar specified above, we must recognize that the lower-level constituents "a" and "b" are instances of variables and that "3.5" is an instance of a number. The subexpression "$3.5 \times b$" must be recognized to be a term having "3.5" and "b" as factors, and the complete expression must be recognized as consisting of the two terms "a" and "$3.5 \times b$" joined by $+$.

Since a given context-free language may, in general, be specified by many alternative context-free grammars, it is important to emphasize that a recognition procedure is not inherently associated with a language but is associated with a specific grammar of the language. Every grammar assigns a structure to strings of the language, which allows substructure to be associated with the substrings. Recognition procedures based on a context-free grammar normally make extensive use of the substructure in order to recognize substrings as being instances of a given substructure. For example, a recognition procedure along the lines of the previous paragraph recognizes substrings to be instances of variables, factors, terms, and subexpressions and builds up the structure which represents the complete expression by recognizing a sequence of successively higher-level substructures.

When developing a syntactic recognition algorithm for a language, the user is free to choose between alternative context-free grammars for specifying the language. The criteria for choosing between alternative grammars include (1) the substructure imposed on strings of the language should group constituents into semantically meaningful groupings and (2) the grammar should be such that, subject to the first condition, recognition is as simple as possible.

Each production $X \rightarrow U$ of a context-free grammar essentially specifies that the string U on the right-hand side is an instance of the substructure specified by the nonterminal X on the left-hand side. Recognition procedures essentially treat strings U appearing on the right-hand side of productions as *templates* (pattern specifications), which are to be matched against substrings of the string that is being recognized in order to determine whether the substring is an instance of the structure on the left-hand side.   Syntactic recognition may be thought of as a specialized form of *sequential pattern matching* by matching a sequence of subpatterns and using matched subpatterns as constituents when matching higher-level patterns.   Once the pattern has been matched, the sequence of actions initiated as a result of pattern matching is referred to as the semantics associated with the syntactic recognition process.†

When using a production"$X \rightarrow U$" to recognize a substring (pattern) U, we say that U is *reduced* to X, refer to "$X \rightarrow U$" as a *reduction*, and sometimes represent it by "$X \leftarrow U$" to indicate the direction of the transformation.   Recognition of a pattern and replacement of the pattern by the name of the class of patterns to which it belongs is similarly referred to as a reduction.

One of the problems of sequential pattern matching along the above lines is that local matching of a template against a substring may turn out to be inconsistent when the context of the matched subpattern is taken into account.   This leads to erroneous matching, which precludes use of the matched constituents for the purpose of matching another template and may require subsequent retraction of a sequence of matched patterns in order to make the constituents of those matched subpatterns available for combination in alternative patterns.   Such retraction of matched patterns is referred to as *backtracking*.

The problem of backtracking has led to the classification of grammars according to the degree of context that must be examined in order to ensure that matching of a given template can never lead to backtracking.   A context-free grammar is said to be of *bounded context* (m,n) if it is always possible to avoid backtracking by examining the m characters preceding the matched string and the n characters following the matched string. However, it can be shown that there are some languages for which there is no (m,n) such that backtracking can always be avoided by examining merely the (m,n) context; i.e., for any given (m,n) there are always strings in the language for which there is more than one local way of matching a template to the string each of which is consistent with m preceding and n

---

† Note that instruction decoding followed by instruction execution is an example of such a twofold process.   So is symbol-table search followed by delivery of the value of the resulting entry.   Any computation can be thought of as consisting of a syntactic recognition phase followed by a semantic transformation phase.   In function terminology the syntactic phase determines the proper element in the domain of the function, while the semantic phase evaluates the function for this argument.   When evaluating numerical functions, determination of the proper element of the domain is assumed to be trivial.   However, when the arguments of the function are objects with a complex structure such as programs, the syntactic phase of the computation becomes nontrivial.

following characters and such that only one of the choices of matching leads to matching of the pattern associated with the complete string. Such a grammar is said to be of unbounded context.

Example: $S \rightarrow a|aSa$ is of unbounded context since for any bounds (m,n) a string a^{2k+1} can be chosen such that $k > m + n$. For this string, there is always an internal symbol such that we cannot tell by examining a context (m,n) whether it is the middle symbol and can be reduced to S or whether reduction must wait until a sequence of reductions starting at the middle symbol has been performed.

Note that any context-free grammar can always be reduced to a grammar of bounded context $(0,0)$ by adding parentheses to the language which explicitly indicate the phrase structure.

Example: $S \rightarrow a|a(S)a$ with $N = \{S\}$ and $T = \{a,(,)\}$ is of bounded context $(0,0)$.

Many actual recognition algorithms scan source-language strings from left to right and reduce a substring to a nonterminal symbol as soon as reduction can be found. Such algorithms run into context problems, just like the previous case, and may require backtracking. However, it may always be assumed that in reducing a given segment of the string all productions to the left have already been applied. The appropriate context to be considered in this case is referred to as a left-to-right (LR) context.

A grammar is said to be an $LR(m,n)$ grammar if when considering a reduction of a substring for which all preceding strings have been reduced, an (m,n) context is sufficient to determine uniquely whether a reduction is to be applied. An $LR(0,n)$ grammar in which the backward context is zero is sometimes referred to as an $LR(0)$ grammar.

Example: $S \rightarrow a|Saa$ is an $LR(n)$ (or $LR(0,0)$) grammar since in a left-to-right recognition process we can tell without looking ahead that an initial substring is to be reduced if and only if it has the form "$Saa \cdots$".

Bounded-context grammars allow recognition algorithms to be developed which do not require backtracking and for which recognition time is therefore a linear function of the length of the string being recognized. However, even when a grammar is of unbounded context, an algorithm which examines a limited amount of context before applying a reduction will greatly reduce the "average" amount of backtracking and thereby speed up the recognition process.

Programming languages having an operator-operand structure can be specified by a subclass of grammars called *operator grammars*. A grammar is said to be an operator grammar if no production has a right-hand side with two adjacent nonterminals; i.e., no production has the form $U \rightarrow xU_1U_2y$, where U, U_1, U_2 are nonterminals and x, y are arbitrary, possibly empty, strings over the terminal and nonterminal alphabets. The arithmetic-expression grammar above is an example of an operator grammar.

Evaluation of expressions with an operator-operand structure is accomplished by the successive application of operations to their operands. In order to capture the semantics of such expressions, recognition should proceed by the successive recognition of phrases corresponding to operators with their operands in the order in which they are evaluated during execution. The order in which operators are applied to their operands is determined in part by parentheses and in part by precedence relations between operators (see Sec. 4.3). When there are precedence relations between operators, as in the case of arithmetic expressions, it is important that the subexpressions which constitute operator-operand combinations be reduced in the order in which they are to be evaluated.

Example: In reducing $a + b \times c$ it is important to reduce $b \times c$ to a term t before reducing $a + t$.

The notion of operator precedence can be formalized by defining a class of context-free grammars called *operator-precedence grammars*. An *operator-precedence grammar* is an operator grammar in which, for every pair of terminals t_1, t_2 which may occur adjacent or separated by a nonterminal in an intermediate derivation, there is a unique precedence relation which determines whether t_1 is part of a phrase (operator-operand combination) which can be reduced prior to reducing t_2, or whether a phrase containing t_2 must be reduced prior to or at the same time as a reduction containing t_1.

Assume that our syntactic recognition process scans the text to be reduced in a left-to-right order and always reduces a phrase as soon as its last character has been scanned. If the grammar is an operator-precedence grammar, we can always determine by looking at the first unscanned terminal whether the portion of the string so far scanned is to be reduced or whether further scanning is required before a reduction can be performed.

The notion of precedence can be defined independently of operator-operand structure by defining precedence relations between arbitrary symbols of a grammar. A grammar is said to be a *pure precedence grammar* if, for every pair of terminal or nonterminal symbols Y_1, Y_2 which may occur adjacent in a partially reduced string, there is a unique precedence relation which specifies whether Y_1 is the last character of a phrase which can be immediately reduced or whether Y_2 must be scanned before a reduction can be performed. Clearly, pure precedence grammars are an example of bounded-context grammars. Moreover, operator-precedence grammars can be reduced to pure precedence grammars by introducing extra nonterminals U' and reductions $U' \leftarrow U$ for transmitting information about the terminal following U' to the terminal which precedes U'.

Example: Let "$I + I \times c$" be an intermediate stage in the reduction of "$a + b \times c$" in which a and b have been reduced to the nonterminal I. In an operator-precedence grammar the decision whether to reduce $I + I$ to a term would be made by comparing the terminals $+$ and $\times$. In a pure precedence grammar only the precedence of adjacent characters may be compared. The precedence relations would be arranged so that $+$ followed by I would require further scanning, I followed by $\times$ would require further scanning, but I followed by $+$ would allow I to be reduced to a nonterminal, say I', having the property that $+$ followed by I' would allow reduction of the phrase $I + I'$ without further scanning. I' effectively serves notice that the operator which follows has a sufficiently low precedence to permit immediate reduction.

The above example indicates how a grammar requiring a context of two symbols can be replaced by a grammar requiring a context of only one symbol by using information-carrying intermediate symbols. This technique can be used to replace grammars requiring any given finite right or left context to grammars requiring a context of only one.

Before leaving the question of recognition we shall briefly consider the question of how recognition algorithms for context-free languages can be implemented. Recognition algorithms can be classified into top-down algorithms which generate strings from the initial symbol in an attempt to match the program string and bottom-up algorithms which perform a sequence of reductions on the program string in an attempt to reduce it to the initial symbol. If grammars are thought of as formal systems with an axiom S, rules of derivation corresponding to productions, and theorems corresponding to terminal strings, then top-down recognition algorithms correspond to theorem proving starting from the axioms, while bottom-up algorithms correspond to theorem proving by working backward from the theorem to be proved.

Both top-down algorithms and bottom-up algorithms require a representation of the grammar (formal system) to be stored in the computer. This representation can be a representation of the syntactic chart, a direct or tabular representation of the set of productions, or some other encoded form of the syntax. One of the more interesting forms of representation is by means of a matrix of zeros and ones with one row for each terminal and each nonterminal of the system and a set of n_i

columns for each production with n_i symbols on its right-hand side and $n_i \geq 2$. The entry in position (j,k) of the submatrix corresponding to the ith production is a 1 if the jth symbol of the grammar occurs as the kth symbol of the production or may be reached by a chain of productions of length 1 from the kth symbol.

Any recognition algorithm for context-free languages both requires an initial representation of the grammar and generates a number of information structures during execution, which keep track of partially recognized strings and other intermediate-level information required by the recognition algorithm. In left-to-right scanning algorithms it is usually convenient to store successively scanned characters in a stack. When algorithms are guaranteed not to require backtracking, recognition of a phrase results in erasing the group of characters which constitutes the phrase, replacing by the nonterminal which names the phrase, and generating of some semantic output. When algorithms may require backtracking, the group of characters which constitutes the phrase must not be erased. The nonterminal which constitutes the tentative phrase structure can be placed in the stack on top of the characters which constitute the phrase, with a pointer to the predecessor symbol in the interior of the stack.

Both top-down and bottom-up algorithms start by matching subpatterns of the string to be recognized and build up successively larger subpatterns until the string is completely matched. Bounded-context and precedence grammars guarantee that any subpattern (phrase) which can be constructed is a valid component of the final pattern, while general context-free grammars may require backtracking. Bounded-context techniques for checking that a reduction is consistent with the context in which it occurs may be used even when the grammar is not guaranteed to be bounded context. Such context checking may drastically reduce and in many instances eliminate backtracking, although provision for the possibility of backtracking is still required.

One convenient technique for keeping track of the compatibility of most recently scanned characters with a production of length n_i is by an n_i-bit vector in which the kth bit keeps track whether the k top symbols in the scanned-character stack are compatible with the given production.† Let the kth bit of such a vector be a 1 if the top k symbols in the stack are a possible initial k symbols of the right-hand side of production. Then updating of this information when scanning a new character can be performed by a simple one-place shift followed by a logical *and* operation with a vector of length n_i for the scanned character. The most recently scanned n_i characters will be compatible with the

† Note that the symbols in the scanned character stack may include both terminals and nonterminals which have been constructed from groups of terminals.

production of length n_i if a 1 appears in the n_ith position of the vector, and a reduction may in this case be performed. When this method is used in practice, the set of vectors for individual productions may be combined into a single vector of length Σn_i, and the logical operations required for pattern matching may be performed in parallel for all productions. The most convenient representation for the grammar in this case is the incidence-matrix representation, since each row of the incidence matrix specifies for a given character precisely the set of positions of all possible productions with which the symbol associated with that row is compatible.

The above approach to recognition, which is due to Domolki, and is not presently available in published form has been used to illustrate the flavor of recognition processes. Examples of specific syntactic recognition algorithms can be found in the literature.

Bounded-context grammars, operator-precedence grammars, and pure precedence grammars are examples of subclasses of context-free grammars for which recognition can be performed in a time that is a *linear* function of the length of the input string. For general context-free grammars, the recognition time for a string of length n can be shown to be of the order of n^3, provided an amount of space proportional to n^2 is available for storing intermediate results.† The minimum storage requirement to parse a string of length n is $(\log n)^2$ [23]. When space requirements are minimized, the time required to recognize a string of length n increases exponentially with n.

Backtracking may be drastically reduced by doing extra context checking at each recognition step and may be altogether eliminated by keeping track of all alternatives in parallel, provided there is enough space. The space and time trade-offs in alternative techniques of syntactic analysis provide an interesting topic for further investigation.

A1.8 SYNTAX-DIRECTED RECOGNITION, COMPILATION, AND EVALUATION

Early programming languages were specified in an ad hoc fashion without the use of a formal grammar, and early recognition techniques involved a sequence of ad hoc rules for recognition of the structure of a program.

---

† The proof of this result is due to Younger [21] and runs along the following lines: Using a bottom-up technique we can successively generate all possible nonterminals for generating terminal strings of length k for $k = 1, 2, \ldots, n$. Since there are k possible ways of combining strings of length less than k to form a string of length k, the time required to compute the set of nonterminals for generating a string of length k from the sets of symbols for generating strings of length less than k is proportional to k. Hence the total computational time is of the order $\sum_{i=1}^{n} k(n-k) \sim n^3$. The total space required in this algorithm is of the order of n^2, since the sets of nonterminals associated with a maximum of $n(n-1)/2$ tree nodes may have to be stored simultaneously.

When the set of strings of a language is specified by a formal grammar, a systematic recognition procedure can be developed which makes direct use of the syntactic specification.   Such a recognition technique is called a *syntactic* recognition technique.

In the case of context-free grammars, we can go even further and specify an algorithm f which, given a context-free grammar G as its data, is converted into an algorithm f_G for recognition of strings of the language $L(G)$.   Such an algorithm f is called a *syntax-directed recognizer*, since the language which it recognizes on any particular occasion is determined by the syntax with which it is primed.   The operation of a syntax-directed recognizer is illustrated in Fig. A1.2.

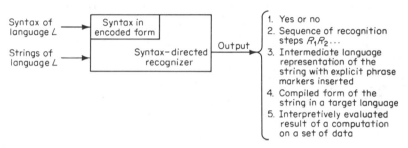

Figure A1.2   A syntax-directed compiler.

Although syntactic recognition algorithms are a fascinating subject of study in their own right, they are of interest to programmers principally because of their usefulness as a first step in the transformation of the strings being recognized.   Recognition of strings prior to their transformation is necessary both during compilation of source-language strings into a target and during interpretive execution of strings of a given language.

In Fig. A1.2 five alternative forms of output from a syntax-directed recognizer are listed.   The simplest form of output is merely "yes" if the string being recognized is in the language and "no" if it is not.   However, if the string is to be used to determine a transformation, some additional information automatically generated by the recognition process is normally provided.   This information may include a specification of the sequence of recognition steps and/or an intermediate-language representation of the string in which explicit markers have been inserted to delimit syntactic groupings so as to make subsequent recognition easier.

If the successive recognition steps recognize semantically meaningful substructures in the order in which they are to be "executed," the recognition process can be directly combined with a transformation process, and each recognition step can trigger a corresponding transformation step, which, in the case of compilation results in symbol-table or output-code generation and in the case of interpretive execution results in an execution step.

The action performed by a syntax-directed recognizer when a syntactic recognition (reduction) step is performed is referred to as a *semantic action*. A syntax-directed recognizer may be thought of as having an associated semantics which is specified by actions taken when successive recognition steps are performed.†

The semantics of a syntax-directed recognizer can be specified by a symbol table containing one entry for each production (reduction). Each entry specifies a semantic action to be taken when that particular production is used as a recognition step. Syntax-directed recognition may be formulated as a process of symbol-table look-up in a symbol table whose first components are templates rather than simple names, as indicated in Sec. 3.4.

Any computation may be thought of as a process which involves a sequence of recognition steps that identify successive operations to be executed, and a set of semantic actions associated with each recognition step. For example, the LISP evaluator and the SECD machine in Sec. 3.9 are organized in precisely this way.

Syntactic recognition techniques have been exploited most extensively in connection with compilation. When syntactic recognition techniques are used for purposes of compilation, the associated semantics specifies generation of output code for executable program segments and symbol-table manipulation for declarative program segments.

The semantics associated with a recognition algorithm for a given grammar G can in principle be changed merely by changing second components of the semantic-action symbol-table. A complete syntax-directed transformation algorithm can be thought of as a function f which must be supplied with a syntactic specification G for recognizing strings of the language and a semantic specification M for determining semantic action for each recognition step. Input of the syntactic and semantic specifications (G,M) transforms the function f into a function $f_{(G,M)}$ for recognition of strings of the grammar G and their transformation according to M.

A syntax-directed transformation program (see Fig. A1.3) is in many respects similar to a macro generator. It contains an initial environment having some system facilities and some powerful macro-

---

† Note that in Fig. A1.2 five alternative semantic models have been suggested to go with a single syntactic recognition algorithm, emphasizing that it is meaningless to talk about the semantics of a language without specifying the context in which it is used.

definition facilities.   The macro-definition facilities allow the specification of the syntactic forms of a language as macro templates and a
specification of the action associated with each of the syntactic forms as
macro bodies.   The nonterminals of a syntactic definition constitute
formal parameters of the definition for which terminal strings of the type
specified by the formal parameter may be substituted, just as in the case
of syntax macros in Sec. 3.4.   The differences between syntax-directed
systems are largely differences in the style of macto-template specification, parameter specification, and macro-body specification.

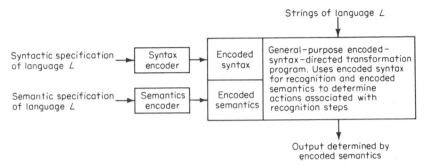

Figure A1.3   A general-purpose syntax-directed transformation program.

Examples: The production $X \to aXbYc$ may be thought of as a macro
specification with a distributed name "$a - b - c$" and two parameters
X, Y which, on substitution, are restricted to be of the syntactic form
specified by X and Y.   In the system of Brooker and Morris [4], the
format of a statement might be specified by the formal specification
"FORMAT[SS] = ⟨variable⟩ = ⟨expression⟩".   This format specification
is essentially a macro-template specification of a macro with a fixed component = preceeded by a parameter of the syntactic type ⟨variable⟩ and
followed by a parameter of the syntactic type ⟨expression⟩.

In early macro systems there were restrictions on the form of macro
templates, macro bodies and parameter types.   These restrictions have
been greatly relaxed in the macro facilities available in syntax-directed
processors.   There is also greater flexibility in the control mechanism
that governs the order in which sequences of macros are to be expanded.
Whereas early macro systems required explicit macro calls to operate on
disjoint, sequential segments of text, syntax-directed macro calls allow
the segments of text transformed by macro calls to be nested.

Sequential matching of macros may be compared to execution of a
sequence of instructions whose operation codes and explicit arguments
are specified by disjoint information fields.   Nested matching of macros

corresponds to replacement of an executed instruction by a value and use of this value as an explicit parameter of a subsequently executed instruction.

Execution of a macro by a syntax-directed processor has the side effect of fixing the local phrase structure of the matched macro template and does not allow the possibility of matching an alternative local phrase structure. In general there may be a number of alternative ways of local matching of lower-level subpatterns, only one of which is compatible with matching at a higher level. In some grammars (precedence and bounded-context grammars), uniqueness of local matching can be established by examining only a limited context in the neighborhood of the matched string. However, there are unambiguous grammars for which no finite amount of context is sufficient to determine uniquely the local phrase structure. In this case backtracking or carrying along of alternatives in parallel may be employed.

The semantics associated with the syntactic forms specified by macro templates depends on the purposes for which the syntax-directed processor is to be used. If the processor is to be used only for recognition, the macro bodies which specify the semantics are required merely to keep track of the point reached in the recognition process. If the processor is to be used primarily for translation, then the macro bodies must include facilities for defining information structures occurring in the target language and for keeping track of name-value correspondences and bound variables by means of symbol tables. If the processor is to be used for syntax-directed execution, then macro bodies must include arithmetic and other transformation facilities.

It is evident that a macro facility is essentially a *definitional facility* for enriching the environment of the program being executed by meaningful syntactic constructs. All higher-level languages have a limited number of definitional facilities for defining procedures, data structures, or macros. In syntax-directed processors we define the complete language rather than merely building additional definitional facilities onto an existing language. However, the definitional facilities in syntax-directed processors can clearly be used to augment the syntactic constructs of a language already defined within the system as well as to define a complete language.

Although definitional facilities for environment modification seem very natural when viewed as macros, there has been a tendency to think of definitional facilities as meta-facilities to be distinguished from ordinary computational facilities in much the same sense that meta-languages for language specification are distinguished from the languages which they specify. As a result, macro systems for syntactic specification and syntax-directed processing are sometimes referred to as *meta-assemblers*.

Further discussion of the relation between syntax-directed processors and meta-assemblers can be found in the paper by Feldman and Gries [19].

Further information regarding specific syntax-directed transformation programs can be obtained by reading the papers listed in Sec. A1.10.

A1.9 HISTORICAL NOTES ON SYNTACTIC ANALYSIS

The formalism for context-free languages developed above was first introduced by Chomsky in 1956.   A good expository account of context-free languages by Chomsky, which contains bibliographical references to earlier work, is given in [1].†   The formalism of context-free languages was first systematically applied to programming languages in the description of the programming language ALGOL 60.   The first ALGOL report appeared in May 1960.   A second version of this report, which removed minor inconsistencies of the first, was published in 1963 in [2].   The formal specification of ALGOL contained in [2] is given in Appendix 2 but with a different verbal commentary from that in [2].

The first computer programs for the syntactic analysis of programming languages were developed in 1960 and 1961 by Irons [3] and Brooker and Morris [4].   The concept of a reductive grammar was introduced at about this time by Floyd [5], who went on to develop the concept of a precedence grammar [6] and of bounded-context grammar [7].   A similar concept was also developed by Irons [8].   It should be noted that the use of precedence matrices and precedence functions for language recognition was first introduced in a nonsyntactic context by Bauer and Samelson in [9].   Perlis claims that this concept originated even earlier in the United States and was in fact introduced to Europe by Sir Walter Raleigh along with the potato.‡

The special case of context for left-to-right translatable languages was examined by Knuth [10].

On the practical side, one of the first operational algorithms for syntactic compilation was that of Cheatham and Sattley [11], who worked in the same consulting company as Floyd.   The discussion of the comparative efficiency of a number of different syntactic analysis methods by Griffiths and Petrick [12] should be brought to the attention of the reader.   The systematic association of semantics with production and with reduction steps was discussed in the early papers by Irons [3],

---

† The first known published systematic application of syntactic techniques to the study of languages occurred in the sixth century B.C. with the publication of the Ashtadhyayi of Panini [18].   This text specifies a grammar for Sanskrit in a manner that has many similarities with the techniques used to specify context-free grammars.

‡ Remark made during presentation of a paper at the Compiler Symposium, Washington, D.C., November, 1960.

Brooker and Morris [4], and Floyd [5]. The two papers by Wirth and Weber [13] systematically develop the concept of pure precedence grammars, introduce the concept of semantics associated with syntax in a semiformal manner, and also give a worked example for a larger and more realistic language fragment than is available elsewhere in the literature. A syntactic-analysis scheme for ALGOL with some error-recovery facilities was developed by Evans [14] at the Carnegie Institute of Technology. Feldman [15] developed a formal semantic language for associating actions with successive recognition steps. This work preceded the work of Wirth and Weber but is not so accessible. A different notation for syntactic specification by labeled ordered recognition rules is developed by McLure [16]. An alternative programming system and notation for syntactic analysis and semantic specification is described by Reynolds [17].

A recent report by Feldman and Gries [19] surveys the field of syntactic analysis. Many of the above papers have been collected in [20]. The formal and mathematical aspects of language theory are discussed by Ginsburg [22], and Hopcroft and Ullman [23].

A1.10 ANNOTATED BIBLIOGRAPHY ON SYNTACTIC ANALYSIS

1. Chomsky, N.: Formal Properties of Grammars, in Luce et al. (eds.): "Handbook of Mathematical Psychology," John Wiley & Sons, Inc., New York, 1962. An excellent review paper both of Chomsky's early work in this field and of other early work. Contains a good bibliography. See also two companion chapters in this volume written jointly with G. A. Miller.

2. Naur, P. (ed.): Revised ALGOL Report, *Commun. ACM*, January, 1963. A revision of the first systematic application of context-free languages to the description of actual programming languages. The publication of this report in April–May, 1960, marked a great step forward in understanding the structure of actual programming languages.

3. Irons, E. T.: A Syntax Directed Compiler for ALGOL 60, *Commun. ACM*, January, 1961. The first paper on syntactic compilation, this discusses both a top-down implementation of a syntactic compiler and the way in which semantics might be associated with generation steps of the syntactic compiler.

4. Brooker, R. A., and D. Morris: "A General Translation Program for Phrase Structure Grammars," *JACM*, January, 1962. This paper summarizes the design and machine-oriented characteristics of a syntax-directed compiler, indicating both syntactic and semantic features of the compiler.

5. Floyd, R. W.: A Descriptive Language for Symbol Manipulation, *JACM*, October, 1961.   The first discussion of reductive grammars, the association of semantics with syntactic recognition steps is directly illustrated.

6. Floyd, R. W.: Syntactic Analysis and Operator Precedence, *JACM*, July, 1963.   This paper defines the notion of an operator grammar, a precedence grammar, precedence matrices, precedence functions, and a number of other concepts.   Examples of precedence grammars and nonprecedence grammars are given.   Floyd's "precedence grammars" are here called "operator precedence grammars."

7. Floyd, R. W.: Bounded Context Syntactic Analysis, *Commun. ACM*, February, 1964.   This paper introduces the basic concepts of bounded-context grammars and gives a set of conditions for testing whether a given grammar is bounded-context (m,n).

8. Irons, E. T.: Structural Connections in Formal Languages, *Commun. ACM*, February, 1964.   The concept of structural connectedness defined in this paper is essentially the same as the concept of bounded context defined in [7].   The author refers to the dependence of local phrase structure on the surrounding context as a *structural connection* between the given phrase and the surrounding grammar.   This approach yields a "geometrical" insight into the phrase configurations which result from bounded-context grammars.

9. Bauer, F. L., and K. Samelson: Sequential Formula Translation, *Commun. ACM*, February, 1960.   The first systematic paper on the translation of programming languages from left to right using precedence techniques.   However, this paper was written before the concept of using the syntactic specification of a language as the basis of compilation had become known.

10. Knuth, D. E.: On the Translation of Languages from Left to Right, *Inform. Control*, December, 1965.   The concept of a grammar which permits translation from left to right with forward context k($LR(k)$ grammar) is developed and analyzed.

11. Cheatham, T., and K. Sattley: Syntax Directed Compiling, *Proc. Spring Joint Computer Conf.*, 1964.   A description of one of the earliest operational top-down syntax-directed compilers.

12. Griffiths, and S. Petrick: On the Relative Efficiencies of Context Free Grammar Precognizers, *Commun. ACM*, May, 1965.   A comparative discussion of syntactic compilation techniques.

13. Wirth, N., and H. Weber: A Generalization of ALGOL and Its Formal Definition, I, II, *Commun. ACM*, January and February, 1966. The first discussion of pure precedence grammars and of their use in the recognition of ALGOL-like languages. Many of the concepts introduced by previous authors are discussed in an illuminating way.

14. Evans, A.: An ALGOL 60 Compiler, *ACM Natl. Conf., Denver*, 1962. The first application of a reductive syntax with labeled productions and error-recovery rules to the design of a compiler.

15. Feldman, J. A.: A Formal Semantics for Compiler Languages and Its Application in a Compiler Compiler, *Commun. ACM*, January, 1966. A description of a formal semantic language which can be used in conjunction with a language for describing syntax to specify a syntax-directed compiler.

16. McLure, R. M.: TMG—A Syntax Directed Compiler, *Proc. 20th ACM Conf.*, 1965. A description of a compiler in which the syntax is specified by an ordered sequence of labeled productions and in which semantics can be explicitly associated with productions.

17. Reynolds, J. C.: Cogent Programming Manual, *Argonne Natl. Lab. Rept. AN1-7022*. A description of a programming system for syntactic analysis and compilation.

18. Vasu, S. C. (ed.): "The Ashtadhyayi of Panini," 2 vols, Motilal Banarsidass, Delhi, 1962. A grammar of Sanskrit, originally published in 600 B.C., whose rules are similar in form to context-free grammars.

19. Feldman, J. A., and D. Gries: Translator Writing Systems, *Stanford Univ. Computer Sci. Dept. Tech. Rept.* 69, June, 1967. A survey in depth of syntactic-analysis techniques, with an extensive bibliography.

20. Rosen, S. (ed.): "Programming Systems and Languages," McGraw-Hill Book Company, New York, 1967. A well-chosen collection of many of the better papers in the field of programming languages and programming systems.

21. Younger, D. H.: Recognition and Parsing of Context Free Grammars in Time N^3, *Information and Control*, February, 1967. This paper describes an algorithm for determining in time N^3 whether a string s is accepted by a grammar G, provided a memory of the order N^2 is available.

22. Ginsburg, S.: "The Mathematical Theory of Context Free Languages," McGraw-Hill Book Company, New York, 1966. A formal presentation of the basic concepts and theorems in context-free languages.

23. Hopcroft, J. E., and J. D. Ullman: "Formal Languages and Their Relation to Automata," Addison-Wesley Press, Inc., Cambridge, Mass., to be published. Presents the basic concepts and theorems of automata theory, formal languages, and computability.

APPENDIX 2

THE SYNTAX OF ALGOL 60

A2.1 BASIC SYMBOLS AND CHARACTER CLASSES

Grammars were first extensively used in the definition of programming languages in defining ALGOL 60 (see Ref. 2 of Chap. 4). The present section will develop the syntactic structure of ALGOL 60 using the style of syntactic definition of the ALGOL report.

The notation to be used in describing the grammar of ALGOL 60 is a slight variant of that of Appendix 1. The grammar G to be described consists of four components $G = (N,T,S,P)$ just as in Appendix 1, but the nonterminal characters will be distinguished from terminal strings by enclosing them in special angle brackets. For example, the nonterminals "letter" and "digit" will be respectively denoted by ⟨letter⟩ and ⟨digit⟩.

The production format differs from that of Appendix 1 in that the symbol $\rightarrow$ is replaced by the somewhat more cumbersome symbol $::=$. For example the production "digit $\rightarrow$ 0" is written as "⟨digit⟩ $::=$ 0".

The terminals of ALGOL 60 include alphabetic and numeric characters, operator characters, and also a number of composite symbol strings such as **for, begin, end,** etc. Composite terminals have exactly the same status as terminals consisting of single characters. They are represented by strings of characters in boldface type for mnemonic purposes but are to be thought of as single characters.

There are 116 terminal characters in the grammar for ALGOL. These 116 characters can be grouped into character classes by the following productions:

1. ⟨letter⟩ $::=$ a|b|c|d|e|f|g|h|i|j|k|l|m|n|o|p|q|r|s|t|u|v|w|x|y|z|A|B| C|D|E|F|G|H|I|J|K|L|M|N|O|P|Q|R|S|T|U|V|W| X|Y|Z
2. ⟨digit⟩ $::=$ 0|1|2|3|4|5|6|7|8|9
3. ⟨logical value⟩ $::=$ **true**|**false**
4. ⟨delimiter⟩ $::=$ ⟨operator⟩|⟨separator⟩|⟨bracket⟩|⟨declarator⟩| ⟨specificator⟩

5. ⟨operator⟩ ::= ⟨arithmetic operator⟩|⟨relational operator⟩|
   ⟨logical operator⟩|⟨sequential operator⟩

6. ⟨arithmetic operator⟩ ::= +|−|×|/|÷|↑

7. ⟨relational operator⟩ ::= <|≦|=|≠|≧|>

8. ⟨logical operator⟩ ::= ≡|⊃|∨|∧|¬

9. ⟨sequential operator⟩ ::= **go to**|**if**|**then**|**else**|**for**|**do**

10. ⟨separator⟩ ::= ,|.|$_{10}$|:|;|:= |"blank"|**step**|**until**|**while**|**comment**

11. ⟨bracket⟩ ::= (|) | [|] | ' | ' | **begin**|**end**

12. ⟨declarator⟩ ::= **own**|**Boolean**|**integer**|**real**|**array** |**switch**|
    procedure

13. ⟨specificator⟩ ::= **string**|**label**|**value**

Thus the 116 ALGOL terminal characters consist of 52 letters, 10 digits, 2 logical values, 6 arithmetic operators, 6 relational operators, 5 logical operators, 6 sequential operators, 11 separators, 8 brackets, 7 declarators, and 3 specificators.

In many implementations it is impractical to distinguish between capital and small letters, so that the number of letter terminals is reduced to 26.

Arithmetic operators have both numerical arguments and numerical values; relational operators have numerical arguments and logical values; Boolean operators have logical arguments and values; and sequential operators are operators which determine sequencing and may be thought of as having labels as their values.

Separators are effectively punctuation symbols.

ALGOL permits four kinds of brackets. Parentheses are used for parenthesizing functions and expressions, brackets are used as parentheses for array subscripts, single quotation marks are used as parentheses for literal strings, and the parentheses **begin end** are used to delimit program segments.

Declarators are used to define the type of ALGOL names. Specificators are similar in function to special kinds of declarations.

Having defined the set of terminals and grouped them into character classes, we shall next define the structure of numbers and then go on to define higher-level structures of the language.

A2.2 NUMBERS AND STRINGS

An integer can be defined in terms of the character class ⟨digit⟩ as follows:

14. ⟨unsigned integer⟩ ::= ⟨digit⟩|⟨unsigned integer⟩⟨digit⟩

15. ⟨integer⟩ ::= ⟨unsigned integer⟩| + ⟨unsigned integer⟩| −
    ⟨unsigned integer⟩

A number may be either an integer, a decimal number consisting of two unsigned integer components separated by a period, or a decimal number followed by an exponent and optionally preceded by a sign.

16.   ⟨decimal fraction⟩   ::= .⟨unsigned integer⟩
17.   ⟨exponent part⟩   ::= $_{10}$⟨integer⟩
18.   ⟨decimal number⟩   ::= ⟨unsigned integer⟩|⟨decimal fraction⟩|
      ⟨unsigned integer⟩⟨decimal fraction⟩
19.   ⟨unsigned number⟩ ::= ⟨decimal number⟩⟨exponent part⟩|
      ⟨decimal number⟩|⟨exponent part⟩
20.   ⟨number⟩   ::= ⟨unsigned number⟩| + ⟨unsigned number⟩| − ⟨unsigned number⟩

Following the ALGOL report, the format of strings will now be defined. ALGOL has no facilities for manipulating strings other than by defining string-manipulation procedures whose body is coded in some other language (see production 10).

21.   ⟨proper string⟩ ::= ⟨any sequence of basic symbols not containing string quotes⟩|⟨empty⟩†
22.   ⟨open string⟩   ::= ⟨proper string⟩|'⟨open string⟩'|⟨open string⟩⟨open string⟩
23.   ⟨string⟩   ::= '⟨open string⟩'

That is, a string is any sequence of characters with matching quotes which is surrounded by an outer layer of quotes.

Objects in ALGOL are named by identifiers, which consist of a letter followed by an arbitrary number of letters or digits.

24.   ⟨identifier⟩ ::= ⟨letter⟩|⟨identifier⟩ ⟨letter⟩|⟨identifier⟩ ⟨digit⟩

A2.3 VARIABLES

Variables in ALGOL may be either simple, consisting of an identifier, or subscripted, consisting of an identifier followed by a subscript list in brackets.

25.   ⟨variable identifier⟩   ::= ⟨identifier⟩
26.   ⟨simple variable⟩   ::= ⟨variable identifier⟩
27.   ⟨subscript expression⟩ ::= ⟨arithmetic expression⟩
28.   ⟨subscript list⟩   ::= ⟨subscript expression⟩|⟨subscript list⟩,⟨subscript expression⟩
29.   ⟨array identifier⟩   ::= ⟨identifier⟩

† ⟨empty⟩ is a nonterminal which expands into the null string.

30. ⟨subscripted variable⟩ ::= ⟨array identifier⟩[⟨subscript list⟩]
31. ⟨variable⟩   ::= ⟨simple variable⟩|⟨subscripted variable⟩

A2.4 FUNCTION CALLS

Function calls in ALGOL may occur in expressions in any position that a variable occurs.   Function calls consist of a procedure identifier followed by a list of actual parameters in parentheses and separated by commas. Function calls are referred to as *function designators*.   Productions 34 and 35 allow comments to be interspersed with actual parameters.

32. ⟨procedure identifier⟩   ::= ⟨identifier⟩
33. ⟨actual parameter⟩   ::= ⟨string⟩|⟨expression⟩|⟨array identifier⟩|⟨switch identifier⟩|⟨procedure identifier⟩
34. ⟨letter string⟩   ::= ⟨letter⟩|⟨letter string⟩ ⟨letter⟩
35. ⟨parameter delimiter⟩   ::= ,|)⟨letter string⟩:(
36. ⟨actual-parameter list⟩   ::= ⟨actual parameter⟩|⟨actual-parameter list⟩ ⟨parameter delimiter⟩ ⟨actual parameter⟩
37. ⟨actual-parameter part⟩ ::= ⟨empty⟩|(⟨actual-parameter list⟩)
38. ⟨function designator⟩   ::= ⟨procedure identifier⟩ ⟨actual-parameter part⟩

Another class of strings that may appear in place of variables in expressions is the class of library functions.   Library functions normally include sin, cos, ln, exp and other standard functions.

A2.5 EXPRESSIONS

Expressions in ALGOL may be arithmetic, Boolean, or designational (label-valued).   The syntax of arithmetic and Boolean expressions reflects the fact that they contain operators having different precedence and that operators of given precedence are always applied to operands in a left-to-right order.

39. ⟨expression⟩ ::= ⟨arithmetic expression⟩|⟨Boolean expression⟩|⟨designational expression⟩

Arithmetic expressions may contain the six arithmetic operators $+ - \times / \div \uparrow$, where / is regular division, $\div$ yields an integer result by translation, and $\uparrow$ is exponentiation.   The definition of arithmetic expressions below permits conditional as well as unconditional arithmetic expressions.

40.   ⟨adding operator⟩ ::= $+|-$
41.   ⟨multiplying operator⟩ ::= $\times|/|\div$
42.   ⟨primary⟩ ::= ⟨unsigned number⟩|⟨variable⟩|⟨function designator⟩|(⟨arithmetic expression⟩)
43.   ⟨factor⟩ ::= ⟨primary⟩|⟨factor⟩ ↑ ⟨primary⟩
44.   ⟨term⟩ ::= ⟨factor⟩|⟨term⟩ ⟨multiplying operator⟩ ⟨factor⟩
45.   ⟨simple arithmetic expression⟩ ::= ⟨term⟩|⟨adding operator⟩ ⟨term⟩|⟨simple arithmetic expression⟩⟨adding operator⟩ ⟨term⟩
46.   ⟨if clause⟩ ::= **if** ⟨Boolean expression⟩ **then**
47.   ⟨arithmetic expression⟩ ::= ⟨simple arithmetic expression⟩|⟨if clause⟩ ⟨simple arithmetic expression⟩ **else** ⟨arithmetic expression⟩

Boolean expressions may contain both logical operators and relational operators which have arithmetic arguments and logical values. The arguments of relational operators may in turn contain arithmetic operators. In an expression which contains arithmetic, relational, and logical operators such as $A + B > C \wedge D$, arithmetic operators take precedence over relational operators, and relational operators take precedence over logical operators, so that the above expression is implicitly parenthesized as $((A + B) > C) \wedge D)$.

Each of the logical operators is in a precedence class of its own, the order or precedence being $\neg \wedge \vee \supset \equiv$. Thus the expression $A \equiv B \supset C \vee D \wedge \neg E$ is implicitly parenthesized as $(A \equiv (B \supset (C \vee (D \wedge (\neg E)))))$. This order of precedence is reflected in the following syntax for Boolean expressions:

48.   ⟨relation⟩ ::= ⟨simple arithmetic expression⟩ ⟨relational operator⟩ ⟨simple arithmetic expression⟩
49.   ⟨Boolean primary⟩ ::= ⟨logical value⟩|⟨variable⟩|(⟨function designator⟩|⟨relation⟩|(⟨Boolean expression⟩)
50.   ⟨Boolean secondary⟩ ::= ⟨Boolean primary⟩| $\neg$ ⟨Boolean primary⟩
51.   ⟨Boolean factor⟩ ::= ⟨Boolean secondary⟩|⟨Boolean factor⟩ $\wedge$ ⟨Boolean secondary⟩
52.   ⟨Boolean term⟩ ::= ⟨Boolean factor⟩|⟨Boolean term⟩ $\vee$ ⟨Boolean factor⟩
53.   ⟨implication⟩ ::= ⟨Boolean term⟩|⟨implication⟩ $\supset$ ⟨Boolean term⟩

54. ⟨simple Boolean⟩ ::= ⟨implication⟩|⟨simple Boolean⟩ ≡
⟨implication⟩
55. ⟨Boolean expression⟩ ::= ⟨simple Boolean⟩|⟨if clause⟩
⟨simple Boolean⟩ **else**
⟨Boolean expression⟩

In addition to arithmetic expressions and Boolean expressions ALGOL permits label-valued expressions, referred to as *designational expressions*. Since there are no infixed designational operators, the structure of designational expressions is simpler than that of arithmetic or Boolean expressions. However, label-valued arrays (switches) and conditional designational expressions are permitted.

56. ⟨label⟩ ::= ⟨identifier⟩|⟨unsigned integer⟩
57. ⟨switch identifier⟩ ::= ⟨identifier⟩
58. ⟨switch designator⟩ ::= ⟨switch identifier⟩ [⟨subscript
expression⟩]
59. ⟨simple designational expression⟩ ::= ⟨label⟩|⟨switch
designator⟩|(⟨designa-
tional expression⟩)
60. ⟨designational expression⟩ ::= ⟨simple designational expression⟩|
⟨if clause⟩ ⟨simple designational
expression⟩ **else** ⟨designational
expression⟩

The above syntax indicates the format of the basic forms of expressions in ALGOL. We shall next consider the basic types of statements permitted in ALGOL.

A2.6 STATEMENTS

The principal statement forms of ALGOL are the assignment statement, go to statement, dummy statement, procedure statement, for statement, conditional statement, compound statement, and block. A complete ALGOL program in turn consists of a single block. The syntax of statements is as follows:

61. ⟨unlabeled basic statement⟩ ::= ⟨assignment statement⟩|⟨go to
statement⟩|⟨dummy state-
ment⟩|⟨procedure statement⟩
62. ⟨basic statement⟩ ::= ⟨unlabeled basic statement⟩|⟨label⟩:
⟨basic statement⟩
63. ⟨unconditional statement⟩ ::= ⟨basic statement⟩|⟨compound
statement⟩|⟨block⟩

64. ⟨statement⟩ : : = ⟨unconditional statement⟩|⟨conditional statement⟩|⟨for statement⟩
65. ⟨compound tail⟩ : : = ⟨statement⟩ **end**|⟨statement⟩; ⟨compound tail⟩
66. ⟨blockhead⟩ : : = **begin** ⟨declaration⟩|⟨blockhead⟩;⟨declaration⟩
67. ⟨unlabeled compound⟩ : : = **begin** ⟨compound tail⟩
68. ⟨unlabeled block⟩ : : = ⟨blockhead⟩;⟨compound tail⟩
69. ⟨compound statement⟩ : : = ⟨unlabeled compound⟩|⟨label⟩: ⟨compound statement⟩
70. ⟨block⟩ : : = ⟨unlabeled block⟩|⟨label⟩:⟨block⟩
71. ⟨program⟩ : : = ⟨block⟩|⟨compound statement⟩

Assignment statements have the following form.

72. ⟨left part⟩ : : = ⟨variable⟩ := |⟨procedure identifier⟩ :=
73. ⟨left-part list⟩ : : = ⟨left part⟩|⟨left-part list⟩ ⟨left part⟩
74. ⟨assignment statement⟩ : : = ⟨left-part list⟩ ⟨arithmetic expression⟩|⟨left-part list⟩ ⟨Boolean expression⟩

Go to statements have the form

75. ⟨go to statement⟩ : : = **go to** ⟨designational expression⟩

Dummy statements have the form

76. ⟨dummy statement⟩ : : = ⟨empty⟩

Conditional statements have the form

77. ⟨if clause⟩ : : − **if** ⟨Boolean expression⟩ **then**
78. ⟨unconditional statement⟩ : : = ⟨basic statement⟩|⟨compound statement⟩|⟨block⟩
79. ⟨if statement⟩ : : = ⟨if clause⟩ ⟨unconditional statement⟩
80. ⟨conditional statement⟩ : : = ⟨if statement⟩|⟨if statement⟩ **else** ⟨statement⟩|⟨if clause⟩ ⟨for statement⟩| ⟨label⟩:⟨conditional statement⟩

For statements have the form

81. ⟨for-list element⟩ : : = ⟨arithmetic expression⟩|⟨arithmetic expression⟩ **step** ⟨arithmetic expression⟩ **until** ⟨arithmetic expression⟩|⟨arithmetic expression⟩ **while** ⟨Boolean expression⟩

82. ⟨for list⟩ ::= ⟨for-list element⟩|⟨for list⟩,⟨for-list element⟩
83. ⟨for clause⟩ ::= **for** ⟨variable⟩ := ⟨for list⟩ **do**
84. ⟨for statement⟩ ::= ⟨for clause⟩ ⟨statement⟩|⟨label⟩:⟨for
      statement⟩

Procedure statements have the form

85. ⟨actual parameter⟩ ::= ⟨string⟩|⟨expression⟩|⟨array identifier⟩|
      ⟨switch identifier⟩|⟨procedure identifier⟩
86. ⟨actual-parameter list⟩ ::= ⟨actual   parameter⟩|⟨actual-param-
      eter list⟩ ⟨parameter delimiter⟩
      ⟨actual parameter⟩
87. ⟨actual-parameter part⟩ ::= ⟨empty⟩|(⟨actual-parameter list⟩)
88. ⟨procedure statement⟩ ::= ⟨procedure identifier⟩ ⟨actual-
      parameter part⟩

A2.7 DECLARATIONS

Declarations occur in blockheads and serve to specify the range of values
and mode of access to identifiers.   Declarations are classified into type
declarations,   array   declarations,   switch   declarations,   and   procedure
declarations.

89. ⟨declaration⟩ ::= ⟨type declaration⟩|⟨array declaration⟩|⟨switch
      declaration⟩|⟨procedure declaration⟩

Type declarations serve to specify the type of real, integer, and
Boolean variables, and have the following form:

90. ⟨type list⟩ ::= ⟨simple variable⟩|⟨simple variable⟩,⟨type list⟩
91. ⟨type⟩ ::= **real**|**integer**|**Boolean**
92. ⟨local or own type⟩ ::= ⟨type⟩|**own** ⟨type⟩
93. ⟨type declaration⟩ ::= ⟨local or own type⟩ ⟨type list⟩

Array declarations have the following form:

94. ⟨lower bound⟩ ::= ⟨arithmetic expression⟩
95. ⟨upper bound⟩ ::= ⟨arithmetic expression⟩
96. ⟨bound pair⟩ ::= ⟨lower bound⟩:⟨upper bound⟩
97. ⟨bound-pair list⟩ ::= ⟨bound pair⟩|⟨bound-pair list⟩,⟨bound
      pair⟩
98. ⟨array segment⟩ ::= ⟨array identifier⟩[⟨bound-pair list⟩]|⟨array
      identifier⟩,⟨array segment⟩
99. ⟨array list⟩ ::= ⟨array segment⟩|⟨array list⟩,⟨array segment⟩

100.   ⟨array declaration⟩ ::= **array**⟨array list⟩|⟨local or own type⟩ **array**⟨array list⟩

Switch declarations have the following form:

101.   ⟨switch list⟩ ::= ⟨designational expression⟩|⟨switch list⟩, ⟨designational expression⟩
102.   ⟨switch declaration⟩ ::= **switch** ⟨switch identifier⟩ := ⟨switch list⟩

Procedure declarations have the following form:

103.   ⟨formal parameter⟩ ::= ⟨identifier⟩
104.   ⟨formal-parameter list⟩ ::= ⟨formal parameter⟩|⟨formal-parameter list⟩,⟨formal parameter⟩
105.   ⟨formal-parameter part⟩ ::= ⟨empty⟩|(⟨formal-parameter list⟩)
106.   ⟨identifier list⟩ ::= ⟨identifier⟩|⟨identifier list⟩,⟨identifier⟩
107.   ⟨value part⟩ ::= **value** ⟨identifier list⟩; |⟨empty⟩
108.   ⟨specifier⟩ ::= **string**|⟨type⟩|**array**|⟨type⟩ **array**|**label**|**switch**| **procedure**|⟨type⟩**procedure**
109.   ⟨specification part⟩ ::= ⟨empty⟩|⟨specifier⟩ ⟨identifier list⟩;| ⟨specification part⟩ ⟨specifier⟩ ⟨identifier list⟩;
110.   ⟨procedure heading⟩ ::= ⟨procedure identifier⟩ ⟨formal parameter part⟩; ⟨value part⟩ ⟨specification part⟩
111.   ⟨procedure body⟩ ::= ⟨statement⟩|⟨code⟩
112.   ⟨procedure declaration⟩ ::= **procedure** ⟨procedure heading⟩ ⟨procedure body⟩|⟨type⟩ **procedure** ⟨procedure heading⟩ ⟨procedure body⟩

The ALGOL grammar $G = (N,T,S,P)$ has as its set N the set of all nonterminals appearing on the right-hand sides of productions. Its set of terminals T consists of the set of 116 listed basic symbols. The distinguished symbol S is the symbol ⟨program⟩. The set of productions P is precisely the 112 production sets listed above.

Although the above grammar generates all ALGOL programs, there are certain strings which, although they are generated by the grammar, would not represent semantically meaningful programs. For example, the above grammar permits two declarations of an identifier with a given name in the same blockhead. It permits an identifier to appear within a block in which it is not declared. Even if a given identifier is declared precisely once, there is no restriction in the grammar against applying incompatible operators which expect arguments to have a type different from that specified in the identifier declarations.

The semantic requirement that identifier declarations match uses of the identifier in the block in which they are declared cannot be specified by context-free grammars. On the other hand, the question of compatibility between use and declaration of identifiers can certainly be determined from the static structure of the program by a mechanical algorithm. Checking for compatibility of identifiers can be embedded in syntactic compilation algorithms or interpretive execution algorithms which use a representation of the above context-free grammar as a basis for recognizing valid ALGOL program structures. The validity of identifiers can be checked by building tables of declared identifiers and imposing the restriction that identifiers used in a given block must occur in the symbol table of declared symbols.

This appendix gives only the syntax of ALGOL 60. The semantics of ALGOL 60 is discussed in Chap. 4. Ambiguities and suggested corrections to ALGOL 60 are discussed in Ref. 20 of Chap. 4.

INDEX